OXFORD EARLY CHRISTIAN STUDIES

General Editors

Henry Chadwick   Rowan Williams

THE OXFORD EARLY CHRISTIAN STUDIES series will include scholarly volumes on the thought and history of the early Christian centuries. Covering a wide range of Greek, Latin, and Oriental sources, the books will be of interest to theologians, ancient historians, and specialists in the classical and Jewish worlds.

REGNVM CAELORVM,

Patterns of Future Hope in Early Christianity

CHARLES E. HILL

CLARENDON PRESS · OXFORD

1992

Oxford University Press, Walton Street, Oxford OX2 6DP

Oxford New York Toronto
Delhi Bombay Calcutta Madras Karachi
Petaling Jaya Singapore Hong Kong Tokyo
Nairobi Dar es Salaam Cape Town
Melbourne Auckland

and associated companies in
Berlin Ibadan

Oxford is a trade mark of Oxford University Press

Published in the United States
by Oxford University Press, New York

British Library Cataloguing in Publication Data
data available

Library of Congress Cataloging in Publication Data
Hill, Charles E. (Charles Evan), 1956–
Regnum caelorum: patterns of future hope in early Christianity
(Oxford early Christian studies)
Revision of thesis (doctoral)—Oxford University.
Includes bibliographical references and index.
1. Eschatology—History of doctrines—Early church, ca. 30–600.
2. Eschatology—Biblical teaching.   3. Bible.   N.T.—Theology.
4. Kingdom of God—History of doctrines—Early church, ca. 30–600.
5. Millennium—History of doctrines—Early church, ca. 30–600.
6. Intermediate state—History of doctrines—Early church, ca. 30–600.   I. Title.II. Series.
BT819.5.H55   1992   236'.09'015—dc20   91–30765
ISBN 0-19-826738-X

Typeset by H. Charlesworth & Co. Ltd., Huddersfield
Printed in Great Britain by
Bookcraft (Bath) Ltd., Midsomer Norton

ACKNOWLEDGEMENTS

The expenses necessary to complete this work would have been prohibitive without the substantial help provided by my parents-in-law, Burton and Betty McPheeters; by the Committee of Vice-Chancellors and Principals of the Universities of the United Kingdom; by the Managers of the Crosse studentship; and by my parents, Merlyn and Iris Hill. Other significant financial contributions have been received from the Trustees of the Bethune-Baker Fund, the Tyndale House Council, the Hort Fund, Fieldstead and Company, Northwestern College, and Mike and Connie Pfefferle. To all of these I express my sincere thanks. My debts to Michael Thompson in general computer wisdom, to Conrad Gempf and Mark Vellinga for their abilities to conjure up lost information from damaged diskettes, to E. W. Kennedy and Joan Anderson for their advice in German and French translation, cannot go unacknowledged. None of these of course is responsible for any errors or deficiencies which remain.

Special thanks go to the Supervisor of my doctoral work, of which this book is a revision, Professor Rowan D. Williams. His enlightening comments and suggestions, flowing from an astonishingly broad expertise, have been a constant stimulation throughout the course of this research.

Deepest gratitude is reserved for my wife, Marcy, who has supported me in this venture in so many ways. This work is affectionately dedicated to her.

CONTENTS

Abbreviations   ix

Introduction   1

I. REGNVM CAELORVM TERRESTRE

1. Irenaeus: Chiliasm and the Intermediate State   9
2. Other Ante-Nicene Chiliasts   18
3. The 'Pharisaic–Apocalyptic' Sources   41

II. REGNVM CAELORVM CAELESTE

Introduction   64
1. The Apostolic Fathers   66
2. The Apologists   89
3. Christian Pseudepigrapha   94
4. Early Martyrologies   105
5. Hippolytus   111
6. Clement of Alexandria   120
7. Origen   127
8. Dionysius of Alexandria   141
9. Cyprian   143

III. SOME OBSERVATIONS ON NEW TESTAMENT ESCHATOLOGY

Introduction   154
1. The Intermediate State in the New Testament outside the
   Book of Revelation   155
2. The Book of Revelation and Chiliasm   163

IV. SUMMARY AND CONCLUSIONS

1. Millennium and Intermediate State   178
2. Distribution of Eschatological Views   181
3. Irenaeus and Chiliasm   184
4. A Non-Chiliastic Exegesis of Revelation 20   188
5. Eschatology in the New Testament   192

viii   Contents

Table of Eschatological Views   194

Appendix: Cyprian, the Carthaginian Confessors, and
Revelation 20   196

Select Bibliography   203

General Index   226

ABBREVIATIONS

1. ANCIENT CHRISTIAN AUTHORS

(Abbreviations of Biblical books follow established usage.)

ActThom.	*Acts of Thomas*
ApostConst.	*Apostolic Constitutions*
Athenagoras	
Plea	*A Plea for the Christians*
Augustine	
CivDei	*De civitate Dei*
3Bar.	*3 (Greek) Baruch*
Clement of Alexandria	
EclProph.	*Eclogae propheticae*
JohPrim.	*in Epistola Johannis Prima*
Paed.	*Paedagogus*
Protr.	*Protreptikos*
Qds	*Quis diues salvetur*
Strom.	*Stromata*
Theod.	*Excerpts from Theodotus*
Clement of Rome	
1Clem.	*1 Clement*
2Clem.	*2 Clement*
Commodianus	
Instr.	*Instructions*
CarmA	*Carmen Apologeticum*
Cyprian of Carthage	
Demetr.	*Ad Demetrianum*
Ep.	*Epistula*
Fort.	*Ad Fortunatum (De exhortatione martyrii)*
Hab.	*De habitu uirginum*
Idola	*Quod idola dii non sint*
Laps.	*De lapsis*
Mort.	*De mortalitate*
OpEl.	*De opere et eleemosynis*
Orat.	*De dominica oratione*
Pat.	*De bono patientiae*
Un.	*De catholicae ecclesiae unitate*
EpApost.	*Epistula Apostolorum*

EpDiogn.	*Epistle to Diognetus*
EpRheg.	*Epistle to Rheginos*
EpV&L	*Epistle of Vienne and Lyons*
Eusebius of Caesarea	
HE	*Historia Ecclesiastica*
PalMart.	*The Martyrs of Palestine*
Filaster	
DivHer.	*Diversarum heresion liber*
GospNicod.	*Gospel of Nicodemus*
Hermas, *The Shepherd*	
Mand.	*Mandates*
Sim.	*Similitudes*
Vis.	*Visions*
Hippolytus	
Antichr.	*Treatise on Christ and Antichrist*
ApostTrad.	*Apostolic Tradition*
CD	*Commentary on Daniel*
Noet.	*Against Noetus*
Ref.	*Refutation of All Heresies*
Song	*On the Great Song*
Ignatius	
Eph.	*To the Ephesians*
Magn.	*To the Magnesians*
Phd.	*To the Philadelphians*
Polyc.	*To Polycarp*
Rom.	*To the Romans*
Sm.	*To the Smyrnaeans*
Tr.	*To the Trallians*
Irenaeus	
AH	*Adversus Haereses*
Dem.	*Demonstration of the Apostolic Preaching*
Fr.	*Fragment*
Justin	
1Apol.	*1 Apology*
2Apol.	*2 Apology*
Dial.	*Dialogue with Trypho the Jew*
MartJustin	*The Martyrdom of Saints Justin, Chariton, Charito, Evelpistus, Hierax, Paeon, Liberian, and their Community*
Lactantius	
DInst.	*Divine Institutes*
Epit.	*The Epitome of the Divine Institutes*
Melito of Sardis	
PP	*Peri Pascha*

Methodius of Olympus
  Res. — Treatise on the Resurrection of the Body
  Sympos. — The Symposium
OdesSol. — Odes of Solomon
Origen
  Cels. — Contra Celsum
  CJohn — Commentary on John
  CMatt. — Commentary on Matthew
  CPs 4 — Commentary on Psalm 4
  CRom. — Commentary on Romans
  CSSol. — Commentary on the Song of Solomon
  DialHeracl. — Dialogue with Heraclides
  ExhMart. — Exhortation to Martyrdom
  FragmRm. — Fragments on Romans
  HomEzech. — Homilies on Ezekiel
  HomGen. — Homilies on Genesis
  HomJer. — Homilies on Jeremiah
  HomLuke — Homilies on Luke
  HomNum. — Homilies on Numbers
  Hom1Sam. 28.3-25 — Homily on 1 Samuel 28.3-25
  Princ. — De principiis
  ScholApoc. — Scholia on the Apocalypse
Polycarp
  Phil. — To the Philippians
Pseudo-Justin
  Mon. — On the Sole Monarchy of God
Tertullian
  An. — De anima
  Fem. — De cultu feminarum
  Marc. — Adversus Marcionem
  Mart. — Ad martyras
  Monog. — De monogamia
  Pat. — De patientiae
  Pud. — De pudicitia
  Res. — De resurrectione carnis
  Scorp. — Scorpiace
  Spect. — De spectaculis
  Ux. — Ad uxorem
  Val. — Adversus Valentinianos
Theodoret of Cyrus
  EcclHist. — Ecclesiastical History
Victorinus of Pettau
  CA — Commentary on the Apocalypse
  Mundi — De fabrica mundi

2. OTHER AUTHORS OF ANTIQUITY

(Abbreviations for Qumran texts follow J. A. Fitzmyer, *The Dead Sea Scrolls: Major Publications and Tools for Study*, Sources for Biblical Study 8 (Missoula, Mont., 1975).)

ApocAbr.	*Apocalypse of Abraham*
ARN	'Aboth d'Rabbi Nathan
AssMos.	*Assumption of Moses*
2Bar.	*2 (Syriac) Baruch*
BibAntiqq.	Pseudo-Philo, *Biblical Antiquities*
1En.	*1 (Ethiopian) Enoch*
2En.	*2 Enoch*
4Ez.	*4 Ezra*
2Macc.	*2 Maccabees*
3Macc.	*3 Maccabees*
4Macc.	*4 Maccabees*
VGAE	*Life of Adam and Eve (Apocalypse of Moses)*
Josephus	
Ant.	*Antiquitates Judaicae*
BJ	*Bellum Judaicum*
Philo	
Abr.	*De Abrahamo*
Cher.	*De cherubim*
Conf.	*De confusione linguarum*
Congr.	*De congressu eruditionis causa*
Gig.	*De gigantibus*
Plant.	*De plantatione*
QSGen.	*Quaestiones et solutiones in Genesin*
PsSol.	*Psalms of Solomon*
SibOr.	*Sibylline Oracles*
TB	*Babylonian Talmud*
TestAsher	*Testament of Asher*
TestDan	*Testament of Dan*
TestJob	*Testament of Job*
TestJud.	*Testament of Judah*
TestLevi	*Testament of Levi*
Test3Pats.	*Testament of the Three Patriarchs*

3. MODERN WORKS OR SERIES

AB	The Anchor Bible
ACW	Ancient Christian Writers

AJT	*American Journal of Theology*
AK	Arbeiten zur Kirchengeschichte
ALBO	*Analecta Lovaniensia Biblica et Orientalia*
ANF	Ante-Nicene Fathers, ed. A. Roberts and J. Donaldson, 10 vols., rev. A. C. Coxe (Grand Rapids, 1978 repr.)
ANT	*The Apocryphal New Testament*
ApF	The Apostolic Fathers. A New Translation and Commentary, ed. Robert M. Grant, 6 vols.
ATANT	Abhandlung zur Theologie des alten und neue Testaments
ATR	*Anglican Theological Review*
Aug.	*Augustinianum*
BAGD	*A Greek–English Lexicon of the New Testament and Other Early Christian Literature. A translation and adaptation of the fourth revised and augmented edition of Walter Bauer's Griechisch–Deutsches Wörterbuch zu den Schriften des Neuen Testaments und der übrigen urchristlichen Literatur by William F. Arndt and F. Wilbur Gingrich,* 2nd ed. rev. and augmented by F. Wilbur Gingrich and Frederick W. Danker from Walter Bauer's 5th ed., 1958 (Chicago/London, 1979)
BAP	*Bibliothèque des Archives de Philosophie*
BEBT	*Bauer Encyclopedia of Biblical Theology*
BEHESR	*Bibliothèque de l'École des Hautes Études: Sciences Religieuses*
BETL	*Bibliotheca Ephemeridum Theologicarum Lovaniensum*
BL	*Bibel und Leben*
BLE	*Bulletin de littérature ecclésiastique*
BHT	Beiträge zur historischen Theologie
BibZ	*Biblische Zeitschrift*
BR	*Biblical Research*
CBQ	*Catholic Biblical Quarterly*
CC	Corpus Christianorum
CIJ	*Corpus Inscriptionum Iudaicarum,* 2 vols., ed. J-B. Frey (Vatican City, 1936, 1952)
CNT	Commentaire du Nouveau Testament
ConB	Coniectanea Biblica
CP	Corona Patrum
CPG	*Clavis patrum Graecorum,* 4 vols., ed. Mauritii

	Geerard, Corpus Christianorum (Brepols, 1974–83)
CSCO	Corpus scriptorum Christianorum orientalium
CSEL	Corpus scriptorum ecclesiasticorum Latinorum
CUAPS	The Catholic University of America Patristic Studies
CTM	Calwer Theologische Monographien
DACL	*Dictionnaire d'archéologie chrétienne et de liturgie*
DB	*Dictionnaire de la Bible* (Paris, 1908)
DCA	*A Dictionary of Christian Antiquities*, ed. William Smith and Samuel Cheetham, 2 vols. (London, 1880)
DCB	*A Dictionary of Christian Biography, Literature, Sects and Doctrines*, ed. William Smith and Henry Wace, 4 vols. (London, 1877)
DHG	*Dictionnaire d'histoire et de géographie ecclésiastiques* (Paris, 1912–)
DHI	*Dictionary of the History of Ideas* (New York)
DS	*Dictionnaire de spiritualité*
DTC	*Dictionnaire de théologie catholique* (Paris, 1923–50)
EB	*Encyclopaedia Britannica*
EBib.	Études bibliques
EEC	*Encyclopedia of Early Christianity*, ed. Everett Ferguson et al. (New York/London, 1990)
EHR	*English Historical Review*
EJ	*Encyclopedia Judaica*, 16 vols. (Jerusalem, 1972)
EK	Einführung in die alte Kirchengeschichte
EPEKTASIS	*EPEKTASIS. Mélanges patristiques offerts au cardinal Jean Daniélou* (1972, no place of publication)
EPROER	Études préliminaires aux religions orientales dans l'empire romain
ER	*The Encyclopedia of Religion*, Mircea Eliade, editor in chief, 15 vols. (New York/London, 1987)
EvQ	*The Evangelical Quarterly*
Expos.	*The Expositor*
ExpT	*The Expository Times*
FLDG	*Forschungen zur christlichen Literatur- und Dogmengeschichte*
FF	*Forma Futuri. Studi in onore del Cardinale Michele Pellegrino* (Turin, 1975)

FRLANT	Forschungen zur Religion und Literatur des Alten und Neuen Testaments
GCS	Die griechischen christlichen Schriftsteller der ersten drei Jahrhunderte
Greg.	*Gregorianum*
Herm.	*Hermathena. A Series of Papers on Literature, Science, and Philosophy, by Members of Trinity College, Dublin*
HJb	*Historisches Jahrbuch*
HNT	Handbuch zum neuen Testament
HTR	*Harvard Theological Review*
HTS	Harvard Theological Studies
HUCA	*Hebrew Union College Annual*
ICC	International Critical Commentary
IESS	*International Encyclopedia of the Social Sciences*, ed. David L. Sills, 17 vols. (1968)
ISBE	*The International Standard Bible Encyclopedia*, fully rev., 4 vols. (Grand Rapids, 1986 rev. from 1915 and 1929 edns.)
JbAC	*Jahrbuch für Antike und Christentum*
JBL	*Journal of Biblical Literature*
JNES	*Journal of Near Eastern Studies*
JPT	*Jahrbücher für protestantische Theologie*
JSNT Suppl.	*Journal for the Study of the New Testament Supplement Series*
JSS	*Journal of Semitic Studies*
JThC	*Journal for Theology and Church*
JTS	*Journal of Theological Studies*
LCC	The Library of Christian Classics
LCL	Loeb Classical Library
LSJ	*A Greek–English Lexicon*, compiled by Henry George Liddell and Robert Scott, revised and augmented by Henry Stuart Jones, Roderick McKenzie, *et al.*, 9th edn. (Oxford, 1985)
MBT	Münsterische Beiträge zur Theologie
MeyerK	H. A. W. Meyer, Kritisch-exegetischer Kommentar über das Neue Testament
MNTC	The Moffatt New Testament Commentary
Mus.	*Le Muséon*
NCE	*New Catholic Encyclopedia*, 16 vols. (New York, St Louis, *et al.*, 1967)
NPNF	*A Select Library of Nicene and Post-Nicene Fathers of the Christian Church*, 2nd ser., ed.

	Philip Schaff and Henry Wace
NTA	*New Testament Apocrypha*, ed. E. Hennecke, W. Schneemelcher, and R. McL. Wilson (ET, Philadelphia, 1963–5)
NtAbh	Neutestamentliche Abhandlungen
NTS	*New Testament Studies*
OECT	Oxford Early Christian Texts
OTM	Oxford Theological Monographs
OTP	*The Old Testament Pseudepigrapha*, ed. J. H. Charlesworth, 2 vols.: i (New York, 1983); ii (New York, 1985)
PG	*Patrologiae Graecae*
PGL	*A Patristic Greek Lexicon, with Addenda et Corrigenda*, ed. G. W. H. Lampe (Oxford, 1987)
PO	Patrologia Orientalis
PTR	*Princeton Theological Review*
PTS	Patristische Texte und Studien
RAC	*Reallexikon für Antike und Christentum*
RB	*Revue biblique*
RE	*Realencyklopädie für protestantische Theologie und Kirche*
Rel.	*Religion*
RGG	*Religion in Geschichte und Gegenwart*, 3rd edn. (Tübingen, 1957–65)
RHPR	*Revue d'histoire et de philosophie religieuses*
RivAC	*Rivista di archeologia cristiana*
RPh	*Revue de philologie*
RQH	*Revue des questions historiques*
RTAM	*Recherches de théologie ancienne et médiévale*
SBT	Studies in Biblical Theology
SC	Sources chrétiennes
SCent.	*The Second Century*
SE	*Sacris Erudiri. Jaarboek voor godsdienstwetenschappen*
SD	Studies and Documents
SEÅ	*Svensk exegetisk årsbok*
SJT	*Scottish Journal of Theology*
SM	*Sacramentum Mundi. An Encyclopedia of Theology*
SQ	Sammlung ausgewählter kirchen-und dogmengeschichtlicher Quellenschriften
ST	Studi et Testi
STL	Studia Theologica Lundensia

StTh	*Studia Theologica*
StudHell	Studia Hellenistica
StudPatr.	*Studia Patristica*
SUNT	Studien zur Umwelt des Neuen Testaments
Suppl.DB	*Supplément au Dictionnaire de la Bible*
Suppl.*NovT*	Supplements to *Novum Testamentum*
TDNT	*Theological Dictionary of the New Testament*
Theoph.	Theophaneia. Beiträge zur Religions- und Kirchengeschichte des Altertums
ThH	Théologie historique
ThSt.	*Theological Studies*
TR	*Theologische Realenzyklopädie*
TS	Texts and Studies
TSK	*Theologische Studien und Kritiken*
TU	Texte und Untersuchungen
VC	*Vigiliae Christianae*
VP	*Vivre et penser*
WTJ	*Westminster Theological Journal*
WUNT	Wissenschaftliche Untersuchungen zum Neuen Testament
ZKTh	*Zeitschrift für Katholische Theologie*
ZNW	*Zeitschrift für die neutestamentliche Wissenschaft*

Additional note: par(s). = parallel(s) throughout.

INTRODUCTION

This is a book about early Christian chiliasm, or millennialism, the ancient belief in a thousand-year reign of Christ and his saints on earth between his second coming and the last judgement. As such, it adds its title to a venerable and rather lengthy body of literature, scholarly and not-so-scholarly, on this topic of perennial interest. For millennialism, in an immense variety of forms, has played a not insignificant role in the Church's long life and claims even today millions of devout adherents, and not a few intrigued onlookers. As a historic expression of Christian eschatology which stresses the intrusion of God's kingdom of justice, in relentless combat with the oppressive structures of this world, it has, for example, supplied inspiration to recent theologians of liberation. Its very name, so suggestive of radicalism to some social historians and social anthropologists, so pregnant with associations of the arcane, the visionary, and the potentially violent or revolutionary, has been lifted from its birthplace in Christian theology and made to serve as a sociological classification which aims at describing numerous popular religious or ideological movements throughout history.[1]

[1] Talmon, 349, 'The term ... is now used not in its specific and limited historical sense but typologically, to characterize religious movements that expect imminent, total, ultimate, this-worldly, collective salvation.' See also Cohn, 13, the 1957 edition of whose book, *The Pursuit of the Millennium*, was signally responsible for this adaptation of the term; Michael Hill, 206–7; Schwartz, 521 and the recent bibliography in Jewett, 203–6. Only two observations will be made here on this definition. (1) Definitions such as the one just quoted, while intending to be broad enough to encompass even the 'original' forms of millennialism, are, in my judgement, not well-suited to the millennialism we shall be studying. For instance, Schwartz allows that 'Not all millenarians', in his use of the term, 'expect an interim paradise before an ultimate heavenly assumption', yet an interim phase in world redemption is crucial to the millennialism we are concerned with; to deny such a phase is to remove oneself from the millennialist camp. (2) Despite these careful definitions, sociologists often use the term millennialism as if it entailed some form of active social dissidence. See Tuveson, 224; Isenberg, 28, 35, along with the criticisms of this use by, for example, McGinn, 29–30. Schwartz indeed says, 'Few millenarians remain entirely passive, quietly awaiting a supernatural transformation of the world.' In our period we might say the opposite: few millenarians, with the participants in the Bar Cochba revolt perhaps the glaring exception, took it upon themselves to initiate the expected transformation of the world. The closest thing to socially disruptive behaviour which can be credited to early Christian millennialists would be the ecclesiastical 'schisms

But this book is also about early, orthodox (non-Gnostic) 'non-chiliasm', as an alternative and competing interpretation of the primitive Christian hope. As such, it is seemingly in search of a genre, and anybody acquainted with the study of early Christian eschatology will know why. Can there really be anything deserving of the name 'orthodox non-chiliasm' to study, before the merely 'literary' protest against chiliasm by Gaius of Rome at the turn of the third century and the devastating remonstrances of Origen a few decades later?[2] And is it not true that, when they did appear, the first ecclesiastical opponents of chiliasm were purely negative in their opposition, offering no positive alternative to chiliasm, no constructive exegesis of the twentieth chapter of the book of Revelation,[3] wherein chiliasm is 'canonically formulated',[4] and tending in fact to repudiate that book altogether, as did the so-called Alogi?[5] Is not the acceptance of chiliasm by Justin Martyr the philosopher, in the words of Adolf Harnack, 'the strongest proof that these enthusiastic expectations were inseparably bound up with the Christian faith down to the middle of the 2nd century'?[6] One prominent source goes so far as to say that for the first two hundred years of Christianity, 'chiliasm, inherited from Jewish political messianism, governed religious thinking'.[7] Again, it has been reported that 'Nearly all researchers are united in this, that the end-time conception and doctrine designated . . . as "chiliasm", dominated the whole Church until the great Alexandrians, and the West even into the third and fourth centuries.'[8] If chiliasm was 'inseparably

and defections of whole churches' reported by Dionysius as taking place in Arsinoë at around the middle of the third century (Eusebius, *HE* VII. 24. 6).

[2] 'A literary dispute occurred first of all with Gaius of Rome . . . But only the Alexandrians met this early church eschatology with force, for many areas and times almost deadly', Maier, 88; cf. Harnack, *Lehrbuch*, i. 619; Semisch–Bratke, 808; Bietenhard, *Reich*, 7; Montgomery, 258; Dolan, 853.

[3] Swete, 265, 'no thorough examination of this passage [i.e.: Rev 20], with a constructive purpose, seems to have been undertaken by the Alexandrian school. To Augustine the Church owes the first serious effort to interpret Apoc. xx. (*de civ. Dei* xx. 7 ff)'. Cf. Maier, 68, 'Only Tyconius and Augustine, by reinterpreting the old eschatology [i.e. the chiliastic one] in keeping with the spirit of their age, succeed in weakening its efficacy'; Bousset, 59; Ford, 350.   [4] Maier, 105.

[5] Maier, 50. On the Alogi, see Norris, 27. Dionysius of Alexandria, an outspoken critic of chiliasm, is often accused of denying the book's authenticity, e.g. O'Rourke Boyle, 6; Montgomery, 358.   [6] Harnack, EB 496.

[7] Schürer, ii. 547. Cf. also Maier, 47–8; Lightfoot, *Supernatural* 151.

[8] Maier, 87. According to Maier, 89, the form of chiliasm described and opposed by Origen in *De principiis* II. 11 was 'the traditional eschatology of the entire Church' ('die hergebrachte gemeinkirchliche Eschatologie').

bound up with the Christian faith' for this long, one might reasonably expect that attacks made on it during this period might also be constrained to direct themselves against other central tenets of this faith. Thus scholars such as Hans Bietenhard find the first dissent from the Church's chiliastic testimony in a scattered chorus of 'hellenistic spiritualisers' whose tendency was to dissolve the Church's faith in the resurrection.[9] Thus Semisch and Bratke already (in 1897) regarded the Old Roman Creed's confession of the resurrection of the flesh as implying a belief in chiliasm.[10] One is frequently left with the decided impression that the earliest Christian non-chiliasts, whoever they were, were also antagonistic to the idea of a bodily resurrection. Unlike the doctrine of the bodily resurrection, however, chiliasm did eventually fall into disfavour and was for ages considered heterodox by the Churches of East and West. The story of chiliasm's drift from the centre to the periphery and finally over the edge is usually told by citing some of the following developments: (i) chiliasm's (alleged) association with Montanism, which is thought to have brought opprobrium upon the doctrine in the eyes of the larger Church, (ii) the influence of Origen's spiritualizing of eschatology and allegorizing of Scripture, (iii) the related infiltration of the Church by 'Greek philosophy' or at least the Hellenistic *Zeitgeist*, which counteracted more Hebraic and 'realistic' modes of thought, (iv) the progressive deterioration of the Church's once vibrant hope of Christ's return, a decay aided by the peace of Constantine, and finally, (v) the authoritative and enormously influential rejection of chiliasm by Augustine.

Yet, some readers who are familiar with this analysis of early Christian eschatology may also recall observing a crack or two in its foundation. Harnack's conclusion from the example of Justin appears to lay one of these faults open to view. While Justin affirms that he and many others 'who are right-minded Christians on all points' are 'assured that there will be a resurrection of the dead and a thousand years in Jerusalem', he admits none the less that 'many who are Christians of pure and pious mind do not acknowledge this' (*Dial.* 80. 2). Justin goes on indeed to mention a second group of non-millennialists who pass under the name of Christian,

---

[9] Bietenhard, SJT, 14, 16.

[10] Semisch–Bratke, 808. Cf. Harnack, *Lehrbuch*, i. 615, n. 1, who indicates that when the Church lost its chiliastic hope, it lost its living faith in Christ's imminent return.

but these, Justin is at pains to make clear, are godless, impious heretics who, among their other aberrations, deny the resurrection of the body. But as to the former group of non-millennialists, it is nowhere indicated that they deny the resurrection, in fact, had Justin known that they did so it is beyond belief that he would have designated them Christians of the pure and pious faith. Here we are justified in assuming the existence of orthodox non-chiliasts known to Justin. But into the questions of their identity and the shape of their eschatological beliefs scholarship has never mounted a serious investigation.

Later in the second century Irenaeus too will mention some who are considered to be orthodox (*qui putantur recte credidisse*) who were not millennialists and whom he engages in polemic on the matter (*AH* v. 31–32. 1). Though attempts have been made to identify these non-millennialists, the results gained so far (to be examined below) are open to question.

One more instance of what ought to be recognized as non-chiliastic future expectation, even before the dawn of the second century, will be mentioned here. It is conserved in Hegesippus' story of Jude's grandsons standing before the emperor Domitian. As related by Eusebius (*HE* iii. 20. 4), 'They were asked concerning the Christ and his kingdom, its nature, origin, and time of appearance, and explained that it was neither of the world nor earthly, but heavenly and angelic, and it would be at the end of the world, when he would come in glory to judge the living and the dead and to reward every man according to his deeds.'[11] Here there is not only no mention of an earthly millennium but language which apparently rules out the possibility of there ever being one. The kingdom of Christ comes to earth at his second coming and in conjunction with the last judgement.

But if outspoken critics of chiliasm are hard to find before Gaius and Origen, have we still no alternative but to surmise that Justin's unnamed non-chiliast acquaintances were few and far between in his day, that the grandnephews of the Lord must have kept their eschatology to themselves and that chiliasm, in terms of distribution and influence, was at least the controlling eschatological outlook amongst Christians of the period?

To answer this question we must know a little more clearly what

[11] English translations from Eusebius, *HE*, unless otherwise noted, will be those of Lake and Oulton in LCL.

we mean by chiliasm and non-chiliasm. Estévao Bettencourt offers us an excellent compendium of the chiliastic scheme in Christian theology:[12]

(i) the second coming of Christ, in majesty; (ii) the first resurrection, that of the just only; (iii) a general judgment, of the nations as a whole, not of individuals; (iv) a messianic kingdom lasting a thousand years; (v) the second resurrection, that of all men; (vi) last judgment, of all persons individually; (vii) the eternal destiny, reward or punishment.

Yet, it would be desirable for our investigation that our definition not be so specifically Christian as to exclude contemporary or antecedent Jewish expressions. We cannot, to cite the obvious example, use the term 'second coming' in our basic definition. Nor may we insist on the figure of a thousand years (thus strictly making the terms chiliasm and millennialism misnomers), even though this figure became normative for Christian chiliasm after acceptance of the book of Revelation, for it was not normative for Jewish writers.[13]

Chiliasm or millennialism as used here will signify belief in a temporary, earthly, Messianic kingdom to be realized sometime in the future: temporary, for, whereas it covers an extended period of time, it is not viewed as the ultimate state of things; earthly, as it takes place on this earth, typically with Jerusalem as its capital; and Messianic, as an individual deliverer(s) plays a central role in it. Whereas many Jewish works may be seen to contain one or two of these components, it is probably best to regard such documents[14] as 'defective' stages towards and possible sources for the full-blown

[12] Bettencourt, 43.
[13] See Prigent, 'Le Millennium', 147–50 for the proposed lengths, ranging from 40 to 7,000 years.
[14] *The Apocalypse of Weeks* (1En. 91. 12–17, 93. 1–10) attests the practice of dividing history up into segments and looks to a final state of 'weeks without number', in which 'sin shall no more be heard of forever' (91. 17), but no Messianic figure plays any part in establishing a temporal triumph of righteousness. *The Book of the Watchers* (1En.) 10–11 prophesies an era of exuberant fecundity in the human and vegetable worlds and its description probably influenced the author of 2Bar. 29. But this time of bliss appears to come after the great judgement and to be eternal, though life is conceived of in material and earthly terms (and men perhaps still die). Similar to this is the view of the *Testaments of the XII Patriarchs* in which the earthly golden age under the Judaic king and the Levitical priest is of endless duration, inaugurated by a general resurrection (TestJud. 25. 1–5). In neither Jub. nor SibOr. III is there any clear demarcation between a temporary and an eternal age of blessedness (cf. Volz, 226). For a discussion of the Qumran documents, see §I.3.2 below.

chiliasm which we find in the Jewish apocalypses 2 *(Syriac) Baruch* and 4 *Ezra*, and to reserve the term chiliasm for those places where all three components converge.

The somewhat more opaque term 'non-chiliasm', being essentially privative, denotes no more than the failure to embrace chiliasm. The non-chiliasm (or amillennialism) of the Christian sources reviewed here, however, can usually be said to have a specific content, the belief—as reflected in the words of Jude's grandsons— in an eschatological return of Christ and his kingdom to earth for a final judgement of the quick and the dead, ushering in the ultimate and eternal state of salvation or ruin for humanity, with no intervening, earthly, golden age. This alternative to chiliasm may be distinguished as 'orthodox' non-chiliasm, where a comparison with Gnosticism is in view.

A besetting problem in assessing the distribution and influence of eschatological views in the second and third centuries is the corpus of early Christian writers who are practically silent or seemingly ambiguous on the matter of millennialism. Important Christian writers such as, among others, Clement of Rome, Ignatius of Antioch, Polycarp of Smyrna, and the author of the *Epistle to Diognetus* have at times been lined up on either side of the question or have been prudently dismissed as witnesses to either view. If we could somehow gain access to their thought relative to chiliasm and non-chiliasm our view of the branches of Christian eschatology might be brought much more sharply into focus, and the origins and influence of both eschatologies as well as the causes of chiliasm's eventual decline might be made more intelligible. But without any new 'key' to their minds we have been forced to live with our limitations.

In the present work, however, we are testing such a key, one taken from the hand of 'le théologien du chiliasme',[15] Irenaeus of Lyons. That key is the doctrine of the intermediate state,[16] that

[15] Gry, *Millénarisme*, 76.

[16] The term has at times been used in Roman Catholic theology in the sense of an 'intermediate place', i.e. purgatory. It is today, moreover, often rather curiously assumed to be inappropriate to the idea of blissful heavenly existence after death, and is reserved instead for some attenuated, semi-conscious existence, of indefinite relation to time or space. The operative factor, however, is that this post-mortem state must be an interim one, anticipatory of a future resurrection or other consummate state of blessedness.

is, the state or condition of the person or, usually more exactly, the disembodied soul in the interim between death and the eschaton.[17]

This key, at first sight, is indeed not a very promising one. The doctrines of the millennium and the intermediate state are seldom represented as standing in anything like a close internal relationship to one other. None the less, their connection is very real to Irenaeus and we shall at length see just how important it was in early Christian eschatological thought. Though the debate was never formulated in exactly these terms by its participants, we may in one sense resolve the matter into the question whether the *regnum caelorum* (understood as the interim reign of Christ) would have as its capital the terrestrial or the celestial Jerusalem.

Finally, a word about some of the inherent limitations of the present investigation. We take for our main objects of study only those texts which offer us intelligible information concerning their authors' views of the end of the world or of the intermediate state. Though we venture up to the gates of the Arian controversy to survey the views of certain chiliasts, with occasional reference to even later writers, our study is intended to be comprehensive only up to the mid-third century, that is, to the time of Origen, Dionysius, and Cyprian. It is hoped that occasion will yet be found to carry the investigation through to Augustine, but, such a scope being too formidable for the present, we must be satisfied in reaching the end of an earlier epoch in the history of chiliasm. Even with this restriction, no claim is made that every relevant source has been found and fully exploited. In particular, I have not attempted to incorporate into this study, to any significant degree, findings from non-literary sources. While convinced of the interest and importance of this material, I am not persuaded that its inclusion in the present work would either change appreciably our conclusions or enhance the subject to the degree necessary to justify the rather extended space needed to deal adequately with the mass of evidence.[18]

[17] For convenience' sake, the 'body' in 'disembodied' and the 'corpus' in 'incorporeal' will in our usage stand for the earthly body which is laid in the grave and which no longer serves as the natural locus of the soul. In our investigation we shall encounter varying attempts to deal with the 'body–soul' relationship. Ours, however, is not a study of this problem *per se*.

[18] On grave inscriptions, see, for example, Stuiber and the critical reviews of his work (by de Bruyne, among others). Elsa Gibson, 139, has justly said concerning

The NT writings are treated last and separately in this study and under purely historical interests this method is open to question. However, 'purely historical' interests, if indeed they are possible, are not being claimed here and the method adopted reflects my easily perceived hope that this study will be viewed as having some bearing upon the understanding of NT eschatology. The terrain of the NT, of course, cannot begin to be properly covered in a work such as the present one. Still, the observations made at the end of this study will give an idea of the relevance of our findings for the questions of NT eschatology.

the tombstone evidence, 'One must not expect tombstones to reflect precisely, completely, and in exact proportion the habits and religious tenets of the deceased. There were customs in tombstones in both language and design.' On representations of the afterlife in ancient Christian art see Gauthier, and the bibliography she gives.

REGNVM CAELORVM TERRESTRE

1. IRENAEUS: CHILIASM AND THE INTERMEDIATE STATE

1. Two Groups of Objectors to Chiliasm

Against Heresies v. 30. 4 closes with an introduction to 'the times of the kingdom, that is, the rest, the hallowed seventh day' in which Christ will restore to Abraham 'the promised inheritance'. This introduction prepares the reader for Irenaeus' expository discourse, by far the most extensive and best reasoned in Christian literature to date, on the millennium. But instead of launching straight away into this discourse in the thirty-first chapter, before amassing arguments from Scripture, tradition, and from proper hermeneutical practice, Irenaeus has to deal with a preliminary difficulty.

But since certain of those reckoned to be orthodox overstep the order of the promotion of the righteous and are ignorant of the method of the preparation for incorruption, they hold among themselves heretical opinions.

For the heretics, despising the handiwork of God and not maintaining the salvation of their flesh, moreover, condemning also the promise of God and overstepping God entirely in their opinions, say that they, as soon as they have died, shall overstep the heavens and the Demiurge and go to their 'mother' or to that 'father' who is a further invention of theirs. They[1] therefore disallow an entire resurrection and as much as they are able seek to remove it from the midst. Is it any wonder if they [these heretics] know not the order of the resurrection?[2]

There are some who are considered orthodox (*qui putantur recte credidisse*) who do not share his belief in a future, earthly millennium. In a manner reminiscent of Justin (*Dial.* 80, see Introduction),

---

[1] *Qui*. I take this to be a continuation of the reference to the *haeretici*, not a reference back to those who are 'reckoned to be orthodox'. Reasons for this will be stated below.

[2] My translation, based on the text of SC 153. Other translations from *AH*, unless otherwise noted, are those of Alexander Roberts and W. H. Rambaut in *ANF* i.

Irenaeus perceives opposition to his millennial views emanating from both orthodox and heretical circles. Part of his response to this problem will be the allegation that the orthodox non-chiliasts have been influenced in some manner and degree by the heretical. As the ensuing argumentation unfolds he has both groups in mind, ostensibly dealing with the Valentinians from 'For the heretics . . .' (line 4, SC) through the rest of the chapter. Only at the beginning of 32. 1 do the orthodox come back to the fore: 'Inasmuch, therefore, as the opinions of certain [orthodox persons] are derived from heretical discourses . . .'.

It is important to be as precise as possible about this segregation of the opponents of Irenaeus, for our conclusions here will profoundly affect our appraisal of non-chiliasts at the time of Irenaeus. It has been maintained by some,[3] most recently and most forcefully by Irenaean scholar Antonio Orbe, that the heretics themselves receive but a passing notice in chapter 31, that everything Irenaeus says of his opponents from 'They therefore disallow . . .' (line 10, SC) has reference to 'ecclesiastics'. This would mean that these non-chiliastic ecclesiastics, who considered themselves orthodox, denied the resurrection of the flesh no less than did the heretics. Orbe identifies these 'reputed orthodox' with the anonymous opponents of Irenaeus in v. 2. 2–3, people who 'condemn the entire dispensation (of God) and disallow the salvation of the flesh . . . maintaining that it is not capable of incorruption'.[4] These, Orbe thinks, are Platonic, allegorizing Christians, the likes of whom had already been encountered by Justin (*Dial.* 80. 3–5), were later combated by Tertullian (*Res., passim*) and who resemble both the

[3] Including Waszink, *Anima*, 556, and Finé, 33.

[4] Orbe believes the arguments from the eucharist employed in v. 2. 2–3 by Irenaeus against the anonymous opponents demand that they are not recognized heretics but ecclesiastics who agreed with Irenaeus in eucharistic practice and, to some extent, in teaching (10, 37–41). Yet iv. 18. 4–5 must at this point come under consideration. Here the same arguments are deployed (namely, that the heretics are inconsistent with themselves, (1) offering the bread as the body and the cup as the blood of the Lord when all of these elements—bread, wine, body, blood—are part of the material creation which they despise; (2) saying that the flesh of the faithful which is nourished with the body and blood of the Lord goes to corruption and does not partake of life) against those who are expressly labelled *haereticorum synagogae*: heretics who, like the Marcionites, maintain 'that the Father is different from the Creator' and who, like the Valentinians, maintain 'that the things around us originated from apostasy, ignorance, and passion'. These none the less celebrate the eucharist in a manner close enough to the custom of Irenaeus for his arguments to have force.

author of the *Epistle to Rheginos* and Origen ('origenistas *ante Origenem*').[5] But there are decisive objections to this view.

First, when Irenaeus says (v. 31. 1 line 13, SC) 'if these things are as they say . . .' he must still have in mind the heretics just mentioned and not the orthodox for the latter have not yet 'spoken'. He must be referring back to those who 'say that they, as soon as they have died, shall overstep the heavens and the Demiurge and go to their "mother" or to that "father" who is a further invention of theirs', who are plainly distinguished as heretics and, as several parallels show, are in fact Valentinians. The followers of Valentinus taught that the 'pneumatics' (i.e. themselves) imbued with the pre-existing seed of their 'mother' Achamoth, would at death ascend past the hebdomad, where the 'psychics' (i.e. the catholics) have their post-mortem repose in the presence of the Demiurge, and on into the 'middle-place' (μεσότης) or ogdoad where Achamoth dwells.[6] 'If these things are as they say', he continues, then the Lord himself would have departed on high immediately after expiring on the cross (and so on).

Second, if in the remainder of chapter 31 Irenaeus has primarily in view the teaching of these 'reputed orthodox' ecclesiastics and not the Valentinians, these opponents are so much like Valentinians as to make any distinction imperceptible.[7] (a) Irenaeus says that they disallow a resurrection of the entire man,[8] that is, of the body along with the soul. This naturally makes us think of heretics Irenaeus has mentioned many times before in his treatise (see e.g. I. 27. 3, Marcion; I. 14. 5, Basilides; v. 1. 2, Valentinians; IV. 18. 5,

---

[5] Orbe, 19.

[6] *AH* I. 5. 4; I. 7. 1; I. 21. 5; I. 30. 14; II. 29. 1; II. 30. 1–2, 5–7; IV. 19. 1–3, also Tertullian, *Val.* 31–2; Origen, *Cels.* VI. 31. See also *The Exegesis on the Soul* II. 6 (Robinson, *NHLE*, 180–7); *EpRheg.* 45. 24–46. 2 (a resurrection of a 'spiritual' flesh though it takes place at death); 47. 19–20 and note Orbe's interesting discussion, 18–36.

[7] Finé, 34, finds a distinction in that Irenaeus seems to speak as if they presupposed that Christ had only a bipartite and not a tripartite or quadripartite nature as did the Christ of the Valentinians. But it is hard to read a specific Christology from the words of v. 31 where indeed the main purpose in citing the example of Christ is simply to prove that there is a fundamental law of human existence to which even Christ conformed, which says that the souls of the dead depart to an infernal realm until they are reunited with their bodies before being allowed to rise to the presence of God.

[8] *Universam reprobant resurrectionem.* Rousseau (SC 153) translates adverbially, 'qui rejettent catégoriquement la resurrection'. Orbe, 13, however, correctly relates this to v. 31. 2 lines 45 ff. where Irenaeus refers to 'rising in their entirety (*perfecte*), that is bodily'. Cf. Tertullian, *Res.* 22.

heretics). In v. 4. 1 this is the teaching of those who postulate a
God above the Creator, a God who can only quicken 'those things
which are immortal by nature' and not the entire man. (b) They
also deny a descent of Christ into Hades to announce salvation to
the souls of the saints, holding that Paul's words 'in the lower parts
of the earth' (Eph. 4: 9) refer not to Hades but 'to this world of
ours'. This is at any rate neither the teaching of Clement of Alexandria nor of Origen nor of Tertullian's opponents in *De anima* 55 (see
§I.2.3 below), all of whom believed in a *descensus ad inferos*.[9] Even
Marcion did not deny this but only reinterpreted it (I. 27. 3).[10]
(c) The 'inner man' which, the opponents assert, ascends at death
to the supercelestial lap of Achamoth is practically a Valentinian
technical term (I. 13. 2; I. 21. 4–5; II. 30. 7; v. 19. 2). (d) The *supercae-
lestem locum* (v. 31. 2 lines 39–40, SC) to which the liberated 'inner
man' ascends is likewise common parlance in the Valentinian sects
for the ogdoad or the dwelling of Achamoth above the merely
'celestial place' of the Demiurge (I. 5. 4; I. 15. 2; I. 21. 3; II. 17. 9;
II. 28. 9; III. 10. 4; III. 16. 6; IV. 19. 1; v. 33. 1; v. 35. 2;[11] cf. Origen, *Cels*
VI. 38; VIII. 15). Are the opponents not therefore Valentinians?

Finally, the reference to Justin will not serve Orbe's argument
well. Justin does indeed know some who are 'called Christians' and
whose teaching resembles that of Irenaeus' heretical opposition in
v. 31. But in *Dial.* 35 Justin had already unmasked imposters 'called
Christians' whom he expressly identifies as Marcionites, Valentinians, Basilidians, Saturnilians, and others similarly dubbed according to the founder of their particular sect, and whose description

[9] Filaster, *DivHer.* LV. 5, on the other hand, speaks of (Gnosticizing?) heretics
who 'assert that this world is the lower world, and declare the resurrection to be
that which takes place every day in the human race by the procreation of sons, not
that which they announce who expect the future and glorious resurrection of
immortality'.

[10] Attestation to a Valentinian reinterpretation of Christ's descent is possibly to
be seen in I. 30. 12. There the vocabulary would indicate that the narration of the
descent ('on His descending into Hades, and on their running unto Him . . .', I. 27. 3;
for the righteous in Hades 'running' to Christ see also *OdesSol.* 42. 15) is reflected
in the account of Christ's descent to this world to attract the remnants of light:
'They further declare that he descended through the seven heavens . . . For they
maintain that the whole besprinkling of light rushed to him, and that Christ,
descending to this world, first clothed his sister Sophia, and that then both exulted
in the mutual refreshment they felt in each other's society . . .'. Like these Valentinians, the opponents of Irenaeus in v. 31. 2 say that Christ descended only to 'this
world'.

[11] See Méhat, *FF*, 286–90 (where however III. 16. 6 appears as III. 6. 6 and IV. 19. 1
as IV. 19. 9) for discussion of the passages.

answers remarkably well to these heretics of chapter 80.[12] It appears
that it is these, and not 'reputed orthodox' ecclesiastics, that Justin
is alluding to again in 80. 3–5. The full parallel between the
accounts of Justin and Irenaeus should be recognized. Justin also
mentions pious, true Christian non-chiliasts (80. 2) and so, it would
seem, does Irenaeus.

Both writers then implicate heretical and orthodox non-chiliasts
and the resemblance between the two descriptions is notable.[13]

We conclude that it is Valentinian dogma which Irenaeus openly
confronts in v. 31 but with the motive of also refuting a teaching
of certain non-chiliastic catholics which approximates the heretical
notion in view. We have then no indication that the orthodox non-
chiliasts known to Irenaeus objected to the resurrection of the flesh.
This is shown again in that when he does return to these orthodox
non-chiliasts in 32. 1 (*Quoniam igitur ... quorundam*) he does not
criticize them for denying the salvation of the flesh but merely for
being 'ignorant ... of the mystery of the resurrection of the just,
and of the kingdom which is the commencement of incorruption'.
That is, they do not believe that the just will rise a thousand years
before the rest of mankind.

2. The Stumbling Block to Chiliasm

It must be kept in mind that the purpose of Irenaeus here is to
clear the way for his exposition of millennialism by explaining why
there are some from among those who *putantur recte credidisse*
who 'are ignorant of the methods by which they are disciplined
beforehand for incorruption', that is, who are not chiliasts. By
giving no place to an earthly millennium these orthodox thus leave
out a crucial step in the *ordo promotionis justorum*. In this, says
Irenaeus, they resemble the heretics, whose compunction against
an earthly millennium is understandable, enemies that they are of
the handiwork of God and the salvation of the flesh. But the real

---

[12] The heretics in 35. 5 teach 'to blaspheme the Maker of all things, and
Christ ... and the God of Abraham, and of Isaac, and of Jacob'; the heretics in 80. 4
also 'venture to blaspheme the God of Abraham, and the God of Isaac, and the God
of Jacob'. In 35. 5 these heretics are known to be 'atheists, impious, unrighteous,
and sinful, and confessors of Jesus in name only'; the heretics in 80. 3 also 'are
called Christians, but are godless, impious heretics, [who] teach doctrines that are
in every way blasphemous, atheistical, and foolish'. See Prigent, *Justin*, 72–3.

[13] Gry, *Millénarisme*, 79–80, wonders, with good reason, whether Irenaeus in *AH*
v. 31 was inspired by this passage. Prigent, *Justin*, 32–3, so believes.

common ground between these two groups is not the denial of an 'entire' resurrection.[14] The common ground with the heretics, the reason why certain orthodox cannot acquiesce to millennialism, is evidently the belief that the righteous go immediately after death into the presence of God in heaven.[15]

If it is true, continues the bishop, with an eye on both groups of non-millennialists, that the soul departs on high at death, then this must have obtained also for our Lord—but such was not the case. For three days 'He dwelt in the place where the dead were' and ascended to the Father only after he had risen in the flesh. No disciple is above his master, and none of the redeemed will enter into the presence of God except by observing the same pattern (the 'law of the dead') followed by their Lord, who awaited the resurrection of his flesh before quitting Hades. Therefore, they too will 'go away into the (invisible) place allotted to them by God',[16] where they will await the resurrection of the just and the millennium. This allotted place is a region in the netherworld ('the heart of the earth', Matt. 11: 40; 'the lower parts of the earth', Eph. 4: 9; and the nethermost hell, Ps. 86: 23).[17]

Irenaeus counters the Gnostic-sounding obstacle to the adoption of chiliasm by teaching that the souls of the righteous are detained in Hades until the day of resurrection. We must pause at this point to observe that earlier in his great treatise Irenaeus had himself allowed for the admittance of Christians into heaven before the resurrection. In iii. 16. 4 he speaks of the innocents slaughtered by Herod, 'For this cause, too, He suddenly removed those children belonging to the house of David, whose happy lot it was to have been born at that time, that He might send them on before into His kingdom; He, since He was Himself an infant, so arranging it that human infants should be martyrs, slain, according to the Scriptures, for the sake of Christ ...'. Similarly in iv. 33. 9, 'Wherefore the

[14] Contra Finé, 33.

[15] Schmidt, 520, 'These are genuine Gnostics; with them their opponents have in common only general points of contact, which are documented in the view of the immediate ascent of the souls after death, but they proceed from entirely different presuppositions.'

[16] Animae abibunt in invisibilem locum definitum eis a Deo, but the Greek survives in the Sacra Parallela (Holl, 81): Αἱ ψυχαὶ ἀπέρχονται εἰς τὸν τόπον τὸν ὡρισμένον αὐταῖς ἀπὸ τοῦ θεοῦ.

[17] It is curious that Schmidt, 495–8, thinks this is a superterrestrial paradise. He is mistaken in equating this 'appointed place' with the paradise of v. 5. 1 whose inhabitants are still in their flesh.

Church does in every place, because of that love which she cherishes towards God, send forward, throughout all time, a multitude of martyrs to the Father.' It is usually presumed that he, like Tertullian, held a consistent and integrated view which acknowledged a special dispensation for the martyrs to be excused from Hades and to enter heaven.[18] There are, however, at least four grounds for challenging this presumption. First, although these two texts do specify martyrs, another text intervenes which speaks in the same terms but apparently of the saints in general. In IV. 31. 3 he compares the Church to Lot's wife who was turned into a pillar of salt, 'indicating that the Church also, which is the salt of the earth, has been left behind within the confines of the earth, and subject to human sufferings; and while entire members are often taken away from it, the pillar of salt still endures, thus typifying the foundation of the faith which maketh strong, and sends forward (*praemittens*), children to their Father'.[19] *Fragment* 26 (Harvey, ii. 492–3) may also be cited.[20] Irenaeus is commenting on the floating axehead in 2 Kings 6: 6.

This was a sign that souls should be born aloft (ἀναγωγῆς ψυχῶν) through the instrumentality of wood, upon which He suffered who can lead those souls aloft that follow His ascension. This event was also an indication of the fact, that when the holy soul of Christ descended [to Hades], many souls ascended and were seen in their bodies.

This text states that souls follow Christ in his ascension to heaven. It also relates that the appearance of the resurrected bodies of some of the saints at the time of Christ's ascension (Matt. 27: 52) was part of an ascending company of souls 'seen' in their bodies, and this is linked with Christ's descent into Hades. We do not know when the work was written of which this fragment is a part. But in Irenaeus' only other reference to this incident from the life of Elisha (*AH* v. 17. 4, written close to the time when his millennial chapters were penned), while the typology of the wood cast into the water as prefiguring the cross still governs the citation, it is

---

[18] Kirchner, 328; Massuet (dissert. 3, art. x, n. 122, *PG* vii, col. 380); Ermoni, 382; Gry, *Millénarisme*, 73–4 all citing IV. 33. 9; Wünsche, 517, incorrect in any case, opens the door for patriarchs and prophets too in the thought of both Irenaeus and Tertullian.

[19] Similarly at III. 11. 8 we also read that the new covenant 'renovates man, and sums up all things in itself by means of the Gospel, raising and bearing men upon its wings into the heavenly kingdom.'

[20] With some reserve. See next note.

significant that we find a different interpretation of the typological meaning of the axehead.[21] *AH* IV. 31. 3 and *Fragment* 26 (if allowed) appear to weaken the position that a fundamental distinction was made by him between martyrs and the rest of the faithful and tend to show that before writing *AH* V Irenaeus gave credence to the view that the souls of all the faithful would ascend to heaven at death.

Second, V. 31–32 is Irenaeus' only extended discussion of the topic of the intermediate state and in it no exceptions are made for any, *not even for Christ*, to the *lex mortuorum*, which is that all souls depart into their sub-earthly abodes until reunited with their flesh before ascending therefrom.[22] To have gone on to heaven would have made them 'servants above their master'.

Third, he says expressly in V. 32. 1 that even those who were afflicted in this life and 'slain because of their love to God' must be revived to reign in that very creation in which they suffered. Thus consolation even of martyrs is assigned to the millennial earth and not to the celestial courts.

Fourth, the case of Tertullian is instructive. We shall have more to say about it later, but we may pre-empt our discussion to say that early in his career he believed all the righteous would go at once to heaven at death. His later 'martyrs only' position, taken in *De anima* and *De resurrectione carnis*, is clearly a break with the former and looks then like a compromise between two extreme views. It appears most likely therefore that in the course of composing the *AH* Irenaeus too changed his view on the subject or at the very least sorted out in book V what had been a lightly held tangle of traditional beliefs. And if this is true the question arises naturally whether this change of position may not signify a concomitant turn towards the embracing of a chiliasm not held before. More will be said on this later when further evidence has been drawn from other quarters.

We may now reflect on the implications of Irenaeus' connecting of these two doctrines of the millennium and the intermediate state and on the place of this connection within his distinctive defence of millennialism.

[21] The authenticity of this fragment has been denied by Devreesse, 24, (repeated in *CPG* i. 115) who, however, offers no explanation or discussion of the matter. If the incongruency with *AH* V. 17. 4 is the only point against it, we might just as easily theorize that the fragment was written before *AH* V. See § II. 2. 2 below.

[22] Those select few who were translated to paradise (V. 5. 1) were translated bodily and so formed no exception either.

Irenaeus' objective in placing this discussion as prefatory to his extended treatment of the millennium should by now be plain. On the view of the non-chiliast orthodox (similarly with that of the heretical dualists) the righteous may enter the *conspectus Dei* immediately after death. These people must therefore be taught that there remains, before the just can be considered worthy to enter the divine presence, first a period of waiting in infernal abodes, then the resurrection of the just and the reign of the millennium. The millennium for Irenaeus serves the necessary purpose of training and gradually accustoming the righteous to apprehend God and his glory (*paulatim assuescunt capere Deum*, v. 32. 1; cf. v. 35. 1–2).[23]

Irenaeus thus exposes a logical and systematic connection between belief in a heavenly intermediate state and refusal of the notion of a future, temporary kingdom of Christ on earth. It is a logical connection because, if souls are ushered into heaven, into the very presence of God and Christ, immediately after death and not detained in refreshing sub-earthly vaults, a future, earthly kingdom would seem at best an anticlimactic appendage to salvation history, at worst a serious and unconscionable retrogression. The millennium is then entirely redundant.[24] It is a 'systematic'

---

[23] We cannot pass this by without remarking on the intriguing likelihood that Irenaeus' own depiction of the millennium was in fact influenced by his Valentinian opponents' depiction of the intermediate state. In v. 31. 1 and v. 35. 2 the millennium is that time in which the just are 'trained beforehand for incorruption' and grow and flourish in the kingdom (*modos meditationis ad incorruptelam* v. 31. 1 line 3 SC; *justi praemeditantur incorruptelam et parantur in salutem* v. 35. 2 lines 105–6, SC; *vere praemeditabitur incorruptelam et augebitur et vigebit in regni temporibus* v. 35. 2 lines 113–15, SC). In I. 7. 5 Irenaeus had indicated that in Valentinianism the πνευματικά also undergo after this life a stage of further training and nourishment in the μεσότης before being counted worthy of final perfection. 'But they assert that the spiritual principles which have been sown by Achamoth, being disciplined (παιδευθέντα) and nourished (ἐκτραφέντα) here from that time until now [i.e. until the consummation] in righteous souls (because when given forth by her they were yet but weak), at last attaining to perfection . . .' (Cf. Tertullian, *Val.* 26.)

[24] It is necessary to go back to some of the older writers on patristic eschatology to find any recognition of this. Ermoni, in a most perceptive, if overly dogmatic, analysis, wrote that the theological problem which faced chiliasm was 'the destiny of the soul after death' (379); 'they taught therefore that the just would not be admitted to the beatific vision until after the thousand-year reign and the general resurrection; this was the natural consequence of their system . . .' (380). Wünsche, 517, similarly, speaking in general of the chiliast view, said, 'The souls of the righteous, accordingly, could not go immediately into heaven after death but would have to spend the time until the parousia in an intermediate state.' Cf. also Tixeront, 227, regarding Justin.

connection because it would appear by inference that the heavenly intermediate state, in the system of his orthodox dissenters, is the opposing counterpart of the earthly millennium in the system of Irenaeus. As introducing the redeemed into direct fellowship with their Saviour and their God this heavenly, post-mortem existence *takes the place of the millennium.*

Just how valid, in a historical/theological sense, are these connections which Irenaeus alleges to have existed between millennial views and ideas of the intermediate state? Do they justify a re-examination of early Christian eschatology in their light? Examples already spring to mind of early Christian writers who entertained the hope of an immediate removal to heaven at death. Does Irenaeus really mean to imply that these are all amillennialists, or at the very least, confused and inconsistent in their millennialism?

In the next section we shall begin to test these connections by examining the writings of other known, pre-Nicaean chiliasts to inquire into their notions of the intermediate state.

2. OTHER ANTE-NICENE CHILIASTS

1. Papias

The days will come, in which vines shall grow, each having ten thousand branches, and in each branch ten thousand twigs, and in each true twig ten thousand shoots, and in each one of the shoots ten thousand clusters, and on every one of the clusters ten thousand grapes, and every grape when pressed will give five and twenty metretes of wine. And when any one of the saints shall lay hold of a cluster, another shall cry out, 'I am a better cluster, take me; bless the Lord through me.' In like manner [the Lord declared] that a grain of wheat would produce ten thousand ears, and that every ear should have ten thousand grains, and every grain would yield ten pounds of clear, pure, fine flour; and that all other fruit-bearing trees, and seeds and grass, would produce in similar proportions; and that all animals feeding [only] on the productions of the earth, should [in those days] become peaceful and harmonious among each other, and be in perfect subjection to man.

Thus runs Papias' famous description of the wonders of the coming earthly kingdom, a description he claims he received from the elders who saw John the disciple, who in turn is said to have received it directly from the Lord (Irenaeus, *AH* v. 33. 3). It may be unfortunate that we have no scrap of tradition under the name of Papias which directly concerns the intermediate state of the righteous dead. We are, however, not left in complete ignorance about his view.

We have already alluded to Irenaeus' doctrine of paradise preserved in *AH* v. 5. 1–2, according to which the only human inhabitants of paradise in the present age, apart from Christ, are that tiny proportion of humanity thought to have been translated bodily before meeting death.

Where, then, was the first man placed? In paradise certainly, as the Scripture declares: [citing Gen. 2. 8]. And then afterwards, when [man] proved disobedient, he was cast out thence into this world. Wherefore . . . those who were translated were transferred to that place (for paradise has been prepared for righteous men, such as have the Spirit; in which place also Paul the apostle, when he was caught up, heard words which are unspeakable as regards us in our present condition), and that there shall they who have been translated remain until the consummation [of all things], as a prelude to immortality. (*AH* v. 5. 1)

. . . and those who were translated do live as an earnest of the future length of days. (v. 5. 2)

As will become clearer as our study proceeds, this view of the inhabitants of paradise is indeed but the correlative of Irenaeus' understanding of the intermediate state: there is a 'law of the dead' according to which the souls of all the dead descend to Hades, there to await the resurrection. It is therefore only those who have been preserved from death, such as Elijah, who was caught up to heaven in a fiery chariot, who may reside in the otherworldly paradise until the return of Christ.

Now, Irenaeus twice expressly tells us (*AH* v. 5. 1; 36. 1) that he got his doctrine of paradise from 'the elders who were disciples of the apostles' and this naturally leads to the assumption that the channel of this paradise tradition was none other than Papias. Indeed, Lightfoot and Bacon have all but demonstrated this.[25] If they are correct, and if we may accept that Papias himself had adopted this tradition, we may then attribute to Papias too belief

---

[25] Lightfoot, *Supernatural*, 198–202; Bacon, 176, 182–6. Körtner, 36–43, it seems to me, is overly restrictive in denying the link between the 'elders' and Papias. If he is correct, our conclusions with respect to Papias would apply instead only to the impersonalized 'words of the elders' which Irenaeus allegedly received from another source.

in the correlative teaching of a subterranean intermediate state for
the righteous dead, and regard him as almost certainly a chief
source of Irenaeus' view of the intermediate state expressed in
v. 31–32.

2. Justin

Many scholars would argue that Justin never achieved consistency
in his view of end-time events. Not only does Justin omit any
mention in his Apologies[26] of an expected earthly kingdom of
Christ—an omission which, as has often been pointed out, could
be excused on grounds of expediency—but his teaching there and
even in parts of the *Dialogue* seems hard to reconcile with such an
expectation. He castigates the Romans for assuming, when they
hear that the Christians look for a kingdom, that this kingdom is
a human one 'whereas we speak of that which is with God'. 'For
if we looked for a human kingdom, we should also deny our Christ,
that we might not be slain; and we should strive to escape detection,
that we might obtain what we expect' (*1Apol.* 11. 1–2). This would
seem an uneasy partner to a chiliastic hope[27] and shows more
affinity with the anticipation of Christ's kingdom expressed by the
grandsons of Jude (*HE* iii. 20. 4, see Introduction). In *1Apol.* 52 and
in *Dial.* 45. 4; 113. 3–5; 139. 5 Justin awaits a general resurrection,
a final judgement and the establishment of an eternal (not a temporary) kingdom on the renewed earth to ensue upon the parousia.
Nevertheless, chapters 80–1 of the *Dialogue* are openly if not enthu-
siastically chiliastic. L. W. Barnard has justly said, 'It is a hopeless
task to reconcile this belief in an earthly millennium in Jerusalem
with Justin's other opinion that the new Jerusalem will be an
immediate, spiritual, eternal land or inheritance.'[28] Barnard seeks

[26] The question whether the apologies were originally one or two will not occupy
us. We shall refer to them under their traditional headings.
[27] Gry, *Millénarisme*, 76–7; Harnack, *Lehrbuch*, i. 614–15; Stonehouse, 17. Though
Goodenough, *Theology*, 286, n. 2, disagrees, 'The mention of the future kingdom in
Ap. i. 11 is nothing more than an extremely awkward attempt to avoid the subject.'
[28] Barnard, *Justin*, 165. See Goodenough, *Theology*, 285, 'There seems to be no
way of reconciling the millennium with the clear implication of Justin's other remarks
that the new Jerusalem will be an eternal inheritance'; Stonehouse, 18, 'Justin's
teaching on the millennium finds no essential place in his theological thinking and
even seems to be inconsistent with his customary mode of expression'; Skarsaune,
403, 'Justin at least in some of these passages [i.e. on Jerusalem] is dependent upon
a source which was not millenarian and which located the final redemption in the
land and Jerusalem'; Grant, *Apologists*, 64.

to explain the conflict by recurring to Professor Moule's theory of the influence of circumstances on eschatology.[29] Whether or not this can provide a satisfactory solution,[30] I wish above all to observe here a similar and a corresponding equivocation on the matter of the intermediate state.

In his apologies and in the account of his martyrdom we find the following view of life after death.[31]

And when Lucius answered, 'Most certainly I am [a Christian],' he again ordered him also to be led away. And he professed his thanks, knowing that he was delivered from such wicked rulers, and was going to the Father and King of the heavens. (*2Apol.* 2. 18, 19)

'If you are scourged and beheaded, do you believe that you will ascend to heaven?'

'I have confidence from my perseverance,' said Justin, 'if I endure. Indeed, I know that for those who lead a just life there awaits the divine gift even to the consummation.'

The prefect Rusticus said: 'You think, then, that you will ascend?'

'I do not think,' said Justin, 'but I am fully convinced of it.' (*MartJustin* 5)[32]

It is thus expected that the Christian, when he dies, will ascend to heaven to be with the Father and King of heaven. But in the *Dialogue* we find only criticism of this view. Placed alongside other enormities of certain false Christians, namely their blasphemy of the OT God and their denial of the resurrection of the flesh, is their boast that 'their souls, when they die, are taken (ἀναλαμβάνεϲθαι) to heaven' (ch. 80). Though the quarrel with 'so-called Christians' who showed disaffection toward the OT God and who spurned the hope

---

[29] Moule, *JTS*, 1–15; Barnard, *Justin*, 158, 'His eschatological language varies according to circumstance, as with the New Testament writers, and this is the cause of his apparent contradictions.'

[30] I must confess my doubts. That circumstances affected his eschatology is patent, but this does not change the meaning of 'contradiction', or reconcile 'irreconcilable' beliefs. This observation does not force us to the alternative that Justin was 'a simple-minded, uncritical, muddled Christian' (*contra* Barnard, *Justin*, 167–8). Laguier, 193, sees in Justin's contradictions a lack of firm conviction in any one eschatological system. Cf. also Osborn's discussion, *Justin*, 197–8. Goodenough, *Theology*, 291, is doubtless too quick to find disharmony but it still seems necessary to say that Justin's writings incorporate varying Christian eschatological traditions.

[31] Translations of the *Dial.* and the apologies are those of Roberts and Donaldson, *ANF* i.

[32] The translation of Musurillo, *Acts*.

of bodily resurrection had by this time a long history,[33] this is
apparently the earliest recorded Christian censure of the notion of
the soul's immediate (ἅμα) ascent to heaven at death. It is most
significant that this, also Justin's *only* expression of antipathy
towards the doctrine, occurs precisely in his defence of chiliasm.
What alternative to this belief about the righteous dead does Justin
offer? It is but an inference from this passage that souls should
remain instead in Hades.[34] But in *Dial*. 99. 3 Justin says that those
who were ignorant of who Christ was, 'fancied they would put Him
to death, and that He, like some common mortal, would remain in
Hades'. To remain in Hades, then, is the lot of the 'common man'.[35]
This is also the position of Irenaeus in *AH* v. 31.

Again, as with the views of Irenaeus, these two views of Justin
on the intermediate state are sometimes assumed to have been
reconciled and integrated into a single one which held that martyrs
alone could be excused from Hades and allowed direct access into
heaven.[36] After all, both instances cited above for the belief in a
heavenly intermediate state concern martyrs. But again, we find no
articulation of this position, and there are indications that such a
position was not his. It would demand that martyrs were considered
by Justin as in a class with Christ above the κοινοὶ ἄνθρωποι who
remain in Hades until the judgement. But Justin never espouses
such a view:

and if men by their good works show themselves worthy of His design,
they are deemed worthy, and so we have received—of reigning in company
with Him, being delivered from corruption and suffering. For . . . those who
choose what is pleasing to Him are, on account of their choice, deemed
worthy of incorruption and of fellowship with Him. (*1Apol*. 10. 2–3)

---

[33] e.g. Ignatius, *Trall*. 9, 10, *Smyrn*. 1–4; Polycarp, *Phil*. 7 where he who impugns
the resurrection and coming judgement is called the 'first born of Satan', an epithet
later applied personally to Marcion (according to Irenaeus, *AH* iii. 3. 4). Docetic
opinions, of course, are encountered at least as far back as the epistles of John
(1 John 4: 2; 2 John 7). See Gunther, *VC*.

[34] An inference drawn by Trollope, 21.

[35] Finé, 83, 'Justin alone [sc. of all the Apostolic Fathers and Apologists]
appears . . . to presuppose a general stay in Hades for all men.' In ch. 5 the philosopher who had introduced Justin to Christianity is reported to have said that 'the
souls of the pious remain in a better place (ἐν κρείττονί ποι χώρῳ μένειν) while those
of the unjust and wicked are in a worse, waiting for the time of judgement. Thus
some which have appeared worthy of God never die' (5. 3). Fischer, *Todesgedanken*,
241, judges no doubt correctly that both places are in the underworld, 'as likewise
an old Jewish tradition taught'.

[36] Quasten, i. 219.

And when you hear that we look for a kingdom, you suppose ... that we speak of a human kingdom; whereas we speak of that which is with God, as appears also from the confession of their faith made by those who are charged with being Christians, though they know that death is the punishment awarded to him who so confesses. For if we looked for a human kingdom, we should also deny our Christ, that we might not be slain; and we should strive to escape detection, that we might obtain what we expect. But since our thoughts are not fixed on the present, we are not concerned when men cut us off; since also death is a debt which must at all events be paid. (*1Apol.* 11)

they become our benefactors when they set us free from sufferings and necessities of this life ... (*1Apol.* 57. 3)

Christians in general, not only martyrs, look for this kingdom which is 'with God' (μετὰ θεοῦ ch. 11). 'Being delivered from corruption and suffering', mentioned in chapter 10, if it is the same thing as being set 'free from sufferings and necessities of this life' of chapter 57, refers to the time of death, and hence the reigning in company with God (in the kingdom which is μετὰ θεοῦ) is something the worthy may receive at that time.

There are problems then for assuming that Justin held a consistent 'martyr élitist' view akin to what we later find in Tertullian. It is more likely that he is simply the indiscriminate heir of divergent Christian traditions. There is yet another possible explanation. Quasten and many others maintain that the *Dialogue*, is 'not altogether a literary convention', but that the 'real conversations and discussions' on which the work is based very probably took place in Ephesus not long after the failure of Bar Cochba's revolt (*Dial.* 1, 9).[37] According to Justin's words in chapter 80, it was his admissions on this very subject of a coming, earthly reign in Jerusalem— so 'Jewish' a teaching that Trypho is surprised to hear it confessed by the Christian philosopher—which led Justin to promise that he would put this admission into writing in the form of a record of their debate. That is, their discussion on the chiliastic question (a matter of considerable ferment in the wake of the late attempt to re-establish a Jewish kingdom in Palestine) is in some sense the genesis of the *Dialogue* itself as a literary piece.[38] Thus, unless this promise was a pure literary fiction on Justin's part, we might expect a concern with staying true to his opinion as expressed in the

[37] Ibid. 203.
[38] On Justin's motives for writing and his intended audience, see Nilson.

historical debate to have competed with the fact of evolution in his theology over the course of more than twenty years before the treatise was published (after the first apology, *Dial.* 120). It may be then that Justin, having adopted a chiliastic eschatology soon after his conversion,[39] saw that eschatology change over the years, a process surely facilitated by his long sojourn in Rome, where chiliasm was never part of the mainstream.

However the confusion in Justin's eschatology is best accounted for, we only emphasize here that the two doctrines of chiliasm and the intermediate state seem to fall out consistently along the lines drawn by Irenaeus. Where Justin is advocating chiliasm we find antipathy towards the idea of an immediate entry of the soul into God's presence at death, an idea replaced by the view that even the righteous are detained in Hades to await there the resurrection. Where Justin on the other hand presses a view of the kingdom as residing with God in heaven and not as something the Christian could attain by preserving his life on this earth, we also find the idea that the righteous dead go to be with the Father in this heavenly kingdom at the time of death.

3. *Tertullian*

Tertullian the chiliast adamantly rejected the idea that the soul of the Christian, when it takes leave of the body at death, has its repose in the celestial presence of God. We noted above that Irenaeus may have been influenced in *AH* v. 31 by Justin's *Dial.* 80. In turn, Tertullian's most explicit treatment of the subject comes in *De anima* 55,[40] a passage materially dependent upon Irenaeus, *AH* v. 31.[41] In *De anima* 55 Hades is described as 'a vast deep space in the interior of the earth, and a concealed recess in its very bowels'. Tertullian warns the reader,

you must suppose Hades to be a subterranean region (*regionem inferum subterraneam*), and keep at arm's length those who are too proud to believe

[39] Skarsaune, 'Conversion', 73.

[40] In a recent article, Hill, *VC*, I have shown reasons for regarding the fragment *De universo*, formerly attributed to Hippolytus, as the work of Tertullian or of one strongly influenced by him. This fragment, which possibly is from Tertullian's lost *De paradiso*, (cf. *An.* 55. 5; *Marc.* v. 12) gives an even fuller description of Hades, the home of righteous and wicked souls awaiting the resurrection. The fragment is found in the *Sacra parallela* of pseudo-John Damascene; in Holl's edition, 137–43.

[41] Waszink, *Anima*, 554; Finé, 86. Waszink's Latin text of *De anima* is followed; I rely, with some revisions, upon S. Thelwall's English translation in *ANF* iii.

that the souls of the faithful deserve a place in the lower regions (*inferis*). These persons, who are 'servants above their Lord, and disciples above their Master', would no doubt spurn to receive the comfort of the resurrection, if they must expect it in Abraham's bosom. 'But it was for this purpose', say they, 'that Christ descended into Hades, that we might not ourselves have to descend thither. Otherwise, what difference is there between heathens and Christians, if the same prison awaits them all when dead?' How, indeed, shall the soul mount up to heaven, where Christ is already sitting at the Father's right hand, when yet the archangel's trumpet has not been heard by the command of God . . . To no one is heaven opened . . . When the world, indeed, shall pass away, then the kingdom of heaven shall be opened. (55. 2–4)

Tertullian's retort to the effect that his opponents 'would no doubt spurn to receive the comfort of the resurrection, if they must expect it in Abraham's bosom' shows that these opponents did believe in the resurrection. They are thus to be distinguished from the heretical non-chiliasts named by Justin and Irenaeus but form an agreeable likeness to their orthodox non-chiliasts.[42] Elsewhere Tertullian will inform us that 'No other persons, indeed, refuse to concede to the substance of the body its recovery from death, than the heretical inventors of a second deity' (*Res.* 2. 2). Further, Tertullian's opponents did not object to a descent of Christ into Hades, as did the Valentinian non-chiliasts Irenaeus faced (*AH* v. 31. 2, see our discussion above); they merely view the motive and result of that descent differently from Tertullian (and Irenaeus): 'No, but in Paradise',[43] they answer Tertullian, 'whither already the patriarchs and prophets have removed from Hades in the retinue of the Lord's resurrection' (55. 4).[44] This statement also shows the distance

[42] *Pace* Finé, 91, 'They are the Christian Gnostics (probably the Valentinians).'

[43] Thus note the contrast with 'the elders', Papias, and Irenaeus on the population of paradise.

[44] Waszink, *Anima*, 557, believes Tertullian confutes in this chapter two different groups, one (in para. 2) which denied the very existence of such a *regio inferum subterranea*, another (in para. 3) who believed that Christ's mission to the underworld had liberated the just and had transferred them to heaven, thus relieving Christians from having to sojourn there at all. But attention turns towards the latter group beginning at least with 'you must suppose Hades to be a subterranean region, and keep at arm's length those who . . .' in para. 2, for the opponents mentioned here are the same ones who say in para. 3 that Christ's descent frees them from the necessity of having to sojourn in Hades, obviously presupposing that such a place as Hades exists. It is these who, Tertullian mocks, would even spurn a resurrection if it must take place in Abraham's bosom—meaning that they do not deny the resurrection. As we saw above, Irenaeus in *AH* v. 31 deals explicitly only with advocates of the first view. Tertullian, on the other hand, though he borrows

between these opponents and Marcion, according to whom the patriarchs and prophets, as disciples of the OT God, remain in Hades to this day (Irenaeus, *AH* I. 27. 3; Tertullian, *Marc.* III. 24. 1).

One more component of the opposing view merits our attention. The soul is supposed to mount up to paradise, or, synonymously, 'to heaven'. Tertullian objects, 'To no one is heaven opened . . . When the world, indeed, shall pass away, then the kingdom of heaven shall be opened' (55. 2–4). This heavenly paradise to which the (orthodox) opponents expect the soul will fly is also the 'kingdom of heaven'. This already reminds us of Justin's words in *1Apol.* 10. 2–3; 11 and *2Apol.* 2. 18–19 to the effect that Christians seek a kingdom which is with God and to which they go when they die. Irenaeus too said that Christ 'sent on before into his kingdom' those innocents slaughtered by Herod according to Matthew 2: 16 (*AH* III. 16. 4). Tertullian himself will admit that martyrdom secures one for the 'kingdom of heaven' (*Scorp.* 6; 10). This use of the terminology of kingdom for the heavenly realm to which Christians (whether only martyrs or others as well) go will gain in importance as our study proceeds.

As we have already intimated, in his earlier writings Tertullian himself had clung to the belief that all Christians go immediately to Christ in heaven at death. Waszink refers to *Apol.* 47. 13[45] and we might also adduce Tertullian's early uses of Philippians 1: 23, Paul's longing to depart and be with Christ, that being far better than remaining in the flesh.[46] In *De anima*, however, Tertullian's

extensively from that chapter, deals at length only with those who take the second. Waszink states that at this time the adherents of the view Tertullian opposes 'are mentioned by him only', confessing that it is 'very surprising that Irenaeus does not say anything about them'. We should instead say that Irenaeus did indeed have something to say about these 'certain orthodox', and thus realize that Tertullian depends on Irenaeus *AH* V. 31 in his refutation of them.

[45] Waszink, *Anima*, 554, 'before becoming acquainted with Marcion, he held a different view, as is shown by *Apol.* 47. 13: *si paradisum nominemus, locum divinae amoenitatis recipiendis sanctorum spiritibus destinatum, maceria quadam igneae illius zonae a notitia orbis communis segregatum*' ('And if we speak of Paradise, the place of heavenly bliss appointed to receive the spirits of the saints, severed from the knowledge of this world by that fiery zone as by a sort of enclosure . . .'). See also Finé, 80, who shows that Tertullian's expanded use of the term *inferi*, as well as his use of the parable of Dives and Lazarus dates from his conflict with Marcionism and Gnosticism (211 or later).

[46] See especially *Spect.* 28 (Quasten, ii. 293, AD 197) along with *Ux.* I. 5 (Quasten, ii. 302, AD 200–6); *Pat.* 9 (Quasten, ii. 299, AD 200–3). Even in *Exh.* 11, written in his 'semi-Montanist period' (Quasten, ii. 302), he can say of a deceased Christian wife that she is 'already received into the Lord's presence' (*iam receptae apud*

ardour would surely have barred the gates of heaven from everyone but Christ. His unrestrained statements may be cited: 'To no one is heaven opened' (*An.* 55. 3); 'Hades is not in any case opened for (the escape of) any soul' (*An.* 57. 11); 'All souls, therefore, are shut up within Hades' (*An.* 58. 1, cf. *Res.* 42. 3). Yet the pressure from Christian revelation and tradition (besides his having written an exhortation to martyrdom which would have betrayed him) lies so heavy upon him for the inclusion of the martyrs that even he must give way. Tertullian is, at the end of the day, only able to challenge his opponents with the assertion that John the author of Revelation saw under the altar in the regions of paradise *only* the souls of the martyrs and that 'the most heroic martyr Perpetua on the day of her passion saw only her fellow-martyrs there' (*An.* 55. 4).[47] No degree of holiness or piety will suffice; virgins and infants, whose condition of life was 'pure and innocent', know no higher abode than the good section of Hades (56. 8): 'The sole key to unlock Paradise is your own life's blood' (55. 5).[48]

But to allow them this key is, strictly speaking, to rescind Irenaeus' *lex mortuorum*, a law which Tertullian alludes to in *An.* 55. 2.[49] For the martyrs have not ascended, like Jesus did, in their resurrected bodies after a layover of the soul in Hades. The exception made for the martyrs seems therefore to be a concession, a compromise position between the view of Tertullian's opponents (and his former self) and the view which his position of chiliasm

dominum, cf. the allusion to Phil. 1: 23 in ch. 12), though Finé, 199, thinks this may be merely rhetorical. This is not repeated in his later work on marriage, *Monog.*, where, in ch. 10, a deceased husband may be 'sent on before' to have *refrigerium* in peace, but with no mention of his being 'with the Lord'.

[47] His only references to 2 Cor. 5: 6–8, Paul's insistence that to be at home in the body is to be away from the Lord and vice-versa, come from the later period when *An.* was written (AD 210–13). In harmony with his new position, he attributes these verses to Paul as martyr, not to Paul as Christian: 'For no one, on becoming absent from the body, is at once a dweller in the presence of the Lord, except by the prerogative of martyrdom, he gains a lodging in Paradise, not in the lower regions' (*Res.* 43. 4, Quasten, ii. 283, AD 210–12).

[48] See also *Res.* 43. 4; *Mart.* 3; *Scorp.* 12. Tertullian too, like Papias and Irenaeus, does allow that the translated (Enoch and Elijah) are preserved in the heavenly paradise (cf. *Res.* 58; *Marc.* IV. 22; V. 12), but he can no longer assert that these are its only human occupants.

[49] So Waszink, *Anima*, 566. 'With the same law of His being He fully complied, by remaining in Hades in the form of a dead man.'

demanded of him.[50] Several scholars have opined that millennialism too was adopted by Tertullian well into his Christian life through conversion to Montanism.[51] This would put his adoption of millennialism at perhaps roughly the same time as we find his new position on the intermediate state emerging. At any rate they are ultimately wedded quite happily and produce in the thought of Tertullian a conception which, while stimulated by recent admonitions of the Montanist paraclete, is seemingly original to him. Advancing beyond Irenaeus, Tertullian uses the conjunction of Hades and the millennium to the advantage of the 'order of the perfection of the just'. Enjoyment of the millennium is postponed for the less righteous of the righteous by a longer stay in the 'prison' of Hades until the last farthing is paid off (Matt. 5. 25, 26) (*An.* 7; 35. 3; 58. 8 compared with *Marc.* iii. 24. 6 and *Res.* 48. 10). The 'first resurrection' releases the just from Hades in shifts and is thus drawn out over a good part of the thousand years of the saints' earthly rule.[52]

We may conclude that Tertullian knows Christian opponents of his subterranean version of the intermediate state who are neither Valentinians (for they do believe in a future bodily resurrection) nor Marcionites (for they believe the OT righteous have been removed by Christ from Hades to heaven). With respect to their doctrine that the saved no longer need visit Hades but may ascend immediately to Christ's heavenly presence at death, these Christians match Irenaeus' orthodox, non-chiliast opponents (*AH* v. 31–2). It is, further, quite conceivable that the same view had been held by the orthodox non-chiliasts introduced to us by Justin. If it is indeed the same doctrine which is countered by both Irenaeus and Tertullian it is highly significant that Tertullian's antagonists evidently use the terminology of kingdom for this heavenly intermediate state. For we noted above the unmistakable inference from the words of Irenaeus that a heavenly post-mortem existence occupies the place of the millennium in the system of his orthodox non-chiliasts.

[50] Tertullian never focuses attention directly on the connection with chiliasm, though we must say this in the absence of his lost treatise on the millennium, *De spe fidelis.*
[51] eg. Ermoni, 370; Gry, *Millénarisme*, 82–3; Leclerq, 1186; Waszink, *Anima*, 592. Bardy, 1762, rightly allows also for the influence of Irenaeus.
[52] See Waszink, *Anima*, 592; Finé, 108. On the relation of this idea to the doctrine of purgatory see Mason, *JTS*, 598–601; d'Alès, *Tertullien*, 133, 134; Waszink, *Anima*, 593.

4. Commodianus

More materialistic in his millennialism[53] but at the same time less definite and certainly less polemical in his doctrine of the intermediate state is the Christian poet and apologist Commodianus.

Estimates of his understanding of the intermediate state have differed. While M. Richard lists Commodianus as an adherent of the subterranean view,[54] Antonio Salvatore has concluded, and not entirely without reason, that Commodianus taught a version of Christ's descent into Hades identical to that contained in the *Gospel of Nicodemus*, according to which Adam, with the rest of the OT righteous, is actually delivered from Hades to ascend to paradise with Christ.[55]

We read in line 314 of the *Carmen apologeticum* that, 'Hades gave way that Adam might be raised (*leuaretur*) from death'. On the other hand, it may be that being 'raised' or 'alleviated'[56] from death is not necessarily equivalent to being raised up out of Hades and into heaven. Commodianus' language is certainly no stronger than that employed by Irenaeus in his citation of the Jeremiah apocryphon in *AH* v. 31. 1, 'and he descended to them to bring them out (*extrahere*) and to save them', where it cannot be maintained that Irenaeus believed this to signify an already accomplished 'extraction' from Hades (cf. Tertullian, *An.* 55. 2).[57]

---

[53] For reviews of his chiliasm see Brewer, 283–9; Martin, *Studien*, 12–13, 133–7; Durel, 49–60; Gagé, 355–78. The only notices of this man in Antiquity come from Gennadius (*De viris inlustribus* 15) and in the list of proscribed authors in the pseudo-Gelasian decretals. His dates are not agreed upon. Some follow Brewer, who located Commodianus in the mid-fifth century. Others such as Young, 610; Durel, 313 and Thraede, 110–11 believe his language, style and the content of his writing reveal a 3rd-cent. African. Gagé, 355–78, makes a case for dating Commodianus' two works, the *Instructions* in two books and the *Carmen apologeticum*, between the years 258–62. For the purposes of our study we shall assume that he belongs to the 3rd cent.

[54] Richard, 'Hippolyte', 567.   [55] Salvatore, 154.

[56] See Durel, 248, on the various senses for *leuare* found in Commodianus, 'to remove, to take away, to relieve or heal, to resuscitate' (enlever, ôter, relever ou guérir, ressusciter).

[57] Daniélou, *TJC*, 236–7, thinks this version of the apocryphon (which Irenaeus cites six times but never in exactly the same words) speaks 'not simply of a salvation won by Christ which would be completed at the resurrection of the dead, but of a liberation, a resurrection already accomplished'. But despite appearances, Irenaeus cannot have intended this for it is in this very context that he is making the point that all the righteous dead are still in Hades until the resurrection. His purpose in adducing the apocryphon here is merely to show that Christ made a real descent to a real place *ubi erant mortui*. A more satisfactory accounting for the differing versions of the apocryphon in Irenaeus is to be found in Skarsaune, 452.

What is more, the remaining references of Commodianus to the state of the righteous dead seem to suppose a habitation still in Hades and not in heaven.

> For to him who has lived well there is advantage after death.
> Thou, however, when one day thou diest,
>   shalt be taken away in an evil place.
> But they who believe in Christ shall be led into a good place,
> And those to whom that delight is given are caressed.
>   (*Instr.* i. 24. 18–21)[58]

The opposition of 'good place' to 'evil place' is vague in itself but evokes the words of the philosopher to Justin in *Dial.* 5. 3, 'the souls of the pious remain in a better place while those of the unjust and wicked are in a worse, waiting for the time of judgement', and those of Tertullian in *An.* 56. 8, 'which of its two regions, the region of the good or of the bad (*aut bonos aut malos inferos*)' (cf. Lactantius, *DInst.* vii. 7. 7, cited below). Besides enjoying 'delights' and 'caressings' (*blanditia* and *amoenitas*), the soul, Commodianus says, also may expect refreshment and rest (*refrigerium* and *requies*) in death (ii. 13. 19, 20; cf. ii. 32. 7). These same words (*refrigerium*, *Idol.* 13; *Marc.* iii. 24; iv. 34; *An.* 58. 1, and *requies*, *Marc.* iv. 34; *An.* 57. 11) had earlier been used by Tertullian to describe the life of the righteous soul in Hades.

According to Commodianus, while the wicked dead are tormented, Abel, who was the first martyr (*Instr.* ii. 17) and therefore a candidate for immediate heavenly bliss in the compromise view of Tertullian, 'lives and occupies the place on the right hand' (*uiuet et loca dextera tenet*, *Instr.* i. 26. 33–4). This 'place on the right' is surely that good section of Hades which the author of the fragment *De universo* also says is 'on the right' (line 23). There the righteous are 'enjoying always the contemplation of the blessings which are in their view, and delighting themselves with the expectation of others ever new' (lines 26–8).[59] The left and right sections in Hades, according to *De universo*, are places to which the evil and the good are 'conducted' at death (lines 24, 33, 35), just as we read also in

---

[58] The text is found in Martin, CC, 19. Translations of the *Instructions* are those of R. E. Wallis, *ANF* iv.

[59] It is true that Hermas knows a 'right hand of the sanctuary' (Vis. 3. 2.1) as a station in heaven for the redeemed but for him the left hand side is also in heaven; the distinction pertains only to saints. For Commodianus, whose colloquy here is with a 'wicked one', the left hand side would be where the tormented are.

Commodianus (*Instr.* I. 24. 19).[60] Judging then from his statement concerning Abel, Commodianus would seem to restrict access to heaven more severely even than Tertullian did.[61] He knows of no heavenly concession for the martyrs.

Though death is to Commodianus not absolute non-existence (*Instr.* I. 27. 1) in that the soul remains even then susceptible to pains or pleasures, immortality is something which is presented by Commodianus as being bestowed only at the resurrection in the future golden age, that is, in the millennium. 'The golden age ... shall come to thee if thou believest, and again thou shalt begin to live always an immortal life' (*Instr.* I. 34. 18–19); 'We shall be immortal when six thousand years are accomplished' (*Instr.* I. 35. 6; cf. also I. 29. 10; I. 44. 4). It is only at the time of the 'golden age', and not at the time of death, that men shall be made 'associates' with God (*CarmA.* 669–72).

Richard then is justified in listing Commodianus as an exponent of a subterranean intermediate state for the righteous. Being also a defender of chiliasm, Commodianus joins Justin, Irenaeus, Tertullian, and most probably Papias, as a witness to the conjunction of these two eschatological doctrines.

5. Novatian

We do not leave this period just following the midpoint of the third century without a comment on the doctrine of Novatian expressed in book I of his great treatise on the Trinity.

[60] For Tertullian too there is an angelic 'arrainger of souls' who brings each soul to its infernal lodgings (*An.* 53. 6). See Finé, 54–63.

[61] We might add that though the codex Mediomontanus (Cheltenhamensis, ninth century, first used by Dombart in 1887 and made the basis of Martin's recent edition) reads at I. 36. 8–10 ... *mundo, qui numquam transmutat animos in Domini credere crucem. Venit in herrorem* ... , the earlier editions of Rigaltius (1649), Oehler (1847) and Ludwig (1877) (based on the seventeenth-century codices Parisinus and Leidensis) read ... *mundo, qui numquam transmittit (transmittat,* Ludwig) *animos in deum. Credere crucem venit in horrorem* ... If the latter reading ('... the world which never transmits souls to God') could be preferred a strong statement against a heavenly intermediate state would result. While neither *transmuto* nor *transmitto* is used elsewhere by Commodianus, the latter finds at least some conceptual support in that death is conceived by him as a 'transition' for the soul to rest and refreshment in II. 13. 19, 20 (*Expecta requiem futurorum transitu mortis*). Further, Tertullian criticizes Valentinians who use this type of language, 'The souls of just men, that is to say, our souls, will be conveyed (*transmittentur*) to the Demiurge in the abodes of the middle region' (*Val.* 32), so it is quite believable that Commodianus too would censure it.

And truly, what lies beneath the earth (*infra terram iacent*) is not itself void of distributed and arranged powers. For there is a place whither the souls of the just and the unjust are taken (*ducuntur*), conscious of the anticipated dooms of future judgment.[62]

We find in the remaining works of Novatian no evidence of chiliasm. On the other hand, we find no assurance that he was not a chiliast. Perhaps this view of the intermediate state for the pious was derived purely and simply from Tertullian,[63] in which case Novatian may have taken it over with or without Tertullian's corresponding chiliasm.

6. Methodius

It is not until 'the dawn of the fourth century'[64] that we find in Methodius of Olympus the first clear disruption of the pattern which we have been observing. Or so it seems at first sight. Although he championed a form of chiliasm along with an eschatology which combated what he saw as the excesses and heresies of Origen, Methodius seems only to know a view of the intermediate state which is quite opposed to that which we have seen in the settled positions of Irenaeus and Tertullian.[65] Commenting on the 'house eternal in the heavens' of 2 Corinthians 5: 1, Methodius concludes,[66]

As then, when the days of our present life shall fail, those good deeds of beneficence to which we have attained in this unrighteous life, and in this 'world' which 'lieth in wickedness,' will receive our souls; so when this perishable life shall be dissolved, we shall have the habitation which is before the resurrection—that is, our souls shall be with God (αἱ ψυχαὶ παρὰ τῷ θεῷ), until we shall receive the new house which is prepared for us, and which shall never fall. (*Res.* II. 15. 7)

Compare also the discourse of Thekla in *Sympos.* 8. 2. But before an irregularity in our pattern is too quickly registered, we must not

[62] I. 1, the translation of R. E. Wallis, *ANF* v.

[63] Fausset, 6, thinks Novatian has Tertullian's *An.* 58 in view at this point. Finé, 74, points to a dependence upon Tertullian's view of 'prejudgement' in the underworld in Novatian's use of the word *praeiudicia*.

[64] Buonaiuti, 263–4. Musurillo, *Methodius*, 9, places the bulk of Methodius' literary activity between 270 and 309.

[65] Fischer, *Todesgedanken*, 309, 'In any case he teaches a post-mortem, heavenly bliss for the righteous, especially for the souls of virgins … The conception of a general interim in Hades is also overcome in this Church father.'

[66] Translations are those of W. R. Clark, *ANF* vi.

fail to observe the oft-noted[67] irregularity of Methodius' chiliasm. For Methodius the millennium would correspond to the first Sabbath after creation and to the Jewish feast of Tabernacles and thus its radical characteristic would be rest. This meant for him that there would not only be no tilling of the ground during the millennium but no eating or drinking whatsoever, 'the fruits of the earth having been gathered in' and God himself resting from his labour of causing the earth to fructify.[68] In contrast to probably all Christian chiliasts before him[69] and certainly to Lactantius who would follow (*DInst.* VII. 24), Methodius held that there would be no marrying or procreating on the millennial earth by any of the saints (*Sympos.* 9. 1). In fact, Lesètre appears to be correct in saying that 'it is only after the judgment that the saints are supposed to enjoy on the earth a repose for a thousand years with Christ. *Sympos.*, IX,1,5'.[70] If this is so, it necessitates a reassessment of Methodius' relation to the chiliast tradition. The seventh millennium is so spiritually conceived of because it is in fact part of the 'new and indissoluble creation', the first stage of the blessedness of the resurrected beyond the great assize. 'I ... on the first day of the resurrection, which is the day of judgment, celebrate with Christ the millennium of rest ...' (*Sympos.* 9. 5). Is Methodius' view then to be regarded as a modified chiliasm or a modified non-chiliasm?

According to Bietenhard, Methodius 'occupied middle-ground between a Biblical realism and a Platonic spiritualising'.[71] But, though the works of Plato had obviously provided Methodius with untold hours of reading,[72] when we speak of Methodius' eschatology

[67] Lesètre, 1095; Farges, 213; Leclercq, 1189; Gry, *Millénarisme*, 100; Bietenhard, *SJT*, 21–2.

[68] Daniélou, *TJC*, 395, thinks Methodius possibly is developing an old millenarian tradition which occurs in *SibOr.* VII. 145–9. There we read of a time when no plough will cut a furrow and no vine nor corn will grow but when all 'will eat the dewy manna with white teeth'. Quite apart from the problem of dating the seventh book of *SibOr.* (see J. J. Collins, *OTP* i. 408, 'there is nothing in the book to enable us to fix its date with any precision within the second and third centuries'), there is no indication that these conditions pertain to a temporary reign.

[69] Certainly to Cerinthus, Justin (*Dial.* 81), Irenaeus (*AH* V. 35. 1) Commodianus (*Instr.* II. 3) and the chiliasts known to Origen and Dionysius. See also *1En.* 10. 17.

[70] Lesètre, 1095, a conclusion arrived at independently by Stonehouse, 131.

[71] *SJT*, 21. Cf. Blum, 730.

[72] Musurillo, *Methodius*, 221, 'It is here [*Symp.* 8. 3] that Methodius comes closest to uniting the Christian and Platonic notions of heaven'; cf. Fischer, *Todesgedanken*, 307–8. But Musurillo also says, *Methodius*, 17, 'The *Symposium* stands, therefore, as one of the most peculiar phenomena in patristic literature: for despite the vast wealth of Platonic quotation and allusion, one has the definite impression that even

it is probably accurate to say with Gry[73] that it was influenced more by his acquaintance with Origen, the tireless and vocal critic of chiliasm. If he knew the writings of Origen at all well, Methodius knew that it was the materialism of the chiliasts and specifically their teaching that the resurrected in the millennium will need physical nourishment and continue to fill the earth with offspring which had been the battered target of Origen's antichiliast attacks.[74] By transplanting the millennium into the eternal world and by accepting a heavenly in place of a subterranean intermediate state Methodius would seem to have achieved a kind of fusion of the two eschatologies, fated for desuetude though it surely was. As it stands, although he is able to perpetuate traditional chiliastic nomenclature, Methodius' 'millennium' is no longer chiliastic in the important dogmatic sense of it being an interim reign on this earth prior to the last judgement.

7. Victorinus

Nowhere is the native alliance of the doctrines of chiliasm and the subterranean intermediate state set in sharper relief than in a few statements of Methodius' contemporary, Victorinus of Pettau. His *Commentary on the Apocalypse*, written probably in the closing years of the third century, seems to have been highly regarded in Antiquity but its witness to chiliasm was stifled by Jerome,[75] who replaced its original explanation of Revelation 20 and 21 with his own non-chiliastic exegesis. The original, undoctored version was not published until 1916.[76]

where Methodius has not positively misunderstood Plato and failed to comprehend the complexities of his system, he was not really interested in its doctrinal content.'

[73] *Millénarisme*, 101, 'As far as one is able to judge the ideas of Methodius on this point, he seems, doubtless under the influence of Origenism, to have singularly modified and attentuated the traditional conception of the thousand year reign.'

[74] See *Princ.* II. 10. 3; 11. 2; *CMatt.* XVII. 35; *CSSol.* prol; *CPs* 4 in *Philocalia* XXVI. 6. Methodius, as if impersonating Origen, castigates the Jews for their 'fluttering about the bare letter of Scripture' and being 'intent upon things earthly', esteeming rather 'the riches of the world than the wealth which is of the soul' (*Sympos.* 9. 1). In the passage cited above from *Res.* II. 15. 7 Methodius broaches an interpretation of Luke 16: 9 which is also found in Origen's *Homilies on Jeremiah* II. 3.

[75] See Jerome's comments in the preface to his edition, Haussleiter, 14–15.

[76] Haussleiter's edition, which is used here. Translations are those of Robert Ernest Wallis, *ANF* vii. Curti, 419, refers to the chiliastic fragment on Matt. 24, codex Ambrosianus i. 101, which Mercati and C. H. Turner, (see Turner, 'Fragment', 227), had suggested might have belonged to our Victorinus. Souter, 608–21, however, in the same year showed that it had been written by the Ambrosiaster.

The chiliasm of Victorinus is robust and moves us back (away from the Methodian revision) squarely within the traditional framework.[77] Like Commodianus, he believed the Antichrist would be Nero returned from the dead (*CA* 12. 6; 13; 17. 3, cf. Commodianus, *Instr.* I. 41. 7; *CarmA.* 825–7). The 144,000 mentioned in Revelation 7. 4–8 are Jews who will be converted under the preaching of Elijah just prior to Antichrist's advent. These evidently will all be slaughtered for they rise in the first resurrection of Revelation 20. 4–6 and stand with Christ on Mount Zion, as depicted in Revelation 14. 1 (*CA* 12. 4; 20. 1, cf. Commodianus, *Instr.* I. 41. 8; *CarmA.* 833, 839). It is in Judea where the saints shall assemble together 'in the seventh millenary of years' (*Mundi* 6) to worship the Lord (*CA* 1. 5). Of life in the millennium, we learn that the godly will reign with Christ 'over all the Gentiles' (*CA* 20. 2, cf. Commodianus, *Instr.* II. 35. 15–16; *CarmA.* 998). John's vision of the New Jerusalem descending from heaven and the ensuing description of the eternal city are transposed from Revelation 21 to supplement Victorinus' description of the millennial earth. There will be saints alive at the coming of the Lord (*CA* 12. 4; 20. 2) and, presumably, these will continue to multiply on the earth, for Paul's words 'and we shall be changed' (1 Cor. 15: 52) pertain to a transformation to take place only at the close of the thousand years (*CA* 20. 2). The saints certainly continue to 'drink from the fruit of the vine' (Matt. 26: 29) in this kingdom with Christ (*CA* 21. 5–6). Victorinus shows, in reliance upon Irenaeus and possibly Papias, that this kingdom will be a time of prodigious fruitfulness when he augments Matthew 19: 29, 'multiplied by a hundred parts', with the words 'ten thousand times larger and better'.[78]

Victorinus reveals his view of the intermediate state of the just in his comment on Revelation 5: 3–4 (*CA* 5. 1). John sees that 'no one in heaven or on earth or under the earth was able to open the scroll or to look into it'. Victorinus paraphrases, 'There was none

---

[77] This is true even if it is admitted with Curti, 432, that 'The adherence of Victorinus to millennialism is not total and unconditioned, since his formation was permeated by two cultures, the "Asiatic" and the "Alexandrian", to which he was in some measure indebted.' Curti's conclusion is based largely upon Victorinus' abandonment of purely literal exegesis in his comments on Revelation 20, 21 and his adoption of certain allegorical explanations possibly due to influence from Origen.

[78] Cf. Irenaeus *AH* v. 33. 3, *Venient dies in quibus vineae nascentur singulae decem millia palmitum habentes* ... Haussleiter, 154, states that Victorinus drew upon Papias.

found worthy to do this. Neither among the angels of heaven, nor among men in earth, nor among the souls of the saints in rest ...' (*CA* 5. 1). The souls of the saints are at rest under the earth.[79]

Not only does Victorinus make no allowance for the martyrs, as a special class of saints, to rise beyond the confines of the underworld, he advances a brilliant solution to Tertullian's problem with the book of Revelation (leaving aside, however, the *Passion of Perpetua*). Tertullian could not get around Revelation 6: 9–11, which pictured the souls of the martyrs under the heavenly altar. Victorinus in *CA* 6. 4 begins with the observation that the law commanded not one but two altars to be made, 'a golden one within and a brazen one without'. Now, the golden one is symbolical for heaven, as we perceive when the Lord tells us to 'leave thy gift before the altar' (Matt. 5: 23, 24). 'Assuredly prayers ascend to heaven. Therefore heaven is understood to be the golden altar which was within'. Likewise, as the priests of old entered before this altar once in the year, so Christ has entered once for all into the presence of the heavenly altar. The reader may guess how Victorinus will continue:

(As the golden altar is acknowledged to be heaven) so also by the brazen altar is understood the earth, under which is Hades (*infernum*),—a region withdrawn from punishments and fires, a place of repose for the saints (*requies sanctorum*), wherein indeed the just are seen and heard by the impious, but they cannot pass over to them.[80] He who sees all things wishes us to know that these saints, therefore—that is, the souls of the slain—are awaiting vengeance for their blood, that is, for their body, from those that dwell upon the earth.

The souls under the altar are therefore *sub terra* and in Hades! It is a reasonable conjecture that in executing this ingenious exeget-

[79] The unknown author of the *Carmen adversus Marcionem* shows in several places that he must have had a copy of Victorinus' commentary; he reproduces this allegorical exegesis and the doctrine it was designed to preserve in IV. 172–91. This interpretation of the altar as symbolizing earth and the souls as having their repose in the infernal realm survived Jerome's censorship and is repeated in modified form in the anonymous *De septem sigillis*, which Matter believes was composed sometime between AD 500 and 633. The interesting modification is that instead of saying that the souls under the earth are 'souls of the saints' this text merely refers to 'spirits' (line 6). Matter, 117, says this interpretation thus 'became a commonplace' in medieval explanations of Rev. 5: 3. The wicked too, of course, have their abode in Hades; Nero rises from Hades to play his role of Antichrist (*CA* 12. 6; 13 and 17. 3, see Commodianus).

[80] A reference to Luke 16: 26, thus signifying that this is also 'Abraham's bosom', understood similarly by Tertullian and the author of *De universo* (if they be not the same).

ical manœuvre Victorinus was consciously intending to alleviate Tertullian's difficulty. At any rate, Victorinus is now able to maintain a consistent position on the place of the Christian dead—even the apostles are comprehended among those who sleep, who 'have in their darkness a light such as the moon' (*CA* 12. 1), certainly the nocturnal light which illumines the restful region of Hades,[81] mentioned also by the author of *De universo*.[82]

Not to be confused, however, with the righteous dead are the two witnesses in Revelation 11: 3–12. Victorinus relates that many Christians believe the second witness, with Elijah, will be Elisha or Moses. But Victorinus objects that these are disqualified because, unlike Elijah, these others died. 'On the other hand, the death of Jeremiah is not discovered. It has been handed down through all our ancients that it is Jeremiah'.[83] God's own prophecy about Jeremiah, namely, that he should be a prophet unto the nations (Jer. 1: 5), remains outstanding to this day, thus marking out for Jeremiah a prophesying ministry with Elijah reserved for the last days (*CA* 11. 3). As these two are 'the candlesticks which stand before the Lord of the earth' (Rev. 11. 4) they are, says Victorinus, 'in paradise' (*CA* 11. 4). The supposition is that paradise contains only those select of the elect who were translated from this world bodily, before death. This, as we have seen, is the very doctrine of Papias, the elders and Irenaeus.

8. Lactantius

Writing not many years before the council of Nicaea,[84] Lactantius devotes the seventh book of his great work *The Divine Institutes*

---

[81] So Fischer, *Todesgedanken*, 270.   [82] A χωρίον φωτεινόν (line 24).

[83] Just who these ancients might have been is a mystery, unless they bear some relation to Papias' 'elders'. This tradition of Jeremiah's preservation from death is possibly attested in 5 *Ezra* 2. 18 where an eschatological return of Jeremiah is expected, also perhaps in relation to Rev. 11: 3, and by Origen who refutes the opinion of the Jews in Matt. 16: 14 that Jesus was Jeremiah (*CMatt* xii. 9). It is definitely repeated in the *Carmen adversum Marcionem* iii. 245–6, whose author must have got it from Victorinus: 'it is agreed that by no death nor slaughter was the hero ta'en away' (Thelwall's translation, *ANF* iv). Though, unlike Victorinus, the author of these verses also believes Enoch is in the ranks of the translated. Irenaeus, Hippolytus, Tertullian, and the author of the *Apocalypse of Peter* each give Enoch as the partner of the eschatological Elijah, a name Victorinus strangely passes by. The Tishbite alone is mentioned also by Commodianus and Lactantius and the author of *SibOr*. ii. See below, § i. 3, n. 169.

[84] According to Quasten, ii. 397, the seventh book 'presupposes the edict of Milan in 313'.

to a defence of the Christian *vita beata*. Chapters 14, 22–6 (but announced already in book iv. 12) form, in Blum's words, the 'High-point of chiliasm in the West'.[85] Here we possess an expansive collection of traditional chiliastic teaching, paraded forth under the indiscriminate sponsorship of prophet, poet and Sibyl.[86]

> Then they who shall be alive in their bodies shall not die, but during those thousand years shall produce an infinite multitude, and their offspring shall be holy, and beloved by God; but they who shall be raised from the dead shall preside over the living as judges. But the nations shall not be entirely extinguished, but some shall be left as a victory for God, that they may be the occasion of triumph to the righteous, and may be subjected to perpetual slavery.
>
> ... and the earth will open its fruitfulness, and bring forth most abund-ant fruits of its own accord; the rocky mountains shall drop with honey; streams of wine shall run down, and rivers flow with milk ... Throughout this time beasts shall not be nourished by blood, nor birds by prey; but all things shall be peaceful and tranquil ... In short, those things shall then come to pass which the poets spoke of as being done in the reign of Saturnus. Whose error arose from this source,—that the prophets bring forward and speak of many future events as already accomplished. (*DInst.* vii. 24; cf. *Epit.* 72)

The chiliasm of Lactantius is completely oblivious to any threat of anti-materialistic criticism. Its every element corresponds to tradi-tional chiliastic teaching and could be reproduced from the collected writings of Irenaeus, Tertullian, Commodianus, and Victorinus.[87] Of special relevance, therefore, will be Lactantius' thinking on the intermediate state.

Concerning the soul and its post-mortem existence, Lactantius is sure he finds corroboration of the Christian view in the founder of Stoicism. 'Zeno the Stoic taught that there were infernal regions,

---

[85]   Blum, 731.

[86]   Fàbrega, 146, is probably correct that the ground motive for the chiliasm of Lactantius is none the less his understanding of OT prophecy and especially of the prophecy of Rev. 20: 1–10 (134–7); but cf. Daniélou, *VC*, 15 and Bietenhard, *SJT*, 26. Fàbrega, 137, points to the Persian astrological world-week as one supplementary source for Lactantius, who knew and used the *Oracle of Hystapes* (*DInst.* vii. 15. 19; 18. 2). On Lactantius' combination of the chronology of Theophilus with the cosmic week theory, see Nicholson, 308. The translation is William Fletcher's, *ANF* vii.

[87]   Fàbrega, 142, 'Lactantius stands with his chiliasm on the ground of a firm biblical and churchly tradition. As in other spheres so is he also in this point a collector of handed-down opinions. That the chiliastic doctrine was contested among orthodox theologians is a fact which Lactantius, with the decided chiliasts, never once intimates'. See also Daniélou, *VC*, 14.

and that the abodes of the good were separated from the wicked; and that the former enjoyed peaceful and delightful regions, but that the latter suffered punishment in dark places, and in dreadful abysses of mire: the prophets show the same thing' (vii. 7. 7). Lactantius mentions but recoils from a later Stoic teaching, that the soul returns to a heavenly place of origin at death (vii. 20).[88] To the contrary, he insists in Tertullianic terms that the just and the unjust alike 'are detained in one and a common place of confinement (*in communi custodia*), until the arrival of the time in which the great Judge shall make an investigation of their deserts' (vii. 21. 7, cf. *An.* 55. 5 and *De universo* lines 47–8). This common place of confinement is the infernal Hades which houses in separate compartments the souls of both godly and ungodly.[89]

Lactantius, however, gives no hint of a possible concession for the martyrs. What we have seen then in the works of Commodianus, Victorinus, and Lactantius, as well as in our discussions of the views of Justin and Irenaeus, strengthens our conclusion that Tertullian's allowance for the martyrs was an innovation designed to prevent a clash of two conflicting traditions, rather than the mere formal statement of a long-held, systematic view of large numbers of Christians.

Once again chiliasm and a conception of the soul's post-mortem existence in the netherworld awaiting the resurrection appear in tandem. Lactantius does not expound their connection in any way. But the fact that they recur here in so traditional an expression of chiliasm attests once again to their perceived congruency.

9. Summary

Of the chiliasts Cerinthus, Coracion, and Nepos we have no remaining writings. But of those chiliasts who also reveal their views on the subject of the intermediate state, only Methodius seems to sever the bond between chiliasm as a view of the end of history, and the doctrine that the believer's soul remained in an infernal sheol/Hades until the resurrection—and Methodius' chiliasm is in fact quite suspect on other grounds. In Papias, Justin, Tertullian, Commodianus, Victorinus, Lactantius, and signally in

---

[88] On the question whether this was an actual Stoic view, see Doignon, *RPh*, 43–55 and the discussion in Doignon, *Lactance*, 167–70.

[89] Fischer, *Todesgedanken*, 273.

the shrewd formulation of Irenaeus, there is to be seen a link, indeed an alliance between these two eschatological teachings.[90] This Christian doctrine of Hades is occasionally noted as the 'common' view of the second and third centuries,[91] or as a peculiarly western phenomenon.[92] Its connection with chiliasm, however, has gone virtually without recognition.[93] Conversely, it is also the case that of the adherents of this view of the intermediate state, none whose doctrine of the parousia may be known were other than chiliasts.[94] Irenaeus is the only one who explains the connection between the two doctrines but we may believe that his explanation was noted and accepted by Tertullian, Victorinus, and Lactantius.

In the next section we undertake to clarify what appears to be the source of this connection. Several obvious links between Christian chiliasm and the eschatology of certain Jewish apocalypses have long been acknowledged. Not as well known, however, is the fact that in the same documents, and in the hopes they embody, lie the main sources of the chiliasts' view of the intermediate state.

---

[90] Pseudo-Barnabas might permit a very tentative classification here. In 15. 3–8 he seems to accept a chiliastic scheme (though his chiliasm is denied by F. C. Grant, 201–2; Haeuser, 126; and most learnedly by Hermans, 849–76) and in 19. 1 he speaks of an 'appointed place' (ὡρισμένος τόπος) to which the just repair after death. The location of this realm is indeterminable from the rest of the letter, but it is interesting that in its precise form this ὡρισμένος τόπος reappears only in Irenaeus' chapter on the intermediate state, and there it means a dwelling place of souls under the earth. All things considered, however, Pseudo-Barnabas' relation to chiliasm is still dubious.

[91] Waszink, *Anima*, 553–4; Perrin, 519; Schürer, ii. 541, n. 96. Waszink concludes from the studies of Clemen, 146–51, and Gschwind, 155, n. 2, that this was the doctrine of 'Justin, Clem. Alex., Novatian, probably also Irenaeus'. The reference to Clement is surely misplaced, as we shall see later; Clemen cites Clement only in reference to an allowance made by the latter for the martyrs to go to heaven (though in Clement's thought this was not a privilege restricted to martyrs).

[92] Richard, 'Hippolyte', 567, naming Tertullian, Novatian, Commodianus, Lactantius, and Victorinus: 'To our knowledge it has never been noted in the Greek fathers.' Daniélou, *OLC*, 393, would appear somewhat closer to the mark when he says, 'In the case of all three writers [Justin, Irenaeus, and Tertullian] this position [of an underworldly intermediate state] seems to be connected with the dispute with Gnosticism and especially with Marcion.' But what of Novatian, Commodianus, Victorinus, and Lactantius (possibly Pseudo-Barnabas)? Advocacy of chiliasm, especially in the case of Irenaeus, was also connected with the dispute with Gnosticism.

[93] Though see above § I. 1, n. 24, the statements of Ermoni and Wünsche.

[94] Novatian and the author of *De universo* (if he is not Tertullian) do not allow a judgement. A possible exception is the Clementine *Recognitions* (I. 52. 4–5), which does not seem to be chiliastic. But see § I. 3, n. 170 below.

3. THE 'PHARISAIC–APOCALYPTIC' SOURCES

The purpose of this section is to see if we can locate the sources
of the phenomenon observed above in the Christian chiliasts, the
conjunction of the subterranean intermediate state with a chiliastic
view of future history. Even under the limitations imposed by our
present study I believe we may determine that the matrix of this
doctrinal conjunction is in all probability the very womb of chiliasm
itself, that is, a strand of Jewish piety which probably owes its
definitive form to the fall of Jerusalem,[95] which (for reasons given
below) might very casually be styled 'Pharisaic–Apocalyptic', and
which comes to expression most clearly in the contemporary apocalypses 2 Baruch and 4 Ezra.[96] We shall proceed in three steps: first,
to show that the same conjunction of eschatological doctrines is to
be found in these two works; then to show that outside these works
this conjunction is rare or non-existent in Jewish literature; and
finally, to show that these two apocalypses and others which are
like them in important respects were known and used by the
Christian chiliasts.

1. The Conjunction in 2 Baruch and 4 Ezra

In the two apocalypses 2Bar. and 4Ez. we find the full conjunction
of the two doctrines in question. These two apocalypses are among
the surprisingly few which reveal a concern for situating the righteous dead[97] and are at the same time also the only proponents
among their peers of an easily discerned, temporary, earthly reign

---

[95] Moore, *Judaism*, ii. 333, 338, 343–5; Strack–Billerbeck, iii. 824, 'Only the post-
Christian synagogue distinguishes between the days of the Messiah and the final
perfection in the ʿolam ha-ba, that is, in the future world'.

[96] Despite certain differences in the theologies of these two works, their numerous
and basic affinities have long been recognized. Some have thought 2Bar. to be
dependent upon 4Ez.; Klijn, *OTP*, i. 617 thinks they knew a common source and
dates 2Bar., as the later of the two, in the first or second decade of the second
century. It is widely agreed that 4Ez. 3. 1 is to be trusted as an indication that the
book was written in or very close to AD 100 (see Metzger, *OTP*, i. 520). Bogaert, (SC
144, 270–96; BETL, 49), while sticking to this date for 4Ez., thinks 2Bar. is the
earlier of the two, originating in AD 95–6. I am inclined to agree with him.

[97] 'Actually there are only a few passages which display an intentioned reflection
on the problem [of the intermediate state]. These are En. 22 . . . and IV Ezra 7 and
the parallel apocalypse II Baruch . . .', Hanhart, *Intermediate*, 25. Unreflective statements are no less important than reflective ones, however, and a few more of the
former type do exist.

of the Messiah.[98] Even the conceptions of the intermediate state
held by those rabbis who promoted belief in a temporary period
known as the days of the Messiah[99] are difficult to track down.
Three other works, *The Book of the Watchers* (1En. 1–36), Pseudo-
Philo's *Biblical Antiquities* and *SibOr.* ii, while not out of precisely
the same mould in these respects, bear special relationships to the
eschatologies of *2Bar.* and *4Ez.*, and so also fall under our notice
here.

(a) The Book of the Watchers (1En. *1–36*).   *1 Enoch* 1–36,[100] cannot
properly be called chiliastic. Its 'golden age' seems to lack a Messianic deliverer and would appear to be everlasting and not temporary. As to the individual eschatology of the book, chapter 22 shows
us in the travels of the hero a great and high mountain in the west
which is said to contain 'three beautiful (or hollow) corners'.[101] Here
the spirits or souls (the terms are near equivalents) of the dead are
gathered 'until the day of their judgement and the appointed time
of the great judgement upon them' (22. 5). Two corners for the
wicked are distinguished according to whether judgement had been
executed upon them in their lifetimes. But the righteous spirits,
even that of slain Abel (a pre-Maccabean version of a 'martyr')
whose plaintive cry continually assaults the heavens until all of
Cain's seed is exterminated, are kept in a submontane region
awaiting the great day of judgement.

(b) 2 Baruch.   The author of *2Bar.* transposes *1En.*'s description
of the fabulous exuberance of nature in the world to come (*1En.*
10. 17–19) into a description of the land of delights in the numbered
days of King Messiah (29. 1–30. 1; cf. on the temporary Messianic
kingdom 29. 1–8, 39. 7–40. 2; 70. 9–74. 4). Palestine will be divinely
protected when the Messiah comes to judge the nations of the earth
(29. 2; 72. 2–6; 39. 8; 40. 1–2). A time of prodigious bounty and peace

[98] Wilcke, 48, 'Besides in the Apocalypse of John, the idea of a Messianic
intermediate kingdom appears in the pseudepigraphic apocalypses only in 4 Ezra—
possibly also in Syriac Baruch.' It is of course a matter of some debate whether
such a view of the Messiah's reign is taught elsewhere. Bailey's is a more liberal
assessment, 170–87, but according to the definition we are using (see Introduction)
Wilcke is closer to the mark. See our comments below.

[99] See e.g. Strack–Billerbeck, iii. 823 ff; Moore, *Judaism*, ii. 375–9.

[100] Usually dated from the pre-Maccabean period. See E. Isaac, 7; Nickelsburg,
Literature, 48, though in *Resurrection*, 134, he is less certain.

[101] The variants being κοιλοι and καλοι.

ensues (29. 5–6; 32. 2–9; 48. 32; 73. 3–7; 74), with no more untimely deaths (29. 7; 73. 2–3) and a banishing of pain in childbirth (73. 7). This period eventually gives way, when Messiah's days are fulfilled, to the day of resurrection and judgement (30. 1; 48. 47) when souls rise from the 'treasuries of souls' (21. 23; 24. 1) in sheol to be reunited with their bodies (30. 1; 50. 2). Sheol is often alluded to in 2Bar., evidently as the realm of all the dead, good and bad (11. 6; 21. 23; 23. 5; 48. 16; 52. 2; 56. 6; 83. 17). When the righteous leave this world to take up their abodes in sheol, they do so with joyful confidence in the expectation of the world promised them (14. 3).[102]

In 2Bar., we learn that paradise was taken away from Adam, in a local sense, and is being preserved along with 'the city' in the presence of God (4. 2–6; 59. 8). After the resurrection it will again be spread out for those who have been 'saved because of their works'. But to Baruch himself is not to befall the common lot of death and descent to sheol, he is rather to 'depart from this world, nevertheless not to death but to be kept unto (the end) of times' (76. 2, cf. 25. 1; 13. 3), that is, to be taken up (46. 7; 48. 30) and preserved bodily (evidently in paradise) along with others translated there, and to be revealed when 'the time will awake' (25. 1–4).

(c) 4 Ezra.   In this apocalypse we find once again the chambers in Hades accommodating the spirits of the righteous dead (4. 42; 7. 32). The souls of those who have 'kept the ways of the Most High,' 'first of all . . . see with great joy the glory' of God, then after seven days (7. 101) they are gathered into their habitations in Hades (4. 41; 7. 32)[103] in seven orders (7. 78–101), 'guarded by angels in profound quiet', and awaiting the glory that will be theirs in the last days. Even the spirits of the wicked apparently begin the afterlife by adoring the glory of the Most High (7. 78),[104] but instead of entering habitations, they 'immediately wander about in torments, ever grieving and sad, in seven ways' (7. 80).

While the souls of the righteous in Hades are awaiting the resurrection, the earth above them awaits the revelation of the Davidic Messiah (7. 27; 13. 32). When he comes he will upbraid and

[102] This promised world, as also in 4Ez., is not the temporary, Messianic kingdom, for the latter is not preceded by a resurrection.

[103] Strack–Billerbeck, iv. 1023. I can see no warrant at all for Volz's statement (248) that 7. 95 speaks of a 'situation above the earth' (cf. 257, 259).

[104] Strack–Billerbeck, iv. 1026.

then destroy Rome and the nations (12. 32–33; 13. 5–11, 37, 49) and will deliver Israel (12. 34; 13. 12, including the returned ten tribes (13. 40–47)). The hidden city and land will then appear, full of wonders, and the Messiah with the surviving remnant rejoices for 400 years (7. 27–28; 12. 34). Then the Messiah and all who draw human breath die. After seven days of silence, the new and incorruptible world is aroused and the dead are raised for judgement.[105]

The heavenly (4. 7–8) 'paradise of delights' is in *4Ez.*, as in *2Bar.*, the eschatological resting place (7. 36) granted to the faithful after Messiah's reign. But Ezra, with 'those who are like' him, that is, those who are removed from this life without suffering death,[106] is 'taken up from among men' to live with God's Son 'and with those who are like you, until the times are ended' (14. 9). We may surmise that the place to which the translated go is the superterrestrial (4. 7–8) paradise.[107] The last days will reveal these 'men who were taken up, who from their birth have not tasted death' (6. 26). These are doubtless those who (just as in *2Bar.*) come with the Messiah when he brings his 400 years of rejoicing to those then on earth (7. 28, cf. 13. 52). The statement, 'And after these years my son the Messiah shall die, and all who draw human breath' (7. 29) naturally then comprehends even the translated.

(d) Sibylline Oracles *ii*. Mention could be made here of the Jewish substratum of *SibOr.* ii.[108] Lines 170–6 record the belief in a future recalling of the lost ten tribes from the East and a dominion of faithful Hebrews over the subjected gentiles.[109] Whether we may

---

[105] The account of Jewish Messianic hope given by Hippolytus, *Ref.* ix. 30, corresponds remarkably to the plan of 4Ez.

[106] Bauckham, rightly, *JBL*, 451; unfortunately misapprehended by Volz, 248, 259, as the dwelling of all the righteous. Cavallin, 80, 82–4, similarly confuses the appearance of the Messiah 'with his companions' preceding the kingdom (7. 28) with a resurrection of these companions. The companions are rather those who have been preserved from death and have no need of a resurrection.

[107] In post-talmudic conceptions of paradise, according to Bamberger, 84, the Messiah is represented in several writings as being in paradise awaiting the day of redemption. But unlike the paradise of 4Ez., this one houses not merely the translated few but apparently all the righteous.

[108] This Jewish substratum is from Phrygia but its date is more problematic. Collins, *OTP*, i. 331, following Kurfess, thinks it comes from around the turn of the era. He points to some weaknesses of Geffcken's position that both Jewish and Christian stages date from the third century AD.

[109] Obviously from a Jewish hand (Collins, *OTP* i. 330). For the Christian chiliasts—even those who looked for a return of the lost tribes as an eschatological sign—the future kingdom would emphatically not be a Jewish one.

call this chiliastic is open to question, for it may be that the kingdom here, as in the scheme of *1En.* 1–36, is envisioned as everlasting. It is perhaps the Jewish author again, and not the Christian redactor, who records the judgement scene in which God's angels will lead out from Hades 'all the souls of men from the murky dark to judgement' (217–18, 227–30). The near conjunction of the two doctrines in question resembles closely that of *1En.* 1–36 and may be seen as just a step away from the full-fledged chiliasm of *2Bar.* and *4Ez.*

(e) *Pseudo-Philo.* Many scholars have noted the special relation-ship which exists between the *Biblical Antiquities* of Pseudo-Philo and the contemporary[110] apocalypses *2Bar.* and *4Ez.*[111] Harrington believes that the feature of a temporary, Messianic kingdom is absent altogether from Pseudo-Philo.[112] Chapter 62. 9 does, how-ever, record the hope of a future Davidic kingdom of some order and the return and the death of Phinehas/Elijah (48. 1, see § I. 3. 3.d below) may presuppose a limited reign, such as we find in *2Bar.* and *4Ez.* But the three works undeniably share a common view of sheol. For Pseudo-Philo too the souls of the righteous are peacefully stored (23. 13) in underground treasuries (*promtuaria*, 32. 13; 31. 7) or 'secret dwelling places of souls' (*occultis animarum*, 21. 9 cf. 28. 8, *invisibilis loci*). This sheol (*infernus*), where the dead receive announcements (24. 6; 31. 7; 32. 13; 61. 6; cf. *2Bar.* 11. 6–7), will pay back its debt (3. 10; 33. 3; cf. *2Bar.* 21. 23, *4Ez.* 4. 41–43; 7. 32) at the resurrection.

Pseudo-Philo 48. 1 reveals that the preternatural Phinehas (Num. 25: 11), who is also Elijah,[113] will be 'lifted up into the place where those who were before you were lifted up, and you will be there until I remember the world. Then I will make you all come, and you will taste what is death.'[114] Exempted from death and from sojourning with the rest of the godly in Hades, this élite class of

---

[110] James, *Antiquities*, 29–33 thought Pseudo-Philo to have written after AD 70; Harrington, 299, opts for a date around the time of Jesus.

[111] Harrington, 300, 302. See especially, James, *Antiquities*, 46–58, who concludes, 'Philo is a product of the circle from which both *Baruch* and *4 Esdras* emanated: and it seems to me clear that the writer of *Baruch* at least was acquainted with Philo' (58).   [112] Harrington, 302.

[113] Cf. Origen, *CJohn* VI. 7 and the midrashim cited by James, *Antiquities*, 210–11.

[114] Recognizing this view of paradise and its inhabitants in Pseudo-Philo makes sense out of an otherwise bewildering individual eschatology (cf. Cavallin, 78).

saints, Pseudo-Philo, *2Bar.* and *4Ez.* agree, is secreted away to a higher elevation to be preserved until the last days. We have already noted that this was the doctrine of Papias and the elders, Irenaeus, and Victorinus.

In the chiliastic works *2Bar.* and *4Ez.*, as in the related works *1En.* 1–36, Ps.-Philo, *BibAntiqq.* and *SibOr.* ɪɪ, the position is taken that the souls of the righteous dead await the resurrection while detained in the netherworld. This view was doubtless widespread in the Judaism of our period. Josephus, we note, identifies it as the Pharisaic view.

According to the Jewish historian, the Pharisees (like the Essenes) maintain the incorruptibility of every soul, 'but that the soul of the good alone passes into another body,'[115] while the souls of the wicked suffer eternal punishment' (*BJ* ɪɪ. 163). The Pharisees also believe that 'souls have power to survive death and that there are rewards and punishments under the earth (ὑπὸ χθονός) for those who have led lives of virtue or vice: eternal imprisonment is the lot of evil souls, while the good souls receive an easy passage to a new life' (*Ant.* xvɪɪɪ. 14). Whether or not we are to suppose that this view was essential to Pharisaism, it does at least follow from this contemporary review that an underworldly, preliminary remuneration for all souls, bad or good, pending the resurrection was especially associated with the Pharisaical school. Josephus also tells us that the Pharisaical was the 'leading' (*BJ* ɪɪ. 162) outlook in late first-century Judaism. He even attributes partially to this very doctrine Pharisaic popularity amongst the townsfolk (*Ant.* xvɪɪɪ. 15), so it may well have been more generalized than its particular association with the Pharisees would indicate.[116]

Judging from the way he states his own view, Justin Martyr seems to regard it as being also that of the Jews who crucified Jesus, and as being acceptable to his second-century Jewish interloc-

---

[115] Not metempsychosis, but Josephus' version of resurrection language. See Fischer, *Eschatologie*, 154–5.

[116] The Hellenistic Jew Jason of Cyrene (or his epitomist), writing perhaps in the early first century BC (Russell, *Jews*, 187; Nickelsburg, *Literature*, 121), represents the worthy and venerable Eleazar, in delivering himself up to martyrdom, as challenging his judges to kill him and 'dispatch him to Hades at once' (*2Macc.* 6. 23). The author of *3Macc.* writing probably about the same time (Anderson, '3Macc', 512), similarly regards Hades as the abode of the righteous immediately upon death (4. 8; 5. 42; 6. 31). It is possible that both authors used ᾅδης in the sense of 'the grave' but it is notable none the less that there is no hint in either document of a heavenly reward even for martyrs.

utor Trypho: 'so likewise Christ declared that ignorance was not on His side, but on theirs, who thought that He was not the Christ, but fancied they would put Him to death, and that He, like a common man, would remain in Hades' (*Dial.* 99. 3). This teaching Justin may take for granted when debating Trypho.

2. Comparisons with Other Jewish Views

Belief in an underworldly waiting place must have been common to a great segment of the Jewish population throughout this period, even if the same cannot be said of a chiliastic Messianic expectation. But if this combination cannot be found elsewhere in the Judaism of the period, what sorts of options were entertained?

(a) *Josephus' Sadducees and Essenes.*   Josephus points to Sadducean pessimism and to what can only be termed Essene Hellenism. He informs his Gentile readers, 'the Sadducees hold that the soul perishes (cυναφανίζει) along with the body' (*Ant.* XVIII. 16). 'As for the persistence of the soul after death, penalties in the underworld,[117] and rewards, they will have none of them' (*BJ* II. 165). But the 'Pharisaic' view of underworldly rewards and punishments is still the foil against which the Sadducees must react.

The Essenes 'regard the soul as immortal (ἀθανατίζουcιν)' and as pre-existing in the pure aether above before descending into this world of sense (*Ant.* XVIII. 18). This sect teaches further that while the souls of the base go away at death 'to a murky and tempestuous dungeon, big with never-ending punishments', the souls of the just, in Josephus' blatant attempt to patronize pagan audiences, rejoice, and are borne aloft to an abode beyond the ocean, the 'isles of the blessed' of Greek myth (*BJ* II. 155–6).[118]

(b) *The Qumran Community.*   The mention of Essene eschatology leads to the community of Qumran. Attempts to analyse the eschatology of the Qumran community labour, at present, under several debilitating difficulties, among them the fragmentary and corrupted state of the scrolls; the likelihood of evolution in eschatological thought amongst a sect whose existence at Qumran must have spanned approximately 200 years; the question of the place to be

---

[117] Reading with C, καθ' ᾄδου.
[118] For the view of Josephus himself, see § II. 1. 1 below.

accorded to those writings found at Qumran but whose provenance
was probably elsewhere (such as the *Temple Scroll*, CD, *TestLevi*,
TestJud., *1En.* minus the *Similitudes*, and *Jub.*); and the ancient
testimonies of Philo, Josephus, and Hippolytus to the eschatology
of the Essenes, the close resemblance of which testimonies to the
literary remains at Qumran, and indeed to each other, has not been
readily seen by scholars.[119] To be added to this is the factor of
compositeness which probably pertains to a few of the writings,
namely to 1QS, 1QM, and CD, according to P. R. Davies, and to *Jub.*
according to Davenport.[120]

It seems to me that little can be said with certainty about the
Qumran sectaries' notions of the intermediate state. The analysis
which says that for the Qumranites individual eschatology was
wholly realized in the present,[121] however, could perhaps stand re-
examination. There is at Qumran the strong hope of an 'eschaton'
(1QM VII). And, the inheritance of the desired 'lot of angels'
(1QH III. 19–23; VI. 13; XI. 10–14; 1QS XI; 1QapGen II cf. *Wisd.* 5. 5;
Jub. 15. 27) and the return of 'the glory of Adam' (1QS IV. 23; CD

---

[119] For analyses of the sources and testimonies of Josephus and Hippolytus, see
Black, 'Essenes', 172–5; Smith, *HUCA*, 297, who argue that the material common to
both was taken independently from a common source. Burchard, 77–96, however,
seems to have proved that Hippolytus used only Josephus, supplementing him with
Christian amplifications (see Fischer, *Eschatologie*, 149).

[120] Davies, *JBL*, 48. Davenport, *Jubilees*. It is to be noted, however, that Wintermute, *OTP*, evidently disregards Davenport's conclusions and continues to speak
of a single author.

[121] Laurin, 346, 355, writing in 1958, was convinced that the sectaries had no
doctrine of survival, bodily or soulish, after death (cf. Nickelsburg, *Resurrection*,
144). Nickelsburg reflects recent learned opinion in emphasizing the importance of
'ideas of continuity and present participation in eternal life', found especially in
certain of the *Hodayot* (1QH), for the determination of Qumranite individual eschatology (*Resurrection*, 166–167). J. J. Collins, *CBQ*, 35, states that death is not a
theological problem in the *Hodayot*, 'because the community believed that it had
already transcended death by passing over into the community of angels'. But here
crops up another contentious factor: the generalizations of Nickelsburg, Collins, and
Kuhn (*Enderwartung*, to whom the two former are indebted), are based in very large
part upon the *Hodayot*. Even apart from the matter of the date of the *Hodayot*, their
poetical character and imagery, resembling the Biblical Psalms, raises a difficulty
for Davies that prevents him even including them in an analysis of Qumranite
eschatological notions: 'it remains to be argued, rather than assumed, that their
thanksgiving for deliverance betrays, any more than the Psalms, a belief in individual
transcendence of death or participation, whether present of future, in an eternal
order'. I do not see the need for such scepticism; there do appear to arise from the
Hodayot some distinctives of Qumran (and contemporary) theology, as compared
with the Biblical Psalms, for instance. But Davies is right to call into question the
overarching extrapolations often drawn from a few passages in these songs.

III. 20; 1QH XVIII. 15; 4QpPs*) could with much intelligibility be placed at this time of the great judgement and the renewal of creation (1QH IX. 10–14 (cf. XII. 11–12); 1QS IV), even if a prolepsis of this was perceived in the community's worship (but also in its coming war with the sons of darkness, CD XII; 1QSb IV). This interpretation still leaves the interim between death and the judgement without definition.[122] Nickelsburg concludes that the minimizing of the significance of physical death in the scrolls 'is most compatible with a theology of immortality (Wisd. Sol.) or immediate assumption (Test. Asher)'.[123] There are significant links between Qumran and *Wisd.*, but on the matter of the place of the righteous souls, *Wisd.* is not as clear as might be thought (see below). Nor does the *TestAsher* afford any clarification beyond its representing the departing soul as being either harassed by the evil spirit it served during earthly life, or introduced to the angel of peace and entering eternal life (6. 5). These expressions might be compatible either with an assumption to heaven or with a peaceful continuance in the chambers of souls in Hades (recall *2Bar.*, *4Ez.*, and Tertullian, *An.*54!). It may be significant that in *TestLevi*, portions of which have been found at Qumran, the visionary Levi sees only archangels and the Lord (and no saints) in the third heaven (3. 8). Among the fragments of *1En.* found in the caves, 4QEnᵉ 1. xxii preserves part of *1En.* 22, the chapter which locates the souls of all the dead in various subterranean compartments until the great judgement.[124]

As for national or cosmic eschatology, we find that the days of the Messiahs (royal and priestly) are turbulent days of war, forty years long,[125] which, if laid beside the schemes of *2Bar.* and *4Ez.*, correspond not to the age of peace and beatitude but to the days of battle which prepare for that age. The militaristic, royal Messiah

---

[122] If this seems to assume a doctrine of resurrection at Qumran, the statement in 1QS IV, that after 'the appointed time of judgement' God will refine 'the human frame by rooting out all spirit of falsehood from the bounds of his flesh' (cf. 1QH VI 29–30, 34; *Jub.* 23. 30; *AssMos.* 10. 8–10; CD 7. 6) may at least be claimed. Josephus' seemingly forgotten testimony that the Essenes were 'confident that they would receive them [i.e. their souls] back again' (*BJ* II. 153, bringing him back into line with Hippolytus, *Ref.* IX. 22) appears to assume a doctrine of resurrection, at least for the godly.

[123] Nickelsburg, *Resurrection*, 167.   [124] See Milik, 229–31.

[125] There is a notable coincidence here with the view of Akiba, who believed the days of the Messiah would be forty years (Pesikta Rabbati 1. 7). If Wise, 161–6, is correct in his interpretation of the Temple Scroll, the days of the Messianic king may have been longer than this in the mind of the redactor of this document.

arises 'at the time of the affliction of those who seek God' (1QSb IV),
the time of great distress for Israel, as appears from 1QM I, XV;
4QFlor II; 4QpPs^a. The 'renewed creation' most likely should be
seen as the outcome of the last judgement.

(c) *The* Similitudes *of Enoch and Other Jewish Apocalypses.* The
Similitudes of Enoch (1En. 37–71), written probably before the end
of the first century AD,[126] represent another important alternative.
For this writer the righteous dead are already in heaven, in the
presence of the Lord of Spirits and the Messiah (39. 4–5; 45. 2; 47. 2;
61. 12, called here the garden of life; 70. 3–4).[127] We must emphasize
that in this book there is no trace of an expected earthly kingdom
of limited duration; it is only after the resurrection and forensic
last judgement that the elect inherit a transformed earth (45. 4–6;
51. 1–5).[128]

Whatever the date of the *Similitudes*, this belief that the intermediate abode of the just is to be in the highest heaven, in God's
presence, is encountered in Jewish apocalypses which can be
securely dated from the period 200 BC–135 AD far less frequently
than might be expected.[129] We may mention *The Life of Adam and*

[126] The question of the precise date of this pseudepigraphon is somewhat delicate,
though a consensus has now appeared. 'Repeatedly the specialists on 1 Enoch have
come out in favour of the *Jewish* nature of this section of 1 Enoch, and its first-
century C.E. origin, and probable pre-70 date', (Charlesworth, SNTS, 89; note his
list of concurring specialists, to which add now G. R. Beasley-Murray, *Jesus*, 63–8).
In Charlesworth's words (SNTS, 110), 'the real issue remains open. Are these Jewish
Parables pre-Christian and a source for understanding either Jesus' *ipsissima verba*
or the theologies of the Evangelists? Or, are they post-Christian and a significant
development independent of the canonical gospels, or a Jewish reaction to Christianity?' Much of the focus of this debate rightfully concerns Messianism and the use
of mediatorial titles. I propose that some fruit might come of a study of the
Similitudes' notion of the intermediate state in relation to that of other first-century
Palestinian Jewish documents.

[127] There may be an inconsistency in 51. 1–2 where the righteous seem to be
included among the souls delivered up by sheol (Volz, 261; Bietenhard, *Welt*, 175).
Elsewhere sheol is only 'oppressive' (63. 10).

[128] See Black, *JTS*, 2.

[129] In *3Bar.*, which is possibly from the period named, the souls of the righteous
are birds in the third heaven (out of five or seven) (ch. 10). Yet it is not clear whether
this element is Jewish or Christian (cf. the Slavonic version). I am not at all persuaded
by Volz, 262, that *1En.* 102–4 depicts an immediate entry into heaven at death. The
righteous descend to sheol (102. 5, 11, see Nickelsburg, *Resurrection*, 123) as do the
wicked (103. 7) though without the latter's torments and with the hope of future
glory; the rewards of 104 concern the time of the last judgement. It may be different
for the author of *1En.* 108, but this chapter is evidently a late appendage (Isaac, 7).

Eve,[130] in which we read that the soul of the deceased Adam embarks on an upward journey (ἄνοδος, 13. 6) at death; his spirit is borne up (ἀναφερόμενον) to his Maker (32. 4). (The body of Adam is taken to paradise, but this is the same earthly paradise from which it had been taken by its Creator, 40. 6.)[131] But is Adam's case exceptional, as is suggested by Bertrand?[132] Other souls too, we are told, migrate (μεθίστημι, 43. 3) from earth, though their destination is not revealed. It is notable that *VGAE* also strongly affirms the hope of resurrection and immortality in a restored paradise (10. 2; 28. 4; 41. 3; 43. 2) but bears no witness to the hope of an intermediate earthly kingdom.

Paradise is often said to be situated for the author of *2En.* in the third heaven. But what is actually disclosed in *2En.* is that Enoch, while flying about in the third heaven, sees paradise when he looks downwards. Chapter 42. 3 recalls Enoch's visit to the East 'into the paradise of Eden ... And it is open as far as the 3rd heaven; but it is closed off from this world.' F. I. Andersen says, 'The language suggests that this paradise is on the level of earth even though Enoch "ascends" to it. Its location in the east, beyond where the sun rises is more like the abode of the blessed in Mesopotamian tradition...'[133] It is even doubtful whether any of the righteous have yet entered paradise[134] with the exception of the prodigy Melkisedek who is taken there as a child for preservation through the coming deluge and to remain there forever (71. 28; 72. 1–7). Enoch himself is translated not to paradise but the 'highest heaven' to stand before the Lord for eternity (53. 1; 55. 2; 67. 2).

---

[130] The Greek version of this work has often been called, following Tischendorf, *The Apocalypse of Moses*, a title which, as Bertrand, 38, argues, should be abandoned. Bertrand believes the original was a Jewish production of the first century BC or the first half of the first century AD (31).

[131] According to 37. 5 the body of Adam is taken to a paradise 'in the third heaven' after being washed three times in the lake of Acheron (37. 5, cf. 13. 6; 32. 4). But the situating of paradise in the third heaven is, according to Bertrand, plainly recognized as a later Christian addition to the text (Bertrand, 62, 139–40). If this is allowed then Bertrand is surely correct that paradise in *VGAE* is never other than a terrestrial garden (140).

[132] Bertrand, 135.

[133] Andersen, *OTP*, 168, note c. 'In the case of Enoch the impression is given that entrance to heaven is possible only if death is circumvented' (ibid. 138, note j).

[134] It appears from 42. 3–5 that the righteous wait outside the portals of paradise until the arrival of the last of the redeemed. Enoch's guided tour of paradise in chs. 8–9 reports no human soul there, but only the 300 angels. In 65. 10 and 66. 8 paradise is part of the eschatological inheritance of the righteous after 'the LORD's great judgement' and in 'the great age' for eternity.

The *Apocalypse of Abraham* apparently holds the same conception of the location of paradise (chapter 21). The garden of Eden is on or near the earth. But when the ascended Abraham looks down into paradise he sees, unlike Enoch in *2En.*, not an empty garden but 'men doing justice in it, their food and their rest'.

(d) *Hellenistic Judaism.*   *Wisd.*, *4Macc.*, and the writings of Philo are commonly held up as prime examples of a 'Hellenistic Judaism' which is said to have replaced the doctrine of resurrection with that of the immortality of the soul.[135] Philo's place in this category is secure. 'Philo's eschatology is wholly expressed in terms of a Platonic immortality of the soul.'[136] For Philo the soul or the mind is inherently immortal and this immortality is a consequence of the soul's (or mind's) heavenly pre-existence. 'So when they have stayed awhile in their bodies, and beheld through them all that sense and mortality has to shew, they make their way back to the place from which they set out at the first. To them the heavenly region, where their citizenship lies, is their native land; the earthly region in which they became sojourners is a foreign country' (*Conf.* 78; see *Cher.* 120; *Abr.* 258; *Gig.* 12). Though, unlike Plato, Philo evidently regarded this heavenly pre-existence as a created pre-existence.[137] The doctrines of bodily resurrection and last judgement are absent, or, perhaps more accurately, reinterpreted. We may see in his work a 'demythologizing' of the concepts of heaven and Hades; for Philo 'place' can have no application to the 'presence' or the 'absence' of God, as it has no application to God Himself (*Congr.* 57).[138] 'In Philo there is no clear presentation of either an afterlife with rewards and punishments, as there is in Palestinian Judaism, or of a heaven and hell.'[139]

The individual eschatology of *Wisd.*, on the other hand, seems rather close to that of many documents originating at Qumran. For the author of *Wisd.*, God created man for incorruption (ἀφθαρcία,

---

[135] Schürer, ii. 540; Volz, 118.

[136] Chadwick, 'Philo', 157, n. 3. See the texts he cites.

[137] *Conf.* 35. 179; *Fug.* 13. 69; see Wolfson, i. 389. Goodenough, *HTR*, 101–3, sees as the dominant strain in Philo's statements on immortality the anticipation of impersonal reabsorbtion into God. This interpretation is contested, however, by Burnett, 456, n. 40; 464; 470, who, with Wolfson, i. 396, inclines to the view that for Philo the soul always continues as an entity distinct from God. See Goodenough's important concession, *HTR*, 103, and compare Cavallin's assessment, 138.

[138] See Goodenough, *HTR*, 89.

[139] Burnett, 464. See also Héring, 'Eschatologie', 446–50.

2. 23). Death, through the devil's envy, engulfs its own, while the souls of the righteous are in the hand of God; no torments touch them and they are indeed sustained by Him in their departure (2. 24–3. 2). They are now 'in peace', and 'their hope is full if immortality (ἀθανασίας)' (3. 3–4). But it is only at the time of their 'visitation' (cf. 1QS IV) that they will shine forth, judge nations and when 'the Lord shall reign over them for evermore' (3. 7–8, cf. 1QM VIII!);[140] until then the 'location' of these peaceful souls remains undisclosed.[141] The author hopes in a future time of vindication after which an eternal reign of the righteous will follow. Though we could wish for greater explicitness, a belief in some form of resurrection is not denied and may well be presupposed.[142]

Less typically 'Jewish' is the eschatology of 4Macc. This is said not so much because we find in it a heavenly estate for the souls of the righteous (at least the martyrs) after death, standing beside the divine throne[143] (17. 18, see also 9. 22; 14. 5; 16. 25; 17. 12; 18. 3, θεία μερίς 23), but because we have in it no evidence whatever for an accompanying belief in the resurrection of the body, in marked contrast to its literary source 2Macc.[144]

In none of the three authors just treated is there in evidence the hope of a temporary, Messianic kingdom.[145]

(e) The Rabbis. If the conception of the righteous dead awaiting the eschaton in the infernal chambers of sheol is common in the literature we have observed so far, it must be said this view vanishes in the Talmud and related literatures. The reason for this is obscure, but it is not unlikely that such a view may have been suppressed by the compilers of the traditions and that this suppression may be related to the variously explained phenomenon of the

[140] Though some early Christian writers, notably Clement of Alexandria and Origen, will use this text to establish their views of the intermediate state.

[141] Even if Volz, 249, is correct that Wisd. assumes an immediate entry into heaven (and this is very doubtful to me, though see Nickelsburg, Resurrection, 88–90), I see no justification for his conclusion that Wisd. teaches the pre-existence and natural divinity of the soul (Volz, 118). See Cavallin, 131, on 8. 19–21; Urbach, i. 236.

[142] Cavallin, 127–8, rightly compares the 'visitation' of 3. 7 with the many instances in contemporary literature which would link it to the resurrection, but is reticent to make the link in Wisd. itself.

[143] Cf. TB Shabbath 152b.

[144] Nickelsburg, Resurrection, 110; Schürer, ii. 542 note 99; Cavallin, 123, is more reserved.

[145] For a review of Philo's political hopes for the world see Wolfson ii. 395–426.

absence of apocalyptic imagery in this literature.[146] For being the successors of the Pharisees, these compilers conform surprisingly more closely to Josephus' Essenes than to his Pharisees in the matter of individual eschatology.

It is in the Talmud where we first encounter the term Arabot (taken from Ps. 68: 4 interpreted by Deut. 33: 26) as a name for the seventh heaven where reside both the souls of the departed righteous and, notably, the pre-existing souls and spirits of the unborn (in the גוּף of TB Yebamoth 62a) in the presence of the Almighty and His throne (Hag. 12b cf.).[147] This celestial framework is also adopted in the Hekalot texts where, however, no real interest attaches to the region of Arabot but only to the site of the throne of glory now placed above Arabot.[148] The souls of the dead are often situated beneath the throne of glory (ARN version A, 12; TB Shabbat 152b, etc.). A slight adjustment is entertained by rabbi Abbahu, in the first half of the fourth century.[149] A heretic said to R. Abbahu,

> You maintain that the souls of the righteous are hidden under the Throne of Glory: then how did the bone [-practising] necromancer bring up Samuel by means of his necromancy?—There it was within twelve months [of death], he replied. For it was taught: For full [twelve months] the body is in existence and the soul ascends and descends; after twelve months the body ceases to exist and the soul ascends but descends nevermore. (TB Shabbat 152b–53a)[150]

Abbahu is willing to postpone for twelve months the final ascension of the soul to the throne of glory in heaven. But what has happened to the chambers in sheol? Again in Genesis Rabbah xii. 10 Abbahu says, this time in the name of rabbi Johanan, that all descend to sheol but that the penitent may escape. Sheol elsewhere in this literature becomes synonymous with Gehenna and both are taken to refer to an infernal abode which exists only

---

[146] See Saldarini, 355–8.

[147] The enumeration of seven heavens in this text is attributed to Resh Lakish (c. 300). Urbach, i. 238, is convinced that this notion of pre-existence is 'not found before the third century'.

[148] Chernus, 89. A counterpart presents itself in the ogdoad of the Christian Gnostics and Clement of Alexandria, though here the storehouse of pre-existing souls is absent.

[149] According to TB Hagiga 13a–b, Abbahu also engaged in merkabah speculation.

[150] Translations of the Talmud, unless otherwise noted, will be from Epstein's edition.

for the torture of the wicked immediately after death (e.g. TB Baba
Mezia 58b; TB Sanhedrin 105a; 110a; 111a).[151] This relatively brief
sojourn in Hades before a definitive arrival in heaven is just the
reverse of the doctrine of *4Ez.*, where the godly soul is allowed a
seven-day gaze at the divine glory before nestling into its infernal
dwelling.

The hands of redactors are possibly evident in the reworking of
a tradition ascribed to rabbi Eliezer ben Jose the Galilean on the
fate of souls after death. In Sifre on Numbers 139 he says, 'As long
as a man is alive, his soul is kept safe in the hand of his Creator
(Job. 12,10); when he is dead, it is put into the treasury (בַאוֹצר),
as it is written, "The soul of my lord will be bound up in the bundle
of life" (I Sam. 25,29)'.[152] The 'bundle of life' is the 'treasury' (אוֹצר),
which could be easily identified with the treasuries of souls in
Hades of *4Ez.* and *2Bar.*[153] But in TB Shabbat 152b Eliezer is
credited with saying something quite different: 'The souls of the
righteous are hidden under the Throne of Glory, as it is said, *yet
the soul of my lord shall be bound up in the bundle of life.*' Now
the treasury is in Arabot, under the throne of Glory.[154] The true
background for this transition is found in TB Hagigah 12b where
we read in a list of the contents of Arabot—the tradition no longer
attached to the name of Eliezer but associated with Resh Lakish
(c.300)—'The souls of the righteous, for it is written: *Yet the soul
of my lord shall be bound up in the bundle of life with the Lord
thy God. The spirits and the souls which are yet to be born, for it*

---

[151] Moore, *Judaism,* ii. 391; Milikowsky, 239–40. But see Lieberman, 496–501;
consistency never prevailed in this.

[152] Moore's translation, *Judaism,* ii. 390. The connection between 'bundle' and
'treasury' is not self-evident in English. Targum Jonathan, however, shows the link
in translating צרור of 1 Sam. 25: 29 with גנז (treasury), a synonym of אוֹצר. There
is also inscription evidence for this belief in afterlife derived from 1 Sam. 25: 29. A
tomb in Antinoopolis from the early second century AD reads נוח נפשו בצרור החיים
(*CIJ* 1534) and a tomb in Spain from probably the sixth century reads נשמתה
שלום אמן החיים בצרור נפשה הבא העולם לחיי (*CIJ* 661).

[153] In *2Bar.* 21. 23; 24. 1 and 30. 2 the treasuries are אוֹצרא, the Syriac equivalent
of אוֹצרוט. This word also occurs in the Syriac version of *4Ez.* 4. 35, 41; 7. 32, 80,
85, 95, 101, where the Latin translator rendered variously, *promptuaria, habitationes,
habitacula.* אוֹצרוט therefore was probably the Hebrew original in each instance.

[154] This same exegesis of 1 Sam. 25: 29 is repeated in Ecclesiastes Rabbah iii. 21. 1
(on Eccles. 3: 21), attributed to rabbi Jose b. Halafta, a contemporary of Eliezer,
though rabbininsts, interestingly, do not regard these words attributed to Jose as
trustworthy (Milikowsky, 241, 247, n. 19); and in Deuteronomy Rabbah x. 4 (on Deut.
32: 1), attributed to rabbi Hanina.

is written: *For the spirit that enwrappeth itself is from Me, and the souls which I have made* [Isa. 57. 16, cf. TB Yebamoth 62a].'

If indeed the attribution to Eliezer of the 'under-the-throne' dicta represents a perversion of his original belief in subterranean 'treasury' of souls (analogous to Ambrose's reinterpretation of the subterranean treasuries of 4Ez. as heavenly compartments in *De bono mortis* 10–11), it would be significant for our study. This Eliezer lived near the middle of the second century and is said to have believed in a thousand-year reign of the Messiah (Pesikta Rabbati 1. 7; Psalms Rabbah 90. 17).

We come perhaps no closer in the Babylonian Talmud to the subterranean view than in the folksy and quasi-comical exchange between the aging sons of Hiyya, who expatiate on the question whether the dead are aware of the sufferings of the living (TB Berakot 18b). It is presupposed here that the souls (spirits) of some of the dead remain at the tomb but at certain times can wander about (unless buried in a matting of reeds!) and ascend even behind the 'curtain' to hear divine decrees. But the sons of Hiyya also know that dead rabbis go where living rabbis long to be. In the world beyond the grave there is a continuation of the rabbinic academy, the 'academy of the sky' (comparable to Origen's *schola animarum?*), in the 'region of fiery sparks and flaming tongues' (TB Baba Mezia 85a–b; 86a; TB Berakot 18b and the texts cited by Chernus, 93). This notion is also shared with the literature of merkabah mysticism.[155]

Another more familiar intermediate-state abode is paradise. But, 'the rabbinic texts are extraordinarily vague on the location of the eschatological paradise',[156] just as they are on the arrival of the 'world to come'. Paradise may be an intermediate abode for the soul awaiting the resurrection, as it apparently is in the deathbed saying attributed to R. Johanan ben Zakkai (TB Berakot 28b); or it may be a zone which has never yet been revealed (TB Berakot 34a). According to Chernus, 'The major focus of eschatological interest [in the rabbis] was ... the garden of Eden or paradise where the souls were re-joined with their resurrected bodies'.[157] This latter view

---

[155] Chernus, 93–4.

[156] Chernus, 89, citing Genesis Rabbah 15. 2, p. 136; TB Berakot 34b; TB Sanhedrin 99a; etc.

[157] Chernus, 94–5; cf. Moore, *Judaism*, ii. 391, 'in many cases it is not evident whether the abode of disembodied souls or of the re-embodied ... is meant.'

would coincide with several apocalyptic sources (see below), but it does not disclose the place of souls before the resurrection.

These elements resist systematization; it is impossible to speak of even a prevailing rabbinic view of the intermediate state for the just. But there is a decided preference for situating the souls of the just in the higher spheres of the universe, in the very throne-room of God, and a very conspicuous abandonment of the subterranean view which is so abundant elsewhere.

(f) Summary. Our brief survey of Jewish sources leads to a few tentative but, I believe, essentially trustworthy conclusions. First, despite its poor attestation in the rabbinic sources, the belief that the souls of the righteous would spend an interim before the resurrection in infernal abodes was widely diffused amongst Jews in the period of the birth and early growth of Christianity. Second, the belief in an interim, Jewish, Messianic kingdom before the last judgement was rather less common, though it shared certain ideals (restoration of national supremacy, redressing of injustice on the earthly plane, supernatural abundance of earthly produce) with other forms of Jewish eschatology. Third, the confluence of both ideas is virtually reserved, in literary sources, to *2Bar.*, *4Ez.*, and possibly Pseudo-Philo's *Biblical Antiquities* (though we admit suspicion about some of the early rabbis whose views may have been quietly censored from the talmudic literature).

We also note some tendencies where a heavenly afterlife is hoped for within Judaism. In these cases there is no manifest concern for a temporary triumph of righteousness on earth to precede the last judgement (*Similitudes*, *3Bar.*, *Life/ApocMos.*, see also *TestJob*, *Test3Pats.*, *AssMos.*). In some places where a heavenly afterlife is believed, a heavenly fore-life is assumed, thus approaching Greek ideas of immortality (Philo; TB Hagigah 12b; Josephus' Essenes) and problems can arise with the doctrine of the resurrection of the body (Philo; *4Macc.*).

3. Dependence on the Part of the Christian Chiliasts

It is indeed remarkable that the two ideas of chiliasm and a subterranean intermediate state—complete with its distinctive understanding of the inhabitants of paradise—have appeared together in *2Bar.* and *4Ez.* (and possibly Pseudo-Philo), and, to our knowledge, nowhere else in Judaism. This alone is certainly enough to warrant the conjecture that the Christian chiliasts drew some of their eschatological inspiration from these two books or from communities of the sort which would have valued them highly. And this conjecture can be further supported. The debt of the Christian chiliasts to 4Ez., 2Bar., and to other pseudepigraphal Jewish apocalypses in matters eschatological is documentable.

(a) Identifiable Citations.   It is generally thought that Pseudo-Barnabas 11. 9, under the formula 'And again another Prophet says . . .', quotes or paraphrases 2Bar. 61. 7.[158] Further, Pierre Bogaert argues plausibly that 2Bar. 32. 4 (cf. 28. 2) is in view in Pseudo-Barnabas' reference to an eschatological temple in 16. 6.[159] It would appear that for Pseudo-Barnabas 2Bar. contains the words of a real prophet. Many also believe he alludes to 4Ez. 4. 33 and 5. 5[160] in 12. 1.[161]

Commodianus derived his expectation of a return of the lost tribes of Israel (Instr. I. 42. 2–3, 30–35) almost certainly from 4Ez.[162] but perhaps also from SibOr. II. 170–3.

(b) Millennial Fecundity.   Reference is frequently made to the extraordinary correspondence between the description, transmitted from the elders to Papias to Irenaeus, of miraculous millennial fecundity and the description in 2Bar. 29. 5–8 of the days of the Anointed One. These two passages are moreover compared to 1En. 10. 17–19, which was probably a source for 2Bar. The mutual relationships, from here on, are unclear. Papias received his description from 'the elders' (but claiming as the ultimate source Jesus himself). It is clear that 2Bar. and Papias are too similar to make viable any theory that they are independent developments of the 1En. tradition. But the expansions in Papias' account[163] would seem

---

[158] Bogaert, SC 144, 272–3.   [159] Ibid. 273–5.

[160] If he knows either pseudepigraphon Pseudo-Barnabas could scarcely have written during the reign of Nerva. Richardson-Shukster, in their proposal for a Nervanic date, do not deal with these probable citations.

[161] See the editions of Lake; Bihlmeyer. Prigent, Testimonia, 116–19, though he thinks the citation is not directly from 4Ez. calls the version in 4Ez. the 'primitive seed' of a testimony tradition.

[162] Brewer, 280; Durel, 58–60.

[163] See Gry, VP, 116. See de Jonge, 46–7, on the talking cluster. Though he thinks this feature of self-presenting foods derives from 'a stock element in the account of utopian lands', de Jonge shows that the entreaty of the cluster, 'bless the Lord through me', 'creates the impression of being due to someone who was familiar with

to argue that his 'dominical agraphon' could have been dependent (perhaps not firsthand) on 2Bar. but not vice-versa.[164] The apparent use of 2Bar. by Pseudo-Barnabas would make this more believable, but in any case we may be confident that Papias' report originated in quarters thoroughly steeped in the type of Jewish apocalyptic piety that is reflected in 2Bar.[165]

(c) Prelude to Incorruptibility. One of Irenaeus' descriptive phrases for the millennial kingdom is 'prelude to incorruptibility' (principium incorruptelae AH v. 32. 1). It is a striking coincidence that in 2Bar., which so closely resembles the eschatology of Irenaeus in its doctrine of the intermediate state, in its doctrine of paradise (see below) and in its portrayal of the earth in Messiah's days, we read that the temporary age of peace brought in by the Messiah is 'the end of that which is corruptible and the beginning of that which is incorruptible' (74. 2). The present age is the age of corruption, the world to come is incorruption, the Messiah's days are the transition between the two; he will have dominion 'until the world of corruption has ended' (40. 3, cf. 44. 12). This is precisely Irenaeus' view of the transitional character of the millennium as it relates to the process of the apprehending of incorruptibility. Though for the author of 2Bar. the Messianic kingdom did not, as it did for Irenaeus, have the function of further training and nourishing the resurrected for the visio dei (v. 32. 1; v. 35. 1,2)—because for this author the resurrection would take place only after the kingdom—Irenaeus' use of the terminology 'prelude to incorruptibility' may well betray first-hand knowledge of 2Bar., though it might also have been mediated through Papias.[166]

For the apostle Paul, the raising of the dead and the transformation of those alive at the sound of the last trumpet heralding Christ's parousia, is when 'this corruptible shall have put on incorruption, and this mortal shall have put on immortality' (1 Cor. 15: 51–3). For Irenaeus, (a) those alive at Christ's coming do not undergo transformation to a final glorified, incorruptible state, rather, 'those that are left shall multiply upon the earth' (AH v. 35. 1, explaining Isa.

Jewish religious observances'. For Rabbinic Judaism 'held that even if a man ate only grapes, he had to say a benediction'.

[164] Bacon, 182.   [165] Gry, VP, 119; Körtner, 102.
[166] Schultz, 168, sees another correspondence between the two authors in the phrases 'the skill of creation' (2Bar. 54. 18) and 'skill of God' (AH iv. 39. 3).

45: 21) and (b) the period following the resurrection of the just is still a period of training for incorruption (v. 35. 2). Though Irenaeus takes Paul's depiction of the renewed creation in Romans 8: 18–25 as a prophecy of the millennium, for Paul any notion of further training or preparation for incorruption in the world he speaks of must be far from his mind: 'Because the creature itself also shall be delivered from the bondage of corruption into the glorious liberty of the children of God' (Rom. 8: 21).

This modification of the Pauline notion of future incorruption is understandable if Paul is read through the filter of a work such as 2*Bar.*

(d) *Paradise and its Inhabitants.*   The claim is often made that especially in the later apocalyptic works the afterlife of the soul is associated with paradise.[167] Still less accurately, Joachim Jeremias remarks that 'throughout apocalyptic it [i.e. paradise] is the present abode of the souls of the departed patriarchs, the elect and the righteous and Enoch and Elijah, who were translated thither during their lifetime'.[168] For 1*En.* 1–36,[169] Pseudo-Philo, 4*Ez.* and 2*Bar.*, however, paradise is manifestly not the domain of righteous souls before the resurrection; on the contrary, we have seen that this domain was the underground sheol/Hades. In the last three named works, paradise houses only those men who were translated from this world bodily without tasting death. This doctrine of paradise, quite significantly, is precisely that of Papias and the elders, Irenaeus, Victorinus of Pettau, and the Clementine *Recognitions*. It was modified by Tertullian to include martyrs.

---

[167]   e.g. Russell, *Method*, 283, paradise 'is transcendental and heavenly in character and is identified as the abode of the souls of the righteous (cf. I Enoch 61. 12; 70. 3f.; II Enoch 8. 1ff.; II Bar. 4. 3; 51. 11; II Esd. 6. 26; 7. 28, 36ff.; 13. 52; 14. 9, 49)'.

[168]   Jeremias, "παράδεισος", 767–8.

[169]   In 1*En.* 32, paradise is in the extreme East, is apparently not heavenly, and is devoid of any human occupants, though this is before Enoch himself has been 'taken'. For talmudic or post-talmudic statements on the number of those who entered paradise alive see Kallah Rabbathi, iii. 26 Baraitha; Derek Erez Zuta 1. 18 (Cohen, ii). The two lists vary; according to the first, seven have entered, according to the last, nine. Enoch appears only in Derek Erez Zuta 1. 18, Ezra and Baruch are absent from both. 'Enoch has been eliminated from Rabbinic tradition generally, and in the *Mid. rabb.* to Genesis ch. 25, the opinion that Enoch did not die is expressly refuted' (Box, *Ezra-Ap.*, 78). We add that in this midrash those refuted are certain 'sectaries' who claim that Enoch has been translated just as was Elijah. Perhaps there is a clue in this for the disappearance of Enoch in the accounts of the return of Elijah in Commodianus, Victorinus and Lactantius.

In the tradition stemming from the elders, Papias and Irenaeus (AH v. 5. 1), which agrees with 4Ez. (3. 6), paradise, as originally created, was separate from the mundane world. The only real antecedent parallel I am able to find to this tradition's three-tiered stratification of the coming world into 'the city', 'paradise', and 'heaven' (v. 36. 1–2), or, paradise, heaven, and earth (*De universo*) occurs in the *TestDan* 5. 12–13.

Again, Irenaeus' conception (AH v. 5. 1) that the translated remain in paradise until the consummation (ἕως cυντελείαc) is exactly the same as that preserved in 4Ez. (the translated are taken up 'until the times are ended' (*usquequo finiantur tempora*) 14. 9), in 2Bar. (to be 'kept unto (the end) of times' 76. 2 cf. 13. 3; 25. 1) and Pseudo-Philo 48. 1 ('until I remember the world'). The same idea occurs in the Clementine *Recognitions*.

as is clearly related in the writings of the law concerning a certain righteous man, that God translated him. In like manner others were dealt with, who pleased His will, that, being translated to Paradise, they should be kept for the kingdom (*serventur ad regnum*). (*Recogn.* i. 52. 4–5)[170]

Just as in Pseudo-Philo, 2Bar. and 4Ez., paradise, for the elders, Papias, Irenaeus, Victorinus (CA 11. 3–4, see above, §I. 2. 7), and the (Ebionite?) author of one stratum of the *Recognitions* (i. 52. 4–5), is throughout this age home for only the translated (and the Messiah) who are preserved there for the last days. The striking correspondences noted here, not merely in the doctrine itself but even in certain details of its expression, point to very close intercourse at some point between these two lines of tradition, one Jewish, one Christian, both chiliastic.

(e) Personal Contacts with Jewish Chiliasts.   Alongside the literary relationships noted above, we may easily believe that even

---

[170] For this author the souls of all other righteous men *servarentur in bonis laetisque regionibus*, probably in an underground Hades. The relation of this author to chiliasm is obscure; we have the full text of the *Recognitions* only in the Latin translation of Rufinus, who may well have expunged certain unorthodox elements, such as chiliasm (cf. Quasten, i. 61; J. Irmscher in *NTA* ii. 534). The kingdom, in the passage cited above, might easily be understood as a chiliastic one, corresponding thus with the reappearance of the translated in the chiliastic authors mentioned above. Jerome did charge that the Ebionites were chiliastic (*In Esiam* 66. 20), though I have found no sure confirmations of chiliasm elsewhere in our present text of the *Recognitions*. The Clementine *Homilies* preserve a belief in a subterranean Hades apparently even for the just (ii. 30; iii. 32–3; xii. 14), though this would be contradicted in xvii. 10. The *Homilies* do not mention inhabitants of paradise, nor, like the *Recognitions*, do they exhibit any sure signs of chiliasm.

throughout the period of the most intense nationalistic Jewish Messianism (70–135 AD), when relations between Church and Synagogue were increasingly strained,[171] there remained significant personal contact and interaction, friendly or otherwise, between Messianic Jews and chiliastic Christians. This may, in some cases, have facilitated Christian adaptations of Jewish Messianism. William Horbury posits the continuation of Christian dependence on Judaism in 'Messianism' in the second century, citing as one piece of evidence the attraction some Christians felt towards nationalistic Jewish hopes which seemed close to fulfilment near the time of the Bar Cochba revolt.[172] To what extent Judaizing actually took place in this situation is certainly debatable,[173] but Christian awareness of Jewish nationalistic hopes during this period was unavoidable. And to 'dialogue' with Jews at this time meant to deal with Jewish hopes of a restoration of Jerusalem as the fulfilment of Biblical promises. It is to this period which we may attribute the eschatological currents which left their marks in the writings of Papias, Pseudo-Barnabas, and chapter 80 of Justin's *Dialogue*.

As Tertullian (including *De universo*) and, to a lesser degree, Lactantius in particular show, we must say that Christian conceptions of an interim existence in Hades were developed in rapport with pagan as well as with Jewish notions and that the adoption of this view of the intermediate state was not entirely due to a desire to remain faithful to the heritage of Judaism. Finé has shown that the battle with Valentinianism and Marcionism was decisive for Tertullian's acceptance and defence of an infernal intermediate state; Daniélou rightly sees this concern in Justin and Irenaeus as well.[174] The justification for Tertullian lay most probably closest at hand in the writings of Irenaeus (and in such Biblical footholds as he could find) and not in the Jewish sources we have dealt with, though we know he was acquainted with at least *1En.* (*Fem.* I. 2–3; II. 10). For Novatian, in turn, it lay in the writings of Tertullian. But

---

[171] Frend, *Rise*, 123–6.

[172] Horbury, *Aug.* 83–4, mentions in addition Justin's remark that Bar Cochba had Christians severely punished for not denying Jesus as Messiah (Justin, *1Apol.* 31; Eus. *HE* IV. 8. 4); Justin's acknowledging that some Christians he knows have gone over to Judaism (*Dial.* 42. 4–5); and 'the great praise of the martyrs who would not confess a false Christ of the Jews, in the Ethiopic text of the Apocalypse of Peter' (*ApocPet.* 2 in *NTA* ii. 669).

[173] *ApocPet.* (for which see below, § II. 3. 2), shows how martyrdom was deemed preferable.

[174] Finé 80; Daniélou, *OLC*, 393.

with Irenaeus himself it was a different story. Though he may have seen some justification in the occasional remarks of Justin and Pseudo-Barnabas, we also know that the eschatology of the chiliastic Jewish apocalypses *2Bar.* and *4Ez.* reappears materially in his eschatology, whether this was transmitted entire from Papias or whether it came partly through his own direct knowledge of these writings. We know too that one or both of these apocalypses, or something very near to them, were utilized by Pseudo-Barnabas, Papias, and probably by Commodianus.

From all that we have seen we are compelled to ask whether it is not necessary in fact to broaden our view of chiliasm and to regard it as entailing a view of both general and of individual eschatology. Should we not indeed consider the subterranean version of the intermediate state as one defining characteristic of the eschatology we call chiliasm, at least in our earliest Jewish and Christian sources? The example of Methodius would stand in the way of this, but his example may certainly be viewed as pioneering a new path away from the well-trodden chiliastic road, a trail which was closed up behind him by the chiliasts Victorinus of Pettau and Lactantius.

II

REGNUM CAELORUM CAELESTE

INTRODUCTION

In Chapter II we shall examine the reverse side of the connection made by Irenaeus. We have already studied those pre-Nicaean Christian authors who may, in my opinion, be said to exhibit a chiliastic view of future history and who also reveal their understanding of the intermediate state. We saw that amongst them the thesis of Irenaeus, that chiliastic eschatology rightfully entails a doctrine of an infernal intermediate state, held up astonishingly well. We have also located with extreme probability the roots of this conjunction of eschatological doctrines in the Jewish apocalyptic soil from which chiliasm itself sprang, concluding that this version of the intermediate state was virtually indigenous to earliest chiliasm.

We are led by statements of Justin, Irenaeus, and Tertullian to believe that each of these men knew of pious or orthodox Christians who were not millennialists. Those known to Tertullian were neither Marcionites nor Valentinians. And the clear inference drawn from Irenaeus, but deriving support from all the evidence collected in § I.1–2 above, is that the non-chiliasm of these orthodox might be revealed by their belief in an intermediate state in heaven, for this belief constituted the stumbling block to their adoption of chiliasm.

The authors whose views are represented in the present chapter all hold, in my judgement, to one form or another of the expectation of an immediate entry into heaven for the righteous at death. None of them, so it will be shown, can be credited with positive chiliastic views (where I go against any prevailing opinion on a particular author, it will be made clear).

The non-advocacy, and sometimes outspoken repudiation, of chiliasm by the authors canvassed in this section has to be seen therefore as reinforcing Irenaeus' contention that the doctrines of the millennium and the intermediate state were interdependent. But each author may be classed (ideally at least) in one of two sub-groups. First, there will be those whose statements, before we come to ask about their understanding of the intermediate state, already allow a reasonable and equitable assessment that their general or cosmic eschatology was not chiliastic. These will naturally form the backbone of the establishment of the reverse side of Irenaeus' connection, that is, they will confirm that orthodox non-chiliasts also believed that the soul departs to heaven at death. Second, there will be authors whose near silence or ambiguity relating to the subject cannot in advance furnish a confident evaluation of their eschatology in terms of chiliasm or non-chiliasm. Yet our estimation of these writers must consequently be affected by the implications drawn from the pattern identified by Irenaeus. For, to the extent that this pattern is thought to hold true and to have characterized early Christian eschatology, to such an extent will it be thought likely that these Christian authors were truly non-chiliastic in their cosmic eschatology.

It has been thought best, rather than to subdivide these authors into the categories 'definite non-chiliasts', 'possible non-chiliasts', to treat them all instead in a more or less chronological fashion using traditional categories such as Apostolic Fathers, Apologists, Martyrologies, etc. This is due primarily to the wish to preserve the natural affinities and continuities which exist between many of the documents and which through another method of treatment might be lost. It is also hoped that the method adopted will be less tedious to the reader. Each author's classification will be summarized by a chart at the end of our study.

One point of special interest, as we go, will be the role of the doctrine of the bodily resurrection, for it is sometimes thought that a denial of this doctrine must have been on the agenda of the earliest non-chiliasts and that a heavenly intermediate state such as Christianity generally came later to adopt, may only 'artificially' be combined with a doctrine of resurrection.[1]

Finally, we shall try to be alert to any evidence of how non-chiliasts regarded the book of Revelation and, in particular, how they might have dealt with the millennial chapter, Revelation 20. Previous research, we remind ourselves, would tell us there is no serious non-chiliastic approach to this chapter recoverable before Tyconius, Jerome, and Augustine.

---

[1] Schürer, ii, 542, 546–7.

1. THE APOSTOLIC FATHERS[2]

1. Clement of Rome

Clement, who probably sent his letter to the Corinthians before the appearance in Rome of the book of Revelation,[3] is only infrequently claimed as a chiliast, and always without good, textual bases.[4] It is true that he refers in 42. 3 to a future coming of the kingdom of God and in 50. 3 to the future visitation of Christ's kingdom, when the dead shall arise from their tombs. But this is the visitation on earth of an already-existing kingdom or lordship which Jesus possesses at the Father's right hand in heaven, as Clement's traditional use of Psalms 2 and 110 (through the medium of the book of Hebrews) in 36. 3–6 shows. Even chiliasts, however, believed in a present lordship of Christ. More revealing might be Clement's apparent expectation that the parousia will bring with it eternal rewards for everyone (34. 3), which, strictly speaking, would exclude the possibility of an intervening millennium.[5] Yet it is perhaps pressing his language a bit to derive such a definite expectation from his imprecise scriptural citation in 34. 3.

The evidence then, such as it is, flows more easily towards non-chiliasm than towards chiliasm. Still, we are left somewhat in the shadows on the relation of his eschatology to chiliasm if we must rely solely on explicit statements about the resurrection or the kingdom. Can his view of the intermediate state then contribute anything to our understanding of his form of eschatology?

In the opinion of J. A. Fischer, Clement's reference in 50. 3 to the 'place of the godly', that is, to the place of the godly after death, signifies 'the interimistic, better places of abode (Aufenthaltsräume)

[2] Greek texts of the Apostolic Fathers cited here (excepting Hermas) are from Bihlmeyer. Translations from *1Clem.* are my own.

[3] Welborn's arguments for a Trajanic or Hadrianic date for *1 Clement*, apart from his calling into question the evidence for a Domitianic persecution, are not convincing. T. J. Herron, at the Tenth International Conference on Patristic Studies in Oxford, August, 1987, challenged the traditional date of 95–6, which has been based almost entirely on the testimony of Eusebius. For reasons which we cannot enter into now, I am not persuaded by Herron that the letter was written before AD 70 (Clement's use of the present tenses in chs. 40–1 is taken by Herron to signify that the temple in Jerusalem was still standing when Clement wrote), but a date of, say, 80–90 does not seem to me unreasonable.

[4] e.g. Semisch-Bratke, 808, hearing 'echoes' of chiliasm in 50. 3. Knoch, 109, note 26, maintains only that Clement was influenced by a chiliastic 'Vorstellungskreis'.

[5] Recall the example of Jude's grandsons (*HE* III. 20. 4), cited in the Introduction.

in Hades'.[6] This position is amplified through further research by Otto Knoch. If it is correct, and if the taxonomy of eschatological notions provided by Irenaeus is followed, we would thus have grounds for presuming that Clement held to an early form of chiliasm. The compilation of the evidence made by Fischer and Knoch, however, calls for re-examination.

Both scholars begin their studies of Clement's view of the intermediate state with 20. 5, where Clement, remarking on the universe's harmonious subservience to the decrees of God, says that 'The unsearchable places of the abysses and the unfathomable judgements of the lower world (νερτέρων) are controlled by the same ordinances'. Both see these 'judgements'[7] as pertaining only to the wicked, but Knoch goes on to assert that Clement conceives of Hades as the common 'dwelling place of the dead, notwithstanding their particular post-mortal fate'.[8] Clement's two uses of the term Hades, however, both appear in reference to the OT story of Dathan and Abiram (Num. 16). It is not to be missed that Hades, in Clement's only uses of the term, receives only wicked people, his prime examples of jealousy and sedition (4. 12; 51. 4).

Determinative stress is laid by both Fischer and Knoch on 50. 3–4:

All the generations from Adam until this day have passed away; but those (persons) who were perfected in love according to God's grace have a place among the godly (ἔχουσιν χῶρον εὐσεβῶν), who shall be manifested in the visitation of the kingdom of Christ. 4. For it is written, 'Enter ye into the chambers for a very little while, until my wrath and fury pass away, and I will remember a day of good and I will raise you up out of your graves.'

Fischer and Knoch draw the not unreasonable conclusion from the combined proof texts adduced by Clement (Isa. 26: 20 and Ezek. 37: 12, linked by words from an unknown source) that this 'place among the godly', into which all the righteous since Adam have been collected, is synonymous with the chambers (ταμεῖα) of Isaiah 26: 20. These chambers are then assumed to be the same as the 'Hadeskammern', the 'treasuries of souls' which we have encoun-

---

[6] Fischer, *Todesgedanken*, 235.

[7] κρίματα (cf. Origin, *CCels.* v. 42). Lake (*ApF*), however, would emend to κλίματα (regions), a reading which, Professor R. D. Williams has called to my attention, would furnish a very intelligible parallelism. If this reading is accepted, there is no reference here at all to a dwelling place of souls.   [8] Knoch, 164.

tered already in *4Ez.* and *2Bar.*[9] 'Place among the godly' of itself is completely unclear as to location; the term is found in pagan funerary poetry and may have had early associations with Orphism.[10] Clement perhaps does regard the 'chambers' of Isaiah 26: 20 as the interim abode of righteous souls (though they might also have signified the tombs, cf. *5Ez.* 2. 31; Tertullian, *Res.* 27), but the connection with anything underworldly still has to be supplied from without. The fact that he, or his source,[11] turns directly to Ezekiel 37: 12 for a promise that God will raise his people, that is, their bodies, from their graves is not determinative, for in any case the interim abode for the soul, whether in heaven or in Hades, is different from the grave itself, the receptacle of the corpse alone. What, for instance, is to prevent Clement from having in mind something like the 'many mansions' in the Father's house (John 14: 2) when he speaks of 'chambers'?[12]

If this text leaves us in doubt as to the location of the souls of the righteous it at least gives us one important principle. For Clement all the elect dead have gone to the same place: 'In love were all the elect of God made perfect'; 'those (men) who were perfected in love according to God's grace have a place among the godly' (49. 5; 50. 3). It is not the case that martyrs, as in the later scheme of Tertullian, or apostles or virgins are in heaven while the rest of the righteous are in Hades. This becomes important as we come to chapter 5, where the post-mortem fates of Peter and Paul are in view.[13] Knoch recognizes this principle and therefore deter-

[9] Fischer *Todesgedanken*, 235; Knoch, 165. Grant–Graham, *Clement*, 81, adds *1En.* 22.

[10] Fischer *Todesgedanken*, 235, citing Franz Cumont; L. Sanders, 104.

[11] Daniélou, *TJC*, 95–96.

[12] Knoch, 166, n. 17, wishes to stress that Clement cannot have known John's Gospel (14: 2), so, no parallel between John 14: 2 and Clement can be used to determine that for Clement the afterlife abode is in heaven. But it is at least as impossible that Clement could have known *2Bar.* or *4Ez.* By the same logic we ought to conclude that he could not therefore have believed in an abode in Hades.

[13] Contra Harnack, *I. Clemensbrief*, 107. That Peter and Paul are not alone in their abode, wherever it is, is made plain in 6. 1–2, where it is said that 'a great multitude of the chosen' have been 'gathered' to them. This is not merely a gathering into 'the imaginary arena . . . , in which the contests of the "Christian athletes" take place' (Altaner, *HJb*, 27). Cυνηθροίcθη has a strong locative connotation and is commonly used for Christian assemblies, Luke 24: 33; Acts 12: 12; Ignatius, *Magn.* 4. 1; *ApostConst* v. 19. 3, 6; v. 30. 2; vii. 34. 10. Compare also the common description of the reward of each group (in 5. 4–7 and 6. 1–2) as 'noble (γενναῖον), and the common use of both groups as surpassing examples of endurance. Peter and Paul are not brought forward as examples simply because they are martyrs or apostles

mines that the resting places of even Peter and Paul, the martyrs and every other redeemed individual are in Hades as well.[14]

Purely from the standpoint of method, it should be remembered that 50. 3–4 comes late in the epistle and after several informative sections on intermediate-state blessings. Chapter 5 especially must lay the foundations for our understanding of Clement's view of the intermediate state.

As jealousy is at the root of the Corinthian fracas, Clement embarks in 3. 2 on a sort of biblical-historical study of this vice, exhausting his store of OT examples in chapter 4, and in chapter 5 bringing his readers to their own generation. The greatest and most righteous pillars of the Church were persecuted and contended unto death (5. 2), because of jealousy against them. The examples of Peter and Paul are then spotlighted, the results of whose faithful endurance and witness give the readers their first glimpse of Clement's view of the intermediate state:

Peter ... having given his witness went to his due place of glory (ἐπορεύθη εἰς τὸν ὀφειλόμενον τόπον τῆς δόξης). On account of jealousy and envy Paul showed the prize of endurance ... he received the noble fame of his faith ... thus he departed (ἀπηλλάγη) from the world and was taken up to the holy place (εἰς τὸν ἅγιον τόπον ἀνελήμφθη) ... (5. 4–7)

The expression used for Peter's abode, the due place of glory, apart from its repetition by Polycarp (*Phil.* 9. 2), appears to be unique in ancient literature. Although the good section of Hades is thought of as 'a locality full of light' by the author of *De universo*, it is straining this conception more than a little that this locality should be called a place of glory.[15] If we may accept Polycarp's

and therefore possess rewards peculiar to an élite class, but because they constitute the most worthy examples for the readers' emulation. Both the lives of the apostles and martyrs and their present heavenly rewards are paradigms, so, the exemplary value of the rewards rests upon their being rewards available to the Christians whom Clement is addressing, not all of whom could have been conceived of as probable candidates for martyrdom.

[14] Knoch, 170, 'But where is this place situated? According to the connection with 50. 3, in Hades ... Clement has then a comparatively simple conception of the post-mortal fate of men. All arrive in Hades as the place of the dead.'

[15] With OT worthies and others in mind Clement says, 'But they who endured in confidence obtained the inheritance of glory and honour; they are exalted, and were enrolled by God in his memorial for ever and ever' (45. 8). Though it is true that glory (δόξα) and honour (τιμή) can also apply to worldly rulers (61. 1–2), this use of the categories as pertaining to the exaltation of the departed invites comparison with Heb. 2: 6–9, where Jesus is the one who has been 'crowned with glory and honour' (Ps. 8: 5–7). Jesus, like the righteous in Clement's epistle, has been

expansion (*Phil.* 9. 2), Hades is in fact decisively ruled out as the
location of this due place of glory and heaven is shown to be
intended (see below). But Knoch, for one, will not accept Polycarp's
elucidation, which he regards as an attempt to fuse Clement's view
with Paul's.[16]

But the assertion that Clement held to an interim existence in
Hades for the just irretrievably flounders at the words 'he was
taken up to the holy place' (5. 7). 'The holy place' to which Paul
has been taken up,[17] especially as is indicated by the use of the
article, can hardly refer to Hades and would seem to be appropriate
for nothing but the heavenly sanctuary.[18] The *earthly* temple is
called 'the holy place' (ὁ ἅγιος τόπος) in *2Macc.* 1. 29; 2. 18; 8. 17;
3Macc. 2. 14 and by Jesus in Matthew 24: 15. In Acts 6: 13–14
Stephen is falsely accused of speaking 'against this holy place and
the law'. Τὰ ἅγια is the customary name used by the author of
Hebrews for the holy place, or the holy of holies, whether the

'perfected through suffering' (Heb. 2: 10). Clement uses here the word 'inherited';
Jesus, in Heb. 1: 14, has *inherited* (after death) a name superior to that of the angels
(indeed he is heir of all things, 1: 2), and there are believers worthy of imitation
who through faith and patience are *inheriting* the promises (Heb. 6: 12 cf. 1: 14,
angels minister to those about to *inherit* salvation).

[16] Knoch, 169, n. 26; 172.

[17] Both Greek MSS have ἐπορεύθη (he went), but ἀνελήμφθη (he was taken up) is
presumed by the Syriac, Latin, and Coptic versions. Since ἐπορεύθη here may
also be accounted for as an assimilation to v. 4, ἀνελήμφθη is preferred by Harnack,
I. Clemensbrief, and Lake, *ApF*. It is also adopted by Bihlmeyer, though not by
Jaubert. Knoch assumes ἐπορεύθη and does not even mention the variant. Confusion
over the variants ἀνελήμφθη and ἐπορεύθη is evident in the volume by Grant and
Graham, *Clement*, 26, in that the former is presupposed by the commentary, while
the latter appears in the translation (the words 'into the holy place' are, moreover,
altogether absent from the translation). If ἀνελήμφθη is original, it would, of course,
be very unsuitable for depicting a removal to Hades but utterly natural for depicting
an ascension to heaven. We shall see below that the martyrs in the *EpV&L* (*HE*
v. 2. 3) were counted worthy by Christ ἀναληφθῆναι upon their confession, though,
by contrast, Irenaeus' system allows the saints ἀναληφθῆναι only after the resurrection of their flesh, at the parousia (*AH* v. 32. 1).

[18] L. Sanders devotes considerable attention to a comparison between *IClem.* 5
and the Cynic–Stoic diatribes which exalt the heroes of virtue. He implies that even
Clement's conception of Paul's ascension to heaven corresponds to an element in
these forms (31–4, 39). There are two essential differences, however. First, heavenly
rewards in the literature cited by Sanders are reserved to a small class of idealized
heroes whose heavenly ascension meant deification (Hercules, Castor, Pollux, Asclep-
ius, etc.). For Clement, Peter and Paul have a reward no different in kind than do
other Christians, and Clement's religious commitments did not allow for such a
concept of deification (Knoch, 167). Second, Clement's terminology, the due place of
glory and the holy place, is not found in the examples cited by Sanders and indeed
has a specifically Christian or Judaeo-Christian derivation.

earthly (9. 8(?), 25; 13. 11) or the heavenly (8. 2; 9. 12, 24; 10. 19). It is moreover significant that in Hebrews, which almost certainly Clement knows,[19] we have clear evidence of the belief that the 'spirits of just men made perfect' now congregate at the cultic precincts of the heavenly Mount Zion (12. 22–4).[20]

Another very important parallel occurs in the speech which Clement's Jewish contemporary at Rome, Josephus, claims to have made to his companions towards the close of the siege of Jotapata, counselling them against suicide (*BJ* III. 374). While the darker regions of Hades receive the souls of suicides, those who die

in accordance with the law of nature and repay the loan which they received from God, when He who lent it is pleased to reclaim it, win eternal renown (κλέος);[21] that their houses and families are secure; that their souls, remaining spotless and obedient, are allotted the most holy place in heaven (χῶρον οὐράνιον λαχοῦcαι τὸν ἁγιώτατον), whence, in the revolution of the ages, they return to find in chaste bodies a new habitation.[22]

This teaching is remarkable for its resemblance to that of *1Clem.*, whatever the assessment of its credibility as coming from the mouth of a first-century Jew;[23] it is indisputably nearer to Clement than are the views of *2Bar.* and *4Ez.* In it the 'most holy place' is expressly set in heaven.

Within a few decades another document of Roman Christian provenance will assume the same conception, by portraying the celestial lot of Christian martyrs after death as the 'right hand portion of the sanctuary (τοῦ ἁγιάcματος)' (Hermas, *Vis.* 3. 1.9; 3. 2.1, see our discussion of this text below), a place also characterized by glory.

In one other place Clement uses the word τόπος to denote 'the post-mortal place of honour'.[24] This time, in an ironical jab at the Corinthians, he is speaking of the lot of deceased presbyters. 'Blessed are the presbyters who have gone on before (προοδοιπορή-cαντες) us, such as had a fruitful and perfect departure. For they

---

[19] See especially, Hagner, 179–95 and Ellingworth.
[20] See reference to this text in Ch. III below.
[21] Cf. *1Clem.* 5. 6, τό γενναῖον τῆς πίcτεως αὐτοῦ κλέος ἔλαβεν.
[22] H. St J. Thackeray's translation (LCL).
[23] Glasson, 43, notes the protestations against this being a genuinely Jewish teaching.
[24] Knoch, 166. Lightfoot, *AF*, 1. 2, 136, is probably correct to suggest also an allusion to τόπος in the sense of office, but he too recognizes a primary reference to the place of the departed.

have no fear that anyone will dislodge them from their established place' (44. 5). The directional quality of προοδοιπορήσαντες, not merely 'predecessors' but those who have travelled or gone before,[25] is reinforced by the clear terminus for the journey in the τόπος of the departed. Despite, then, *prima facie* resemblance to Irenaeus' 'appointed place' (ὡρισμένος τόπος *AH* v. 31. 2), Clement's 'established place' (ἱδρυμένος τόπος) represents a conception of the place of the dead entirely at odds with that notion. There is every reason to assume that the teaching here is of a piece with that of chapter 5, in which the due place of glory and the holy place must be understood as the heavenly sanctuary and not as a subterranean holding place.

What we have seen of Clement's understanding of the intermediate state and what we have seen of his view of Christ's kingdom fall in line with Irenaeus' thesis of a connection between the two doctrines. According to this thesis, Clement's notion of an interim existence in heaven for the godly, before the bodily resurrection, should signify that he was not a chiliast. Thus our cautious, preliminary verdict based on what he says about the kingdom and the return of Christ, that Clement's eschatology tended away from chiliasm, would be confirmed.

Finally, it must be noted that absolutely no tension can be detected, in Clement's mind, between his heavenly version of the intermediate state and his evident non-chiliasm on the one hand, and a vigorous Christian doctrine of the resurrection of the body on the other (chs. 23–7; 50. 4).

2. Ignatius of Antioch[26]

It is well known that the letters of Ignatius of Antioch provide no direct testimony to chiliasm. He may not have known the book of Revelation; it certainly did not hold the appeal for him that Paul and his epistles did. Ignatius' use of the phrase 'kingdom of God' is perhaps surprisingly infrequent and, apart from its futuristic

---

[25] Cf. Ignatius, *Eph.* 9. 2, Christians are σύνοδοι (fellow travellers) on the path which leads up to God.

[26] Translations of Ignatius are my own. We shall be using the 'traditional' (since Lightfoot and Zahn) corpus of his writings (texts from Bihlmeyer). On the recent theories of authenticity by Ruis-Camps and Joly, see Hammond Bammel.

reference, in itself unremarkable.[27] It occurs only twice (Eph. 16. 1;
Phd. 3. 3), both times in warnings, reminiscent of Paul's, about
certain people not inheriting it.[28] We shall comment later on Ignatius' notion of 'inheritance'. It may be that when he speaks of his
own inheritance, as he often does, he is thinking of it as laid up in
'the kingdom of heaven'. Thus, attaining his inheritance may well
mean for Ignatius inheriting the kingdom of God.

The Ignatian corpus is a unique portal to the mind of a man
bearing about the sentence of death for being a Christian. Ignatius
has thus left us a vital and intriguing source for early Christian
notions of the afterlife.

(a) Attaining God (('Επι)τυγχάνω θεοῦ). His most characteristic
referent for what will happen to him if he faithfully endures unto
death is the unusual expression, 'to attain God' (ἐπιτυχεῖν θεοῦ).[29]
'Επιτυγχάνω appears twenty times in Ignatius, nine times in his
letter to Rome. Thirteen times God is either the expressed or implied
(Rom. 8. 3; Phd. 5. 1) object. Twice the object is Christ (Rom. 5. 3,
bis). Ignatius uses the unemphatic form τύγχανω in a similar way.
But by appealing to Ignatius' use of τυγχάνω with the ἐπι- prefix
when speaking of his own death and his use of τυγχάνω without
the prefix for Christians in general, it has been said that Ignatius
conceived of his own death, being that of a martyr, as conferring
upon him a glory of a different order from that which he allows to
non-martyred Christians.[30] Yet besides the inherent difficulty in
believing all this to be summed up in the prefix,[31] other factors
combine to negate such a conclusion.

[27] It is not accurate, however, to represent him as not possessing an eschatology,
or even as unconcerned about the topic of the return of Christ and the end of the
world. 'No more than Paul (Phil. 1: 19–26) does he insist upon general eschatological
notions as he confronts his own death', Grant, Ignatius, 17. Ignatius, at Eph. 11. 1
in particular, sounds more than a faint echo of eschatological urgency. Polycarp is
counselled by his elder fellow-bishop to await (προσδόκα) the coming of Christ.
Neither is there any flagging in Ignatius' expectation of the believers' bodily resurrection at the parousia (Tr. inscr.; 9. 2; Sm. 5. 3; 7. 1, possibly Polyc. 6. 1).
[28] Ignatius does believe that the incarnation had wrought a dissolution of the
'ancient kingdom' of evil, with which is associated magic and 'every bond of
wickedness' (Eph. 19. 3).
[29] See Bauernfeind; BAGD, 829; Willis; and Bower, who relates ἐπιτυγχάνω in
Ignatius to the theological concept of 'union'.   [30] Willis, 88.
[31] Bower, 1, 'Even more striking is the similarity of Ignatius' use of these two
verbs'. Corwin, 254, and Schoedel, Ignatius, 29, agree that little can be made of any
difference in meaning from the use of the two verbs.

First, Ignatius does in fact once use the unemphatic form for his own fate, including himself along with the Magnesian Christians in stating that 'we shall attain God' (θεοῦ τευξόμεθα, Magn. 1. 2). The requisite antecedent for so attaining is stated to be the enduring and finally the escaping of all the evil treatment of the devil, an enterprise in which Ignatius sees himself (Tr. 4. 2; Rom. 5. 3; 7. 1), no less than the Christians to whom he writes (Eph. 13. 1; 17. 1), as vitally engaged.

Second, he does on one occasion use the emphatic form for someone other than himself, namely, Polycarp (Polyc. 2. 3).

Third, Ignatius, who is concerned about remaining stalwart to the end and thus attaining his lot or inheritance (Tr. 12. 3; Rom. 1. 2; Phd. 5. 1) once identifies his lot as 'the lot of the Ephesian Christians' (Eph. 11. 2). Attaining this 'lot' (κλῆρος) can be practically synonymous with attaining God. Both appear as objects of the verb ἐπιτυγχάνω in the same context (Tr. 12. 2–3),[32] and, the construction of Tr. 12. 3, in which Ignatius requests prayers on his behalf that he might be made worthy of attaining his lot, is parallel to the constructions of Magn. 14. 1 and Tr. 13. 1, 3, in which prayers are likewise requested that he might attain to God. It certainly appears that Ignatius does not perceive his lot of attaining God as materially higher than or different from that of other Christians.

If it is the case then that ἐπιτυχεῖν θεοῦ describes an inheritance essentially the same as that denoted by τυχεῖν θεοῦ, why does Ignatius customarily use the strengthened form when referring to his own destiny? The prefix probably serves only to lend force or intensity[33] to the expression when the immediacy of final attainment, due to the close proximity of death itself, is felt. It is the thought rather of death as a believer than of martyrdom in any technical sense (far less, a 'martyr theology') which attracts the use of emphatic forms in Ignatius' speech.[34] It is important to remember that for Ignatius the 'normal' Christian life is itself a life of suffering and endurance (Magn. 1. 3 and Sm. 9. 2).[35]

(b) Time and Place.   It has been recognized by most readers of Ignatius that the phrase 'to attain to God' represents the thought

---

[32] Schoedel, Ignatius, 160, n. 5; Corwin, 252. Compare EpV&L (Eus. HE) v. 1. 10; 1. 26; 1. 48.   [33] LSJ, 623 (G.III. 4); Grant, Ignatius, 43.

[34] Aune, 162, 'There is no evidence in the letters of Ignatius to suggest that martyrs alone could "attain God" '; Baumeister, 288, 'The goal of all Christians is the attaining to God and Christ. Martyrdom is the sure and direct path to this goal'; cf. Schoedel, Ignatius, 28–29.   [35] Rebell, 464, n. 13.

of transport to the presence of God in heaven immediately upon death.[36] This indeed is the natural impression. It will be advantageous for our purposes to establish beyond doubt whether he does in fact consider 'attaining God' to be an intermediate-state blessing, entered, temporally, immediately upon death and, spatially, in God's presence in heaven.

For a start, there is a near identity in Ignatius' mind, based on the notion of life or eternal life as inhering already in the Christian (John 5: 24; 11: 25–6),[37] between physical death and entry into life (Tr. 2. 1; Eph. 20. 2; Sm. 3. 2). So radically has death been devastated, so completely has its stranglehold been reversed that Ignatius can paradoxically enjoin the Romans, referring to his approaching death, 'do not hinder me from living, do not wish me to die' (Rom. 6. 2).

That the temporal dimension was not absent from his mind is seen in several of his expressions. He assures the Trallians that his spirit is consecrated to them not only now, 'but when I attain God' (Tr. 13. 3). The use of ὅταν (when) here shows that he has a definite time in mind when he will attain to God (also note ὅταν in Eph. 12. 2 and see below on Rom. 6. 2), and this time cannot intelligibly be the day of resurrection for on that day the Trallians will presumably be with him. The immediacy of his hope is thrown into striking relief in his statement to the Smyrnaeans, 'to be near the sword is to be near God, to be with the beasts is to be with God' (Sm. 4. 2). These instruments of death will be his direct passageway to God; to be near them is to be near to attaining his desired end.

Likewise, it can be shown that this immediate removal to God at death was indeed perceived in spatial terms. He implores the

---

[36] See e.g. Corwin, 213 (cf. 254).

[37] Rebell, 461–2, believes that Paul's dynamic tension between the already and the not yet is lost on Ignatius who has replaced it with the wish for gaining the victory in the struggle through martyrdom—leaving little of Paul's 'already'. But for Ignatius 'life' is possessed by the Christian here and now: Christ has breathed incorruption (ἀφθαρσίαν) on the Church (Eph. 17. 1)—even though the proof of possessing it lies in our willingness to die for Christ (Magn. 5. 2). Aune, 165, attributes the marginal role of realized eschatology in Ignatius to the dialectic between the individual and the community. Still, due consideration must be given to the phenomenon of self-depreciation in Ignatius. His appraisals of his Christian readers manifest his willingness to accord to them 'realized' Christian virtues which he will not allow to himself or will allow to himself only if he successfully completes his course towards martyrdom. This is the case with his use of the terms μαθητής and ἄνθρωπος (see Eph. 1. 2: Rom. 6. 2, etc.): Schoedel, Ignatius, 29; 182, n. 6.

Romans, 'Let me receive the pure light. Having arrived at that place (ἐκεῖ) I shall be a man' (Rom. 6. 2). This statement depicts a transport of some kind to a locality of pure light distinct from this world.[38] Receiving the pure light must be analogous to 'attaining to God'.[39] Surely relevant in this context is Colossians 1. 12 and the connection with Ignatius' notion of his inheritance (κλῆρος). The author of Colossians 1. 12 summons his readers to render thanks to the Father, 'who has qualified us to share in the inheritance (κλήρου) of the saints in light'. This in turn should be compared with other statements attributed to Paul in Acts 20. 32; 26. 18 and Ephesians 1. 18.[40] We have already seen that, for Ignatius, 'attaining one's lot' can be a circumlocution for 'attaining God' (and possibly for 'inheriting the kingdom of God'). When these NT texts (in which κλῆρος and κληρονομία are used synonymously) are laid alongside Ignatius' teaching concerning his κλῆρος what emerges is that the inheritance which in the canonical writings is spoken of with an air of ambiguity is conceived by him as belonging definitely to the sphere of heaven and as capable of being entered at death (see also Tr. 12. 3 and Rom. 7. 2).

In Romans 2. 2 Ignatius exploits the circumstances of his journey, from the land of the sun's rising to the land of its setting, for imagery that will give expression to his own desire to 'set' from this world and 'rise' (ἀνατέλλω) to the Father. The thought is much the same as that in 1Clem. 5. 7, wherein the apostle Paul, whom

---

[38] The notion of death as the conduit to another location is presupposed also in *Magn.* 5. 1, 'and each one is about to remove to his own place (τὸν ἴδιον τόπον)' (cf. Acts 1: 25; Polycarp, *Phil.* 9. 2; 1Clem. 5. 4, 7; 44. 5). Also relevant is Ignatius' curious reference to his coming death as a birth or birthing process: 'the time of birth is upon me' (Rom. 6. 1). A noteworthy contrast to this is to be seen in 4Ez. 4. 41–42 where the 'birth' is from the intermediate state to the eternal at the time of the resurrection; for Ignatius it is from this life to the intermediate state at the time of death. More comparable to Ignatius is 4Macc. 16. 13, though it is quite contestable that Ignatius was directly dependent upon this document (pace Perler, *RivAC*, 56–7). With regard to Perler's theory of literary dependence see the remarks of Hammond Bammel, 72–3; Baumeister, 288.

[39] Corwin, 167. Schoedel, *Ignatius*, 183, sees a connection with Gnosticism here but rightly remarks, 'The idea presupposed here of the ascent to the other world appears elsewhere in Ignatius and is comprehensible against a wider background than Gnosticism' (183). Similarly, Hammond Bammel, 76. See also 1 Tim. 6: 16; Athenagoras, *Plea*, 16.

[40] This may explain why it is especially the lot of the Ephesian Christians which he singles out as his own (11. 2): the words of Paul in Acts 20: 32 were spoken to the Ephesian elders and the words from Ephesians 1: 18, obviously, are from the letter traditionally assigned to that locale.

Ignatius also may have had in mind as his model in the passage before us, is extolled as having taught righteousness to all the world, having come 'to the limits of the West', who gave his testimony before the rulers and thus passed from the world and was taken up ($\dot{\alpha}\nu\epsilon\lambda\dot{\eta}\mu\phi\theta\eta$) into the holy place. This parallel would suggest that the rising Ignatius here speaks of is not a reference to the bodily resurrection at the last day but a rising $\epsilon\dot{\iota}c$ $\theta\epsilon\acute{o}\nu$ at the time of his death.

Apart from him let nothing be pleasing to you, in whom I bear about my bonds, spiritual pearls, by which ($\dot{\epsilon}\nu$ $o\dot{\hat{\iota}}c$) may I rise ($\dot{\alpha}\nu\alpha\sigma\tau\hat{\eta}\nu\alpha\iota$) as the result of your prayer, of which may I ever have a share, in order that I may be found in the lot of the Ephesian Christians ... (Eph. 11. 2)

Is Ignatius here speaking about a resurrection of his flesh at the last day? The physical resurrection (or any resurrection) would be very oddly conceived of as a rising, 'even in his bonds or fetters'.[41] Lightfoot thinks 'he can hardly mean that he desired literally to rise in his chains' but still refers this resurrection to the general resurrection of the body.[42] Schoedel is sensitive to the incongruity and sees that 'his talk of rising in his bonds is not intended to clarify the state of human beings in the other world but to express his hope of seeing his martyrdom through.'[43] The problem of Ignatius 'rising in his fetters' is alleviated by the recognition that he is rather thinking of his bonds, that is, his bondage, as the means through which he will be brought to death and thus rise unto God. $\dot{E}\nu$ $o\dot{\hat{\iota}}c$ should be translated as a dative of means, 'by which', rather than as a locative, 'in which'. This thought is paralleled in Rom. 4. 1–3, where this time it is the wild beasts 'through whom I can attain God'. He there indicates that, though he is now bound, if he suffers (death), 'I shall become a freedman of Jesus Christ and I shall rise ($\dot{\alpha}\nu\alpha\sigma\tau\dot{\eta}\sigma\omega\mu\alpha\iota$) in him free'.

Therefore, the 'rising again' through their prayers[44] in Ephesians 11. 2 is best taken not as his rising 'in the flesh ... even in his bonds or fetters' but as his incorporeal rising at death, his coming to, his attaining to God.[45] $\dot{A}\nu\acute{\iota}\sigma\tau\eta\mu\iota$ is thus, along with $\dot{\alpha}\nu\alpha\tau\acute{\epsilon}\lambda\lambda\omega$, shown to be part of the possible vocabulary for such an ascension.

---

[41] Grant, Ignatius, 43.   [42] Lightfoot AF, II. 2, 62.
[43] Schoedel, Ignatius, 72, n. 2.
[44] Ignatius elsewhere asks for prayers on his behalf, with the focus being his attaining God through endurance to the end (Phd. 5. 1; Sm. 11. 1; Tr. 12. 3; Magn. 14. 1; Eph. 12. 2).   [45] Schoedel, Ignatius, 72,n. 2.

(c) The Old Testament Righteous. From what we have seen of
Ignatius' doctrine of the intermediate state and in keeping with the
principle that the full enjoyment of Christ's benefits for the redeemed of the new era ought to be provided for those of the old as
well, we would expect to find the saints of former times in heaven.
While this is not stated explicitly, it should probably be inferred
from *Magnesians* 9. 2. The OT prophets, the only saints of former
times whose lot is mentioned by Ignatius, have been made the
subjects not only of a preaching tour[46] but of a resurrection performed by Christ in the underworld.

How shall we be able to live apart from him whom the prophets, being
his disciples in the Spirit, awaited as their teacher? And therefore when
he came for whom they righteously were waiting, he raised (ἤγειρεν) them
from the dead. (*Magn.* 9. 2; see also *Phd.* 5. 2)

The text itself does not make clear whether this resurrection is
of the soul alone or of the body as well. It may well be a variant
tradition concerning the events reported in Matthew 27: 52.[47] We
have already seen, however, that the words ἀνατέλλω and ἀνίστημι
can be used by Ignatius to depict the ascension of souls to God.
This is almost certainly then an early representation of Christ's
rescue of the souls of the OT saints from Hades and a transportation
into heaven.[48]

Ignatius too, like Clement but much more abundantly than he,
attests to the acceptance of the belief in the Christian's immediate
removal to the divine presence at death. Nothing stands in the way
of our classifying his eschatology as non-chiliast, and the typology
of eschatological beliefs provided by Irenaeus substantiates this
classification.[49]

3. Polycarp of Smyrna

We have in Polycarp's epistle to the Philippians no cause for
evaluating him as a chiliast.[50] He once reminds his readers that 'if
we walk as citizens worthy of him, we shall also reign with him'
(5. 2). But neither the duration of this joint reign nor the time when
it is entered into is specified.

[46] Camelot, 89.   [47] Daniélou, *TJC*, 237.
[48] Schoedel, *Ignatius*, 124. cf. Irenaeus, *Fragm.* 26 (cited above, in § I. 1).
[49] More will be said of Irenaeus and the eschatology of Ignatius in § IV. 3 below.
[50] Wood, 36, claims to find chiliastic teaching in Polycarp, without stating where.

At least one statement concerning the intermediate state, however, does reveal a definite conception of the whereabouts of the righteous dead: 'We are convinced that all these "did not run in vain", but in faith and righteousness, and that they are in their due place with the Lord (εἰς τὸν ὀφειλόμενον αὐτοῖς τόπον εἰσὶ παρὰ τῷ κυρίῳ), with whom also they suffered . . .'.[51] (9. 2).

Polycarp, as mentioned earlier, borrows Clement's expression (1Clem. 5. 7)[52] 'due place', but he fills it out by the specification 'with the Lord', thereby conspicuously portraying a heavenly afterlife. He brings the dominant 'Pauline' strain—fellowship with Christ—which was lacking in Clement's portrayal, back to the fore. It was this same Philippian Church addressed by Polycarp in which Paul had once confided that he wished 'to depart and be with Christ' (Phil. 1: 23). This desire may well have been echoing in Polycarp's mind as he addressed the Philippians: words from Philippians 2: 16 appear in the same sentence, and there is a possible allusion to Philippians 4: 9 in the sentence preceding. Paul is one of those mentioned by Polycarp, along with the rest of the apostles, Ignatius, Zosimus, and Rufus and others formerly of the Philippian congregation, as being now deservedly in Christ's presence (9. 1). The mention of Ignatius points to an agreement with another contemporary's view of afterlife. As we have seen, Ignatius, whose letters Polycarp had read and collected (13. 2), also believed that death ushered the Christian into the presence of God and Christ. These three influences on Polycarp's eschatological thought (Paul, Clement, Ignatius) are easily traceable; Polycarp does not depart from them.

To this should be connected Polycarp's request in chapter 12 that God grant the Philippians and himself 'a lot and portion among thy saints' (sortem et partem inter sanctos suos), reflecting a conception of the 'church above in glory'[53] which must be compared to Paul's 'his glorious inheritance (κληρονομίας) in the saints' (Eph. 1: 18) and 'a share of the inheritance of the saints in light' (μερίδα τοῦ κλήρου τῶν ἁγίων ἐν τῷ φωτί Col. 1: 12), Clement's 'place of the godly' (χῶρον εὐσεβῶν 1Clem. 50. 3) and Ignatius' 'in the lot (κλήρῳ)

---

[51] Translations of Polycarp are my own.

[52] Note as well the paraenetic concern and the appeal to lay eminent examples 'before your eyes', common to both passages. 'This ninth chapter is, so to speak, a commentary on I Clement 5f.', Altaner, HJb, 27. See Lightfoot, AF, I. 1, 149–52 for the evidence that Polycarp possessed Clement's epistle to the Corinthians.

[53] Schoedel, ApF, 35–6.

of the Ephesian Christians' (*Eph.* 11. 2). Entry into his inheritance is a future privilege, and one which cannot be restricted to martyrs or apostles, as it is available to all Polycarp's addressees in the Philippian church.

Nor does Polycarp compromise in any degree on the hope of a bodily resurrection at the last day: 'Whoever says there is neither resurrection nor judgement, he is Satan's firstborn' (7. 1).

It is clear that Polycarp, at whose feet Irenaeus once sat, whose letter to the church at Philippi Irenaeus knew and loved well (*AH* III. 3. 3), cannot be claimed as a source for his most famous student's view of the intermediate state as given in *AH* v. 31–2. On the contrary, his venerated instructor in the faith perpetuated the view which Irenaeus claims is linked to non-chiliasm and which resembles too closely, so he fears in retrospect, the views of the heretics.

4. Hermas[54]

(a) *General Eschatology.*   Daniélou has noted that millenarianism was unable to gain a lasting foothold in Alexandria or in Rome. Of the latter he says, 'The evidence of Hermas shows that there interest was concentrated on the building up of the Church, the completion of which is the condition for the coming of the heavenly kingdom, and the Messianic age seems therefore to be identified with the times of the Church . . .'.[55] Similarly, Pernveden concludes, 'The time of the Church is for Hermas the last remaining time.'[56] Although the *Shepherd* of Hermas, which is here assumed to date, at least in its final form, from around AD 140, is manifestly indebted to the heritage of contemporary Judaism,[57] this evaluation of its eschatological *ordo* appears to be correct. Hermas envisions a time of unprecedented and final tribulation (*Vis.* 2. 2. 7; 4. 2. 5 see also *Sim.* 7. 5)[58]

---

[54] We shall be using Joly's Greek text. Translations are those of Snyder, ApF.

[55] Daniélou, *TJC*, 404.   [56] Pernveden, 271.

[57] The overall Jewish cast of the *Shepherd* has been upheld by several studies, e.g. Audet, 41–82; Daniélou, *TJC*, 36–39; Barnard, *StudPatr*, 4–10; Hinson, 697–701. The Jewish sources of, in particular, its eschatology have been contended for by O'Hagan, 305–11.

[58] Bauckham, *JTS*, 33, 'The great tribulation is therefore the means of transition from this age to the next'; 'Hermas recognizes that the coming of the new age requires not only the purification of the righteous but also the destruction of the wicked: his great tribulation performs both functions and again it follows that its meaning cannot be confined to persecution.'

closely bound up with the last judgement (shown to be the last judgement because it has to do even with Christians and arrives only when the tower/Church is completed),[59] a time set in the future but near enough that an appeal to it implies a dire and urgent warning to the lapsed for their speedy repentance (see especially Vis. 4) and for the rest a serious call for their endurance and perseverance in good works:

5. Consider the judgement which is to come. So let those who have more seek out those who are hungry until such a time as the tower is finished. For after the tower is finished you will wish to do good, but you will not have the opportunity. 6. So you who rejoice in your riches see to it that the needy never groan and their groaning go up to the Lord, and you be shut outside the door of the tower with your goods. (Vis. 3. 9. 5–6, see Sim. 10. 4. 4; Vis. 3. 5. 5)

As to the doctrine of the bodily resurrection in Hermas, Pernveden says that it has been 'replaced by the belief that upon the death of the body, the saved soul directly enters the kingdom of God'.[60] But 'replaced' is not the right word. It should be remembered first of all that Hermas' principal image for the Church is the tower. This image, for all its complaisance, is understandably not well equipped to accommodate the added jolt of the notion of resurrection. We are never told what happens to the tower when the Lord of the tower returns because we always leave the tower allegory before the Lord's advent. Under another image the righteous are like trees waiting to blossom in the summer/world to come (Sim. 4). This presentation is very conducive to the hope of a transformation of some kind.

But, more importantly, a future existence for the body is demanded by Sim. 5. 6. 7, 'For all flesh in which the holy Spirit has dwelled, when found undefiled and spotless, will receive a reward'. In the context, the attention has moved from the reward due to the flesh of Christ for its faithful service to a reward for Christians in the flesh, and this must be an eschatological reward. The Christian must keep his flesh undefiled, 'so that the Spirit that dwells in it may bear witness to it and your flesh may be justified ($\delta\iota\kappa\alpha\iota\omega\theta\hat{\eta}$). Beware, lest it enter your heart that this flesh of yours is mortal

[59] The coming judgement as it affects the ungodly and the heathen is related at least once under the image of a fire which consumes a dry forest (Sim. 4. 4 and perhaps Vis. 3. 2. 8; 3. 7. 2). This is probably signified also in the 'colour of fire and blood' on the monster's head in Vis. 4. 3. 3.   [60] Pernveden, 273.

(φθαρτὴν) and you misuse it in some defilement ...' (5. 7. 1). 'By
δικαιοῦcθαι the judgement naturally is meant',[61] and this requires
that the somatic nature, along with the spiritual, has more than a
temporary significance. 'For both [i.e. flesh and spirit] belong
together and neither can be defiled without the other' (5. 7. 4). The
near silence of Hermas on the resurrection is thus due to the
accepted and uncontroverted place which the doctrine had with
Hermas and his readers.

Hermas thus allows us at the outset to say what we could not
say at the outset of our studies of Clement, Ignatius and Polycarp,
namely, that his general eschatology shows itself to be decidedly
non-chiliastic.[62] The age of the Church is the last age, the coming
tribulation ushers in the return of Christ and the great judgement.
If the correlations made by Irenaeus are valid for the eschatology
of Hermas we would therefore expect to find in the *Shepherd* a
'heavenly' and not a 'underworldly' view of the intermediate state.
This is exactly what we do find.

(b) *Individual Eschatology.* The Two Cities: *Similitudes* 1. In the
first similitude Hermas introduces the dilemma for Christians living
in this world, under an allegory of the two cities. The question of
the identity of the two cities has an important bearing upon our
study. Snyder, following Zahn, contends that, 'The two cities are
not earthly and heavenly ... , but church and state.'[63] But for several
reasons this explanation is wholly unsatisfactory and recourse
must be had again to the view Snyder rejects, that is, that the cities
are the earthly and the heavenly.

Those who are called citizens of another city are the 'servants of
God' (vv. 1, 10). Yet these servants of God are only 'about to dwell'
in their city (ἐν ᾗ μέλλετε κατοικεῖν), they are not now there. They
live rather in a 'foreign place'; 'their' rightful city is far from 'this'
city (v. 1). 'Their' city is in v. 1 contrasted with 'here' (ὧδε), where
they have opportunity to purchase fields, expensive furnishings,
buildings and worthless rooms. They are thus estranged from 'their'
city as regards both space and time. Nor are the Christians exhorted
to vacate 'this' city, which doubtless they would have been if
vacating it meant becoming attached to the church on earth. They

---

[61] Dibelius, 576.
[62] Despite Semisch–Bratke, 808; Wood, 36; Maier, 87.
[63] Snyder, ApF, 95.

are but enjoined to live in 'this' city as sojourners and not to lay up too many treasures here (v. 5). Rich Christians are to 'purchase souls that are in distress, as each is able' (v. 8). For, 'It is much better for you to purchase such fields and possessions and houses as you will find in your city when you go home to it' (v. 9). The Christian readers are told to live by the laws of their own city now while absent from it so that they be not excluded from it when they depart hence. The time will come when the ruler of 'this' city will cast them out as rebels against his law. It is only then that the stranger departs to his own city with rejoicing (v. 6). This cannot mean that one day the emperor will expel them from Rome or the State and they shall then have to join the Church! Surely these Christians are members at once of Church and State. The despot of 'this' city is instead the 'ruler of this age'[64] who seeks to draw Christians away to following his laws—according to *Mand.* 12. 4. 6 it is the devil, not the emperor, who has bitter and licentious commandments which are to be forsaken. This is substantiated as well by the close connection in the passage before us between living by the laws of 'this' city and accumulating worldly possessions to the neglect of spiritual ones, an unnatural connection if the laws of 'this' city are merely the laws of Rome.[65]

In this first similitude Christians are about to dwell in their own city, but their flight ($\dot{\epsilon}\xi\epsilon\lambda\theta\epsilon\hat{\iota}\nu$) there occurs not necessarily when the Lord comes but when the despot of the earthly city expels them after they have stood against his law (1. 6). It should be concluded then that the first similitude assumes and teaches an immediate removal to the heavenly city for the Christian who has kept its laws while here on earth.

The Martyrs/Sufferers. Of the twenty occurrences of the word $\pi\acute{a}\sigma\chi\epsilon\iota\nu$ (to suffer) in Hermas it approaches a technical meaning very close to 'to die' in fourteen.[66] In each of the fourteen the suffering is because of or for the sake of God, Christ or the law and hence

---

[64] So, rightly, Dibelius, 551.

[65] Early Christian witnesses to this extremely popular theme of the two cities, and the related theme of Christians as sojourners in this world, are too numerous to detail here. See, besides Gal. 4: 25–6; Phil. 3: 20; Heb. 11: 13–16; 12: 22–4; 13: 14, the literature cited by Lightfoot, *AF*, I. 2, 5–6. The concept, under several variations, was known in Judaism as well, see *2Bar.* 4. 3–6 (for Philo, besides the texts cited by Lightfoot, *Cher.* 120–121; *QSGen.* III. 10–11). By contrast, in *4Ez.* 10. 7 it is the earthly Jerusalem which is 'the mother of us all'!   [66] Cf. *PGL*, 1049.

martyrdom is in view. All of these occurrences are found in the third vision or the eighth or ninth similitude, which are openly concerned with obtaining a dwelling place in the tower.[67] It is these who have suffered who infallibly have a place in the tower, their sufferings possessing some kind of quasi-atoning or at least ensuring power (Sim. 9. 28. 5–6). Those who are currently suffering are not said to be inhabiting the tower yet, only to have a place reserved there (Sim. 9. 28. 5). A number of the characteristics of those who have suffered demonstrate that their afterlife glory is to be classed under heavenly bliss and not subterranean contentment.

In Visions 3 Hermas is shown by the old woman (another symbol for the Church) his first vision of the erection of the tower. But before he is granted the vision Hermas is bidden to sit down beside the old woman. He is distraught because he is not allowed to sit on her right but only on her left. He is told that the right hand portion belongs to those who have already pleased God and have suffered on behalf of the name (3. 1. 9).[68] Only those who have borne all the afflictions which these have borne may occupy 'the right hand portion of the sanctuary' (τὰ δεξιὰ μέρη τοῦ ἁγιάσματος 3. 2. 1).[69] For the rest there is the left hand portion. But for both groups there are the same gifts, the same promises: only to those sitting on the right also belongs a certain glory (ἔχουσιν δόξαν τινά 3. 2. 1).

Dibelius correctly states that, 'By the sanctuary, the right side of which belongs to the martyrs, is not meant some Christian meeting house but the heavenly sanctuary; the heavenly figure assigns to the wonderfully appearing bench, not to earthly places.'[70] This sanctuary is the one in heaven, where a 'certain glory' may distinguish those on the right from those on the left. Here we refer to the parallels cited above concerning Clement's 'holy place' (1Clem. 5. 7).[71] As to the division between right and left, perhaps it is related to the prom-

---

[67] Vis. 3. 1. 9; 3. 2. 1; 3. 5. 2; Sim. 8. 3. 6; 8. 3. 7; 9. 28. 2 (bis); 9. 28. 3 (bis); 9. 28. 4 (bis); 9. 28. 5; 9. 28. 6 (bis).

[68] The idea that martyrs have 'pleased' God (see also Sim. 8. 3.5) is paralleled in a passage from the ApocPet. (James, ANT, 512, notes the parallel). Cf. Polycarp, Phil. 5. 2.

[69] Clement of Alexandria apparently has this text in mind when he writes that the Gnostic 'martyr' turns his back on country, sustenance and the laws of civil polity ἕνεκεν τοῦ φίλον γενέσθαι τῷ θεῷ καὶ τυχεῖν τῶν δεξιῶν μερῶν τοῦ ἁγιάσματος, καθάπερ καὶ οἱ ἀπόστολοι πεποιήκασιν (Strom. IV. iv. 5. 4 see also IV. vi. 30. 1).   [70] Dibelius, 457.

[71] Ἁγιάσμα represents the earthly temple or holy place in 1Macc. 1. 21, 37, 39; Sirach 36. 13; 49. 6; 50. 11, and TestDan 5. 9. Philo, Plant. 50, uses it of the created world as a sanctuary but as 'a copy of the original (ἀρχετύπου)'.

ise of the risen Christ in Revelation 3: 21, 'He who conquers (ὁ νικῶν), I will grant him to sit with me on my throne, as I myself conquered and sat down with my Father on his throne', which throne, of course, is at the right hand of God. In the case of Hermas' sufferers, who have already pleased God and departed this life, the 'right hand portion of the sanctuary' must signify reception into the heavenly holy place as the immediate consequence of death.

In *Similitudes* 8, we are told of a vision in which all who are called by the name of the Lord are given willow branches by a glorious angel. Many return their branches, emblematic of the law and the Son of God, not only green as they had received them, not only budding, but bearing fruit. These fruitful servants are given crowns made from palm trees, dressed in white robes and sent into the tower under the auspices of the archangel Michael.[72] We are told in 8. 3.6 that these servants have suffered for the law. They are distinguished from those whose branches budded but bore no fruit by the fact that though these latter had been persecuted on behalf of the law they had not suffered.[73] In *Similitudes* 9. 28, a different parable, a finer distinction sets off those who gave up their lives (9. 28. 2) cheerfully with their whole heart—whose fruit was more splendid—from those who wavered and cravenly harboured thoughts of denying before they suffered and thereby covered their sins—whose fruit was less splendid. As many as have suffered for the name are glorified (ἔνδοξοί) before the Lord (9. 28. 3). But those who suffered cheerfully have a greater glory before the Lord (μᾶλλον ἐνδοξότεροί εἰσι παρά τῷ κυρίῳ 9. 28. 4). As these sufferers are those who have laid down their lives, the phrase 'before the Lord' should be given a local sense.[74]

The Stones from the Deep. In *Similitudes* 9 four courses of stones are brought up from the deep and fitted unhewn into the foundation of the tower. The first three are identified as the first generations

[72] Those whose branches budded but bore no fruit, as well as those whose branches were simply green as they had been given them, were granted seals and the white robes. All three groups were sent into the tower.

[73] This is why Daniélou's idea, *TJC*, 120–1, that this similitude is concerned with a public rite of penance is untenable; those who have 'suffered for the sake of the law' and 'conquered the devil' are those who have died, not those who have fulfilled a prescribed order of penance.

[74] Clement of Rome speaks of presbyters who, while not martyrs, are deceased and who had 'a fruitful (ἔγκαρπον) and perfect departure', who have gone on before us into an established place (*IClem.* 44. 1, cf. 56. 1).

of the righteous (i.e. before Christ's coming), the last are the apostles and teachers of the preaching of the Son of God (9. 15. 4). All these in common had 'fallen asleep' (9. 16. 3–5). Though they had already the seal themselves, the deceased apostolic men preached in the 'Todesreich' and applied the seal of baptism to those who had previously fallen asleep, that is, they performed in some way the baptism which marks one with the name of the Son of God, without bearing which one cannot enter the kingdom of God.

The details of *Similitudes* 9. 15–16 seem to form a modification of Hermas' original scenario of *Visions* 3. In *Visions* 3, those recovered from the deep are all said to have suffered for the sake of the name of the Lord, which is the equivalent of saying they were all martyrs (3. 5. 2). These stones would thus likely evoke to the first readers intense persecutions of earlier Christian times. The permutation in *Similitudes* 9. 15–16 probably represents an attempt to patch up a tired motif and stuff inside a theological concern (what has happened to the OT righteous?) neglected in the earlier presentation.

The second state of the idea is patently a version of the despoiling of Hades, with a few twists peculiar to our author. We know that the notion was current in Rome about this time also from the fact that Marcion found it in a pre-existing form and contorted it to suit his contempt for the OT heroes and their God (Irenaeus, *AH* i. 27. 3; Tertullian, *Marc.* iv. 24).[75] As it stands in *Similitudes* 9. 15–16, this mission to the underworld may legitimately be termed a 'despoliation', a 'plundering' or 'harrowing'. Its purpose embraced more than a mere announcement of salvation, it effected the release, the raising of the souls who received the name of the Son of God to a station of glory in the presence of God (παρὰ τῷ θεῷ).

Passage with the Angels. In *Visions* 2. 2. 6 it is promised to those who remain workers of righteousness and ward off double-mindedness that they shall have a 'passage with the angels' (ἡ πάροδος μετὰ τῶν ἀγγέλων). In *Similitudes* 9. 25. 2 we are told that the apostles and teachers who preached and taught to the whole

---

[75] A baptism in Hades performed by Christ for the righteous of the old dispensation is known from *EpApost.* 27; *ApocPet.* 14 and probably *OdesSol.* 42. 20, but for Hermas it is not Christ himself but his emissaries who descend and perform the preaching/baptism which leads aloft (perhaps he had read John 4: 2!). See Hippolytus, *Antichr.* 45, for the view that John the Baptist, as part of his mission as forerunner, first preached to those in Hades to announce the coming descent and ransom by Jesus.

world the word of the Lord and always walked in righteousness and truth have this 'passage with the angels'.[76] These historical figures are from a generation freshly bygone, so their passage with the angels is a present reality, rather than a future promise. Exactly what it is to have a passage with the angels is not self-evident. But earlier in the ninth similitude we are told that the Son of God is the gate of the tower, through whom even angels must pass to come before God (*Sim.* 9. 12. 8). Later it is pledged to the simple, harmless, and virtuous believers that they are enrolled in the number of the angels, and that the whole of their seed shall dwell with the Son of God (*Sim.* 9. 23. 5). If these statements may all be amalgamated it would appear that having a passage with the angels denotes having the entrance of glory which the angels have, that is, having access with them through the Son of God who is the gateway to the tower[77] in the heavenly world after death.[78]

That we have found in Hermas, (*a*) a non-chiliastic view of future history, (*b*) a notion that the dead in Christ go immediately to the presence of their Lord in heaven (nothing of Tertullian's 'martyr–élitist' theory), (*c*) the doctrines of the future resurrection of the body and the great judgement taken for granted, speaks powerfully for the validity of the eschatological patterning suggested to us by Irenaeus.

5. 2 Clement

For this Corinthian[79] preacher, the kingdom of God arrives when the 'day of God' appears (12. 1–6). But the coming of 'the Lord',

[76] Exemplary bishops, if they remain unto their end serving the Lord, are glorified in the presence of God (παρὰ τῷ θεῷ) and already have their place (τόπος) with the angels (*Sim.* 9. 27. 3). Cf. *IClem.* 44. 5 and our discussion on it above.

[77] James the Just, according to Hegesippus (Eusebius, *HE* II. 23. 8, 12), was interrogated as to the meaning of 'the door of Jesus,' to which he replied that Jesus was the Saviour. Jesus is 'the Door' in John 10: 9 and the door of the Father in Ignatius, *Phil.* 9. 1.

[78] Further light perhaps emanates from the link several have drawn between Hermas and the Essenes. A prominent side of the eschatological (as the present writer sees it) hope of the Qumranites is represented by the phrase 'sharing the lot of the angels' (see the texts cited in § I. 3 above). At Qumran the notion belongs properly to the hope of the renewed creation, 1QH IX. 10–14 (cf. XII. 11–12). If there is some kind overlap between these ideas and the thought world of Hermas it is noteworthy that what at Qumran resides in the new creation beyond the divide of the last judgement becomes for the Christian Hermas a way of expressing the glorified post-mortem existence of those who bear the name of the Son of God.

[79] Donfried, 1–15, has demonstrated both the high probability that *IIClem.* was written (and first preached) in Corinth and the compatibility of the document with

when unbelievers shall see the rulership of the world in the hands of Jesus, means also 'that day of judgement', the ultimate distribution of rewards and punishments to individuals (17. 4–7, cf. 16. 3). This does not appear to be compatible with chiliasm. Neither does the hope for the pious sufferer in 19. 4 take any account at all of an earthly millennium: 'a time of blessedness awaits him; he shall live again with the fathers above (ἄνω), and rejoice to an eternity wherein is no sorrow'.[80]

Like Hermas, and indeed like 1 Peter and the Epistle to the Hebrews, 2 Clement too speaks of our life here as a sojourn.[81]

Wherefore, brethren, forsaking our sojourning in this world, let us do the will of him who called us and let us not fear to go forth (ἐξελθεῖν) from this world ... And know ye, brethren, that the sojourning which is in this world of this flesh is a little thing and of short duration, but the promise of Christ is great and wonderful and (is) rest (ἀνάπαυσις) of the coming kingdom (μελλούσης βασιλείας) and of life eternal. What then shall we do to attain (ἐπιτυχεῖν) these things ...? (5. 1, 5–6, see also 19. 3–4; 20. 2, 5)

Since the author is trying to embolden his hearers to face the prospect of leaving this world,[82] the 'rest of the coming kingdom' would appear to be a prize that awaits the godly immediately at death (rest is also an eschatological reward in 6. 7). In chapter 8 he concerns himself again with death, exhorting his hearers to repent before they die, for there is no more chance for repentance where they are going. This too shows that he has a conception of the 'place' to which the dead go.

Thus the writer, while giving every appearance of excluding from his future expectation the hope of an earthly reign of peace and blessedness at the same time seems to conceive of an entry into the rest of the kingdom and eternal life at the time of departure from this world in death. Support for this interpretation should also be gained from our comments above on Hermas, Sim. 1. 6. It is evident, moreover, that the author of 2Clem. was not slack in upholding a

the assumption of a relatively early date. Whether it is, as he maintains, a hortatory address composed by one of the presbyters who had lately been deposed and then reinstated (partly due to the effect of the recently arrived IClem.), is more doubtful. See Roberts, 461.

[80] I cannot imagine, therefore, where Semisch–Bratke, 808, saw chiliasm in this letter.   [81] My translation.

[82] Donfried, 118–19, is correct, against Knopf, that this is not an exhortation to martyrdom. The writer is exhorting them to think little of the present, fleeting, life in view of the greatness of the promise of Christ.

traditional doctrine of the future resurrection of the body (see 9. 1; 14. 5; 19. 3).

We mention finally Harnack's interpretation of 20. 4, 'And because of this, divine judgement has injured a spirit which is not righteous and has laden it with chains.' Most translations seem to take the 'spirit' to be a human spirit, and the aorists 'injured' (ἔβλαψεν) and 'laden' (ἐβάρυνεν) as gnomic, thus denoting an ongoing manifestation of God's judgement in human life. Harnack, however, interpreted the unrighteous spirit as Satan. This view has in its favour the fact that the writer does not elsewhere use 'spirit' (πνεῦμα) for the human spirit or as a synecdoche for a human 'person', as he does with the word 'soul' (ψυχή). The aorists 'injured' and 'laden' then, would refer to an event of past history, the binding of Satan (cf. Rev. 20: 1–3), 'he had the opinion, therefore, that the devil already in this age was laden with chains'.[83] Thus the binding of Satan 'with a great chain', which begins the thousand-year kingdom of Christ in Revelation 20, has already happened. I must confess that neither interpretation seems obviously correct within the immediate context of the letter. Yet if we give due weight to the author's non-chiliastic eschatology, in which the coming kingdom may apparently be joined when one begins to rest from life's labours in death (cf. Rev. 14: 13), an allusion to the past binding of Satan cannot at least be seen as incongruous.

2. THE APOLOGISTS

Only a few of the Apologists disclose notions of the intermediate state which may be classified in accord with our interests. We have already studied Justin and his somewhat equivocal eschatology. Here we shall treat the *Epistle to Diognetus* and Melito of Sardis.

1. Epistle to Diognetus

In a manner very similar to Hermas and the author of *2Clem.*, the writer of the *Epistle to Diognetus*[84] views Christians as dwelling in

---

[83] 'Censuit igitur diabolum iam hoc tempore catenis onustum esse', Harnack, Gebhardt–Harnack, 143.

[84] The time which separates these authors, moreover, may not have been great. The arguments of Barnard, *Studies*, 171–3, and Nielsen, *ATR* (cf. also Lienhard, 289) for a date for the *EpDiogn.* before the outbreak of Marcionism appear sound, though Grant, *Apologists*, 178, places it after 176.

their own countries only as sojourners (πάροικοι): they endure all hardships as strangers (ξένοι) (5. 5); their existence is on earth, but their citizenship is in heaven (5. 9). The analogy drawn in 6. 8 between the Christians' relation to the world and the soul's relation to the body provides another angle on the same theme. 'The soul dwells immortal in a mortal tent. And Christians sojourn among corruptible things, awaiting incorruption in the heavens.'

It is worth noting that this incorruption in the heavens has some correspondence to the kingdom of God and the life which also dwell in the heavens. 'To attain life' (τυχεῖν ζωῆς) and 'to enter into the kingdom of God' (εἰσελθεῖν εἰς τὴν βασιλείαν τοῦ θεοῦ) are virtual equivalents (9. 1, 6).[85] But the author conceives of the kingdom of heaven as residing in heaven (τὴν ἐν οὐρανῷ βασιλείαν 10. 2) and this is the kingdom which Jesus has gained and which has been promised to those who have loved him. The 'true life' is also set by our author in heaven (τὸ ἀληθῶς ἐν οὐρανῷ ζῆν); it is this life in heaven that one begins to comprehend when learning to despise the apparent death here below (10. 7). Death for the Christian is no death at all because true life is in heaven, the kingdom of God in heaven is promised to him. It is not difficult to surmise that, to this author, death for those who have loved God means elevation of the soul to obtain life and enter that incorruptible kingdom in heaven. In any case, while his doctrine of the intermediate state can only be inferred, there is no warrant for finding a chiliastic expectation in this epistle, the kingdom of God is only heavenly (or spiritual). When Christ comes again, he shall come as judge (7. 6). It should be said that there is no certain reference in this work to the doctrine of the bodily resurrection, though there is on the other hand no evidence that it was doubted.

2. Melito of Sardis

Melito of Sardis is commonly assumed to have been a proponent of chiliastic eschatology. Several French writers who so regard him seem only to repeat the assessment of Gry,[86] who in turn had followed Harnack.[87] But this assessment rests upon two rather

[85] Meecham, 128, who points to a similar correspondence in Mark 9: 43–7; 10: 17, 24–5. We should also refer to 2Clem. 5. 5, cited above.

[86] Lesètre, 1095; Leclercq, 1186; Daniélou, TJC, 389.

[87] Gry, Millénarisme, 81–2, appealing to Harnack, Geschichte, i. 248.

unsteady pillars. First is the fact that Melito wrote, according to Eusebius, a treatise 'On the Devil and the Revelation of John'. Deducing that he was a chiliast from the mere title of this perished monograph can only be done on the presumption that anyone writing at this time (c.160–80) on this topic must have been a chiliast.[88] But, as we are beginning to see, non-chiliastic eschatology seems to have been more pervasive within Christian theology at this time than Harnack had supposed. Second is a remark of Gennadius of Marseilles at the end of the fifth century in his *Liber ecclesiasticorum dogmatum*[89] to the effect that certain people called 'Melitans' expected something earthly or transitory in the fulfilment of the divine promises. Melito himself is not named by Gennadius as holding to chiliast views, even though Papias, Irenaeus, Tertullian, and Lactantius are. It is more probable, in my opinion, that the millennialists mentioned by Gennadius were adherents not of Melito of Sardis but of Meletius of Lycopolis (this does not necessarily mean that Meletius himself had been a chiliast). Elmenhorst's edition (reprinted in Migne, PL 58), in which the word is *Melitani*, is often cited. But this edition is now listed as the recension of an unknown author of the sixth century.[90] C. H. Turner's text, which is regarded as a more primitive recension, has as a matter of fact the name *Meletiani*: *In diuinis repromissionibus nihil terrenum uel transitorium exspectemus, sicut Meletiani sperant*.[91] *Meletiani* can scarcely be regarded as coming from the name Μελίτων, it seems indeed to refer to followers of some Meletius.[92] In any event, it must be wondered at that in the complete absence of any previous (or later!) notice of such a sect, a group which adopted or was given the name of Melito of Sardis would be known to Gennadius writing at the end of the fifth century, more than three centuries after their namesake's death.[93] On the other hand, we do know that followers

---

[88] It is true that Melito writes in Asia Minor, even from a city addressed in one of the seven letters in John's Apocalypse. But the same can be said of Polycarp, whose eschatology is not of the chiliastic variety. It is quite likely, in my view, that the theme of such a work might have been the binding of the devil, spoken of in Rev. 20: 1–3. As we shall see, this theme is prominent in Melito's extant works and may have influenced the early Irenaeus (see next section).

[89] Frend, *Rise*, 240, Melito 'was regarded in later tradition as a millenarian ...'; cf. Hall, xii. Both cite Gennadius in Elmenhorst's edition in PL 58.

[90] See SE 3 (1961), 211.   [91] Turner, 'Gennadius'.

[92] Another unexplored possibility is that the original read *Milliarii* and was miscopied.

[93] But even if they had derived their name from our Melito, who is to say whether the chiliastic views they held were perceived even by them as stemming from Melito?

of Meletius of Lycopolis flourished well into the fifth century and survived through most of the eighth. Theodoret, referring to them, notes that 'there are in some districts bodies of monks who refuse to follow sound doctrine, and observe certain vain points of discipline, agreeing with the infatuated views of the Jews and the Samaritans' (*EcclHist*. I. 9).[94] We are not told what these infatuated views of Jews and Samaritans are, though chiliasm would easily have been so described by one who had not accepted it. Two later references to Meletians locate Meletian priests and monks (by the thousands, in one report) at Arsinoë,[95] interestingly the stronghold of Egyptian chiliasm already by the time of Dionysius of Alexandria.[96]

The opinion that Melito was a millenarian has occasioned puzzlement, even amongst those who hold this opinion, when laid alongside his view of the Roman state's high calling, to nourish and to grow up side by side with the Christian faith (Eusebius, *HE* IV. 26). Gry calls Melito's conciliation of these two views impossible, illogical, and dangerous; Leclercq quips, 'Perhaps logic worried Melito very little'; Lesètre draws the fabulous conclusion, 'Melito of Sardis considers that the Roman empire, converted to Christianity, will one day establish the millennial kingdom'![97]

It appears that a reliable verdict on Melito's relation to chiliasm is still in suspense. What we can derive from his writings concerning his understanding of the intermediate state, however, seems to place him in the non-chiliast camp.

For Melito, while the bodies of all the pre-Christian dead wasted away in the earth from which they were taken, their souls were shut up (κατεκλείετο) in Hades (*PP* 55–6). But in *PP* 102, lines 760–4, he advances the theory of a rescue from Hades. Christ is pictured as saying,

They might have been called Melitans for some other reason, and their chiliasm may have been a trait not attributed to Melito. Further, if a group of chiliasts in the fifth century had wished to attach a reputable name to their party, why choose that of Melito when those of Irenaeus, Tertullian, Lactantius, or Victorinus might have served the purpose better?

[94] See J. M. Fuller, 891.   [95] See Amann, 535.

[96] Dionysius states that the doctrine 'had long been prevalent' in the nome of Arsinoë, 'so that schisms and defections of whole churches had taken place' (Eusebius, *HE* VII. 24. 6). Though Dionysius at length was able to persuade Coracion and others to abandon chiliasm, it is far from unlikely that the teaching persisted in the region for a long time.

[97] Gry, *Millénarisme*, 81–2 (n. 1); Leclercq, 1186; Lesètre, 1095.

> I am he who destroyed death
> and triumphed over the enemy
> and tread down Hades
> and bound the strong one
> and bore man away to the heights of heaven.[98]

'"Man" is first and foremost the humanity of the Saviour, but in it is included all redeemed humanity.'[99] Here the binding of the strong one (Satan), which is taken from Matthew 12: 29, is applied to Christ's descent to Hades and results in the freeing, the carrying off of man to the heights of heaven.[100]

New Fragment III. 5 (lines 24–36) also expands on the descent to Hades:

> by the cross death is destroyed,
> and by the cross salvation shines;
> by the cross the gates of hell are burst,
> and by the cross the gates of paradise are opened.
> The cross has become the way of saints and martyrs;
> the cross has become the chain of the apostles
> and the shield of faith of prophets. (24–30)

> The cross is the guide of the faithful robber;
> the cross is the destroyer of hell. (35–6)[101]

In other ways of developing the theme, death might be construed as being 'destroyed' by Christ with nobody being dislodged from Hades. But the mention of the gates of paradise being opened, the cross becoming the way of saints and martyrs, the chain of the apostles and the guide of the faithful robber of Luke 23: 43 allows no room for doubt. Melito is speaking of a transferral from Hades to paradise.[102]

---

[98] ἐγὼ ὁ καταλύσας τὸν θάνατον | καὶ θριαμβεύσας τὸν ἐχθρὸν | καὶ καταπατήσας τὸν ᾅδην | καὶ δήσας τὸν ἰσχυρὸν | καὶ ἀφαρπάσας τὸν ἄνθρωπον εἰς τὰ ὑψηλὰ τῶν οὐρανῶν

[99] Perler, SC, 203.

[100] Cf. Fr. 8b 4, lines 42–3; Fr. 13, lines 22–5 (Christ trod down death, bound the strong one and released man), see Hall, xxxiv–xxxvii, xxxix on the authenticity of the latter fragment. Melito's Asian contemporary, Claudius Apolinarius of Hierapolis, also speaks of Christ's binding of the strong man in connection with the passion (Eusebius, *ChronPasc.* praef.). It is probable that this writer also believed in a ravishing of Hades.

[101] The New Fragments are from a Georgian manuscript. English translations here are those Hall has made from Van Esbroek's Latin retranslation of the Georgian.

[102] Cf. NF II. 15 (lines 145–6) 'He perceived the taste of death and pitied those who were below in the condemnation of death. He was buried and he raised the dead . . .'; 16 (line 162) '. . . and restored again Adam and a royal treasure'; 17 (line 165) 'One was buried and many arose'. NF II. 12 (lines 107–19) seems to be a

Melito's conception of a despoiling of Hades, a removal of the
saints to heaven to be with Christ, fits with the non-chiliastic but
is at odds with the chiliastic pattern of eschatology.

3. CHRISTIAN PSEUDEPIGRAPHA

Several works from this extremely broad class of writings from the
second and early third centuries will be dealt with briefly in this
section. Each reveals some idea of a heavenly intermediate state
and none shows any sign of being chiliastic in its view of future
history.

1. Ascension of Isaiah 6–11

Ascension of Isaiah 3. 12–4. 22 is often thought to preserve an early
form of chiliasm. Chapters 6–11, which contain no indications of
chiliasm, abundantly testify to a well-developed doctrine of a heavenly intermediate state for the righteous. This does not, however,
endanger the thesis of Irenaeus concerning the relationship between
the two doctrines, for the majority of scholars of *AscIsa*.[103] have
ascribed these sections, at least in their original forms, to different
authors.[104]

reflection on Matthew's crucifixion story, relating that dead men rose at that time
but specifying that it was the souls of these men which were 'released'. It is
strikingly similar in this respect to what Irenaeus says in Fr. 26 (cited in § I.1.2
above; cf. *AH* III. 23. 1, 6) and thereby confirms both the traditional character of this
teaching and the believability of Irenaeus' early advocacy of it.

[103] R. Lawrence, F. C. Burkitt, and V. Burch were the exceptions when Knibb,
OTP, 148, wrote in 1979. Hall, 'Ascension', 290, also identifies Mauro Pesce, whose
recent article, 'Presupposti per l'utilizzazione storica dell' *Ascension di Isaia*', in
*Isaia, il deletto e la chiesa: Visione ed esegesi profetica cristiano-primitiva nell'
Ascensione di Isaia*, ed. M. Pesce, Testi e recerche di Scienze religiose 20 (Brescia,
1983), 13–48, I have not been able to consult.

[104] Within the *AscIsa.*, which evinces on the surface a bipartite structure (chs.
1–5 and 6–11), there are, according to Knibb (*OTP*, 143, 147–150), three distinct
compositions. Into a Jewish substratum, 1. 1–5. 16, has been inserted a Christian
addition, 3. 13–4. 22. Chapters 6–11 comprise another Christian composition. This
is essentially the same division as was reached by Charles, *Ascension*, xxxvi–xliii;
Tisserant, 59; Flemming and Duensing in *NTA* ii. 643 (the last three also see 11. 2–22
as extraneous to the surrounding material). On the history of the literary problems
up to 1909 see Tisserant, 42–61. Knibb, *OTP*, 147, concludes that chs. 6–11 'not
only circulated independently of chapters 1–5, but also had a quite independent
origin'. There is general agreement that 3. 13–4. 22 comes from near the end of the
first century (Knibb, *OTP*, 149; Charles, *Ascension*, xliv; Tisserant, 60). Knibb

A greater difficulty is that the allegedly chiliastic section, 3. 12–
4. 22, itself seems to assume a heavenly version of the intermediate
state, for here departed saints are represented as descending with
Christ from heaven at the parousia. This too, however, may be
inconsequential. On one plausible hypothesis, it was the final Christian redactor who has edited and reworked the pre-existing material
in chapters 3–4,[105] which he probably did not read as chiliastic.[106]
He then could have been responsible for the element of the dead
saints coming from heaven with Christ at his return, clothed in
their celestial garments.

Chapters 6–11 of *AscIsa.*, taken on their own, are remarkable for
their clear and frequent evidences of a developed doctrine of a
heavenly afterlife (7. 23; 8. 14; 9. 2; 11. 35, etc.). A few of its features
command our special notice. First, we learn that the OT faithful
are in the highest heaven at a time preceding Christ's incarnation,
'And there I saw all the righteous from the time of Adam onwards'
(9. 7, cf. 9. 8ff., 28; 11. 40).[107] Interestingly, the LXX of Isaiah 57: 15,
ὕψιστος ἐν ἁγίοις ἀναπαυόμενος ('the Most High resting among the
holy ones') seems to function as a Scriptural proof for this convic-

believes chs. 6–11 were composed in the second century (*OTP*, 150), Tisserant, 60,
placed them between 100–50. Charles, *Ascension*, xlv, dated them from the end of
the 1st cent. based on what he regarded as dependence on 11. 16 on the part of
Ignatius, *Eph.* 19. But Knibb is correct that dependence is not obvious. Most recently,
Hall, 'Ascension', has argued that the final redaction was complete by the early 2nd
cent.

[105] 'The author composed much of the historical review in reliance on early
Christian tradition, but does quote at least one source (4. 1–18) which she or he
interpolates freely', Hall, 'Ascension', 291; cf. 292.
[106] The alleged chiliasm of this section of *AscIsa.* 4. 14–18 is not exactly unmistakable. In any case, Daniélou's claim that this section expresses a 'standard form' of
early Christian chiliasm has fully taken leave of the evidence. The attempt at fitting
the teaching of this section, and the contents of 1 Thess. 4, 2 Thess. 1, 1 Cor. 15
and Rev. 20 into a common chiliastic *ordo* (*TJC*, 378–9) can be admired only for the
scale of its imagination. It would involve, among other things, the squeezing of the
millennial kingdom into the space comprehended by Paul's 'twinkling of an eye' in
1 Cor. 15. 52; the invention of a *second* transfiguration for those alive at Christ's
coming, something of which no NT document shows the slightest awareness, and
imposing a point of termination onto the eschatological rest mentioned in 2 Thess.
1: 7. If *AscIsa.* 4. 14–18 is set up as a 'standard' form of early chiliasm one would
have to admit—contrary to all modern authorities—that standard chiliasm was not
a champion of the resurrection of the body; the doctrine of bodily resurrection, if it
assumes a continuity between the body which has died and that which is resurrected
or transformed, is not upheld in the present form of this document: 'and their body
will be left in the world' (4. 17).
[107] Even Enoch is there, in the same place with all the righteous; he too is 'stripped
of the garment of the flesh' and in his 'robe of above'.

tion (6. 8; 10. 6, and probably 7. 17). This is quite bold, if indeed
this section dates from the early second century. Of the many early
Christian documents which assume a celestial abode for the righteous, there is seldom a decisive word to indicate that such a state
of affairs obtained before the resurrection and ascension of Christ.
For most, the central, redemptive acts of Christ in history are the
prerequisites of the removal of the righteous from an infernal to a
supernal repose.

Our author still knows and accepts some form of the teaching
of Christ's descent to the angel of death to retrieve certain souls.
Charles and others have determined that these must be the imper-
fectly righteous.[108] But there is no evident concern in *AscIsa.* about
imperfect righteousness or about levels of sanctification amongst
the saints. It might be preferable to view these ransomed ones as
those of the elect who expired close to the time of Christ's own
passion, who had not yet gone on to heaven, perhaps preserved for
the special purpose of being manifested to those still alive (cf. Matt.
27: 52–3) and to follow in the train of the ascending Christ.

Second, what the redemptive acts of Christ do accomplish for
the whole body of the departed saints is that after the Beloved
completes his cosmic circuit these heaven-dwellers are permitted
to don their crowns and to sit on their thrones (9. 10–18) whereas
before this they could wear only their robes of glory. This may be
of great significance. Whereas robes and even crowns[109] do not
necessarily connote a ruling/judging function or status, the same
cannot be said for thrones, in such a context. A striking parallel is
thus afforded both with the twenty-four elders of Revelation who
sit on thrones, are clad in white garments and wear golden crowns
as they participate in the heavenly worship, and with those who
sit on thrones in Revelation 20: 4, who reign with Christ and serve
him as priests during the thousand years. The author of this section

---

[108] Charles, *Ascension*, 63; MacCulloch, 136. Tisserant, 180, sees a simple contradiction.

[109] Daniélou, *Symbols*, 20, regards the crown motif in *AscIsa.* as belonging to the
symbolism of the feast of tabernacles and makes certain links between the bestowal
of leafy crowns in tabernacles rites and the hope of an earthly millennial kingdom,
'The feast of Tabernacles, then, signifies the earthly rule of the Messiah, before
everlasting life' (6). It is all the more significant then that for the author of *AscIsa.*
the bestowal of crowns takes place *not* in an earthly millennium but in the
courts of the seventh heaven during the interval between Christ's ascension and
his return.

of the *AscIsa.* clearly believes in a joint reign of the departed saints with Christ in heaven in the present era.[110]

The third aspect of his conception of the intermediate state reinforces the parallels with Revelation, and that is the participation of the righteous in the heavenly liturgy of worship, song and praises (9. 28–42): 'all the righteous I had seen, and the angels also I had seen, approached him and worshipped him and praised him with one voice' (9. 28). This also has a correspondence in Revelation 20 where those privileged to have a part in the first resurrection 'shall be priests of God and of Christ' while they reign with him.

Not only are chapters 6–11 not chiliastic, the only kingdom they know is one which resides in heaven, in which all the righteous dead have participated ever since the Beloved has returned there from his incarnational voyage. What is most noteworthy are the correspondences between this version of the intermediate state and the description of the millennium in Revelation 20. This is not to say that our author knew Revelation 20, though this cannot be ruled out. But he attests the lively existence of a non-chiliastic outlook from which other Christians may have approached their understanding of that chapter, perhaps an outlook similar to that of the Patmos seer himself.

2. *Apocalypse of Peter*

If R. J. Bauckham is correct about the interpretation of chapter 2 of the *Apocalypse of Peter*, this work should be regarded as a Palestinian, Jewish Christian production written in the face of anti-Christian oppression from the Bar Cochba regime between 132 and 135.[111] Such a *Sitz im Leben* would certainly predispose many to expect to find in it the ardent hopes of a vigilant, chiliastic community. What we actually find, however, in the first six chapters of this work (which seems to be familiar with Rev. 11: 3 in ch. 2) is that the expected parousia of Christ will bring with it the resurrection of all the dead and the final judgement. Here then would be an extremely important witness to the eschatology of Jewish Christians

[110] Knibb, *OTP*, 154, 170, n. i.
[111] Bauckham, *JBL* (1985), 287. Many have accepted as original the fairly obvious reference to Bar Cochba in ch. 2 but Bauckham points out that *ApocPet.* does not record the revolutionary's defeat. 'It is almost impossible, on our interpretation, to imagine its being written outside the immediate context of Bar Kokhba's persecution of Christians' (287).

all too well aware of the nationalistic chiliasm of their non-Christian kinsmen.

In chapters 15–17 we gain a glimpse of a paradise ('outside this world', according to the Akhmim fragment) inhabited not merely by the translated few but by 'the companies of the fathers' in their rest, wearing glistening garments and crowns of plaited flowers. From the citation of Matthew 5: 10 in chapter 16 (Eth.), this paradise appears to have been identified with the kingdom of heaven,[112] as it is in Luke 23: 42–3.

Here again we see the conjunction of a non-chiliastic future expectation with a heavenly—here specified as a paradisaical—intermediate state for the godly.

3. 5 Ezra

Recent study has tended to place this pseudepigraphon within the second century. G. Stanton thinks it comes from a community of Christians shortly after the final quelling of the Bar Cochba revolt.[113] This would put the work in close association with Justin's *Dialogue with Trypho* (even if the final publication of the latter was some years hence), and indeed both works share a preoccupation with matters of Church–Synagogue relations and self-definition.[114]

[112] Here we may mention also the Christian interpolations in *SibOr.* I and II which, at II. 238–338, according to Maurer, *NTA*, ii. 666, are dependent upon *ApocPet.* II. 235–347 also associates the great assize with the return of Christ and situates the final hope of the faithful in the eternal day of a new creation. The writer's view of the intermediate state, however, is not obvious, though the awards mentioned in II. 39–54 (including entry into the heavenly city) would seem to pertain to that state.

[113] Stanton, 70–2. Previous to Stanton's article, Duensing (*NTA*, ii. 689), Schneemelcher and Daniélou (*OLC*, 18, 30) had argued for a late second-century date, though Daniélou had stressed the possibility that *5Ez.* may have been contemporary with the *Shepherd* of Hermas.

[114] This could be significant. 'It is much more plausible to see the community from which 5 Ezra stems as struggling to define itself over against a Judaism which could not be ignored. Israel's privileges are to be transferred to the church without remainder and without modification', Stanton, 77. If it is true that Jewish hopes of a temporary, earthly, Messianic kingdom flowered as never before during the period between the two revolts against Rome, it is quite understandable that such a Jewish hope would have come up in Justin's discussion with Trypho (chs. 80–1). Justin was no doubt motivated by the same desire Stanton observes in 5 Ezra, to adopt all the Jewish hopes into the Christian family as a consequence of the displacement of Israel by the Church, and thus room is made by him also for the Christian version of such a hope, namely, chiliasm. 5 Ezra, it is interesting to note, manifests on the other hand no inclination to adopt these notions of the kingdom.

5 Ezra openly lacks any chiliastic elements, a fact which, to Daniélou, points to a Roman, Jewish–Christian provenance.[115] What then does this document reveal of its author's notions of the intermediate state? Its last verses present a fascinating scene which takes place on Mount Zion. The question for us is whether, as Daniélou and Knibb believe,[116] this is the earthly Mount Zion after the time of the return of Christ or whether, as Myers supposes,[117] it is the heavenly Zion during the present era.

In 2. 38, the section just preceding the vision of Mount Zion, the visionary exhorts to[118]

Receive what the Lord has entrusted to you and be joyful, giving thanks to him who has called you to heavenly kingdoms (*ad celestia regna vocavit*). Rise and stand, and see at the feast of the Lord the number of those who have been sealed. Those who have departed from the shadow of this age have received glorious garments from the Lord. Take again your full number, O Zion, and conclude the list of your people who are clothed in white, who have fulfilled the law of the Lord. The number of your children whom you desired is full. . .[119]

There are numerous correspondences between this exhortation and the vision of Mount Zion which immediately follows it in vv. 42–8, for which vision it seems indeed to be preparing. In v. 8 he calls upon the reader to see the *number* of those sealed; in 2. 42 he himself gazes upon a great multitude which he cannot number. In 2. 39 are mentioned those who have 'departed from the shadow of this age' and have 'received glorious garments from the Lord', evidently these are deceased brethren[120]—they have already fulfilled the law of the Lord (2. 40)—clothed in heavenly garments; in 2. 45 he is told that the innumerable multitude he sees are those 'who have put off mortal clothing and put on the immortal'. This parallel suggests that the immortal clothing is not the body of resurrection received at the last day but the interim garments of glory worn in heaven (cf. Rev. 6: 11; 7: 9, 14; 14: 4). These are, moreover, deceased (perhaps martyrs), as is clear from 2. 45, 'they

---

[115] Daniélou, *OLC*, 23, thus recognizing its affinities with other 'Roman' works, 1 Pet., *IClem.* and the *Shepherd* of Hermas.
[116] Ibid., 'nothing is said about an intermediate state or about the condition of the dead while they wait for the *parousia*'; Coggins-Knibb, *Esdras*, 98, sees the multitude in the vision as resurrected martyrs.
[117] Myers, 153, 158.   [118] The translation of Metzger, *OTP*, i.
[119] Coggins-Knibb, *Esdras*, 97, the author 'believed the end of the world was extremely close'.   [120] Ibid. 97.

have confessed the name of God; now they are being crowned, and receive palms', and 2. 47 'He is the Son of God, whom they confessed in the world'. As they are said to have confessed him *in saeculo*,[121] this Mount Zion is evidently somewhere outside the world, not in the world of an earthly kingdom. The connections with Revelation 7: 9–17 and 14: 1–7 are obvious.[122] Daniélou is right also in noting the substantial correspondence in thought with Hermas, *Sim.* 8, where an angel of God (also of immense size, *Sim.* 8. 1.2 cf. 5Ez. 2. 43) bestows crowns on the faithful. But as we noted above in our study of Hermas, those crowned and sent into the tower are again those who have died and who are thus receiving their heavenly rewards (the crown motif is especially associated with martyrdom in *Sim.* 8. 2.1; 8. 3.6); they too have kept the law (*Sim.* 8. 3.3–5 cf. 5Ez. 2. 40), they too receive white garments (*Sim.* 8. 2.3 cf. 5Ez. 2. 40–1, 45), they too receive palms (woven into their crowns) (*Sim.* 8. 2.1 cf. 5Ez. 2. 45).

It appears then that this scene on Mount Zion takes place in the heavenly kingdom during the interadvent period. This particular instance of an eschatology which holds no evident expectation of an earthly millennium and on the other hand looks to an enjoyment of the kingdom in heaven after death is of special importance because of its manifest acquaintance with the book of Revelation. This causes us to wonder how the author might have understood the millennium of Revelation 20. Once again there is seen in this type of eschatology an important place reserved for the doctrine of the bodily resurrection (2. 16, 23, 31).

---

[121] This is the reading of the 'French' family of mss. The 'Spanish', which on the whole is preferred as earlier by James (TS, lxiii) and Daniélou (*OLC*, 18), reads *in saculo mortali*.

[122] Coggins-Knibb, *Esdras*, 98, 'the whole vision . . . seems to be based on Rev. 7: 9–17'. See also James, ST, lxxix. I must disagree with Stanton, 79–80, who recognizes no literary dependence on Revelation (for more extreme scepticism, see Kraft, *HTR*, 166, who questions the Christian nature of the work). Though 'closer' verbal parallels may indeed be found in Hermas, many elements cannot be accounted for from Hermas: the parallel scene in Hermas does not (expressly) take place on Mount Zion (2. 42), but that in Rev. 14: 1 does; Hermas does not mention the innumerable multitude (2. 42), but see Rev. 7: 9; Hermas does not deal with 'the number of those who are sealed' (2. 38), but see Rev. 7: 4, 'And I heard the number of the sealed, a hundred and forty-four thousand'; Hermas does not mention the singing, 'and they all praised the Lord with songs' (2. 42) but see Rev. 14: 3, 'and they sing a new song before the throne'. Myers, 153, also believes the appearance of the two servants Isaiah and Jeremiah (2: 18) is an interpretation of Rev. 11: 3 (Daniélou, *OLC*, 22, reminds us that Victorinus of Pettau ascribes the identification of the second witness of Rev. 11: 3 with Jeremiah to ancient tradition).

4. *Syrian Pseudepigrapha*: Epistula Apostolorum; Odes of Solomon; Acts of Thaddeus; Acts of Thomas

The *Epistle of the Apostles*,[123] written almost certainly in the first half of the second century,[124] is manifestly non-chiliastic. 'The βασιλεία τοῦ θεοῦ is in heaven; an earthly kingdom with its joys of the Messianic age is never spoken of ...'.[125] Christ's parousia brings no earthly millennium but a resurrection (on the physical nature of which our author could hardly have been more emphatic),[126] a judgement of all the living and the dead (chs. 16, 26, 39) and a bodily ascent for the redeemed to the rest and kingdom in heaven (ch. 21). Neither kingdom nor rest are associated in *EpApost.* with future ventures on earth (chs. 12, 19, 26–8, 32, 42, 44).[127] After the resurrection, in contrast to the teaching of Cerinthus, there will be no more eating and drinking; 'And you will not have part in the creation below, but will belong to the incorruptibility of my Father' (ch. 19 Ethiopic). Against Schmidt,[128] I would even advance the hypothesis that the Cerinthus opposed by the 'epistle' (chs. 1, 7) was a millenarizing and not merely (perhaps not at all) a Gnosticizing one. Though the specific heresy of Cerinthus is not divulged, the author's radical antichiliasm may be seen as a response to an overly-materialistic eschatology such as this heretic is reported by some to have held.[129]

This thoroughgoing stress on the heavenly locus of future glory (ch. 21) contributes to the confusion as to whether and when the author might be speaking of an intermediate state of glory in heaven as opposed to his referring exclusively to the time following the

[123] Translations and chapter numerations follow *NTA* ii.
[124] Gunther, 91, 'before the wave of Marcionism from Rome swept across Syria and the eastern Mediterranean'. This date is corroborated by Deunsing, *NTA*, 191 and Hornschuh, 116–19. Schmidt, 361–402, had settled on a date of 160–70 and an Asia Minor provenance.
[125] Schmidt, 355.   [126] Ibid. 344–51; Hornschuh, 64.
[127] Schmidt, 354; Gunther, 89.   [128] Schmidt, Exkurs i. 401–52.
[129] A well-known problem for the historian of chiliasm is that Gaius of Rome, Dionysius of Alexandria, and many subsequent writers largely dependent upon them charge that Cerinthus taught chiliasm (the later testimonies attribute to him other Judaizing tendencies) while Irenaeus, Hippolytus, and Pseudo-Tertullian give no indication of this and represent his teaching instead as suggestive of Gnosticism. Klijn–Reinink, 5, 8, 19, 72, reject both lines of evidence as unhistorical, though they are rightly criticized by Skarsaune, 407–9, who affirms Cerinthus' chiliasm. An interesting study could be made, however, of the correspondences between the early descriptions of Cerinthus' chiliastic teaching and the contrary eschatological tendencies of our author.

return of Christ. The immediacy of his eschatological expectation[130] also means that the intermediate state is not a matter of prime concern. Nevertheless, there are various hints which seem to show that along with a very evident non-chiliastic outlook *EpApost.* combines a presupposition of the saints' rest in heaven preceding the second coming.

The disciples are to keep the passover until the Master comes again 'with those who were killed for my sake' (ch. 15 Coptic).[131] 'They are the martyrs, who, in conformity with the faith of popular Christianity, become joined with Christ immediately in his kingdom and now follow him in his coming down. . .'.[132] But are the martyrs in heaven alone of their race?

Speaking to his disciples after his resurrection, but before his ascension, Christ says that he has descended to the righteous and the prophets 'that they may come forth from the rest which is below and go up to what is [above] . . .' (ch. 27 Coptic). Daniélou remarks that 'there is, however, no trace of an immediate resurrection with Christ. . .'.[133] But this may well be because in the context of the dialogue Christ himself has not yet gone on to heaven. The transport to the rest above, which is promised to them, is very probably to take place in conjunction with Christ's ascension. In chapter 28 the risen Christ goes on to tell his disciples that, just as he has promised to redeem them from all the power of the archons so he will grant to 'the righteous and the prophets' below, 'that they may come [out of] the prison and the chains of the archons and the powerful fire'. This, especially as it been combined with the idea of a baptism accomplished in Hades (ch. 27), does not give the impression of a postponement of the rise to heaven. The prospect of escaping from prison and the archons has undoubted affinities with Gnostic conceptions but in the case of our present document, since it takes an uncompromising stance against Gnosticizing trends throughout, we should

---

[130] The Ethiopic version sets the date for the Lord's return at 120 years after his resurrection; the Coptic version extends this number to 150.

[131] The Ethiopic has 'until I come from the Father with my wounds', but Hills, 110–15, has convincingly shown that the Greek original must have been τραυματιῶν (slain ones) which was read as τραυματῶν (wounds) by the Ethiopic translator.

[132] Schmidt, 343. Schmidt then refers to the words of Paul in the *Acta Pauli* (*NTA* ii. 386), 'I go to the Lord that I may come (again) with him in the glory of his Father'.

[133] Daniélou, *TJC*, 239.

also be prepared to look for more 'domestic' parallels. Indeed these do exist and come from a Syrian milieu.[134]

Odes of Solomon 17. 10–15 speaks of Christ shattering the bars of iron, loosing all his bondsmen who were bound, blessing and gathering them together. In ode 42. 14–20 the righteous in Hades cry out 'Son of God, have pity on us. And deal with us according to your kindness and bring us out from the chains of darkness'. In ode 22 God is said to have overthrown by the hands of Christ the dragon with seven heads and to have levelled the way for those who believe. This chapter goes on to speak of a resurrection ('It took dead bones and covered them with flesh') of certain ones, concluding, 'And the foundation of everything is your rock. And upon it you have built your kingdom, and it became the dwelling place of the holy ones'.

The archons of *EpApost.* 28, perhaps equivalent to the personified Sheol and Death in *OdesSol.* 42. 11, appear again in the *Acts of Thomas*, a Syrian production of the first half of the third century:[135]

Jesus Christ, Son of compassion and perfect Saviour; Christ, Son of the living God, the undaunted power which overthrew the enemy, the voice that was heard by the archons, which shook all their powers; ambassador sent from the height who didst descend even to Hell, who having opened the doors did bring up thence those who for many ages had been shut up in the treasury of darkness, and show them the way that leads up to the height. (*ActThom.* 10)

[he whom] the Archon feared when he saw him, and the powers that were with him were confounded. (*ActThom.* 143)

who among men was crucified for many, who didst descend into Hades with great power, the sight of whom the princes of death did not endure, and thou didst ascend with great glory, and gathering all those who took refuge in thee thou didst prepare a way, and in thy footsteps they all journeyed whom thou didst redeem, and thou didst bring them to thine own flock and unite them with thy sheep. (*ActThom.* 156)

---

[134] See the Syrian works cited by Klijn, *Acts*, 189–90, and, besides the texts cited below, *Acts of Thaddeus* (Eusebius, *HE* I. 13. 20), 'and was crucified, and descended into Hades, and rent the partition which had not been rent from the beginning of the world, and raised (ἀνήγειρεν) the dead, and he went down alone, but with a great multitude did he go up to his Father', and the long recension of Ignatius, *Tr.* 9, 'He descended, indeed, into Hades alone, but He arose accompanied by a multitude; and rent asunder that means of separation which had existed from the beginning of the world, and cast down its partition-wall.'

[135] Klijn, *Acts*, 26; Bornkamm, *NTA*, ii. 441.

The baptism performed by Christ for the OT saints in *EpApost.* 27, which would seem to be related to *OdesSol.* 17. 15, 'then they received my blessing and lived', and *OdesSol.* 42. 20, 'And I placed my name upon their head', reappears also in Hermas *Sim.* 9. 16. 2–3 and in *ApocPet.* 14, all of which presuppose that the baptized were subsequently taken on to the kingdom in heaven.

Thus it is a solid inference that the author of the *EpApost.* also believed in a transferral of the just from their rest below to their rest above in connection with the ascension of Christ. And thus when Christ commissions his disciples to lead God's children 'into heaven' (ch. 19) and when he promises himself to lead them there, 'to the place [which] my Father has [prepared] for the elect...the chosen kingdom in rest, and eternal life' (ch. 28, cf. ch. 12) it is reasonable to deduce that this happens, pending his return in glory, at life's end, when believers will not have to fear the archons which might otherwise have sought to detain them (cf. *ActThom.* 142; 148; 167).

We have already seen that the Syrian *Acts of Thomas* contains more than one account of Christ's rescue of the saints from Hades. Another aspect of its teaching on the intermediate state now claims our attention. The apostle in 142, speaking of his imminent death for the sake of Christ says, 'Behold, I reign in the kingdom on which even here I have set my hope'. Earlier, speaking as one of the disciples addressed in Matthew 19: 28, he had prayed to Christ, 'thou hast shown us the ascent to the height [cf. ch. 10], having promised us that we shall sit on thy right hand and with thee judge the twelve tribes of Israel' (80, cf. 21–5).

This specimen of early third-century Syrian Christian thought, somewhat Gnostic in tendency but not so thoroughly as is made out by Bornkamm and Georgi,[136] shows up the belief in a heavenly intermediate state in which the heavenly realm is conceived as a kingdom to be inherited and participated in by the righteous (pre-eminently the apostles) immediately at death. In this it is not unlike *AscIsa.* 6–11 and *5Ez.* It knows nothing of a future kingdom on earth.

---

[136] Diverging assessments of the relation of this work to Gnosticism and early Manicheeism are found in Bornkamm and Georgi, *NTA,* ii, 425-42 and in Klijn, *Acts* (see Georgi, *NTA,* ii, 442). Along with Klijn, 34, we must remember that for all its many points of contact with Gnostic spirituality this document does preserve faith in the reality of Christ's earthly body which was crucified and rose, and in the promise of a resurrection for the bodies of his believers (e.g. 158).

4. EARLY MARTYROLOGIES

Much of our information for early Christian beliefs about the intermediate state comes from the literature surrounding Christian martyrdoms, information contained not just in the *acta*, the *passiones*,
and the legends[137] but also in the theological and moral treatises
of many Church leaders.

Here we shall devote some attention to two of the earliest and,
to most minds, the most historically reliable of the *passiones*, two
which bear special relations to Irenaeus (see below and § IV.3), the
Martyrdom of Polycarp and the *Epistle of Vienne and Lyons*.

1. Martyrdom of Polycarp[138]

The *Martyrdom of Polycarp* was written by one Marcianus (20. 1)
on behalf of the Smyrnaean church shortly after the martyrdom
which took place probably between AD 155 and 160.[139] Chapter 14
gives an account of Polycarp's dying prayer in which the saint
shows that he expects that day to join the 'whole race of the
righteous' (τοῦ γένουϲ τῶν δικαίων, synonymous with 'the Christians'
in 17. 1, and not restrictable to martyrs alone)[140] who have departed
this life and are living in God's presence (οἳ ζῶϲιν ἐνώπιόν ϲου).
Polycarp is also to have 'a portion among the number of the martyrs
in the cup of Christ unto a resurrection of life eternal,
of both soul and body, in the incorruption of the Holy Spirit'.
This cup of which he is about to partake is the bitter cup of death/
martyrdom (Mark 14: 36 = Luke 22: 42; John 18: 11; *AscIsa.* 5. 13).[141]
But the most poignant Biblical source is Matthew 20: 22–3 = Mark
10: 38–9 where drinking Jesus' cup (Polycarp's 'cup of Christ'!) has
some connection with sitting at his right or left in his kingdom!
That this Gospel source is behind Polycarp's words is made even

---

[137] The classification of Quasten, i. 176.

[138] Translations of the *MartPolyc.* are my own based on the text of Bihlmeyer.

[139] Lightfoot, *AF*, II. 1, 646–722; Schoedel, ApF, 48; Barnes, *JTS*, 512; Musurillo,
Acts, xiii. On questions of literary criticism see Barnard, *Kyr.*; Baumeister, 292–5.

[140] Cf. also γένοϲ τῶν δικαίων in Hermas, *Sim.* 9. 17. 5; θεοϲεβῶν γένοϲ in Melito
(Eusebius, *HE* IV. 26. 5).

[141] 'Participation in the cup of Christ is essentially identical with κοινωνία in the
suffering of Christ (cf. Mart. pol. 6,2)', Baumeister, 299–300. There may indeed be
eucharistic connotations to this reference to the 'cup' (Barnard, *Kyr.*, 201–3; Baumeister, 299–300) but the connection with death is primary; the eucharist too has to do
with death.

more likely by the fact that both Tertullian and Origen explicitly draw from it the connection between martyrdom and reigning with Christ in his heavenly kingdom.[142] The author, Marcianus, certainly conceives of Polycarp as already in this heavenly kingdom when he expresses the desire (17. 3) that all his readers might become fellow partakers and fellow disciples with the martyrs, who displayed incomparable loyalty 'to their own King and Teacher', and then praises the Father who is 'able to lead us all by his grace and gift into his heavenly[143] kingdom' (20. 2). This is surely, because still future to the author, the kingdom *in* heaven, entered after enduring faithfully unto death.

From 17. 1 and 19. 2 it is clear that Marcianus believes the deceased Polycarp has been crowned with the crown of incorruption, a conception of the departed which has NT roots,[144] one of which was perhaps the 'crown of life' mentioned in the letter addressed to his own church in the book of Revelation[145] (2: 10–11, see also 1 Cor. 9: 24–5; 2 Tim. 4: 6–8; Jas. 1: 12). In the *MartPolyc.* the crown, very notably, is awarded not at resurrection day but upon entering heaven at death. In 19. 2 Polycarp is said to have donned his crown and now, 'rejoicing with the apostles and all the righteous, glorifies the Father and the Son'. This recalls *AscIsa.*

---

[142] Origen: *ExhMart.* 28, 'We learn, besides, that he who drinks of that cup that Jesus drank will sit and rule and judge with the King of kings' (translations of the *ExhMart.*, here and below, are from Oulton–Chadwick, LCC); see also *CMatt.* XVI. 4–6. Tertullian: *Scorp.* 12, 'sitting with the Lord on His throne [Rev. 3: 28],— which once was persistently refused to the sons of Zebedee. Who, pray, are these so blessed conquerors, but martyrs in the strict sense of the word?'; *Pat.* 13, martyrdom is 'the act of ascending the divine seat'. Perhaps also Clement of Alexandria, *Paed.* I. vi. 51. 1–2; *Strom.* IV. xi. 75. 2.

[143] Reading ἐπουράνιον with Mosquensis (a 13th-cent.) MS) and Lightfoot. Bihlmeyer follows *Baroccianus, Hiersolymitanus* and *Parisinus*, all earlier but all from the same family and thus constituting one witness, in reading αἰώνιον. Lightfoot (*AF*, II. 3, 356) states that Mosquensis is 'the most important of the Greek manuscripts, as is shown by the coincidence of its readings with those of Eusebius'. The citation by Eusebius, however, does not extend to this portion of the martyrology. There is a possible corroboration of ἐπουράνιον to be found in the alternate ending, inserted at the end of ch. 19, contained in the MS *Vindobonensis*, of the 11th or 12th cent. It incorporates and works over a section its author omitted from ch. 17 and adds a doxology. But between these it includes a clause which seems to reflect the thought of the reading of 20. 2 we have adopted: καὶ ἐπιτυχεῖν τῆς βαcιλείαc τῶν οὐρανῶν cὺν χριcτῷ ἰηcοῦ τῷ κυρίῳ ἡμῶν. That Jesus is King is affirmed again in Polycarp's answer to the proconsul in 9. 3 and the appended chronology in 21. 1 (though the genuineness of the latter is debated).

[144] Notwithstanding its long use in Stoicism. See Schoedel, ApF, 76.

[145] Cf. Hemer, 65, 74.

9. 10–18 and the texts from Revelation cited above in connection with it.

There are no traces of chiliasm in this document. Yet it still attests a belief in the resurrection of the body and the 'fire of the future judgement and eternal punishment, which is reserved for the ungodly' (11. 2, cf. 2. 3; 14. 2). Its adherence to a belief in an intermediate state in heaven for *all* the Christian dead is unquestionable and thus is true to the trajectory of Polycarp's belief recorded in his letter to the Philippians. The two surviving literary relics of Polycarp's Smyrna in Asia (the province commonly viewed as the hotbed of Christian chiliasm at this time) attest therefore only to this non-chiliastic form of eschatology.

2. *Epistle of Vienne and Lyons*

About 20 years after Polycarp's death, what was probably 'the most bloody persecution' since the Neronian[146] consumed in its fury great numbers from the churches of Vienne and Lyons. A report of the atrocities was soon sent from Gaul to the churches in Asia and Phrygia and to Eleutherus in Rome, with personal letters by some of the imprisoned confessors subjoined (Eusebius, *HE* v. 1. 1; 4. 1). This dossier's portrayal of the status of martyrs is essentially the same as that which we have observed in the *MartPolyc.*, with which document in fact it seems to be familiar.[147]

The martyrs are seen as noble athletes locked in a superhuman conflict with the diabolical enemy (v. 1. 5, 23, 27; v. 1. 16). The heroic Christians, putting on the invincible athlete Christ (v. 1. 23–4, 29, 36, 42), conquer the adversary and garner the crown of incorruption (v. 1. 36, (38), 42). These are true martyrs 'whom in their confession Christ has accounted worthy to be taken up (ἀναληφθῆναι), having set his seal upon their witness through their departure (ἐξόδου)' (v. 2. 3). These are now with God: 'having gone away to God (πρὸς θεὸν ἀπελθόντες), victory-bearers in all things ... with peace they removed to God (ἐχώρησαν πρὸς θεόν)' (v. 2. 7).

Unlike the *MartPolyc.*, the letter from the churches of Gaul has nothing to say of the dead in Christ who were not martyrs. This is probably due alone to the subject matter, and it is probably safe to assume that their doctrine would have mirrored that of the

---

[146] Lightfoot, *AF*, ii. 1, 516. [147] Ibid., 605, 611: Barnard, *Kyr.* 193.

earlier martyrology. The stalwart faith of these Christians in a bodily resurrection is proved from the contemptuous flouting it suffers at the hands of the persecutors, who swept the ashes of the martyr's remains into the Rhone (v. 1. 62–3). Again there is no evidence at all of an adherence to chiliasm.[148]

Yet, the author(s) certainly knows the book of Revelation,[149] invoking Revelation 22. 11 as 'the Scripture' which must be fulfilled (v. 1. 58), alluding to 3. 14 and 1. 5 (v. 2. 3) and to 14. 4 (v. 1. 10). This last verse is put to a fascinating use in describing the fate of Vettius Epagathus, a young, blameless man of position who intervened on behalf of the Christians, who confessed himself to be a Christian and who then was duly martyred. He, in the words of our text, 'was and is a noble disciple of Christ, who "follows the Lamb wherever he goes"'. Such a panegyric can hardly have been carelessly chosen; the language is an application of Revelation 14: 4. The worthy Vettius is viewed thus as one of the 144,000 chaste and spotless ones redeemed from the earth who in Revelation 14 stand with the Lamb on Mount Zion bearing the divine name and singing a new song before the throne. There are many things this does not tell us about the early Gallican exegesis of this passage but it does tell us that the 144,000[150] were viewed as departed (perhaps all martyred) saints. The Mount Zion on which the Lamb and his followers stand is therefore (here as in 5Ez. 2. 42–8)[151] not the earthly but the heavenly one.

There is another possible debt owed to the book of Revelation.

---

[148] Without citing any evidence, both Harnack, *Lehrbuch*, I, 483, and Semisch–Bratke, 808, stated that chiliasm could be found in our epistle. Frend, *Martyrdom*, 16, also attributes the expectation of an earthly millennium to our document, evidently on the basis of the mere expectation of a future Antichrist. But this would not necessarily entail millennialism (cf. Origen, Cyprian, etc.) and the connection with Irenaeus, as we shall presently see, will not easily yield a positive answer to the question of chiliasm.

[149] Frend, *Martyrdom*, 19, 'Clearly, the Fourth Gospel and the Apocalypse were two of the main sources of inspiration to the writer.'

[150] If this number was identified with the 144,000 in Rev. 7, 12,000 taken from each of the twelve tribes of Israel, it is interesting that these do not appear to have been regarded as all racially Jewish, considering the Gentile name of Vettius Epagathus (Frend, *Martyrdom*, 3).

[151] See above, § II. 3. 3. This is important as these two documents furnish us with the earliest remaining witnesses to an interpretation of Rev. 14: 1–5. The same interpretation is taken again by Methodius, *Sympos*. 6. 5 (though he may think all 144,000 are virgins). Charles, *Revelation*, ii. 1–10, like many modern interpreters, insisted on Rev. 14: 1–5 being a picture of the holy coterie on the earthly Mount Zion during the millennial reign.

We read in v. 1. 5 that the persecutions of Christians in Gaul are engineered by Satan, whose pogrom against the churches was viewed as only a prelude (προοιμιαζόμενος) to his future coming ἀδεῶς (v. 1. 5). What does this word ἀδεῶς mean? LSJ gives it as an adverb from ἀδεής, fearless (related to δέος, fear), hence ἀδεῶς, without fear or scruple, confidently, or with impunity. This derivation is well established in Greek usage. The word appears also in *MartPolyc.* 7. 2 (which the author of *EpV&L* knew), where Polycarp requests that his captors allow him to pray for an hour ἀδεῶς. But why would Polycarp request permission to pray without fear or scruple, confidently or with impunity? Roberts and Donaldson translate, 'without disturbance'; Lightfoot, 'unmolested', Lake, 'without hindrance', Goodspeed, 'without interruption', Shepherd, Staniforth, and Schoedel, 'undisturbed'.[152] Again we may ask, why, in the *EpV&L*, would the adversary be said to be coming 'without fear or scruple, confidently, or with impunity'? Possible meanings, perhaps, but Kidd is the only English translator I have seen who renders the word as 'fearless'.[153] Williamson and Bright read ἀδεῶς as a sentence adverb: Williamson, 'his advent, which undoubtedly is imminent', Bright, 'his final coming of which we can be sure'.[154] Lake leaves the word untranslated.[155] Another group of translators offer a different sense. Cruse and McGiffert both render ἀδεῶς by 'unbridled', Pratten and Oulton by, 'without restraint'.[156] *PGL* in fact defines the adverb ἀδεῶς, referring to the two texts we have dealt with so far, as meaning 'freely, without restraint'. This definition, in accord with the last group of translations of *EpV&L* v. 1. 5 and with the translations of *MartPolyc.* 7. 2 cited above, seems to bring us back not to δέος but to δέω, to bind, tie, fetter; adj., ἄδετος, unbound, loose, not clamped together, free.[157] This makes good sense of both passages: it is easy to see why Polycarp would ask leave to pray unmolested or freely; it is understandable that the

---

[152] Roberts and Donaldson, *ANF* i. 40; Lightfoot, *AF* ii. 3, 480; Lake, ii. 249; Goodspeed, 249; Staniforth, 157; Shepherd, LCC i. 151; Schoedel, *ApF*, 60.

[153] Kidd, 95.

[154] Williamson, 194; Bright, *Early Christian Spirituality*, 39.

[155] Lake, *Eusebius*, i. 409.

[156] Cruse, 169; Pratten, *ANF* viii. 778; McGiffert, *NPNF*, 212; Oulton, *Eusebius*, i. 140.

[157] Compare e.g. the similar case of ἀφανῶς, 'invisibly', found in Clement of Alexandria *Theod.* 61. 5, for which there is no recorded adverb ἄφανος but only the verbal adverb ἄφαντος. BAGD seems to utilize both derivations of ἀδεῶς, defining it 'without fear or disturbance'.

Gallican Christians would believe in a future 'unbridled', or unrestrained coming of Satan against the Church. The word in question also appears in this sense in another second-century Christian author, Clement of Alexandria: 'exercise temperance, not encouraging each other to eat ἀδεῶc what is set before us' (*Strom.* IV. XV. 97. 5). Here again, 'unrestrainedly' or perhaps 'greedily' unquestionably fits better than does 'without fear, confidently, or with impunity'.

But if ἀδεῶc does belong to the same word group with δέω, to bind, its appearance in *EpV&L* v. 1. 5 is significant indeed. If Satan's final coming against the church will be unbridled, unrestrained, this means that even the persecution and eventual bloodbath experienced by the Christians in Gaul as reported in this letter was the rampage of an arrested, restrained foe, exercising his servants beforehand (προγυμνάζων) for his final, unbridled onslaught. It would then seem altogether probable that this concept and the use of the word ἀδεῶc come from reflection on the wording of Revelation 20: 2, where it is said with reference to the devil, 'and he bound (ἔδηcεν, from δέω, to bind) him for a thousand years'. In Revelation 20 the binding of Satan means, at least, that for the millennial interval he is deprived of his power to gather the heathen hordes for the final attack on the 'camp of the saints' predicted in Rev. 20: 7–10. The Gallican Christian(s) responsible for this letter understands Satan to be restrained, bound now, in the present age— even while he attacks with all viciousness he can muster—and to be destined for a future release (Rev. 20: 7, cf. 2 Thes. 2: 7–9) and a coming against the Church.

It appears very probable therefore that the author of our letter, who knew Revelation, was familiar with chapter 20 and had employed a non-chiliastic interpretation of the binding of Satan. The 'early' eschatology of Irenaeus confirms this. After twice referring to the fact that Jesus in his first coming had bound the strong man (Matt. 12: 29), 'and spoiled his goods, and abolished death, vivifying that man who had been in a state of death (i.e. Adam) (*AH* III. 23. 1, cf. III. 18. 6), Irenaeus refers to this binding once again in III. 23. 7. But in the last passage, instead of putting the binding in terms of Matthew 12: 29 (binding of 'the strong man') he speaks of the fulfilment of Psalm 91: 13 ('thou shalt trample down the lion and the dragon') in terms of Revelation 20: 2, 'that he should bind "the dragon, that old serpent", and subject him to the power of man, who had been conquered . . .'.[158] This binding too, as a comparison with III. 23. 1 shows, is a binding accomplished at the first coming of Christ. Needless to say, this early interpretation of Revelation 20 is at odds with the one Irenaeus advances in the last chapters of *Against Heresies*. But it is identical to our proposed explanation of *EpV&L* v. 1. 5.

The Gallican Christian community, made up largely of Asiatic immigrants,[159] corresponds in its eschatological outlook to the two other works of Asian provenance we have examined, Polycarp's letter to the Philippians and the account of his martyrdom by Marcianus. This is an outlook which Irenaeus would later characterize as non-chiliastic. Over the years several notable scholars, most recently Pierre Nautin and Robert M. Grant, have maintained that it was the young Irenaeus who authored the *EpV&L*.[160] If this is true (the evidence makes a plausible if not fully conclusive case) it marks with increasing clarity the extent to which his eschatology had changed by the time he wrote *AH* v. In any case we must now recognize among the 'certain orthodox' of *AH* v. 31–2 who do not embrace the hope of an earthly millennium because they believe in a soulish afterlife in God's presence before the resurrection, members of his own churches in Gaul—one of whom we now know was his former self.[161]

5. HIPPOLYTUS

An unavoidable problem in settling any issue in Hippolytan studies at the present time is that the authentic corpus of the writings of Hippolytus is, as it has been for much of the past century, very much under dispute. Many works the MSS of which bear the name of Hippolytus have been discounted by modern scholars and, conversely, some works have been attributed to him which no MS superscriptions would support. In the last century the addition of

[158] It is this type of exegesis which we might imagine was contained in Melito's *On the Devil and the Apocalypse of John.*

[159] Frend, *Martyrdom*, 2–5; Lawlor, *Eusebius*, ii. 154–5.

[160] Nautin, *Lettres*, 54–61; Grant, *Eusebius*, 118–19, who notes that this identification was made by Oecumenius in his *Commentary on 1 Peter*; see also McGiffert, *NPNF*, 212, n. 3. Barnes, *JTS*, 517 regards this theory as incapable of proof or disproof.

[161] For more on the relationship of these martyrologies to Irenaeus' own eschatology see § IV. 2 below.

the *Philosophumena* or *Refutation of All Heresies* to the received list of his works was the major achievement of Hippolytan scholarship, along with the discovery of the full text of the *Commentary on Daniel*. For many years an elaborately constructed solution, a jewel of nineteenth-century learning, held fairly comfortable sway. But Nautin in 1947 shattered this consensus by segregating the *Refutation*, the *Chronicle*, the fragment *De universo*, and the works mentioned on the statue[162] from the rest as the works of, in Nautin's opinion, one Josippus of Rome.[163] Few scholars have supported Nautin in every particular (least of all in the name he bestowed on his discovery) but the theory has forever made scholarship sensitive to the undeniable diversity which exists within the now-traditional mass of Hippolytan writings. More recently, in a volume published in 1977, V. Loi, C. Curti, P. Meloni, and M. Simonetti proposed a division of the works differing only slightly from Nautin's proposal, assigning those works (designated group R) which Nautin had gathered under the name of Josippus to Hippolytus of Rome, the presbyter (not a bishop) who was exiled in 335 to Sardinia, there to die as a martyr.[164] The other works (designated group A) belong to another Hippolytus, presented here as an oriental bishop (perhaps from Asia Minor), the formidable exegetical theologian responsible for the *Commentary on Daniel*, the treatise *On Christ and Antichrist*, *The Blessings of Jacob*, *The Blessings of Moses*, *De David et Goliath*, *Commentary on the Song of Solomon*, the *Contra Noetum*, and possibly others.[165] An even more recent attempt has been made by J. Frickel to reconcile the *Refutation* and the *Contra Noetum* and to reassert a single Hippolytus whose multifarious talents and interests can account for all of the works in question. At least one reviewer remains sceptical of Frickel's solution to the Hippolytan puzzle.[166] If I favour a theory of multiple authorship it is because a study of the eschatology of the documents had already led me to suspicions which were unexpectedly confirmed by the work of the Italian scholars named above.

---

[162] In 1551 the statuary remains of a seated figure were found in Rome. On the chair was inscribed a list of writings which matched to some extent the lists of Hippolytus' works passed down by later writers. The statue itself, thus taken to be a likeness of Hippolytus, M. Guarducci has recently shown to have been originally a feminine figure. See Guarducci.

[163] Nautin, *Josipe*.   [164] Loi, *Ricerche*.

[165] Loi, 'L'identità', 86; Meloni, 97–120; Simonetti 'Ipotesi'.

[166] See Butterworth.

Until recently, most of those writing on Hippolytus have treated the 'traditional' corpus as the product of one man. Among such writers it has long been customary to regard Hippolytus as a chiliast, though this opinion has not gone without occasional, weighty dissent.[167] The conclusion reached here, briefly stated, is that whether he was one or two, Hippolytus cannot assuredly be considered a chiliast. That is, neither the writings of group A nor those of group R reveal positive chiliastic traits.

The two factors which have given rise to the position that Hippolytus was a chiliast are (a) his assiduous labours in the chronicling of history, coupled with his acceptance of the cosmic-week theory[168] (see *CD* IV. 23–24), and (b) excerpts preserved in the twelfth-century Syrian writer Dionysius Bar Salibi's (d. 1171) *Commentary on the Apocalypse, Acts and Epistles*, which Bar Salibi claims to have taken from Hippolytus and which contain a partial exposition of Revelation 20.[169]

But as to the first factor, it must at least be admitted that not every form of a cosmic-week chronology may be equated with chiliasm. Even Daniélou, who classifies Hippolytus as a chiliast, says,

There is a whole tradition, to which Origen in particular is a witness, which understands the sabbath as signifying eternal life (*Hom. Num.* XXIII, 3).[170] All that is involved here is a typology of the week in which the six days of creation represent the time of this world, and the seventh day the world to come. This belongs to Jewish tradition, and was adapted by Philo.[171]

Lightfoot's evaluation, though written before the publication of Bar Salibi's extracts, is still accurate and to the point:

[167] Notably, Lightfoot, A. d'Ales, L. Atzberger, and B. Altaner. Bardy–Lefèvre, SC, 32–3, is cautiously doubtful. See below and Dunbar, *WTJ*, 337. Dunbar, 'Eschatology', 112–28, decides with some reserve in favour of his chiliasm.
[168] Seen as evidence for his millennialism by e.g. Gry, *Millénarisme*, 94; Bietenhard, *SJT*, 19; Daniélou, *TJC*, 401; Blum, 730; Dunbar, 'Eschatology', 120, though at 127 he indicates that this and other evidence is not sufficient to allow a clear-cut judgement.
[169] Text to be found in Sedlacek.
[170] We might add *HomNum.* VII. 1, 4; *CRom.* 11, 13 *CSSol.* III. 12; *SelPss.* (Lomm. xiii. 102–3). In the last named passage Origen even says that the seventh is a symbol for this world and the eighth is a symbol of the age to come.
[171] Daniélou, *TJC*, 401. Altaner-Stuiber, 166, on the other hand think that 'Hippolytus wrote his world chronicle in order to show that the hopes for the coming of the thousand year kingdom, still widespread among Christians, were foolish'.

[Hippolytus] does maintain that the world will last six thousand years, corresponding to the six days of the creation, and that afterwards will come the reign of Christ, of which the Sabbath is the type, but the parallel is not pressed so far as to insist upon the same duration for his antitypical Sabbath as for his antitypical working-day; and he elsewhere speaks of the Second Advent in such a way as to leave no room for a millennium. It is at least remarkable, that though he again and again enlarges on eschatological subjects he is wholly silent on this one point, even where the subject would naturally lead him to state the doctrine [viz., chiliasm], if he held it.[172]

Though he adopts (in the *CD*) the world-week scheme in some form, Hippolytus, like Theophilus of Antioch before him,[173] never speaks of an end to the seventh day (Augustine, *CivDei* xx. 7, points out that the seventh day in Genesis has no evening!). The kingdom Hippolytus speaks of as being instituted on the 'seventh day' is the 'kingdom of the saints' of Daniel 7 (*CD* IV. 23). This kingdom, according to the interpretation of Hippolytus, is given to the saints when Christ returns to render to every man according to his works (*CD* IV. 10. 1–2), *after* the general resurrection (*Antichr.* 65; *CD* IV. 58) and corresponds not to the millennial period of Revelation 20, but to the ultimate and eternal kingdom of the new heavens and new earth of Revelation 21–2 (see the citations of Rev. 22: 15; 21: 8 in *Antichr.* 65 and cf. ch. 5 and *CD* IV. 23).[174] Hippolytus thus draws a distinction between this 'kingdom of the saints' and the 'kingdom of Christ' which has already begun with the ascension of the Son to the Father's throne in heaven (*Antichr.* 61, commenting on Rev. 12: 5; *Noet.* 6, 18).

This present kingdom of Christ, moreover, is a kingdom of peculiar qualities:

[172] Lightfoot, *AF* I. 2. 387. See also Stonehouse, 104. Dunbar, 'Eschatology', 128, admits that 'the entire treatise on the Antichrist contains nothing that would point to a millenarian outlook'.

[173] Daniélou, *TJC*, 401 notes the similarities between Hippolytus and Theophilus on chronology and opines that both imply 'that the year 6,000 will begin the Messianic reign which is to fill the seventh millennium, and that the year 7,000 will be the end of the world and the founding of the heavenly city'. Nicholson, *JTS*, 296, states, however, that Theophilus 'showed no interest in either millennia or the End of the World'. Rather, it was left for Lactantius to combine with the dates worked out by Theophilus 'the pattern of the cosmic week' (308). Grant, *Apologists*, 156, concurs: the chronology of Theophilus 'has no eschatological referent at all, and this is why all his successors except Lactantius neglected it'.

[174] Also, *On the Quails and Manna*, 'What is the Sabbath if not the heavenly kingdom' (Brock, 198), though Brock is uncertain of its authenticity.

And in order that no one entertain the notion that his is a temporary (πρόσκαιρος) or earthly (ἐπίγειος) kingdom which was given to him by the Father, the prophet says, 'his authority is an eternal authority which shall not pass away, and His kingdom shall not be destroyed' [Dan. 7: 14]. Therefore the Father, 'having subjected all things' [1 Cor. 15: 27] to His own Son, 'things in heaven, things on earth and things under the earth' [Eph. 1: 22], demonstrated him to be the firstborn among all things [Col. 1: 18]. (*CD* IV. 11. 4)[175]

But temporary and earthly are precisely what the chiliast millennium must be. Hippolytus appears on the contrary to be *refuting* chiliasm (see also *CD* IV. 9. 3–4). Traces of antichiliastic sentiment are perhaps also to be found in his work, *The Blessings of Moses*. When the saints in general reign with Christ they will have no more need of 'corruptible nourishments' or 'earthly food' but will taste of 'the incorruptible Bread of Life' and be 'watered from eternal beverage'.[176] This denial of literal eating and drinking in preference for the 'Bread of Life' appears again in Origen's polemic against the chiliasts (*Princ.* II. 11. 2–3; cf. *CMatt.* XVII. 35; *CSSol.* prologue) and might fairly be understood against the backdrop of the claims of Cerinthus, Papias, or Irenaeus—or possibly of the overly-expectant Syrian and Pontic bishops he mentions later in *CD* IV. 18–19—that the saints must enjoy material food and drink in the millennial kingdom.

Another claim that Hippolytus was a chiliast has been mounted from the above-mentioned extracts from Bar Salibi. One of these purports to be Hippolytus' answer to the calumnies of 'the heretic Gaius' against the teaching of Revelation 20.[177] It must at least be

---

[175] Translations from the Greek of Hippolytus are my own, based, unless otherwise noted, upon the text of Bonwetsch–Achelis.

[176] Brière–Mariès–Mercier, 197–9.

[177] It has thus been identified as the work *Chapters Against Gaius* mentioned only by Ebed-Jesu, a Syrian who flourished around 1300. John Gwynn, the discoverer of Bar Salibi's commentary, believed the *Chapters* to have been a separate work (Gwynn, 405, 408), a judgement perpetuated by Achelis's arrangement, Bonwetsch–Achelis, 229–47. Lightfoot (*AF* I. 2, 395) believed they were but part of another work on the Apocalypse. (The statue of Hippolytus lists one ὑπὲρ τοῦ κατὰ Ἰωάννην εὐαγγελίου καὶ ἀποκαλύψεως.) Recent Hippolytan scholarship supports Lightfoot. Nautin, *Dossier*, 146, and Prigent 'Hippolyte', 412, echoed by Richard, *StudPatr.*, 69, find no evidence of another work by Hippolytus on the Apocalypse besides the lost *Apology on the Apocalypse and the Gospel of John* and believe the *Chapters* to have been gleaned by Bar Salibi from a work dependent at some stage upon this *Apology*. Ebed Jesu, they conclude, misunderstood Bar Salibi's comments and supposed the *Chapters* to have been a separate work.

said that its exegesis of the thousand years is unique among early[178] Christian expositions. Bietenhard gives the standard explanation when he says concerning this text, 'Hippolytus places the millennial hope within the schema of a universal week of 7000 years'.[179] But here is what the text says:[180]

And the number of the years is not the number of days, but it represents the space of one day, glorious and perfect... 'This is the day which the Lord hath made'... Accordingly, when with the eye of the spirit John saw the glory of that day, he likened it to the space of a thousand years; according to the saying, 'One day in the world of the righteous is as a thousand years.' And by the number he shows that day to be perfect, for those that are faithful.

For this Hippolytus, one day does not equal a thousand years, rather, a thousand years equal one day. That is, the thousand years of Revelation 20 is a figure, a symbol for a single, glorious, and perfect day, and this day has no appearance of belonging to a world-week chronology. This instead is a complete reversal of the normal cosmic-day idea. Such a view does preserve the futurity of the millennium but it stretches to the breaking point the conception of the millennium as a period of earthly rule and, though it is the strongest evidence, it is hardly adequate evidence for Hippolytus being a chiliast.[181]

As to his view of the intermediate state,[182] Hippolytus believes that Christ in his great work of redemption has effected the release of the souls of the righteous dead from Hades (*Antichr.* 45, cf. 26; *Song* fr. 1; *De David et Goliath* 11).[183] Believers who die in the gospel era spend the interim until the resurrection in the blessed environs of heaven (*CD* I. 21. 4–5). One of the most poetic and quotable exhibitions of this is found in *Antichr.* 59, where he develops the metaphor of the church as a ship:

---

[178] We find a somewhat similar explanation made in AD 397 by Hilarianus in his *The Progress of Time* 18. 'To the saints the resurrection will be one day, but this day of the saints will be prolonged so much that to the evil who will be living with pain in the world it will number a thousand years' (translation of McGinn, 53).

[179] Bietenhard, *SJT*, 18.   [180] From Gwynn's translation of the Syriac.

[181] Stonehouse, 107, 'His language... definitely excludes the chiliastic scheme ...'.

[182] I am assuming here that the fragment *De universo*, commonly attributed to Hippolytus, is not from the same author who wrote the *CD*, *Antichr.*, and various other exegetical works placed in Loi's group A. For discussion see Hill, *VC*, which interacts with the contrary assessment of Richard, 'Hippolyte', cols. 542, 565–8.

[183] Garittè, *CSCO*.

The church has mariners on the right and left as holy angels, assessors
through whom she is always governed and defended.

There is in her a ladder which leads aloft to the sailyard as an image of
the sign of Christ's passion, which is drawing the faithful unto the
ascent to heaven.

There are top sails upon the sailyard, being united on high as orders
(τάξεις) of prophets, martyrs and apostles at rest in the kingdom of
Christ.

The souls of the faithful, with the special orders of prophet,
martyr and apostle, are said to be now at rest in Christ's heavenly
kingdom. In chapter 31 he apostrophizes to address the prophets
Daniel and Isaiah whom, though asleep as regards their bodily
condition, he addresses 'as living ones (ζῶσιν), and rightly so. For
you already possess (ἔχετε) the crown of life and incorruption laid
up for you in the heavens'. The same is said of David in *De David
et Goliath* 12. 1. Stephen also is said to have endured and, after his
stoning, to have been crowned by God (*CD* II. 36. 5). Those, again,
who have departed pure from this world now possess (ἔχοντες) their
heavenly crowns (*CD* II. 37. 3).[184]

There is yet one very salient statement of Hippolytus' which
seems to reveal a non-chiliastic exegesis of Revelation 20. In *CD*
II. 37. 4 he states that the one who does not shrink from martyrdom
to rejoin this world of temptation and vice but exits from it worthily
in martyrdom, 'is no longer judged at all but judges, possessing his
own portion in the first resurrection'![185] Bonwetsch's text accents
κρινει (judges) as a future, κρινεῖ (will judge),[186] but the point of the
sentence seems instead to be that the martyr's condition at the time
of his death undergoes a complete reversal as soon as he dies. This
thought is nicely paralleled by a comment on Luke 22: 42 attributed
to Dionysius of Alexandria[187] about Christ's death: 'He passed from
His passion to impassibility, and from death to deathlessness, and
from the position of one judged to that of one judging (καὶ ἀντὶ τοῦ
κρίνεσθαι τὸ κρίνειν), and from subjection under the despot's power

---

[184] See also *ApostTrad.* XXXVI. 5, 12 in the *nones* and *mattins* prayers are mentioned the 'souls of the righteous' who praise and glorify God along with (in the
latter text) the ministering angels.

[185] οὗτος γὰρ οὐκέτι οὐδὲ κρίνεται ἀλλὰ κρινεῖ, μέρος ἴδιον ἐν τῇ πρώτῃ ἀναστάσει ἔχων.

[186] Followed by Lefèvre, SC: 129, 'il sera juge' (Lefèvre); 29, 'c'est lui qui jugera'
(Bardy).

[187] Text found in Feltoe, *Dionysius*, 240. Feltoe, 229–31, doubts its authenticity
as a work of Dionysius but Bienert, 43, expresses a more favourable opinion.

to the exercise of kingly dominion (τὸ βαcιλεύειν).' Here is expressed
the same idea of an immediate exchange of position through the
passage of death—Jesus was judged but now he is judging. This
interpretation of κρινει as present in CD ii. 37. 4 also finds support
in that judging prerogatives for the martyr after death are found
previous to Hippolytus in Clement of Alexandria (Strom. vi. xiii.
106. 2, though not restricted to martyrs), and soon afterwards in
Origen (ExhMart. 28), Dionysius (Eusebius, HE vi. 42. 5) and in the
letter of the Roman confessors to Cyprian (Ep. xxxi. 3), all of which
will be examined below.

Having a part (ἔχων μέρος) in the 'first resurrection', of course, is
what allows the blessed of Revelation 20: 4–6 to 'live and reign
with Christ' during the thousand years. 'Judgement' (κρίμα) is given
to these (20: 4). Thus the initial obscurity of this allusion of
Hippolytus[188] is relieved by the parallels just cited and by the
recollection that in the eschatology of Hippolytus Christ's kingdom
exists in and from heaven and departed saints dwell in it (with
their crowns). This piece from CD ii. 37. 4 only completes the puzzle.
The 'first resurrection' for Hippolytus is apparently the resurrection
of the souls (Rev. 20: 4) of the righteous, pre-eminently those of the
martyrs,[189] to join Christ in the kingdom of heaven (cf. Antichr. 59;
CD iii 31. 3). The millennium of Revelation 20 would thus be the
present age. It is true that this view is contrary to that which is
contained in the Chapters Against Gaius, where the thousand-year
day is entirely future. Perhaps this points to a change of opinion
on the part of Hippolytus. Or, what is more likely, the Hippolytus
responsible for the Chapters is someone other than the author of
the CD.[190] There are more problems posed by the extract on Rev.
20 besides the one already noticed. It deals also with the binding
of Satan in Rev. 20: 2–3. Hippolytus here not only denies that this
binding has yet taken place but he denies, against the objection of
Gaius, that 'the strong one' has been bound in any continuing sense
according to Matthew 12: 29. This is quite difficult to believe in the
light of the distinguished place in Christian preaching and apologetic the theme of Satan's past binding had had amongst his

---

[188] Dunbar, 'Eschatology', 124.

[189] But not exclusively, see especially ii. 38. 5.

[190] Prigent, 'Hippolyte', 411–12 (also 400–1), thinks that the work which Bar
Salibi had before him was not one of Hippolytus' treatises at all but a source book,
a catena of extracts from the exegetical works of Hippolytus.

immediate predecessors (cf. Melito, *PP* 102; Claudius Apolinarius (Eusebius, *ChronPasc.* praef.); Irenaeus, *AH* III. 8. 2; III. 18. 6; III. 23. 1; III. 23. 7; V. 21. 3). Indeed, Hippolytus the author of *CD* IV. 33. 4–5 contends that Christ in his first advent *has* bound Satan (the contradiction is observed by Gwynn)![191] The view of the extract is entirely opposed to this. Moreover, the order of eschatological events in the extract should also be contrasted to that contained in *Antichr.* 5 and *CD* IV. 58.[192] At any rate we appear to have in the self-contained eschatology of Hippolytus' *CD*, his *Antichr.*, and not contradicted by any of the works of his corpus in its widest estimate, the Bar Salibi extract on Revelation 20 excepted, the view that the millennium covers the age of the gospel, while Christ's kingdom bases itself in heaven until it visits the earth in judgement and instigates the eternal dominion of the saints.

Here I add that this analysis, which would separate the *Chapters* from the exegetical works just mentioned, is corroborated by Loi, who also recognizes a disparity between the *Chapters* and the *CD*.[193] Loi places the former work alongside the *Refutation* and the other works mentioned on the statue as the product of the Roman presbyter Hippolytus.

To summarize, if one wants to ascribe to a single Hippolytus all the works listed in, say, M. Richard's or Quasten's treatments we would have, I believe, still no solid grounds for maintaining that this Hippolytus was a chiliast. I would in this case only insist that the fragment *De universo* and the excerpt from the *Chapters Against Gaius* on Rev. 20 be kept separate (but not as products of the same hand) from the author of the writings of group A, as identified above, adding *On the Great Song* to that group. If on the other hand one is prepared to accept the theory of (at least) dual authorship within the Hippolytan canon, what we have observed in this section leads us to conclude that neither Hippolytus stood in the chiliastic line, though the author of the *Chapters Against Gaius*, whoever he was, put forth a different non-chiliastic view than that which shows up in *CD* II. 37. 4. If we accept the *Chapters* as genuine we may conjec-

---

[191] Gwynn, 418.

[192] Other Irenaean themes in this extract (see Dunbar, 'Eschatology', 148) and indeed in other remarks of Bar Salibi's on Rev. 20 (see Prigent, 'Hippolyte', 404–7) are credible as coming through the mediation of one who was a student of Irenaeus. But many of these particular Irenaean parallels find no real correspondence in the remaining works of Hippolytus.

[193] Loi, 'L'identità', 87–8.

ture that its author agreed with Gaius that Revelation 20 taught a future kingdom on earth (hence Gaius' distaste for the book) but that in order to defend the book as apostolic he answered Gaius' antimaterialistic concerns by interpreting the millennium as really a single, glorious day, applying a new twist to the long tortured formula, 'one day is as a thousand years'.

If the Hippolytus of group A was in any sense a student of Irenaeus,[194] it is all the more remarkable that he did not adopt the eschatology with which his mentor had brought his greatest treatise to a climax. The eschatology of this Hippolytus in fact bears a surprisingly close resemblance to the type which draws Tertullian's attack in *De anima* 55 (§ 1.2.3 above).[195] It is an eschatology which views the departed saints as reigning with Christ in his present heavenly kingdom until that great day when he returns in glory to establish the visible reign of the saints.[196] If this Hippolytus wrote in Rome, he will be seen in the trajectory of non-chiliasm represented there in Clement, Hermas, and possibly 5Ez. If he hailed from Asia Minor we will add one more witness to the list of early Asian non-chiliasts which includes at least Polycarp, Marcianus, the early Irenaeus, and most probably Melito.

Moreover, in Hippolytus, whose *CD* we may confidently date to the earliest years of the third century, we would seem to have an intriguing and highly important relic of a non-chiliastic exegesis of Revelation 20: 4–6, wherein John's 'first resurrection' is viewed as taking place when the martyred soul rises to join Christ the judge in his heavenly dominion (*CD* II. 37. 4 cf. III. 31. 3).

6. CLEMENT OF ALEXANDRIA[197]

Clement of Alexandria has more to say about the afterlife than any Christian author we have investigated so far. Nobody familiar with

---

[194] Simonetti, 'Ipotesi', 155–6, believes that both Hippolyti knew the works of Irenaeus.

[195] Waszink, *Anima*, 5*, 6*, is confident that the years 210–13 provide the limits for the composition of this treatise. Hippolytus' *CD* is usually placed about the year 202 and *Antichr.* perhaps just earlier (Quasten, ii. 170; Bardy–Lefèvre, SC, 12, 14).

[196] Hippolytus' doctrine of the bodily resurrection at the last day is, of course, utterly conventional (e.g. *CD* II. 28; IV. 56; *Antichr.* 65).

[197] The Greek text used throughout is from GCS 12; 52 (15); 17. Unless otherwise noted, English translations of *Protr.*, *Paed.*, *Strom.*, and *QDS* are the translations of William Wilson in *ANF* ii and translations of *Theod.* are Casey's, *Excerpta*.

his works will be surprised by the assertion that he was on the one hand a believer in a 'heavenly' intermediate state of the soul and on the other that he was no patron of millennialism.

For Clement redemption is προκοπή, ethical and intellectual 'advancement' upward, both spatially and metaphysically, to the goal of assimilation to God. Death, far from impeding the process of προκοπή, gives it a tremendous boost, at least for the Christian (e.g. *Strom*. IV. vi. 44. 1; IV. vii. 68. 1; VI. xi. 80. 1; *EclProph*. 14. 1).[198] The body, though good and by no means evil by nature, is yet inferior to the soul (*Strom*. IV. xxvi. 164. 3), and the latter, being less susceptible to vice, will find its improvement capabilities enhanced through separation from the body (*Strom*. VI. vi. 46. 3; cf. IV. xxii. 140. 2). Therefore the time after death sees the continuation of education, purification, and even of disciplinary punishments for the great majority of believers[199] until the highest level of advancement is gained in the immediate circle of those who surround God the Father.[200]

---

[198] There is, of course, in Clement's theology a large measure of 'realized eschatology' attainable to the true Gnostic while in this life (*Strom*. IV. xxiii; V. vi. 39. 4–40. 4; V. xi. 73. 3; VI. xii. 105. 1; VII. x. 57. 5; VII. xiii. 82. 2, 5).

[199] See Wytzes, 151. Fischer, *Todesgedanken*, 284, claims that 'The concept of purgatory appears for the first time with him.' Clement's persuasion that most Christians are in need of further training (παιδεία) and purification after death and his articulation of a mechanism for ethical and ontological progress in the other world could be seen as conducive to the rise of a conception of purgatory. But this is only because he includes in his notion of progress the idea of purgation. Irenaeus, as we have seen, implies by his doctrine of the millennium that further exercise in godliness is necessary for the redeemed after death (in fact, after the resurrection), but he seems unaware of any need for purgation or punishment. For the possible Valentinian influence here, see above, § I. 1. 2, n. 23.

[200] Clement gathers testimonies for his heavenly notion of the afterlife, as he does for other aspects of his theology, from pagan poets, playwrights, and philosophers; his cartography of the heavenly world could have been taken from a Valentinian's logbook, complete with angelic customs agents and other attendant angels who populate the skyward path (*Strom*. IV. xviii. 116. 2; 117. 2). He also speaks of an initiation into mysteries in the world above (*Protr*. XII. 118. 4; see also *Strom*. V. xii. 79. 1; VI. xii. 102. 1–2), though Osborn, *SCent.*, 223, is probably correct in stressing that this is merely a subtle metaphorical device (cf. Lilla, 154). It is however very important that for Clement the heavenly journey of the soul, despite the plethora of images borrowed from pagan and heretical thought, is a journey to the home of another, which can only become man's home by adoption, by grace (*Strom*. V. xii. 83. 1) and through moral and intellectual progress (Fischer, *Todesgedanken*, 282). Man, it is true, partook of a divine inbreathing at his creation, 'But it is not as a portion of God that the Spirit is in each of us' (*Strom*. V. xiii. 874–88. cf. IV. xxvi. 167. 4; III. xiv. 94, on which passages, see Héring, *BEHESR*, 32–4). (The aorist ἔγνω in *Strom*. VII. xiii. 82. 5 relates to the Gnostic's former life on earth, not to 'the pre-existent state' of the soul, *contra* Mayer, *Miscellanies* VII, 321.) Pre-

Clement's eschatology is thus bound up very closely not only with this over-arching conception of redemption as upward progress but with his anthropology, his metaphysics[201] and with his peculiar cosmology as well. It will not serve our purpose, however, to give a complete summary of Clement's eschatology, its sources and its integration within these larger contours of his thought. We can only focus here on a few, limited aspects of it which have an immediate relevance to our study.

1. Eschatology and History

Though he shows no disposition to favour millennialism and shows perhaps no awareness of millennialists themselves (though see *Strom.* VI. ix. 75. 1), Clement does believe there will be an end to this present world order (cf. *QDS* 36) and he is convinced that prophecy has revealed a continuation of persecution for the Church until that end arrives (*Strom.* VI. xviii. 167). He believes in a future coming of the Antichrist, in relation to Matthew 24: 24 (*Theod.* 9. 1), and a future return of Christ with his angelic host (*QDS* 42. 18; *JohPrim.*, on 2. 23; *EclProph.* 56. 6). There is a judgement coming, and before it arrives the heretics must be admonished to repent (*Strom.* VII. xvi. 102. 3; cf. VII. ii. 12. 4).

A perceived difficulty for Clement's eschatology is in the preservation of a traditional doctrine of the resurrection of the body.[202] Clement's ambiguous language and his seeming acceptance of Stoic psychology enable Klaus Schmöle to maintain that for Clement the resurrection body, being the 'spiritual body' of 1 Cor. 15. 44, is continuous not with the mortal, physical body but with the soulish-spiritual aspect of man, which is in reality a very refined corporeal

---

existence is expressly denied in *EclProph.* 17. 1–2. The soul's assimilation to God, its deification, is after its own order and 'according to power', it is emphatically not 'according to nature' (*Theod.* 17. 4; *Strom.* II. xvii. 77. 4; IV. xxvi. 168. 2; V. x. 63. 8; VI. xvi. 138. 4; xvii. 150. 3; VII. iii. 13. 2; 16. 6). See also Chadwick, *Classical Tradition*, 49 and J. D. Turner, *NovT*, 342–3 (on the distinction between the *visio dei* in Jewish and in Platonic visionary literatures).

[201] Clement holds to a notion of a chain of being extending from God, the highest and first Principle, to the Logos, then through the several ranks of angelic beings down to man (*Strom.* VII. ii. 9).

[202] The body is 'by nature subject to dissolution' (*Strom.* II. xx. 118. 5) and Clement once says 'conformity with the image and likeness is not meant for the body' (*Strom.* II. xix. 102. 6), though neither of these statements is necessarily a denial of a bodily resurrection.

substance.[203] The resurrection 'of the body' is then the progressive advance and ultimate arrival of the spiritual body (the spiritual man) at its highest stage.[204] Through much of Clement's writings Schmöle's analysis will encounter no obstacles. Still, while we must not hesitate to admit that the force of an intellectual environment in which the idea of a bodily resurrection was repugnant has made itself deeply felt on Clement, Schmöle never gives a satisfactory explanation of the 'visible resurrection'[205] which comes at the end of the world according to QDS 42. 15. And, meditation upon 'the resurrection of the flesh in the resounding skin'[206] (Paed. II. iv. 41. 4) would seem odd if there were no reunion with a transformed, sarkic substance in view. It must also be kept in mind that our assessment of Clement has to be made in the absence of his promised treatise on the subject (see Paed. II. x. 104. 3). Finally, the situation is aggravated by the fact that the bulk of our knowledge of Clement's theology derives from the Stromateis, a composition the peculiar esoteric character of which, when compared to his other works, needs to be taken into account.[207] It is especially in the Paedagogus (e.g. I. vi. 28. 3; x. 92. 1; II. iv. 41. 4; II. x. 100. 3; x. 104. 3) that the doctrine receives a place which seems to be quite in keeping with traditional orthodox emphasis: 'the end is reserved till the resurrection of those who believe' (Paed. I. vi. 28. 3).

2. Individual Eschatology

Hades, once the collecting point for all the dead, now, since Christ's deportation of its righteous captives, receives only the sinful (Strom.

---

[203] Schmöle, 3–7, 128, etc.

[204] Schmöle accordingly believes that the conceptions of advancement, training, teaching, discipleship, purification, assimilation to God, and union may be analysed as 'resurrection' (137–8, cf. 3–7, 128, 135, etc.). Only part of the evidence for this interpretation rests on the controverted assignment to Clement of those sections of Theod. which advance a materialist psychology (see Casey, Excerpta, 10; Sagnard, 87).

[205] Ἀνάcταcιc βλεπομένη. Wilson, perhaps reading ἐλπομένη, translates 'the resurrection for which we hope'.

[206] Τῆc capκὸc τὴν ἀνάcταcιν ἐν ἠχοῦντι τῷ δέρματι. Wilson mistakenly has 'dead' in place of 'skin'.

[207] Marsh, 70, 'We must not forget that there are two Clements, the Alexandrine philosopher and the Christian evangelist.' Cf. Fischer, Todesgedanken, 274; Daniélou, GM, 455, 457. The elaborated eschatological tenets of the Stromateis, consisting of detailed information about the advance of the soul in the hereafter and the gradations of the angelic hierarchy constitute the esoteric, more Gnosticized form of Clement's echatology.

VI. vi. 44. 5–47. 3, where Clement is dependent upon Hermas, cf. IV. vii. 45. 1).

Clement endorses a familiar view of martyrdom and the martyr's lot, one not to be found in Gnosticism. The martyr 'hastens to God' (πρὸς ... σπεύδει (τὸν) θεόν Strom. IV. iv. 13. 2); 'goes to the Lord, his friend' (πρὸς φίλον τὸν κύριον ... ἔρχεται Strom. IV. iv. 14. 2), martyrdom being 'the perfect work of love' (Strom. IV. iv. 14. 3). Martyrdom is the short route to the divine presence (Strom. IV. xi. 80. 1) because it is itself a 'glorious purification' (Strom. IV. xv. 104. 1). But for Clement, the martyr is not essentially distinguished by his loss of blood, for the pure soul 'is a witness both by life and word, in whatever way it may be released from the body,—shedding faith as blood along its whole life till its departure' (Strom. IV. iv. 15. 3). Knowledge as well as martyrdom is 'quick in purifying' and conveys man through 'the mystic stages of advancement' (Strom. VII. x. 56. 7–57. 1) Clement's 'true Gnostic' who dies in peace therefore is also able to 'drink the cup'[208] and to 'tread in the footsteps of the apostles'[209] (Strom. VI. ix. 75. 1–2) and to join those who are to be enrolled in the heavens (QDS 21. 6).

For our purposes, one of the most significant facets of his thought is his frequent allusion to kingdom and reigning, never in relation to an earthly regime but only to a heavenly one. That the time after death can be a time of sharing God's reign in God's heavenly kingdom we learn in QDS 32. 1–6: 'Aspire to dwell in the heavens, and to reign (βασιλεῦσαι) with God. This kingdom a man imitating God will give thee. By receiving a little here, there through all ages He will make thee a dweller with Him' (cf. also 42. 16). Heaven is the 'chosen land' which saints will inherit and rule over as promised in Jeremiah 3: 19 (Strom. V. xiv. 139. 1).

The journey to heaven at life's end is quite clearly in Clement's mind what Jesus meant by his enigmatic 'taking of the kingdom of heaven by force', in Matthew 11: 12; Luke 16: 16 (Paed. III. vii. 39. 1–2; Strom. IV. ii. 5. 3; V. iii. 16. 7; VI. xvii. 149. 5; QDS 21. 3 cf. 42. 19). Receiving the 'eternal habitations' of Luke 16: 9 also

---

[208] A common martyrological phrase, Matt. 20: 22 = Mark 10: 38; Mark 14: 36 = Luke 22: 42; John 18: 11; AscIsa. 5. 13; MartPolyc. 14. 1; Origen, ExhMart. 28; Clement, Strom. I. vi. 51. 1–2.

[209] Another common martyrological phrase, cf. 1 Pet. 2: 21; Ignatius, Eph. 12. 2; MartPolyc. 22. 1; Clement, Strom. VI. xiii. 107. 2; QDS 21. 6.

meant for Clement reigning in God's kingdom directly after death
(QDS 31. 6–32. 6).

That the twenty-four elders in Revelation 4: 4; 11: 16, etc. (Strom.
VI. xiii. 106. 1–108. 1) depict the state of human souls (not angels)
immediately after death (Strom. VI. xiii. 105. 1), or for some, after
an interval of training and purification in the other world, is taken
for granted by Clement. These advanced Christians, distinguished
not by race, not even by position in the earthly Church but by
Gnostic piety, are the presbyterate of the heavenly Church, after
which the earthly presbyterate is patterned. The number twenty-
four is not exact, for this presbyterate is continually being added
to as more perfected Christians, following in the footsteps of the
apostles, enter its ranks from this world, 'who sit on thrones with
other gods that have been first put in their places by the Saviour'
(Strom. VII. x. 56. 5–6). The function of these presbyters in the
Church above is to be both judges and administrators (κριταί τε
καὶ διοικηταί). A question for us is whether this picture of the
heavenly elders might be partially inspired by the profile in Revelation 20 of those who reign with Christ the thousand years.

Clement says of him who is destined to join the heavenly eldership, 'he will sit down on the four-and-twenty thrones, judging the
people (τὸν λαὸν κρίνων), as John says in the Apocalypse' (Strom.
VI. xiii. 106. 2). But the passages in the Apocalypse which concern
the twenty four elders say nothing expressly about their judging
function. Clement may simply have confused with some section of
the Apocalypse one of the Gospel statements in Matthew 19: 28
(used for the intermediate state, as we have seen, in ActThom. 80),
Luke 22: 30, or even Wisd. 3. 8 (which he does cite elsewhere, Strom.
IV. xvi. 104. 2). On the other hand, it is quite possible that Revelation 20: 4, which says of those who 'sat on thrones' that 'judgement
was given to them', has tinted his picture of John's twenty-four
elders.

There is one more possible trace of influence from Revelation
20: 1–9 in Clement's works which adds credence to this suggestion.
Clement frequently indicates that it is the human destiny to become
changed into the nature of angels, but in EclProph. 57. 4 he
enlightens us about the final stages of this transformation. Men
who have been transformed into angels are instructed for a
thousand years by true angels. These angels then are promoted to
the rank of archangel and the trained angelic men become in turn

teachers of the less perfected of humanity. But why the thousand-year interval? Plato in Republic x. 615 and Phaedrus 248–9 posits a period of a thousand years between incarnations of the soul. But Clement did not believe in metempsychosis and it is difficult to imagine why he would have employed Plato's figure for such an alien conception. Clement's conception might be thought to be just as alien to the context of Revelation 20. Yet it conforms rather well to his statements on the twenty four elders, where he says 'the grades (προκοπαί) here in the Church, of bishops, presbyters, deacons, are imitations of the angelic glory', and to his statements about a promotion for some from the heavenly diaconate to the heavenly eldership (Strom. VI. xiii. 107. 2–3). It may thus be seen how the unspecified text in the book of Revelation which furnished him with the idea that the heavenly elders 'will sit down on the four-and-twenty thrones, judging the people (τὸν λαὸν κρίνων)' (Strom. VI. xiii. 106. 2) may have been Revelation 20, which passage also provided him with the number 1000 to meld into such a scheme as we see above. A point in favour of this connection with Revelation 20 is that it provides a background for some of Origen's statements in De principiis II. 11. The heavenly elders in Clement's view sit on thrones ruling and administrating, and those whom he says are ascending through the angelic grades are engaged in teaching those of lower rank. For Origen these functions explicitly meet in the persons of the 'princes and rulers' in Princ. II. 11, as we shall presently see.

We have abundant proof that the non-chiliast Clement, speaking sometimes as he stands at the penumbra of Gnosticism and at other times within more recognizably orthodox margins, believed also that human souls will reign, judge and be part of the administration of the heavenly kingdom following directly upon their earthly sojourn. This is significant in the light of the similar, though less explicit, language of earlier authors about departed Christians participating in some way in Christ's heavenly kingdom, and in the light of comparably explicit language used by Hippolytus, the author of the Acts of Thomas, and by slightly later writers, as we shall see in future sections of our study. Though we cannot be certain that Clement had an interpretation of Revelation 20 (we have noted two cases wherein influence from the passage is possible), an equation of the millennial reign of the saints with Christ as described in Revelation 20: 4–6 with the intermediate state of the soul in heaven, though adapted to a scheme quite unknown to the author of Revelation, would have fit Clement's eschatology perfectly.

7. ORIGEN

The writings of Origen uncover some very important data for our investigation. Though the beginnings of effective opposition to chiliast views are often attributed to him[210] it is generally not recognized that Origen had any constructive interpretation of the millennium of Revelation 20.[211] His contribution is sometimes seen in terms of a more or less complete internalizing of eschatology: 'the focus was not upon the manifestation of the kingdom within this world but within the soul of the believer.'[212] But after an examination of his writings in the light of the connection posited by Irenaeus we shall be able to state positively that for him *the millennium is the intermediate state.*[213]

1. Answering Chiliasm

Origen's lengthiest discussion of millennialism and millennialists is in the relatively early work, *De principiis*. We find in book II, chapter 11 the main points of his reply to chiliasm and these remain fundamentally consistent throughout all of his writings. His onslaught is practically merciless, as he scolds the literalists (the term chiliast was not yet known) for being too lazy to use their heads and too hospitable to their carnal impulses. Yet his method is not simply to overpower by denunciation and ridicule. He gives an answer to many of the concerns of those he is criticizing, points out the direction proper exegesis ought to take and enunciates a

---

[210] Maier, 87–8; Dolan, 853; Montgomery, 358.

[211] Swete, 265; cf. Bietenhard, *SJT*, 20, 23.

[212] Sandeen, 201; cf. Dolan, 853. Hanson, *CHB*, 434, says Origen dealt with the Bible's eschatological language in two ways: by allegorizing it, in Gnostic fashion, into moral, spiritual, or mystical experience, or, by dissolving it within an immense vista of pre-mundane and post-mundane existences.

[213] It is valid, indeed, necessary, to use the term 'intermediate state' in speaking of Origen's thought. In the preface 5 to *Princ.* he calls apostolic the teaching that the soul is rewarded with blessedness or with punishments upon its departure from this world, and he clearly distinguishes this state from the time of the resurrection of the body.

positive alternative to chiliast eschatology. This alternative is nothing other than his doctrine of the intermediate state.

A dominating theme in Origen's condemnation of chiliasm is that
the literalists look for the fulfilment of the promises in a corporeal
world 'according to the manner of things in this life', desiring 'that
what now is should exist again' (*Princ.* II. 11. 2),[214] a world which
to Origen's mind would be unpalatable in the extreme. Their conception of the resurrected body is that it too is so like the present
one as to be again in need of physical aliments and pleasures (*Princ.*
II. 10. 3; 11. 2; *CMatt.* XVII. 35; *CSSol.* prol.; *CPs.* 4 in *Philocalia*
XXVI. 6). These Christians even believe that marital bonds will be
reimposed upon the resurrected (*Princ.* II. 11. 2; *CMatt.* XVII. 35; *CPs.*
4). Consistent with such 'worldliness' is their expectation of an
earthly Jerusalem rebuilt to the literal specifications of the prophecies of Isaiah 54: 11ff; 60: 5–10; Revelation 21 and others (*Princ.*
II. 11. 2; *Cels.* VII. 28) and an anticipation of their own promotion to
positions of lordship over the nations (Luke 19: 17–19), whose
spoils will be laid at their feet (*Princ.* II. 11. 2).

For Origen's part, the chiliast ideal of the resurrection body,
besides deeply offending his sense of what is worthy of divine
promises, is a blatant contravention of Paul's doctrine of the resurrection of a spiritual body (*Princ.* II. 11. 2). The riddle posed by
promises of eating and drinking in the kingdom (Matt. 26: 29, among
others), is solved 'according to the understanding of the apostles'
by recognizing that 'the saints will eat indeed, but ... it will be the
bread of life, which may nourish the soul with the food of truth
and wisdom ...' (*Princ.* II. 11. 3, cf. *CSSol.* prol.; III. 6). In the bosom
of Abraham, Isaac, and Jacob the saints will recline in the Father's
kingdom eating of the tree of life and drinking wine from the true
vine (John 15: 1), the new wine Christ promised in Matthew 26: 29.[215]

OT promises of restored glory to Jerusalem are by all means
precious to the Christian, but only as they are understood to refer
to the heavenly city (*Princ.* IV. 22; *Cels.* VII. 30). Origen also deems
it a consequence of Paul's doctrines of the heavenly Jerusalem (Gal.
4: 26; Heb. 12: 22–3) and the 'Israel according to the Spirit' (1 Cor.
10: 18; Rom. 2: 28–9; 9: 6, 8) that there must be something in heaven
corresponding not only to the holy city but to the entire holy land
circumjacent to it (*Princ.* IV. 3. 7–8; *HomNum.* 28. 2). Thus in *Cels.*

---

[214] This continues to be a concern for Dionysius (Eusebius, *HE* VII. 24. 5).
[215] De Lubac-Doutreleau, homily 16. 4 on Gen. 43: 1.

VII. 29 the chiliasts' interest in the Judea below and their interpretation of prophecies which would seem to relate to this land are discounted on the basis of the curse of God which has fallen upon all the earth. Because this curse comprehends even the land of Judea, the promises of future glory must refer to the holy land in heaven:[216]

The apostle discusses this land ... and has found a meaning not contained by any Jewish mythological interpretation,[217] when he says 'But you have come to mount Sion and to the heavenly Jerusalem, the city of the living God, and to an innumerable company of angels.'

But the Jerusalem above is also that very place to which the 'spirits of just men made perfect' have been gathered (Heb. 12: 23). Hence at this point in his critique in *De principiis* Origen begins to speak of the intermediate state.[218]

By this food of wisdom, the understanding, being nourished to an entire and perfect condition like that in which man was made at the beginning, is restored to the image and likeness of God; so that, although an individual may depart from this life less perfectly instructed, but who has done works that are approved of, he will be capable of receiving instruction in that Jerusalem, the city of the saints, i.e. he will be educated and moulded, and made a living stone, a stone elect and precious, because he has undergone with firmness and constancy the struggles of life and the trials of piety ... And they also are to be understood to be the princes and rulers (*principes et rectores*) who both govern (*regunt*) those of lower rank, and instruct them, and teach them, and train them to divine things.

[216] Chadwick's translation.
[217] According to Daniélou, *GM*, 487, a reference to millennialism. This charge of 'Jewish mythological interpretation' is a recurring one on the part of Origen (and, probably following his lead, on the part of Eusebius, *HE* III. 39. 11, τινα ἄλλα μυθικώτερα) against chiliasm. The charge of Jewishness, made by most early critics of chiliasm, is significant. It is made because this is in fact how many non-Christian Jews interpreted such promises (*Princ.* IV. 3. 2; see Wilken, 304–7). But the scandalous nature of the charge is not always clearly brought out. Its basis is not anti-Semitism. Origen indicates that it is the *result* of this literalism, namely the fostering of false expectations of the Messiah and his kingdom, such as the wolf—'the four footed animal'—and the lamb feeding together (Isa. 11: 6–7, a prime chiliast proof text), which contributes directly to the Jewish rejection of Jesus and their justification of the crucifixion because such prophecies were not 'visibly accomplished' during the advent of Christ (*Princ.* IV. 2. 1; Wilken, 307). This is seen again in Tertullian's third book against Marcion. The Marcionites make common cause with Jewish unbelief in saying that the Christ promised in the OT has not yet come: 'The Jews were themselves quite persuaded that it was some other who came: so they not only rejected Him as a stranger, but slew him as an enemy' (*Marc.* III. 6, cf. III. 21, 23).
[218] Frederick Crombie's translation, *ANF*, iv.

This last sentence also introduces us to Origen's answer to the expectation of ruling over the heathen in the terrestrial kingdom of Christ. There will be those in the worlds of the afterlife more advanced in the things of God who will have governing and teaching authority over others.[219] We read elsewhere that the Gospel promises of authority over five or ten cities (Luke 19: 17–19) and of sitting on twelve thrones judging the twelve tribes of Israel (Matt. 19: 28) pertain apparently both to the intermediate state (*Princ.* IV. 3. 8; *ExhMart.* 14 (cf. Matt. 20: 21–3 in *ExhMart.* 28)) and to the ultimate state of things at the consummation (*HomNum.* 28. 4 (with Matt. 25: 23)).

God has placed within man a thirst for understanding, a desire to comprehend the meaning of the works of God, such as is indicated by Paul in Philippians 1: 23, who desired the far better estate of being with Christ through his exit from this life (*Princ.* II. 11. 5). Thus man will begin in the intermediate state to understand the mysteries of the Bible and of creation: 'not a little time may pass by until the reason of those things only which are upon the earth be pointed out to the worthy and deserving after their departure from life' (*Princ.* II. 11. 6). The departed saints then are enrolled in this divine tuition which, even if it is begun for most in a paradise 'situated on the earth',[220] is an escalating course which leads progressively upward through the many mansions spoken of in John 14: 2 to the kingdom of heaven in heaven. Those who are 'pure in heart, and holy in mind, and more practised in perception' will the more quickly ascend to this kingdom (the martyr most quickly of all, cf. *ExhMart.* 14), following him who passed into the heavens

---

[219] Though the context would make it appear that Origen is speaking of men in these capacities (it answers to the chiliast proposals that 'they are to be kings and princes, like most earthly monarchs who now exist', II. 11. 2), Crouzel says, 'It concerns the angels who instruct the blessed: *PArch.* III. 6. 9; *HomJér.* x. 8' (SC 253, 245, n. 18). I do not see that the passages he cites bear out his conclusion. From Clement's *EclProph.* 57. 4 we should surmise that men as well as angels take part in the teaching (cf. *Princ.* I. 6. 3). See below.

[220] *in aliquo in terra posito.* There is no doubt as to the meaning of these words as they stand. Yet one must wonder whether the 'earth' intended was not, instead of this 'dry land', part of that higher 'heaven and earth from which this present heaven and earth which we now see afterwards borrowed their names' (*Princ.* II. 9. 1), that 'earth' which the meek shall inherit (Matt. 5: 5, *Princ.* II. 3. 7) because, as Crouzel says, 'Usually, Origen allegorizes paradise as the place of origin of rational creatures and the future place of the blessed' (Crouzel, SC 253, 250, n. 43), neither of which places can possibly have been understood by Origen as being situated on this earth.

and said 'I will that where I am, these may be also' (John 17: 24). There in the celestial abodes the rational nature, no longer hindered by the downward pull of bodily things, is able to perceive truth and causes and to feast on its proper food, 'the contemplation and understanding of God' (*Princ.* II. 11. 7).

For Origen, chiliasm, besides employing a wrong-headed, literalistic approach to Biblical promises, besides surrendering to crass conceptions about the nature of resurrected life and the kingdom of Christ, is a misappropriation of promises which largely pertain to the intermediate state.

This is illustrated once again in *Contra Celsum* VII. 28–30. In chapter 28 Celsus alleges that Christians have derived their hope of a 'better land' after death from the Greeks and from Plato in particular. Origen responds to the effect that Moses was dead long before Greek literature appeared on the scene, and that according to this prophet God had already promised to man 'a good land and a large, a land flowing with milk and honey' (Exod. 3: 8). For Origen, this is the fatherland of the faithful in heaven. The fact that Origen immediately turns to counter the objection from 'some' (Jews or chiliasts or both) who suppose this refers to that part of the earth which we call Judea, shows there is at work a conflict not merely of 'hermeneutical principles' (literalism vs. allegorism) but of *patterns of eschatology*. Exodus 3: 8 is only part of a large battery of texts, including Hebrews 12: 22; Psalms 76: 2; 48: 1–2; 37: 9, 11, 22, 29, 34; Isaiah 54: 11–12 and many more, which to Origen speak of the holy land in heaven inherited by the righteous *after death*, but which certain others refer to the land of Judea to be inherited after the resurrection of the body. The idea of the Christian's departure to heaven stands as a given reality, an undoubted article of faith waiting to be supported by Biblical references. For another instance, the symbolism of the Exodus from Egypt may be understood in two ways, according to Origen. On the one hand it speaks of the departure from the darkness of unbelief into the light of true knowledge. On the other hand, it symbolizes[221]

the abandonment of the shadows of this world by the soul ... and its voyage toward another world, given sometimes as the 'bosom of Abraham' in the parable of Lazarus, sometimes as 'paradise' in the episode of the thief who is converted on the cross, sometimes as God knows what places

[221] *HomNum.* XXVI. 4, (Méhat, SC 29, 501–2).

or dwellings, which serve as passage to the soul believing in God to arrive at the 'river which makes glad the city of God' [Ps. 46: 4] and to enter into it in possession of the very inheritance promised to his fathers.[222]

It may be said that Origen taught an Alexandrian rendition of the doctrine of a heavenly intermediate state. As could already have been said for Clement's doctrine, it had had its beginnings in the household of the Bible but had grown up under the watchful care of a stepmother, the assumption of a basically Platonic distinction between the sensible and the intelligible sets of heavens and earths, and amid free speculation about a *schola animarum* and 'leisurely purgation'[223] in the afterlife. But it is the intermediate state none the less which occupies the place of the millennium in his system. His 'Alexandrian' elaboration would not of itself have brought about a repositioning of the doctrine within the system. Moreover, it is just such an interchange between the earthly millennium and the heavenly intermediate state in the Church's eschatology which had already passed under the scrutiny of Irenaeus a full generation earlier, and which indeed, as we have seen, seems to have been around from a much earlier stage.

2. Exegesis of Revelation 20

It is perhaps not surprising that Origen's exegesis of Revelation 20 itself has been hard to pin down. We have no surviving work in which he treats the passage at length and his occasional allusions to it are sometimes quite casual.[224] The recognition that the doctrine

---

[222] Origen even views the ancient Canaanites as a symbol of the angelic hosts of darkness which occupy the heavenly places (Eph. 6: 12 ff.), who are conquered by Christ and his disciples (*HomNum.* vii. 5; xviii. 4).

[223] Hanson, *Allegory and Event*, 341.

[224] One in particular, *On Prayer* 27. 13, is potentially confusing. Rather than providing us with concrete information about his view of the millennium, however, it seems that this text simply shows Origen indulging a sarcastic wit to the belittlement of chiliasm. His allusion of the 'famous period of a thousand years' seems to have the effect of saying, 'if you are going to appeal to Psalm 90: 4 to support a millennialist eschatology, note that the day the Psalmist speaks of is "yesterday that is past", not a tomorrow of the future'. It is this same sort of chiding which we find in Methodius' *On Things Created* 12, where Origen is quoted as responding to the 'clever arithmeticians' who count six thousand years 'from Adam to our time'. Here he concludes that there have therefore been thirteen days (thousand years) since the creation, facetiously correcting his opponents who have forgotten to add on the first seven days to their world-week scheme. The exasperated Methodius gains our sympathy.

of the intermediate state constitutes Origen's alternative to chiliasm and in fact seems to be his positive interpretation of the millennium in *Princ.* II. 11 and *Cels.* VII. 28–30, however, should induce us to see this as a proper backdrop for our understanding of his exegesis of Revelation 20 itself.

(a) The First Resurrection. Origen's understanding of the two resurrections of Revelation 20 is often represented as follows: 'The first, which begins here below by baptism lived in the faith, is progressive, it is realized more and more in proportion to one's spiritual and moral ascent. The second, which coincides with the end of time, the coming of Christ in glory, is perfect and total'.[225] In other words, the first resurrection was understood by Origen in what could be called a typically Tyconian or Augustinian sense as the resurrection to new life in baptism. It is indisputable that Origen does speak of two distinct resurrections in the senses just outlined.[226] Moreover, as Crouzel has shown, the belief in such a resurrection *ex parte*, finds support in Origen's words elsewhere about the three types of mortality and immortality.[227] But this cannot answer our question *a priori*. The issue is whether Origen, when he came to the twentieth chapter of John's Revelation, in fact understood its 'first resurrection' as a spiritual resurrection *ex parte* experienced progressively in this life and associated with baptism.

Origen refers to this 'first resurrection' three times in his extant writings: in *Homilies on Jeremiah* II. 3, in a *Fragment on Luke* and in his *Commentary on Isaiah* XXVIII. The fragment from the twenty-eighth book of his lost work on Isaiah is conserved for us in a Latin translation in Pamphilus' *Defence of Origen*.[228] Here his interpretation differs from that contained in the other two works.[229] He appears to apply the term 'first resurrection' to the resurrection of

---

[225] Crouzel, *Didaskalia*, 19. See also Crouzel, *EPEKTASIS*, 278; Crouzel, *FF*, 986–7; Crouzel, *BLE*, 96; Crouzel, *Origène*, 310, 319. This view is also taken by Hennessey, 301–3.

[226] The chief sources for this are the *CRom.* v. 9, *PG* 14, 1047 C (preserved in a Greek fragment XXIX, see *JTS* 13, 363), *HomEzech.* II. 5, GCS viii. 346 and *CJohn* x. 35. 231–2, SC 157, 522 and cf. *FragmRm.* XXVIII, *HomLuke* XVI. 7, Crouzel–Fourier–Perichon, SC 87, 244; see Crouzel, *Didaskalia*, 4–7.

[227] Stated explicitly in *DialHeracl.* 25. The three senses of 'death' outlined here, however, do not exhaust its meaning (see e.g. *CRom.* v. 10).

[228] Migne, *PG* xvii. 597 B–598B (also in *PG* xiii. 217–18 B).

[229] Crouzel, *Didaskalia*, 8.

the righteous at the last day and the second resurrection to that of the unrighteous on the same day of judgement.

Jesus says in Luke 14: 12–14 that when we throw a feast we ought to call the poor, the maimed, the lame and the blind, for they cannot repay us; we shall instead be repaid at the resurrection of the just. Origen explains in his work on Luke,[230] 'Now here he calls "resurrection of the just", that which John in the Apocalypse labels "first".' Origen does not go on to explain. But here again he could not have understood John's 'first resurrection' as a resurrection to new life experienced here below in baptism; the resurrection in view, because it is the time of reward in Luke 14: 12–14, is obviously something beyond this life, taking place either immediately after death or at the final assize.[231]

Origen's only remaining reference to the first resurrection of Revelation 20: 5–6 is in his second homily on Jeremiah (II. 3):[232]

Blessed therefore is he who is baptized 'in the Holy Spirit' and is not constrained to a baptism which is of fire, but thrice unfortunate is the one who has need of being baptized by fire . . .
And 'blessed is he who has part in the first resurrection' [Rev. 20: 6], who has kept (ὁ τηρήϲαϲ) the baptism of the Holy Spirit. Who is the one who is saved in another resurrection? He who is constrained to a baptism which is of fire, whenever he comes upon that fire, and the fire proves him, and that fire finds 'wood, hay' and 'stubble' [1 Cor. 3: 12–13], so as to burn them up.

The aorist substantive participle ὁ τηρήϲαϲ (the one who has kept) does not invite a progressive interpretation of the 'first resurrection' but indicates instead that participation in this resurrection comes only at the end of one's life, after the baptism of the Holy Spirit may be said to have been *kept*. This is supported by Origen's language in *HomLuke* XXIV. 2, preached probably about a decade earlier.[233]

that whoever after departure from this life desires to pass over to paradise and is in need of purification, he (Christ) baptizes and sends across to the place of his desire. But he does not baptize in a washing of fire him who

---

[230] *Fragment 83*, Crouzel–Fourier–Perichon, SC 87, 540 (Rauer's no. 209, GCS 49).
[231] This fact is not observed by Crouzel (*Didaskalia*, 7, n. 14).
[232] My translation.
[233] Nautin, SC 232, 15–21, puts the homilies on Jeremiah at about AD 242; Fournier, in Crouzel–Fourier–Perichon, SC 87, 81, thinks the homilies on Luke date from the second sojourn at Caesarea in 233–4.

does not have the seal of a prior baptism. For one should first be baptized 'in water and Spirit' so that when he comes to the river of fire he may show that he has kept (*servasse*) the washing of both water and Spirit and at that time still deserves to receive a baptism of fire in Christ Jesus . . .[234]

Here, as in *HomJer.* II. 3, facing the river of fire (associated in *HomJer.* with the need to be raised in 'another resurrection') comes after death. But this passage also clarifies that it is at this time that one shows whether one has 'kept' (*servasse*) his baptism. And, very significantly, it is seen here to be a time *before the resurrection of the body* as it concerns the entry of the righteous soul into paradise, that is, it concerns the intermediate state. After the exit from this life the one who would pass on to paradise must show at that time that he has kept his baptism. The person who has done so, according to *HomJer.* II. 3, takes part in the first resurrection. The person who stands in need of further purification after failing in some respect to have kept his baptism must undergo a baptism of fire.[235]

Close parallels to the idea, even expressed in the same language, are to be found elsewhere, particularly in *2 Clement* 6. 9 and 8. 6, where 'keeping' one's baptism or its seal is the prerequisite for entering the kingdom[236] of God and receiving eternal life, both evidently post-mortem rewards (cf. 7. 6).[237] Origen simply links to this traditional conception the Johannine terminology of having part in the first resurrection.

Further, the context shows that in this portion of the second homily on Jeremiah Origen is indeed concerned with preparation for death and with the rewards which await us after death. As he goes on to say, 'If then we are able before our departure (ἐξόδου) to become pure, and have prepared our works for the departure,

---

[234] My translation.

[235] The *HomLuke* XXIV. 2 differs from *HomJer.* II. 3 in that in the former Origen says that even the one who has kept his baptism will be baptized (painlessly?, so Hennessey, 301, n. 17) in the river of fire whereas in the later homily on Jeremiah he says that 'it is not the same man who is baptized by Jesus in "the Holy Spirit" and "in the fire"'. Rather, it is only the one who has sinned after baptism who must be purified in the baptism of fire.

[236] Lightfoot, *AF* I. 2, 222. See our comments above on *2Clem.*.

[237] See also Hermas, *Sim.* 8. 6. 3; Tertullian, *Spect.* 4. 24; Cyprian, *Ep.* LVIII. 9 (Hartel); Ps.-Hippolytus, *De consummatione mundi* 42; *Acts of Philip* 28; *ApostConst.* III. 16.

having made our exit among them we shall be received among the good and be saved in Christ Jesus.'

The first resurrection here certainly occurs not concurrently with baptism but as a culminating reward after the successful keeping of one's baptism, that is, at a point when the possibility of still violating one's baptism is no longer entertained. In the second homily on Jeremiah and supported to some extent by *Fragment* 83 on Luke this resurrection appears to be understood as the rising of the soul to paradise in the intermediate state. Origen may thus be seen as perpetuating the interpretation given also by Hippolytus in *CD* II. 37. 4.

(b) *The Beheaded.* There are more reasons to think that Origen understood the positive meaning of the millennium of Revelation 20 in this way. In *ExhMart.* 30 he quotes from Revelation 20: 4. This comes in the midst of explaining that to drink the cup which Jesus drank and to be baptized with the baptism with which he was baptized is to be martyred.[238]

Consider whether, just as the Saviour's death brought purification to the world, the baptism of martyrdom may also by the service of those who undergo it bring purification to many. Just as those who attend at the altar (θυσιαστηρίῳ προσεδρεύοντες διακονεῖν) according to the Law of Moses thought they obtained remissions of sins for the Jews by the blood of bulls and goats, so the souls of those 'who have been beheaded for the testimony of Jesus' (Rev. 20. 4) do not attend[239] in vain at the heavenly altar, but mediate remission of sins to those who pray. At the same time we know that, just as the high priest, Jesus Christ, offered himself in sacrifice, so the priests, whose high priest he is, offer themselves in sacrifice and therefore appear by the altar in their proper place.

Here it is plain that the souls who are 'beheaded' for Christ, who in Revelation 20 are (or are among) those who take part in the first resurrection, are martyrs in heaven during the interadvent period. This confirms and elucidates our explanation of Origen's interpretation of the first resurrection given in *HomJer.* II. 3. The martyrs belong to the priestly ministry of heaven, beside whose altar they

---

[238] Koetschau, 3–47. The translation is Chadwick's, LCC. See now the instructive article of P. Bright.

[239] Or, 'who sit alongside' (παρεδρεύουσαι). See below on Dionysius' use of the term πάρεδροι for the martyrs (Eusebius, *HE* VI. 42. 5), for which the present text appears to provide the proper background.

are stationed. This should be compared to *On Prayer* 28. 9 (cf. *ExhMart.* 34) where the martyrs, on the basis of their being likened to the apostles, to whom was given authority to forgive or to retain sins (John 20: 23), are said to be priests of the great high priest.[240] To be observed also is the intermingling of priestly and kingly roles in this conception, comparable to that of Revelation 20: 4–6 itself. Earlier in his exhortation (ch. 28) Origen had interpreted Matthew 20: 22 to signify that 'he who drinks of that cup that Jesus drank will sit and rule and judge with the King of kings'. Later (ch. 37), he states that the martyrs, who imitate the scorn of death displayed by their Master, 'will sit with him and reign in heaven with him' (cυγκαθεδροῦνται αὐτῷ καὶ cυμβαcιλεύcουcιν ἐν τοῖc οὐρανοῖc), in a heavenly reign which takes place before the resurrection of the body.[241] It is highly probable that the term cυμβαcιλεύcουcιν (they will reign with) adverts to Revelation 20: 4, 6, 'and they lived and reigned (ἐβαcίλευcαν) with Christ the thousand years . . . and they shall reign (βαcιλεύcουcιν) with him the thousand years'. Origen is thus also able to see in the words of Ecclesiastes 4: 14, 'From the house of the prisoners he will go forth to be a king', a reference to the 'just man who has fought a good fight, who is departing from the fetter of the body' to be admitted to some kind of royal charge (*DialHeracl.* 24 (SC 67).[242]

Precisely like those who in the second homily on Jeremiah have part in the first resurrection, Ambrose and Protoctetus (the addressees of the *ExhMart.*), if they endure to the end, will not be stopped by the flaming sword which guards the way to the tree of life but will have Christ as their escort through the gates of paradise (*ExhMart.* 36).

(c) *The Binding of Satan.*   There is yet more to be said of Origen's interpretation of Revelation 20. The first three verses of that chapter record the binding of the dragon, the ancient serpent, and his being

---

[240] It is, in my opinion, this likeness to the apostles, who had been given the power to remit sins and to sit on twelve thrones judging the twelve tribes of Israel (*ScholApoc.* xxiv), and *not* the martyrs' 'possession by the Holy Spirit', which lies at the root of the appeal to confessors for absolution. See the Appendix.

[241] With a reference to the future resurrection of the body, 'if we no longer deserve to be divided into two parts'.

[242] See also *ScholApoc.* xxiv where it is intimated that the apostles now sit on the twelve thrones in order to judge the tribes of Israel, 'for anyone to sit with the Father on his throne clearly is to reign wih him: for a throne is a symbol of kingship'.

cast into the abyss. For all chiliast interpreters this foretells a time yet future, a complete arresting of Satan's powers necessary for the implanting of Christ's kingdom on earth. For Jerome and Augustine it was an allegory of the sealing up of Satan within the heart of the unbeliever, symbolized by the abyss.

In the first of his *Homilies on Genesis*[243] Origen recounts the story, told in Genesis 1: 2, of the creation of the (invisible) world and comes upon the phrase 'And darkness was on the face of the abyss.' What is the abyss? 'That undoubtedly in which "the devil and his angels" will be.'[244] The reference is to Revelation 20: 1–3 (cf. for 'his angels' Rev. 12: 9). The next sentence, 'This indeed is most clearly manifested in the Gospel where it is said of the Saviour, "And the demons which he was casting out were asking him that he not command them to go into the abyss",' demonstrates that even in the time of Jesus (Luke 8: 31) the casting into the abyss was still unaccomplished. But later in the same homily there is another reference to 'that water which is below, that is, the water of the abyss in which darkness is said to be, which "the prince of this world" and the adversary, "the dragon and his angels" inhabit (*habitant*).' If the Latin translation of Rufinus may be trusted Origen is here seen to be presupposing that the devil has *since* the coming of Jesus been cast into the abyss of Revelation 20: 1–3. Hence the millennium has begun.

This is supported by the *CRom.* v. 10, where Christ's binding of Satan with respect to Matthew 12: 29 is referred to a binding which took place at the cross, which was then followed by a rescuing of souls out of Satan's house of Hades, the 'spoiling of his goods'. Both NT descriptions of a binding of the devil (Matt. 12: 29; Rev. 20: 1–3) are said to have been accomplished since the time of the crucifixion.[245] In this Origen is like the early Irenaeus.

It is therefore proposed that we have found in the extant works of Origen all the signs of a consistent, if not completely recoverable, non-chiliastic exegesis of Revelation 20 wherein the binding of Satan (20: 2–3) is conceived of as accomplished since the first

---

[243] De Lubac-Doutreleau.

[244] A variant has instead of the future *erit* the imperfect *erat*. But Doutreleau (de Lubac-Doutreleau, 26–7) points out that Origen is here speaking of the pre-existent world and so the devil at that point would not be inhabiting the abyss for which he was destined.

[245] Cf. *On Prayer* 26. 5. where Origen denies that Satan, who has fallen from heaven like lightning, and his hosts are now dwelling in heaven.

coming of Christ, the first resurrection (20: 5–6) is at least once conceived of as a rising of the soul to heaven at death, and the beheaded (20: 4) who reign with Christ and who serve as 'priests of God and of Christ' (20: 6) are identified as the martyrs who even now join in Christ's royal, heavenly session and serve at the heavenly altar. With reference to previous sections of our study we must observe that this interpretation is not something which sprang full grown from the head of Origen. We have seen all of these aspects of Origen's interpretation of Revelation 20 to some degree present in the Church's eschatology before him. What is more, as this exegesis of Revelation 20 locates itself within Origen's development of thought on the kingdom of heaven, the intermediate state, and particularly the intermediate state of the martyrs, it shows up other links with previous eschatological tradition which may not have referred explicitly to Revelation 20 but which tie in with the larger categories mentioned.

3. Thnetopsychiasm

Origen, like many Christians before him, believed that all the dead of former times descended into Hades (*Hom1Sam.* 28. 3–25 (GCS 6, 291)) where they were 'shut up' ($\kappa\alpha\tau\alpha\kappa\lambda\epsilon\acute{\iota}o\nu\tau\alpha\iota$)[246] until the time of Christ's advent there. Even Abraham, when Christ spoke of him in the story of Lazarus and the rich man, had not the ability to pass by the flaming sword which guards the way to the tree of life in an otherworldly paradise. But now, because Christ has bound the devil, who had the power of death (*CRom.* v. 10), and has visited Hades[247] as its master and has delivered all who had awaited him there (*CSSol.* III. 12), Abraham's bosom is identified with paradise (*HomNum.* 26. 4; *DialHeracl.* 23). Only the wicked henceforth must see the interiors of Hades. The righteous immediately at death depart to be with Christ (*DialHeracl.* 23, 24; *Princ.* II. 11. 5), rising to the Jerusalem above (*CMatt.* XII. 20; 43; *CRom.* v. 10) to reign with Him there (*DialHeracl.* 24; *ScholApoc.* XXIV). The martyrs have special privileges beside the altar of the heavenly temple.[248]

But Origen is well aware that not all Christians share with him these conceptions. 'Thnetopsychiasm', which Origen faced in the

---

[246] Klostermann, no. 560 (p. 230).
[247] Even Celsus had heard of this Christian teaching, *Cels.* II. 43.
[248] See Rordorf, *EPEKTASIS*.

synod in Arabia (Eusebius, *HE* vi. 37) and in the *DialHeracl.*, if indeed these do not represent the same occasion, must be classed as a view not only opposed to that of Origen but also distinct from that which belonged to the millennialists we have observed hitherto. The 'subterranean-chiliast' view was comfortable with a notion of the immortality of the soul, being in fact built on the assumption of the soul's continuous survival after death in a conscious, sentient state. But the view encountered in Arabia and possibly elsewhere was more radical. It would hold even these ideas in suspicion, as being more Greek than Biblical. For these Christians the soul must be as mortal as the body, must die with it and must be recreated or reconstituted with it at the resurrection.

Was this a new development, as alien in its origins and character to the 'subterranean–chiliast' view as it was to the 'heavenly'? Or, was it possibly a reactionary offshoot of the former? The 'subterranean' and the thnetopsychiast views have at least this in common, that they both recoil from any affirmation that the souls of the redeemed may enter the divine presence before reunion with the body at the resurrection of the just.

While it cannot be proved,[249] it yet remains a viable hypothesis that certain chiliasts known to Origen, whose chiliasm was of a starker sort than that of Irenaeus,[250] saw the need to adopt a more anti-Hellenic position with regard to the dead in Christ, stating, in order that the resurrected state might come into greater prominence, that there is *no* hope for continued human existence without the resurrected (but very much like the present) body, without the earthly millennium.

4. Conclusion

The clear inference from Irenaeus' critique of the non-chiliast orthodox, that for them the heavenly intermediate state holds the place occupied by the millennium in the system of Irenaeus, is incarnated

---

[249] There are remarkable similarities in the method and the substance of his refutations of the two groups, chiliasts in the preface to the *CSSol.*, thnetopsychiasts in the *DialHeracl.* Crouzel, SC 253, 229, believes that the chiliasts, thnetopsychiasts, and anthropomorphites 'represent three aspects of the same mentality'.

[250] For Irenaeus, those who beget children on the millennial earth are not the resurrected but those who are found alive at the parousia. For the chiliasts whom Origen criticized, just as for Commodianus (*Instr.* i. 44), the resurrected body itself was to take part in the procreative act.

in the work of Origen. From Origen we may draw the reverse inference: the chiliasts take those promises meant to instruct us of the intermediate state of the blessed in heaven and transmute them into a crass hope of an earthly paradise.

Origen perpetuates the non-chiliast tradition which we have observed in a large number of writers before him. If in other points Origen's eschatology represents 'a rupture with tradition',[251] it is also true that his eschatology 'could not possibly be described as making a complete break with the past'.[252] In his doctrine of the intermediate state he has preserved and developed what had certainly been a widespread and very primitive Christian belief that the souls of the righteous go immediately to be with Christ in heaven at death. Origen has also left us with extremely valuable remnants of his non-chiliastic exegesis of Revelation 20 itself. In this exegesis we recognize traces especially from Hippolytus and from previous martyrological thought. For Origen the opponent of chiliasm, the positive meaning of the millennium of Revelation 20 is that it opens up for us a window on the intermediate state. This large and noteworthy specimen of early Christian eschatology could shed some important light on our perception of the preceding non-chiliastic tradition.

8. DIONYSIUS OF ALEXANDRIA

Clearly one of the more important figures in the early history of Christian chiliasm is Dionysius of Alexandria. His consultations with chiliast followers of Nepos in Arsinoë and his resulting publication, On Promises, were not only influential, and controversial, in his own day but exercised an obvious influence on the thought of Eusebius of Caesarea. On Promises became the target of the resurgent chiliast rebuttal of Apollinarius of Laodicea.

Sadly, all we have of the two volumes of On Promises, written probably between 253 and 257,[253] are the segment preserved by Eusebius and a few insignificant fragments.[254] All these are from the second volume of the work, in which Dionysius examines John's Apocalypse. Apart from his 'demonstration' that the book as a

---

[251] Gry, Millénarisme, 96.

[253] Bienert, 194.

[252] Hanson, Allegory and Event, 366.

[254] See Feltoe, Dionysius, 125–6.

whole cannot be understood in the literal sense, and his confession
that its matter is above his comprehension (*HE* VII. 25. 5–6), we are
left with little to inform us about how Dionysius might have interpreted the millennium of Revelation 20.

Eusebius has, however, preserved an interesting and revealing
portion of a letter[255] from Dionysius which recounted to Fabius the
persecutions and martyrdoms at Alexandria under Philip and
Decius (*HE* VI. 41–42). In it Dionysius appeals to the mercy shown
by the martyrs, before they died, towards some of those who had
been charged with sacrificing but who later repented: 'These, the
divine martyrs among us, who now are assessors of Christ and
who share the fellowship of his kingdom, and are partakers of his
decisions and judge along with him . . .' (VI. 42. 5).[256]

Martyrs are believed to be seated with Christ as companions of
his kingdom in heaven and participate, in some sense, in his
decisions (κρίϲεωϲ) and judge along with him (ϲυνδικάζοντεϲ). Such
a conception is irresistibly reminiscent of the blessed partakers of
the first resurrection in Revelation 20, who are seated on thrones,
granted judgement and reign with Christ as his priests during the
thousand years. It is almost certainly this passage to which much
of Dionysius' thought here harks back. We recall Origen's direct
appeal to Revelation 20: 4 to substantiate the idea that martyrs
now attend (παρεδρεύουϲαι) at the heavenly altar (*ExhMart.* 30). This
shows that Dionysius' 'assessors' (πάρεδροι) denote probably not
primarily a governmental but a priestly role, thus we find again the
two roles intermingled, as they are in Revelation 20: 4–6.

This citation from Dionysius also seems to tell us how a kind of
present judging function in heaven could have been acknowledged
without prejudice to a future consummation of that function on the
day of judgement. That is, by associating it with the judging and
ruling prerogative exercised by Jesus Christ himself, a prerogative
acknowledged by all Christians yet with the understanding that it
is being exercised for the remainder of the present age in restraint,
deferring until his second coming its full, compensatory execution.
The participation of the martyrs and others in the present administration of Jesus in heaven would thus be a participation in this
sovereign, but patient, governing economy.

---

[255] Dated 251, according to Lawlor, *Eusebius*, ii. 229.

[256] Αὐτοὶ τοίνυν οἱ θεῖοι μάρτυρες παρ' ἡμῖν, οἱ νῦν τοῦ χριστοῦ πάρεδροι καὶ τῆϲ
βαϲιλείαϲ αὐτοῦ κοινωνοὶ καὶ μέτοχοι τῆϲ κρίϲεωϲ αὐτοῦ καὶ ϲυνδικάζοντεϲ αὐτῷ. . .

In another text (*HE* VII. 22. 4), Dionysius speaks of the martyrs feasting in heaven. This may have to do with an exegesis of such passages as Matthew 8. 11 (Luke 13: 29); 26: 29 (pars.); Revelation 2: 7, interpreted, as by Origen (*Princ.* II. 11. 3, cf. *CSSol.* prol.; III. 6; *HomGen.* 16. 4), to mean spiritual feasting and not the literal feasting for the resurrected which Irenaeus, for example, insisted upon (*AH* v. 30. 4; 33. 1).

Finally it is worth observing that the bodily resurrection at the time of Christ's parousia was an undoubted and non-negotiable article in the theology of Dionysius (Eusebius, *HE* VII. 24. 5). In his letter to Stephen on baptism he threatens, 'if anyone despises the doctrine of the resurrection of the body, let such an one be at once ranked with the dead.'[257]

9. CYPRIAN

The writings of Cyprian, spanning little more than a decade (246–58), were for the most part produced amidst considerable societal or ecclesiastical turbulence and often show the marks of a very intense eschatological consciousness. They reveal that Cyprian too was both an amillennialist and a proponent of a 'heavenly' intermediate state and, quite importantly, they disclose to us his interpretation of Revelation 20: 4–6. To say that he taught the immediate attainment of God's heavenly presence at death is not liable to arouse a dispute, but a few modern writers, at least, have seen cause for claiming Cyprian as a chiliast.[258] The following discussion of Cyprian's eschatology will therefore consist of, first, a look at his eschatological expectancy with regard to the question of millennialism, and then a summary of his teaching on the inter-

[257] Conybeare's translation from the Armenian. Maier's depiction (93) of the opposition between the views of Nepos and those of Dionysius, 'There stood ... Jewish-biblical and Greek-Platonic spirit, realism and mysticism ... over against each other', utterly fails to convince. Note Dionysius' 'realistic' application of Rev. 13: 1–10 (Eusebius, *HE* VII. 10. 2–3, see Bienert, 168–9, 172–4), made in 262 (Lawlor, *Eusebius*, ii. 252–3), evidently *after* writing *On Promises*.

[258] See, Montgomery, 358; Maier, 130, 'It was just in the African homeland of Augustine that, in the words of Harnack, a "massive chiliasm" was at home. We meet it in Tertullian, Cyprian, Commodian, Arnobius and Lactantius...'. No evidence is cited in support of Cyprian's chiliasm by Maier or Montgomery and in fact Maier had earlier stated, 'Cyprian was indeed an antichiliast ...' (106)!

mediate state, including special attention to the exegesis of Revelation 20: 1–6.

1. Millennialism

Cyprian is usually passed by in historical surveys of early chiliasm,[259] indeed, no Cyprian scholar to my knowledge has ever placed him within that camp.[260] In studies of millennialism one none the less occasionally runs across the claim that Cyprian was a chiliast. This claim seems to rest on Cyprian's acceptance of a world-week chronology (see *Fort.* praef. 2 [317]; 11 [338])[261] and on his belief in the imminency of Christ's return and the setting up of the kingdom.

But we have already observed that both Hippolytus and Origen accepted such calculations of the world's age and even seemed to give some credence to a full world-week allegory yet without by any means involving themselves in millennialism. Neither these nor Cyprian indicate that the last 'millennium' either will be literal, as opposed to being symbolic of the eternal sabbath, or that it corresponds to the thousand years of Revelation 20: 1–6. Indeed, we shall see later that Cyprian's own exegesis of this passage is not chiliastic. We can also see that his acceptance of this world-week scheme did not play a formative role in Cyprian's eschatology. This is because by the standard calculations of his day (Theophilus, Hippolytus, Julius Africanus, etc.) Christ was born in the year 5500, which meant that the world had by Cyprian's time another 250 years of life left before the parousia. This squares neither with Cyprian's view that the world in his day was then in its death throes nor with his seeming expectation that Christ would return before he could die a natural death.

For he believed, especially as the dreaded but never-materialized

[259] He is, for instance, completely omitted in the articles on chiliasm by Semisch–Bratke, Leclercq, Bardy, Harnack, W. Bauer, Gelin, H. Kraft, Bettencourt, Dolan, Sandeen, Daniélou (BEBT), Blum, Bietenhard, and in the longer study of Gry.

[260] On the other hand, his place in the history of non-chiliastic thought has gone unrecognized. Express denials that Cyprian was a chiliast are made by Harnack, *Lehrbuch*, i. 616, n. 1; Lesètre, 1095, d'Ales, *Cyprien*, 35–6, though with little discussion of the fact and with no attempt to give the context or the significance of his eschatology.

[261] Cyprian's works are here cited by title and chapter or paragraph number. The number following in brackets indicates the page number in Hartel. Latin citations are from Hartel, English translations, except where noted, are those of Ernest Wallis in *ANF* v.

persecution of Gallus approached, that the return of Christ and the coming of the kingdom were imminent: 'it appears that the Lord also is now returning' (*Ep.* LXI. 4 [697]); 'His second coming draws near (*propinquat*) to us' (*Ep.* LXIII. 18 [716]); 'Let us always with solicitude and caution wait for the sudden (*repentinum*) coming of the Lord, that when He shall knock, our faith may be on the watch, and receive from the Lord the reward of our vigilance' (*Un.* 27 [233]).[262]

As to this belief, however, and its bearing on millennialism, a few points must be made. There are several places where Cyprian expressly looks for the kingdom, or our participation in it, to arrive soon, with this advent of Christ (*Un.* 27 [233]; *Ep.* LVIII. 10 [665]; *OpEl.* 9 [381]; *Orat.* 13 [275–6], 19 [281]; *Mort.* 18 [308]). But it is crucial also to bear in mind that, according to Cyprian, *the time of the parousia is not the only time when Christ's kingdom may be entered.* In one of the texts just mentioned, *De mortalitate* 18, he indicates that Christians seek and desire that the kingdom of God would come quickly.

Why, then, do we pray and ask that the kingdom of heaven may come, if the captivity of earth delights us? Why with frequently repeated prayers do we entreat and beg that the day of His kingdom may hasten, if our greater desires and stronger wishes are to obey the devil here, rather than to reign with Christ (*regnare cum Christo*)?

Although he prays for the speedy arrival of the kingdom (in alluding to the petition of the Lord's Prayer, 'thy kingdom come'), the larger context shows that the 'reigning with Christ' mentioned in the last line is intended not as the reigning which will ensue at that time but the reigning which awards the Christian on his departure from this world. Cyprian, on the basis of the Christian teaching that believers 'go to Christ' when they die, is complaining about the reticence and even heathenish fear with which many Christians are facing the scourge of the plague then afflicting North Africa. Thus he has already (ch. 2 [298]) stated 'Who in the midst of these things, is fearful and sad, save he who lacks hope and faith? For it is for him to fear death who is unwilling to go to

---

[262] This was not the expectation of an 'any moment coming' of Christ, for Cyprian also believed that before Christ could return Antichrist must be manifested, who would engineer a universal deception and spearhead an unprecedented devastation of God's flock. The rampage will be shortlived and will not prevail; Christ is to follow on the heels of his adversary (*Ep.* LVIII. 7 [662–3], see also *Un.* 27 [232–3]).

Christ. It is for him to be unwilling to go to Christ who does not believe that he is beginning to reign[263] with Christ'. He continues,

If you are just, and live by faith, if you truly believe in Christ, why, since you are about to be with Christ, and are secure of the Lord's promise, do you not embrace the assurance that you are called to Christ, and rejoice that you are freed from the devil? (ch. 3 [298]; similarly in ch. 6 [300])

So many persecutions the soul suffers daily, with so many risks is the heart wearied, and yet it delights to abide here long among the devil's weapons, although it should rather be our craving and wish to hasten to Christ by the aid of a quicker death . . . (ch. 5 [299])

That in the meantime we die, we are passing over to immortality by death . . . Who would not crave to be changed and renewed into the likeness of Christ, and to arrive more quickly to the dignity of heavenly glory, since Paul the apostle announces and says, 'For our conversation is in heaven . . .' [Phil. 3. 21] . . . He who is to attain to the throne of Christ, to the glory of the heavenly kingdoms (*ad regnorum caelestium*), ought not to mourn nor lament, but rather, in accordance with the Lord's promise, in accordance with his faith in the truth, to rejoice in this his departure and translation. (ch. 22 [310–11])

This shows that Cyprian is concerned throughout the treatise with an entry into the kingdom, an advance to the throne of Christ, which takes place in the Christian's departure in death. Returning now to chapter 18, his exhortation there will now be understood to mean, 'How can you pray the Lord's Prayer and say that you desire the kingdom to come quickly, when you show by your fear of dying that you would rather remain on earth and serve the devil than pass from this world to reign with Christ in that very heavenly kingdom for which you ask.'

Again, it is true that Cyprian also refers to a participation in the kingdom at the time of the approaching day of judgement in *Ep.* LVIII. 10 [665]. But even this text shows by its mention of greeting the patriarchs, prophets, apostles, and martyrs who are *already* in this kingdom in heaven (cf. *Mort.* 26 [313–14]) that Christians enter the kingdom of heaven upon departure from this world in death. We reserve further comments on this matter until later.

The second reason why Cyprian's 'Naherwartung' does not signify chiliasm is that, as the preceding passage (*Ep.* LVIII. 10 [665]) among others testifies, for Cyprian the coming of Christ would bring with it the final, definitive judgement of the human race.

---

[263] *incipere regnare.* So translated by Hannan, 23. Wallis has 'about to reign'.

'Since now the end of the world is at hand (*proximo*)' (*Demetr.* 23 [367]); 'the day of judgement is now drawing nigh (*adpropinquante*)' (*Demetr.* 5 [354]). This is a judgement such as would suggest to nobody the need of a further, more comprehensive judgement at the end of an intervening, provisional, kingdom on earth. On this see also *Demetr.* 24 [368–9]; *Idola* 14 [31]; *Pat.* 23–4 [415–16].

Finally, there is no indication that the kingdom Cyprian looked for to attend the arrival of Christ in glory was anything other than the eternal, ultimate kingdom of God; there is absolutely no hint that he expected human life to continue, whether for the resurrected or for a race of non-resurrected human beings, in an enhanced 'earthly' condition, with the continued opportunity for marriage and the begetting of children.

Consequently, his expectation of the kingdom arriving with the relatively imminent parousia cannot be seen as an indication of chiliasm. The only earthly kingdom Cyprian ever speaks of is, in fact, one to be renounced. In *De dominica oratione* 13 the desire for *terrena regna* is expressly forbidden and contrasted to the seeking of the heavenly kingdom (*non terrena sed caelestia regna desiderat*).[264] This might be compared to the sentiment expressed by Hippolytus in *CD* IV. 11. 4 (cf. IV. 9. 3, 4).

2. The Intermediate State

It is unnecessary to document fully the evidence that Cyprian believed in an immediate ascension to the Lord's presence in heaven for the departed Christian. His allusions to 'going to' the Lord or to His presence or to heaven are far too numerous to reproduce here, (see e.g. *Epp.* VI. 1 [480–81]; X. 2 [491], 5 [494]; XXXVII. 3 [578]; LVIII. 3 [658]; LXVI. 7 [731–2]; LXXXI [841]; *Hab.* 21 [202], 23 [204]; *Fort.* praef. 4. [319]; *Mort.* 22 [310–11], 24 [312]). We shall only remark briefly on a few aspects of his doctrine of the intermediate state before moving on to consider his understanding of the millennium in Revelation 20: 1–6.

Cyprian three times, twice in *Ep.* LV, uses the word *inferi*.[265] It

---

[264] Moffatt, *Expos.*, 182–3.

[265] Hannan, 76. There are two passages where Cyprian perhaps discloses the idea of a raiding of Hades (*Idola* 13 [29]; *OpEl.* 1 [373]), though these are not so clear as to allow full assurance. It is possible, though less likely, that he believed the saints in all past ages went away to the Lord's presence without ever passing through Hades.

is quite doubtful, despite the *ANF* translation, that he meant by it simply 'the place of the departed'. He is rehearsing to Antonianus his policy of offering absolution and communion to the lapsed who have been under the sentence of penance but who are about to die. In these cases he allows them communion because, 'there is no confession in Hades (*inferos*)' (LV. 17 [636], also 29 [647]). It seems that here Cyprian is entertaining the idea, whether seriously or for argument's sake, that those who depart this life out of communion with the Church are not among the saved, that is, they go not where Christians go but where the wicked go. This appears from his address to the pagan reviler Demetrianus, written about the same time, whom he warns in exactly this same fashion: 'When you have once departed thither, there is no longer any place for repentance, and no possibility of making satisfaction' (*Demetr.* 25 [370]). It is therefore those outside the Church who will abide 'in Hades'. In his one remaining use of word *inferi*, he exhorts Demetrianus to 'seek God in the highest, that you may be free from *inferis*' (16 [362]).

It is remarkable, given Cyprian's high estimate of the glories of martyrdom and especially in the light of his adherence to Tertullian, that for him the rewards of the martyrs are greater indeed[266] but not of a different order than those of other Christians. It is not the case that for Cyprian ordinary Christians must endure after death a period of waiting before arriving at their heavenly homes (e.g. *Fort.* 12 [344–6]).[267] This brings us inevitably to Cyprian's supposed doctrine of purgatory.[268] Pierre Jay has shown how Cyprian's statements in *Ep.* LV. 20 have been misread and hastily applied to the doctrine of purgatory.[269] What Cyprian is talking about when he refers to the 'payment of the last farthing' of Matthew 5: 26 is not

[266] In *Hab.* 21 [202] he mentions the martyrs, the virgins and 'the just of all kinds' as being on the path to heavenly glory. To the martyrs belong the hundred-fold reward, to the virgins the sixty-fold; the inference is that the thirty-fold belong to 'the just of all kinds'.

[267] Contra d'Ales, *Cyprien*, 33 and those cited in the next note.

[268] Affirmations of its existence to be found, among others, in d'Ales, *Cyprien*, 35, who seems to think that all non-martyrs are detained in some manner after death; similarly, Rahner, *ZKTh*, 392; Fischer, *Todesgedanken*, 267–9, who allows that 'Each of the righteous attains directly after death the heavenly blessedness' but maintains that for 'the great host of the ordinary', who are not yet worthy of heaven, there is a post-mortem purgatory where sins are atoned for.

[269] Jay, 133–6. Also Fahey, 275–6. Even Jay, however, holds that the last judgement must intervene before non-martyrs may know the sort of beatitude which the martyrs enjoy straightaway (135, n. 10; 136).

a penal detention beyond the grave for the imperfect but the more or less lengthy period of penitential discipline endured in this life by the lapsed—made even less bearable by the violent upheavals of the times.[270] Ignorance of an idea of purgatory is evidenced not only by Cyprian's assumption that the dedicated Christian attains the same post-mortem bliss as the martyr (see our next section) but by the fact that even the lapsed, if they repent and die while in communion with the Church, are said to 'come to the Lord' when they die (*Epp.* XVIII. 1 [524]; XIX. 2 [525]; XX. 3 [529]). This is language Tertullian would not have used.[271]

Cyprian's conception of the condition of the righteous now in heaven is so lofty, especially where the martyrs are concerned, that it tempts some to regard this condition as the state of bliss beyond which nothing could be imagined. But this would not be accurate. The state of the departed righteous also sounds a note of incompleteness, of forbearance, of endurance. The saints in heaven still entreat the Lord for those on earth (*Ep.* LX. 5 [695]), expecting, desiring, soliciting our salvation (*Mort.* 26 [313]); the martyrs themselves wait unavenged until the day of judgement (*Laps.* 18 [250]). It is still appropriate to use the term intermediate state for this view, for the future consummation, the second coming of Christ in judgement, is still the all-important hinge for the human condition according to Cyprian. It restores soul to body (*Demetr.* 24 [369]) and executes supreme and eternal justice.

3. *Exegesis of Revelation 20: 1–6*

In the preceding we have concluded that there is no real evidence of chiliasm in Cyprian's writings. To what sort of framework then

---

[270] Cf. *Mort.* 25 [312–3], because the world is collapsing and the most terrible things are imminent it is 'the greatest advantage to depart from it as quickly as possible'. This is also the case, despite Fischer, *Todesgedanken*, 269–70, for the pseudo-Cyprianic *De laude martyrii* 13 where in the allusion to Matt. 5: 26 penitential discipline recedes and the payment of the last farthing is the remaining in this life after refusing martyrdom, 'mixed up with the bloody carnage of wasting diseases in a common lot with others' and enduring 'cruel torments and mischievous acts of punishment' which then prevailed against the Christians.

[271] Cyprian in an early letter (*Ep.* I. 2, AD 249) uses the common metaphor of 'sleep' for the death of the believer. Like Tertullian he uses the term *refrigerium* for the state of the dead in Christ (*Mort.* 15 [306]) but unlike Tertullian he saw the locale of that refreshment in heaven.

does his one exposition of Revelation 20: 4–6 belong if a chiliastic one cannot be found?

The main point in his treatment in *Ad Fortunatum* 12 is that the promises held forth in that chapter of the Revelation pertain not to martyrs only but only to them pre-eminently. The one who perseveres in unvanquished faith,

even he also is honoured by Christ among the martyrs (*inter martyras*), as He Himself promises and says: 'There is no man that leaveth house, or land . . . but shall receive seven times as much in this present time, and in the world to come eternal life.' In the Apocalypse also He says the same thing: 'And I saw,' saith he, 'the souls of them that were slain for the name of Jesus and the word of God.' And when he had placed those who were slain in the first place, he added, saying: 'And whosoever had not worshipped the image of the beast, neither had received his mark upon their forehead or in their hand;' all these he joins together, as seen by him at one time in the same place (*quos uniuersos a se in eodem loco simul uisos coniungit*), and says, 'And they lived and reigned with Christ.' He says that all live and reign even whosoever, standing in firmness of the faith and in the fear of God, have not worshipped the image of the beast, and have not consented to his deadly and sacrilegious edicts.

When is this 'living and reigning'? The entire context as well as Cyprian's use of similar language elsewhere establish beyond a reasonable doubt that he has in mind the enjoyment of the millennium of Revelation 20: 4–6 in heaven by the faithful during the interadvent period.

The treatise is an exhortation to martyrdom. Cyprian is concerning himself not with a terrestrial, political regime but with post-mortem rewards of the faithful obtained immediately after death in heaven.[272] The succeeding chapter (13 [347]) shows this quite clearly.

In persecutions, earth is shut up, but heaven is opened; Antichrist is threatening, but Christ is protecting; death is brought in, but immortality follows; the world is taken away from him that is slain, but paradise is set forth to him restored; the life of time is extinguished, but the life of eternity is realized. What a dignity it is, and what a security, to go gladly from hence, to depart gloriously in the midst of afflictions and tribulations;

[272] It is true that among these rewards he also lists accompanying Christ 'when he shall come to receive vengeance from His enemies, to stand at His side when He shall sit to judge', but this privilege is clearly set off from the rest by the use of the future tense.

in a moment to close the eyes with which men and the world are looked upon, and at once to open them to look upon God and Christ! Of such a blessed departure how great is the swiftness (*quanta uelocitas*)! You shall be suddenly taken away from earth, to be placed in the heavenly kingdoms (*terris repente subtraheris, ut in regnis caelestibus reponaris*). . . . In persecution, the warfare,—in peace, the purity of conscience is crowned.

Beholding God and the glorified Christ in the heavenly kingdoms happens *statim*, as soon as the eyes are closed in death. And again the same point is stressed as was made in the preceding chapter, where Revelation 20: 4–6 is used: the reward is granted whether death comes in persecution or in peace, whether the dying one is a martyr in the proper sense or one in spirit only.

The reader is referred back to the instances cited above from *De mortalitate* 2 and 18 where Cyprian alludes to reigning with Christ in the kingdom of heaven (cf. also *Ep.* VI. 2 [481] and the words of the Roman confessors in *Ep.* XXXI. 3 [559]). A long quotation from *De mortalitate* 26 [313–4], intended by Cyprian to stir up the hearts of the readers with the courage (rather, the longing) to die, will be appropriate at this point.

Let us greet the day which assigns each of us to his own home, which snatches us hence, and sets us free from the snares of the world, and restores us to paradise and the kingdom (*paradiso restituit et regno*). Who that has been placed in foreign lands would not hasten to return to his own country? . . . We regard paradise as our country—we already begin to consider the patriarchs as our parents: why do we not hasten and run, that we may behold our country, that we may greet our parents? There a great number of our dear ones is awaiting us, and a dense crowd of parents, brothers, children, is longing for us, already assured of their own safety, and still solicitous for our salvation. To attain to their presence and their embrace,[273] what a gladness both for them and for us in common! What a pleasure is there in the heavenly kingdom (*caelestium regnorum*), without fear of death; and how lofty and perpetual a happiness with eternity of living! There (*illic*) the glorious company of the apostles—there (*illic*) the host of the rejoicing prophets—there (*illic*) the innumerable multitude of martyrs, crowned for the victory of their struggle and passion—there the triumphant virgins . . . there are merciful men rewarded . . . To these, beloved brethren, let us hasten with an eager desire; let us crave quickly to be with them, and quickly to come to Christ.

---

[273] The same hope entertained by Celerinus in *Ep.* XXI. 1 [530].

Entry into the kingdom of heaven, return to a restored paradise,[274] coming to Christ and the blessed of past ages, occurs at death— and very significantly, Cyprian is addressing the event of death by plague, not by martyrdom. This death like any other unites the faithful, communicant Christian with the martyrs, the prophets, the apostles, and all other saints who have been 'sent before' (Ep. XL [586]; Mort. 20 [309]) into that kingdom. Once again, in his Ep. LXXVI. 2 [829] and 7 [832–3], arrival into the presence of Christ, into the 'divine domiciles', into 'paradise', into 'the kingdom of heaven' is anticipated as the immediate consequence of death for the faithful.

This, then, is the natural and the only intelligible way to under- stand Cyprian's exegesis of Revelation 20: 4–6, namely, as a descrip- tion of the privileges of the departed, living and reigning with Christ in heaven during the present age.

A fuller view of the part played by this interpretation of Revela- tion 20 in current martyrological thought is explored in the Appendix.

4. Conclusions

Cyprian's eschatology was not formed under the influence of Origen. The Christian theologian who exercised the most profound effect on him was Tertullian. Yet in some of the central affirmations of his doctrines of the second coming of Christ and of the interme- diate state Cyprian stands much closer to Origen than to his North African 'master'. He is not a chiliast and did not believe in an infernal abode for the non-martyred Christian awaiting the resur- rection but relied upon a vital hope of an immediate rapture into the Lord's royal and heavenly presence at death. Nor is his eschato- logy encumbered, as are those of Clement and Origen, with ontolo- gical and cosmological theories of a continual upward advance by intelligent beings towards the ultimate metaphysical state. It betrays practically no interaction with pagan views and very little speculative originality. It constantly resorts to Biblical phrases and

---

[274] Fischer, Todesgedanken, 267, is certainly correct as over against Atzberger, d'Ales, Cyprien, 33–5, and Rahner, ZKTh, 392–3 (though Rahner expresses some doubt) in affirming that there is no appreciable distinction in Cyprian between paradise and the kingdom of heaven. Hannan, 55, rightly notes the association of paradisi in Mort. 2 [298] with heaven. See also Demetr. 26 [370].

traditional ideas. It is fairly recognizable also as the dominant eschatology at this time in Rome, if we may judge from his Roman correspondence, and, as may be seen in our Appendix, it was the view shared even by Cyprian's ecclesiastical opponents in Carthage, retained by Cyprian even when the chiliastic option would have provided him with a tool for disarming these opponents.

Cyprian's exegesis of Revelation 20: 4–6 places him alongside Origen and, apparently, Dionysius and Hippolytus as a prime witness to an early non-chiliastic understanding of that passage which, though it is seldom actually recoverable amongst other non-chiliasts, might well have had its own influence on the similar eschatologies of many. The thousand-year reign portrayed in Revelation 20: 4–6 was understood not as an earthly but as a heavenly kingdom, wherein martyrs in the first place but the rest of the dead in Christ as well had a portion with Christ the King and High Priest.

The importance of Cyprian's understanding of the millennium and its place in the history of non-chiliastic thought rests therefore not so much in the impact it might have had on later writers but on the witness it bears to the non-chiliast tradition which preceded it and gave it nurture.

III

SOME OBSERVATIONS ON NEW TESTAMENT ESCHATOLOGY

INTRODUCTION

Two implications of our investigation for the study of NT eschatology may now be briefly explored. The first concerns the question of chiliasm in the NT. Irenaeus' observations about the cohesiveness of certain eschatological conceptions have been found remarkably consistent with the evidence not only of Christian writings but also of Jewish works contemporary with or antedating Christianity's first decades. It must be permitted, therefore, to bring the results of our investigation to bear upon the NT writings. So, for those NT authors concerning whom it is often debated whether they held chiliastic hopes, a previously ignored but very significant line of evidence will now be made accessible if we can accurately survey their ideas of heaven, Hades, and the intermediate state. What we have seen up to now strongly suggests that while belief in a subterranean intermediate state did not, of course, infallibly signify chiliasm in the ancient world, chiliasm was congenitally joined to this view of the intermediate state. That is, not all 'infernalists' were chiliasts, but it seems that all chiliasts were 'infernalists'. The subterranean intermediate state was simply one facet of the chiliastic eschatology. On the other hand, belief in a heavenly intermediate state did not belong to the chiliast version of Christian eschatology. Those who held to such an expectation of individual afterlife showed no allegiance to the hope of an intermediate earthly kingdom before the last judgement and the eternal reign of God. In the light of these results we must be led to expect that if a given NT writer adhered to a chiliastic eschatology he also would have believed that Christian souls or spirits abide in an infernal Hades until the parousia. While, on the other hand, if we find in the NT evidence for the belief that the Christian (or his soul or spirit) at the time of death departs to heaven where Christ is, this ought to be counted as evidence of a non-chiliast eschatology. Furthermore, any conceivable prototypes of the later use of the terminology of the 'kingdom' (of God; Christ; heaven) for the realm, the sphere, the location of Christian dead should be given due weight in reconstructing the author's understanding of eschatology.

Second, beyond the obvious relevance this patterning of eschatological doctrines holds for the study of the book of Revelation, we must reckon with the added factor of the discovery of a neglected, early, non-chiliastic exegesis of Revelation 20 which emerges most clearly in the third-century authors Hippolytus, Origen, Dionysius, and Cyprian. We are also, therefore, bound to ask how such an approach as is suggested by this exegesis compares with the interpretative approach of chiliasm. There are, of course, other interpretative approaches to this chapter, but these two are at least the earliest historically attested ones and on that basis they deserve comparison.

1. THE INTERMEDIATE STATE IN THE NEW TESTAMENT OUTSIDE THE BOOK OF REVELATION

The major point to be made in this section is simply that we find in the NT no reason to think that any of its authors believed, as did many of their Jewish contemporaries, that a detainment in Hades awaited the Christian after death (whatever may have been the fate of the godly of past generations).[1] The data left to us on the subject, on the contrary, favour only an immediate presence with Christ in heaven.

We can do little more in our limited space than merely point out a few of the most relevant texts (some will have to be passed over entirely) outside the book of Revelation before going on to a consideration of the eschatology of that book.

1. The Gospels

Of the Synoptic Gospels the most promising materials for our purposes are to be found in Luke. The story of Dives and Lazarus

---

[1] Jeremias, 'ᾅδης', 149.

in Luke 16: 19–31 has long captured the fascination of those interested in the afterlife, yet, even apart from the fact that its parabolic
form keeps many interpreters from accepting it as a source of
information about what Jesus, or Luke, really thought about afterlife, it was capable, as we have seen, of sustaining appeal from
opposing directions. Dives, we are told, was in torment in Hades
(16: 23). But where is the bosom of Abraham to which Lazarus was
carried by the angels? To some the 'far off' of verse 23 indicated
heaven; Tertullian instead concluded that the poor man and the
patriarch were in Hades along with Dives (though at a higher level).
Origen at times seemed to take the former view but at least once
acknowledged that the whole scene takes place in Hades but before
Christ's descent thither and his release of the righteous dead.
Henceforth, the bosom of Abraham is to be found in heaven.

More perspicuous, however, are Christ's words to the thief on
the cross in Luke 23: 42–3. When the thief entreats his fellow-
crucified in this 'peak of the Lucan scene of crucifixion':[2] 'remember
me when you come into your kingdom', Jesus replies, 'Truly, I say
to you, today you will be with me in Paradise'. Here we must reckon
with a virtual identification of Christ's kingdom with paradise. And
this paradise-kingdom is enterable 'today', the day of the thief's
death, the day of Christ's death. The only credible setting for this
paradise-kingdom of Christ is the heavenly realm[3] (cf. 22: 69 and
Col. 1: 13; Rev. 1: 5; 1 Cor. 15: 24–8; see below on 2 Pet. 1: 11). The
emphasis of the 'with me' ($\mu\epsilon\tau$ ' $\dot{\epsilon}\mu o\hat{\upsilon}$) points to a recurring source
of NT consolation and probably to the central factor in the Christian
formulation of the 'heavenly' understanding of the intermediate
state (Phil. 1: 22–3; 2 Cor. 5: 8; John 14: 3; cf. Rom. 8: 38–9).

It cannot be missed that this conception of paradise belongs to
an eschatology quite in contrast with that of the authors of the
chiliastic 4Ez. and 2Bar. As we have seen, for these authors the
paradise of delights could receive in the present age only those few
saints translated bodily from this world before tasting death, and
would be exposed to general human view only at the time of the
general resurrection, after the earthly regime of the Messiah has

[2] Fitzmyer, Luke (X–XXIV), 1508.

[3] The other two uses of the term in the NT, 2 Cor. 12. 4 and Rev. 2. 7 suppose
paradise to be a heavenly realm, as indeed do 4Ez. and 2Bar. There is no justification
even in apocalyptic literature for imagining a paradise in Hades. Bietenhard, Welt,
171–2, suggests a paradise on earth, in the East but such a realm is hard to imagine
as the seat of Christ's kingdom.

spent itself (*4Ez. 7. 37; 2Bar.* 51. 11). Jesus the King opens paradise 'today' for the most miserable of his subjects, whose body, so far from being wondrously translated or from entering resurrection glory, is about to expire and go to dust.

It should also be observed that none of the early Christian chiliasts, aside from one glance by Tertullian (*Pud.* 22, Christ in his passion 'set the robber free'), takes any notice of Luke 23: 43.[4]

In John 14: 2–4 Jesus is about to leave his disciples to return to the Father via the cross. But he promises to prepare a place for them in his Father's house and come again to take them to be with him. Should this return and taking away of the disciples be understood as occurring at the death of the disciple,[5] at a future parousia of the Lord when he shall 'raise them up at the last day',[6] more existentially, in the ongoing union his followers will experience with Jesus after his death, the 'epiphany of the love of God',[7] or in some combination of one or more of these.[8] No interpretation has been able to secure a clear consensus from modern scholarship. Yet the case for its referent at least including post-mortem blessedness in the Father's heavenly presence, besides being probably the most time-honoured (it was used profusely by early non-chiliasts for the intermediate state), has strong exegetical warrant.

This coming of Jesus to take his disciples to where he is can also be spoken of as the disciple's 'following' (ἀκολούθησις) of Jesus in 13: 36. This would seem easiest to understand of the phenomenon of 'departure' in death, especially in view of the suggestive reference in 13: 37 to Peter's willingness to follow Jesus even to death.[9] The

---

[4] Indeed, as Bammel, 48, says, 'It is remarkable that Papias says nothing about the Gospel of Luke . . .'.

[5] e.g. Bultmann, *John*, 601–2. Such an interpretation need not at all be made along the Gnostic and Mandaean lines suggested by Bultmann and, among others, Widengren; e.g. J. C. James, 428, 'The allusion . . . is to the temple, בּיט אלה, in the precincts of which there were many apartments (cf. I K 6[5], Ezr 8[29], Jer 35[2, 4] 36[10]). So around the temple-throne of God there are mansion-thrones for His people (cf. Rev 4[4]).' The existence and significance of the temple imagery in these verses has recently been examined by James McCaffrey.

[6] e.g. Bietenhard, *Welt*, 176–7; Van Hartingsveld, 142. Schnackenburg, *John*, iii. 410 n. 45 lists Bernard, Schlatter, Tellmann, Strathmann, Morris for this view.

[7] Dodd, *Interpretation*, 405. See also Hamilton; Robinson, *Coming*, 178.

[8] Gundry, 68–72.

[9] Schnackenburg (*John*, iii. 60) thinks the closest parallels to the thought are contained in the *Similitudes of Enoch* (cf. Gundry, 71, who does not exploit the full parallels), where (e.g. 39. 4f.; 41. 2; 71. 5–10) the dwellings of the just are in heaven with the angels and it is clear that they are received directly after death.

connection between following Jesus to death and then being where he is was made earlier in 12: 24–6, 'Truly, truly, I say to you, unless a grain of wheat falls into the earth and dies, it remains alone . . . He who loves his life loses it, and he who hates his life in this world will keep it for eternal life. If any one serves me, he must follow me; and where I am, there shall my servant be also.' In the Father's glorious presence is where Jesus 'is', and it is here he desires his disciples to be, with him: 'Father, I desire that they also . . . may be with me where I am, to behold my glory which thou hast given me in thy love for me before the foundation of the world' (17: 25). Isaiah beheld Jesus' glory in his heavenly temple (12: 40–1). Is it not such a vision that Jesus is preparing for those whom he takes to be with himself in his Father's many-roomed temple?

2. *The Pauline Corpus*

Paul's statements in Philippians 1: 22–3 and 2 Corinthians 5: 1–10 have from the earliest to the most recent times been read as signifying a belief in an immediate removal to the presence of Christ at death.

For all the difficulties contained in 2 Corinthians 5: 1–5, it is at least well recognized that vv. 6–8 denote an immediate fellowship 'at home' with the Lord as soon as one is 'away' from the earthly tabernacle.[10] Thus, whatever may be the true meaning of the preceding verses, the author's distance from the chiliastic view of the intermediate state is already made plain. Being at home with the Lord cannot be imagined as spending an interim existence in the segregated compartments of the underworld but naturally evokes the heavenly world where Christ is (1 Cor. 15: 47; Rom. 8: 34; Eph. 1: 20; Phil. 3: 20; Col. 3: 1; 1 Thess. 1: 10; 4: 16; 2 Thess. 1: 7).[11]

Moreover, some interpretations of vv. 1–5 would take Paul's subject here to be a heavenly existence between death and the resurrection. One interpretation which has gained many recent adherents

[10] For the interesting post-reformation history of the interpretation of this 'crux interpretum' see Lang.

[11] It seems to me that this puts Paul beyond Hanhart's category of 'reverent agnostic' (*JBL*, 445, 453) with regard to conceptions of afterlife. Being 'with Christ' is in itself quite a significant definition of the afterlife. If Paul's language here indulges in metaphor which 'resists localization' (Hanhart, 452) the type of metaphors for locale which he uses are at least capable of fruitful comparison with other metaphorical, and with more concrete, forms of expression.

maintains that the 'building from God' in 5: 1 is the resurrection body, elsewhere expected to be bestowed at the parousia but here believed to be inherited at death.[12] While the reception of the ultimate glorified body at death disqualifies the use of the term *status intermedius*, it is still understood as a reception in heaven. On another view, one which appeals to the present writer, the 'building from God' is instead another NT instance of the use of house or temple terminology to denote the habitation of the departed in heaven (cf. John 14: 2; probably Luke 16: 9; Heb. 9: 12; 24; Rev. 6: 9; 11: 19; 13: 6; 15: 5, 8).[13] Paul's heavenly house 'made without hands' mirrors exactly several other NT allusions to the heavenly temple, Acts 7: 48 (cf. 17: 24); Hebrews 8: 2; 9: 11, 24. Lang and Furnish helpfully note the substantial parallels with Philippians 3: 12–21,[14] 'But our commonwealth is in heaven . . .', which widens the conception of the heavenly realm beyond house/temple imagery to city/country imagery.

Paul's assumption in 1 Corinthians 5: 6–8 that being away from the body is being at home with the Lord is reiterated in Philippians 1: 23 in the confession of his desire to depart and be with Christ, that being far better than remaining 'in the flesh' (σαρκί). Neither expression allows room for anything other than the belief in an instantaneous consummation of that expected nearness which we have also noted in the promises of Luke 23: 43 and probably John 14: 3.[15] We need not stress here the possibility that the 'prize of the upward call of God in Christ Jesus' in Philippians 3: 14 refers to this 'ascension' to the Lord's presence in the heavenly commonwealth (cf. *3Bar.* 6. 15; *5Ez.* 2. 37). The 'Christward' focus of his conception of the intermediate state already rules out any attachment to the contemporary notion, which Paul might have held in his former life as a Pharisee, of a subterranean detainment.[16]

It is, again, instructive to observe that the early chiliasts generally

---

[12] Most thoroughly defended by Harris, *Raised Immortal*, whose list of proponents, 255, n. 2, includes C. F. D. Moule, W. D. Davies, and F. F. Bruce.

[13] According to Allo, *Corinthiens*, 139, this approach is found in Ephraem, Photius, Hervé, and Aquinas. See also Hodge, 109–10; Furnish, 294–5; Hanhart, *JBL*, 453–4.

[14] Lang, 184; Furnish, 295.

[15] On the notion of 'soul sleep' see § IV.1 below.

[16] Paul knows the association of 'the dead' with 'the abyss' in Rom. 10: 7 (see Jeremias, 'ἄβυσσος'). In a comparison of this text with his use of Ps. 69: 8 in Eph. 4: 8–10 the acceptance of a notion of a liberation of the righteous captives from an underworldly realm of the dead might be seen. But this has not been accepted by many modern interpreters.

(excepting Methodius) do not engage either of these Pauline passages in their extant writings. Papias, as is well known, makes no certain reference to the writings of Paul at all,[17] and the silence of Justin, and more especially that of Irenaeus, Commodianus, Victorinus, and Lactantius with respect to these passages is nothing less than remarkable. We have already commented on Tertullian's change of position on them.[18] His only references to 2 Corinthians 5: 6–8[19] come from his later period in *Res.* 43 (AD 210–12),[20] where he attributes these verses to Paul as martyr, in order to preserve the position that only martyrs are spared detention in the underworld before the resurrection.[21]

Further research on the relation between Paul's notions of the heavenly commonwealth of Philippians 3: 20, his reference in Galatians 4 to the Christian's celestial metropolis (contrast the *earthly* 'Zion, the mother of us all', in *4Ez.* 10. 7) on the one hand and his perception of the kingdom of God or Christ on the other, could prove fruitful. Paul often alludes to the Christian's inheritance of or in the kingdom of God (1 Cor. 6: 9, 10; 15: 50; Gal. 5: 21 Eph. 5: 5; cf. Jas. 2: 5).[22] Echoing the words of the risen Christ to him (Acts 26. 18), Paul can also link reception of the 'inheritance' to being with the holy ones (Col. 1: 12, cf. Acts 20: 32; Eph. 1: 18).[23] But the description 'to share in the inheritance of the saints in light' (Col. 1: 12) is perhaps significant. Is this light, as it was for Ignatius half a century later (Ignatius, *Rom.* 6. 2), a predicate of the heavenly realm which was to be the lot of the Christian at death? Is this inheritance the 'lot and portion among thy saints' which Polycarp understood as the heavenly inheritance of departed Christians (Polycarp, *Phil.* 12. 2)?[24]

[17] Bammel, 48; Körtner, 42. See especially Nielsen, *ThSt.*

[18] See above, § I. 2. 3.

[19] Tertullian referred the subject of 5. 1–5 to the putting on of the resurrection body at the parousia for all the faithful who would be alive at that day (*Marc.* v. 12; *Res.* 41).   [20] Quasten, ii. 283.

[21] Note the revival of this hypothesis in Schürer, ii. 542–3!

[22] Peter knows of an inheritance 'kept in heaven for you' (1 Pet. 1: 3, 4). Other NT texts also speak of a treasure or reward in heaven (Matt. 5: 12; 6: 20; 19: 21; Mark 10: 21; Luke 6: 23; 12: 33, 34; 18: 22).

[23] Here meaning not the angels, as at Qumran (1QH iii. 22; xi. 11. 12; 1QapGen II) and possibly *Wisd.* 5. 5, but the saints as Acts 26: 18 shows.

[24] In the Qumranite *Genesis Apocryphon* Enoch's sharing 'the lot [of the angels], who taught him all things' (1QapGen II) is such a lot, in heaven. Though for Paul the holy ones are humans and not angels, the concept is in the main the same: an inheritance in heaven.

A final verdict on Paul's relation to chiliasm cannot be given apart from detailed work on 1 Corinthians 15: 20–8 such as cannot be undertaken here. Elsewhere I have shown reasons for concluding that that passage indeed does not evince a chiliastic scheme.[25] What we can say from the present study is that chiliastic eschatology entailed a version of the intermediate state which was undoubtedly known to Paul but decisively rejected by him, and that what he puts in its place is that 'heavenly' version which belonged to a non-chiliastic outlook.

3. Hebrews

Compressed into the three verses of Hebrews 12: 22–4 in a unified picture are several elements of the Pauline conception of the intermediate state. Here is the heavenly Jerusalem/Zion, the scene of angelic worship, the eschatological realm of the Christian which he has 'approached' here and now, and the present realm of the departed saints. Most commentators accept as a matter of course that by πνεύμασι δικαίων τετελειωμένων in 12: 23 the author means 'to the departed spirits of righteous men made perfect' and numbered among the denizens of heaven.[26] Many would also refer 'the assembly of the first-born who are enrolled in heaven', mentioned earlier in the same verse, to the same saintly body. Made perfect through Christ's offering of himself (10: 14), the society of these spirits (of both covenants) forms an integral part in the make-up of the city which has foundations, whose builder and maker is God (11: 10), the city 'to come' (13: 14). Certainly this Mount Zion

---

[25] Hill, *NovT*. J. Lambrecht, *NovT*, has recently responded to this article, criticizing my proposal for the structure of Paul's argument in 1 Cor. 15: 20–8. But while we offer differing analyses of the structure of this passage, Lambrecht agrees with the conclusion that the kingdom of Christ there treated by Paul is the present reign of the interadvent period inaugurated by the resurrection and ascension of Christ.

[26] e.g. Westcott, 415, 418; Moffatt, *Hebrews*, 217–18; Spicq, ii. 406, 408; Héring, *Hébreux*, 119 (martyrs); Montefiore, 232; Hughes, *Hebrews*, 544–5; Attridge, 376. The notable exception is Buchanan, 222–4, who envisions the whole scene as a festival gathering in the restored earthly Jerusalem said to have been shortly expected by the author. Hughes's judgement (546) that if such expectations fell within the scope of the author's reference they are there rather as misconceptions to be corrected is, it seems, much more credible. See also Attridge, 374, n. 54.

A favourable comparison is to be made, as Spicq observes, to the *Similitudes of Enoch* 39. 4–7. 'There [i.e. in the ultimate ends of heaven] I saw other dwelling places of the holy ones and their resting places too. So there my eyes saw their dwelling places with the holy angels, and their resting places with the holy ones. . .'.

embraces for our author the heavenly sanctuary (9: 12; 24) into which the great High Priest has entered, and is more or less synonymous with the heavenly homeland which was the patriarchal desideratum (11: 14–16). Probably therefore it is also that same antitypical land of 'rest' where is celebrated the perpetual Sabbath (the πανήγυρις of 12: 22?) when the labours of life are ended (4: 10, 11; cf. Rev. 14: 13).[27]

4. 2 Peter 1: 11[28]

> so there will be richly provided for you an entrance (εἴσοδος)
> into the eternal kingdom of our Lord and Saviour Jesus Christ.

Is this eschatological entry into the eternal kingdom of Christ to be understood as occurring in death?[29] Death, his own death, is on the author's mind as he writes this epistle of 'reminder'.[30] His expressed purpose in setting his thoughts on paper is to leave to his readers a lasting record of his teaching so that they may recall it at any time after his death (1: 12–14). His death will be the putting off of his 'tent' (1: 14); it will be his ἔξοδος ('departure' 1: 15). Corresponding to this ἔξοδος from his earthly 'tent' (σκήνωμα, cf. 2 Cor. 5: 1) is his anticipated εἴσοδος (entrance) into the eternal kingdom of our Lord and Saviour Jesus Christ.

It is true that the author would direct the hope of the Christian to the ultimate arrival—after the destruction of this world—of the new heavens and the new earth in which dwells righteousness (3: 13, cf. Matt. 25: 34), but there is no reason why he would not have believed, along with other early Christian authors, that the kingdom of God and of Christ exists *already* in heaven.[31]

The understanding of Peter's words in 1: 11 as signifying an entry into Christ's kingdom in heaven when the body is laid aside

---

[27] Spicq, ii. 84; Attridge, 375.

[28] Notwithstanding the several ways of understanding Christ's preaching to the 'spirits in prison' (3: 19–22), I am not persuaded that 1 Peter offers us any firm basis for judging its doctrine of the intermediate state beyond saying that the (Christian) dead are yet alive in the spirit like God (4: 6).

[29] Compare 'you will never fall' of v. 10 with the teleological promise of Jude 24 (Bauckham, *Jude, 2 Peter*, 191).

[30] Bauckham, *Jude, 2 Peter*, 131–2, emphasizes the character of 2 Peter as a farewell speech or testament, 1: 3–11 being one of the main proofs of this.

[31] Cf. Luke 23: 43; John 14: 2; 2 Cor. 5: 6–8; Heb. 12: 22–4; Hermas, *Sim.* 9. 15. 2, 3; 9. 16. 2, 3, 4; 9. 20. 2, 3; 9. 29. 2; 9. 31. 2; Ignatius, *Eph.* 9. 2; *MartPolyc.* 20. 2.

cannot be criticized as anachronistic and should in fact be seen as an interpretation eminently suitable to the context of the epistle. It would thus amount to an equation of the intermediate state of the righteous with the kingdom of Christ in heaven and in this it would stand alongside Luke 23: 42–3.[32]

Though we can by no means assume that all of the NT texts treated above could have been available to the author of Revelation, they point none the less, through the diversity of their authors, to a widespread conviction of a heavenly intermediate state for those who belong to Christ, a conviction surely conventional in at least many segments of the Christian Church by the time the seer of Patmos received his revelations.

2. THE BOOK OF REVELATION AND CHILIASM

We have searched for possible NT representations of the intermediate state outside the book of Revelation and have uncovered no sure evidence for the view we have come to associate with chiliasm, finding instead several apparent examples of that view which is associated with non-chiliasm. We turn now to the book of Revelation.

It is not our task here to present a detailed exegesis of Revelation 20. (A review of the major elements of the millennial scene of Revelation 20: 1–10 as they appear in the non-chiliastic exegesis will be given in § IV.3 below.) The plan of the present work merely allows us some comments on the alternative contexts which chiliasm and non-chiliasm provide for our understanding of the author's eschatology. Since the early non-chiliastic interpretation of Revelation 20: 4–6 sees the teaching of that passage largely in terms of the intermediate state in Christ's kingdom during the present era, we shall begin with a discussion of the book's notion of the intermediate state.

1. The Intermediate State in the Book of Revelation

Tertullian, as we have seen, claimed John's vision in Revelation 6: 9–11,[33] which specifies as martyrs those abiding under the

---

[32] It is quite possible that these are also joined by 2 Tim. 4: 18, 'The Lord will rescue me from every evil and save me for his heavenly kingdom', cf. 1: 11–12.

[33] Along with Perpetua's vision, where it is not at all obvious that Tertullian's claim, to the effect that Perpetua saw only martyrs in heaven, is justified.

heavenly altar, as support for his view that only martyrs and not Christians generally are exempted from Hades before the return of Christ. Without going any further, it should be remembered that even if this were shown to be the view of the author of Revelation, it, strictly speaking, would already signify a break with the chiliastic order: not even martyrs were allowed an exit from sheol in *4Ez.*, *2Bar.* or in the Pharisaic eschatology described by Josephus and exemplified in *2Macc.* and *3Macc.* This is shown again by Victorinus' attempt later in the third century to heal the breach.[34] The presence in heaven of 'the souls of those who had been slain for the word of God and for the witness they had borne' in 6: 9–11 already provides a reasonable cause for viewing 'the souls of those who had been beheaded for their testimony to Jesus and for the word of God' of 20: 4 as souls in heaven during the present era. Are there any other indications in Revelation that the redeemed of the earth may enjoy the life of heaven between death and the resurrection?

(a) *The Multitudes in Heaven.*   Victorinus aside, the famous picture of the 'souls of those who had been slain for the word of God and for the witness they had borne' resting beneath the altar in 6: 9–10 has won near universal recognition as a picture of martyrs in heaven prior to the parousia.[35] The reader of Revelation is, however, frequently presented with visions of multitudes in heaven where John takes no care whatsoever to preserve the impression that these are always literal martyrs.[36]

This heavenly altar under which the souls of the slain reside should be identified with the 'golden altar of incense' (8: 3, 5; 9: 13;

---

[34] See above, § I. 2. 7.

[35] Though Fiorenza, *CBQ*, 554, believes it is questionable 'whether the thought of "a separation of body and soul after death" is here present'. Ladd, 103, is more definite: the scene 'has nothing to do with the state of the dead or their situation in the intermediate state'.

[36] Similarly, in 14: 13 those who reap the blessing of rest are all who die in the Lord henceforth, and not martyrs only. The macarism of 14: 13 has unmistakable sabbatical overtones: 'Blessed are the dead who die in the Lord henceforth ... that they may rest from their labors, for their deeds follow them!' Resting from one's labours must be reflective of God's resting from His labours. But unlike the world-sabbath in the world-week scheme used by many later writers, this rest for the imitators of God takes place in the world beyond death. Though the 'place' of rest is unspecified, there is a parallel here with the condition of the deceased martyrs of 6: 11 who are instructed to 'rest a little longer' under the heavenly altar.

16: 7, etc.) which is 'before the throne' (8: 3).[37] It is evidently these 'martyrs' (and possibly others) under the altar, but called through metonymy simply 'the altar', who concur with the judgements of God poured out from the temple bowls in 16. 7, witnessing, as it were, part of the retribution for which they were told to wait in 6. 11.[38] Echoing the voice of those called 'the altar' in 16: 7 is that of a 'great multitude in heaven', upon the demise of Babylon in 19: 2. We may show the interrelatedness of these three passages by setting them side by side.[39]

6: 9–10	16: 7	19: 2
I saw under the altar the souls . . .[10] they cried out with a loud voice, 'O Sovereign Lord, holy and *true*, how long before *thou wilt judge and avenge our blood* on those who dwell upon the earth?'	And I heard the altar cry, 'Yea, Lord God the Almighty, *true and just are thy judgments*.'	'for *his judgments are true and just*; for he has judged the great harlot who corrupted the earth with her fornication, and *he has avenged* on her *the blood of his servants*'.

It is reasonable to assume that they are the same beings who concur in the righteousness of God's judgements in 16: 7 and 19: 2 who also bear a concern for vengeance upon those who have shed the blood of God's servants in 6: 10 and 19: 2.[40] But the source of the heavenly voice in 19: 2 is not explicitly a martyr throng but a

[37] Charles, *Revelation*, i. 228 'According to Jewish Apocalyptic, therefore, and kindred literature, there is only one altar in heaven.'

[38] Conceivably, 'the altar' could be the 'voice from the four horns of the golden altar' (9: 13). But because this voice is a voice of command, unleashing a judgement of God (probably from ὁ καθήμενος ἐπὶ τοῦ θρόνου), and because the cry of 'the altar' in 16: 7 is rather an echo of response to an accomplished judgement of God, the interpretation above is to be preferred.

[39] 6. 9–10: εἶδον ὑποκάτω τοῦ θυσιαστηρίου τὰς ψυχὰς . . .[10]καὶ ἔκραξαν φωνῇ μεγάλῃ λέγοντες, Ἕως πότε, ὁ δεσπότης ὁ ἅγιος καὶ ἀληθινὸς, οὐ κρίνεις καὶ ἐκδικεῖς τὸ αἷμα ἡμῶν ἐκ τῶν κατοικούντων ἐπὶ τῆς γῆς; 16: 7: καὶ ἤκουσα τοῦ θυσιαστηρίου λέγοντος, Ναὶ, κύριε ὁ θεὸς ὁ παντοκράτωρ, ἀληθιναὶ καὶ δίκαιαι αἱ κρίσεις σου. 19. 2: ὅτι ἀληθιναὶ καὶ δίκαιαι αἱ κρίσεις αὐτοῦ ὅτι ἔκρινεν τὴν πόρνην τὴν μεγάλην ἥτις ἔφθειρεν τὴν γῆν ἐν τῇ πορνείᾳ αὐτῆς, καὶ ἐξεδίκησεν τὸ αἷμα τῶν δούλων αὐτοῦ ἐκ χειρὸς αὐτῆς.

[40] Charles, *Revelation*, i. 175, 'xix. 2 describes the fulfilment of the prayer' of 6: 10. They are probably the same also as the altar and the great multitude in 19. 5, 6 and those who had conquered the beast in 15. 2.

'great multitude'. Is this not the same 'great multitude which no
man could number' already introduced in 7: 9 ff.? These too, like
the golden altar of incense where the souls of the martyrs are
located (6: 9), stand 'before the throne' (7: 9). These saints who have
come out of great tribulation are 'before the throne of God, and
serve him day and night within his temple' (7: 15). That these are
deceased Christians is beyond question: they have come out of the
great tribulation and have whitened their robes in the blood of the
Lamb (7: 14). That they are all martyrs is distinctly possible but is
not mentioned. This multitude in turn bears a close resemblance to
the spotless 144,000 who, in 14: 1–5, stand on Mount Zion with the
Lamb as first fruits of the redeemed. This resemblance enhances
the opinion that this Mount Zion is the heavenly one (Heb. 12: 22),
not the restored Zion of a millennial earth. As we have seen, such
is the earliest extant interpretation of the scene, appearing in 5Ez.
EpV&L, and Methodius of Olympus. It is probably the 144,000
whom John hears singing a new song 'before the throne and before
the four living creatures and before the elders' (14: 3), all of which,
we have previously been shown, are in the heavenly throne room.
Ford notes the substantial parallels between this scene on 'Mount
Zion' and the unmistakably heavenly scene in 5: 6–11: in both we
see the Lamb standing; in both attention is drawn to the presence
of the throne, the living creatures and the elders; in both the sound
of lyres is heard; in both a new song is chanted; in both the Lamb's
redemption of human beings is extolled.[41] Moreover, in 14: 3 we are
told that these 144,000 have been redeemed from ($\dot{\alpha}\pi\acute{o}$) the earth,
which might suggest a non-earthly setting. Finally it is worth
mentioning that a heavenly elevation for this Mount Zion would
complete the accomplishment of the presaging words of 12: 12.
After the dragon has been cast down out of heaven a heavenly
choir (see next section) exclaims, 'Rejoice then, O heaven, and you
that dwell therein! But woe to you, O earth and sea, for the devil
has come down to you in great wrath . . .'. These three, heaven,
earth, and sea, then appear in reverse order in the next three
sections of the prophecy: the woeful sea spawns the first beast
(13: 1), the woeful earth brings forth a second (13: 11), but in 14: 1–5
the rejoicing of the heaven dwellers is heard in song in the presence
of the Lamb whose blood has redeemed them (5: 9; 12: 11).

[41] Ford, 245.

(b) The Heaven-dwellers. A still more definite indication that martyrs are not the only redeemed ones in heaven is to be found in
18: 20, the call to 'rejoice over her [Babylon], O heaven, O saints
and apostles and prophets, for God has given judgment for you
against her!.' Here 'saints and apostles and prophets' stand in
apposition to 'heaven' as if they constituted the inhabitants of
heaven. That this is the force of the rhetorical structure is confirmed
by a comparison with 12: 12 where we find the same form of
exhortation, 'Rejoice then, O heaven and you that dwell therein!'.
It thus appears that saints, apostles, and prophets too are among
those who make their abode in heaven (cf. 13: 6) and who, along
with the martyrs, are avenged by the heavenly justice.

In 6: 11 the souls of the slain residing under the altar are told to
continue their rest (cf. 14: 13) 'until the number of their fellow
servants and their brethren should be complete'. In Revelation
12: 10 we hear a loud voice *in heaven* celebrating the fact that 'the
accuser of our brethren has been thrown down'. The brethren of
the accused cannot be angels (in Rev. 'brethren' are humans and
are distinguished from angels, 19: 10; 22: 9) and, again, must be
children of Adam already in heaven. Significant also is the rhaps-
odic declaration of these human souls in 12: 10 that at the casting
down of the Accuser from heaven the kingdom of God and the
authority of Christ have come in heaven, even though many woes
are still in store for the earth and the sea.

(c) The Conquerors. Most commentators today are hesitant to say
outright that any of the promises to the conquerors in chapters 2
and 3 apply to the time between the conqueror's death and the
descent of the new heavens and new earth.[42] Yet this is not easy
to understand when the use of the term 'to conquer' as applied to
the saints in the rest of the book (12: 11; 15: 2; see 3: 21; 5: 5 on
Christ's conquest through death) and the stress on remaining faithful unto death (2: 10) or keeping Christ's works 'until the end' (2: 26)

---

[42] e.g. Beasley-Murray and Beckwith apply them to the future Messianic kingdom;
Swete is all but silent on the matter. Prigent is probably correct to stress the present
aspect of the promises, evoked especially in baptism, the eucharist, and the reign
already shared with Christ, while not preventing a future reference as well. The
emphasis on conquering and being faithful unto death, however, places the rewards,
proleptically enjoyed here below, properly in a realm beyond death.

are considered.[43] We have observed to be prominent in connection with the intermediate state the themes of paradise (Luke 23: 42–3), temple (John 14: 2; 2 Cor. 5: 1–5; Heb. 12: 22–4), city (Heb. 12: 22–4), and kingdom (Luke 23: 42–3; 2 Pet. 1: 11) in NT writings. All four themes are involved in the promises to the conquerors (paradise, 2: 7; temple, 3: 12; city, 3: 12; kingdom, 2: 27; 3: 21–2). In the light of the rather copious attestations of heavenly afterlife in Revelation we must ask, can the intermediate state be on principle ruled out as a referent for at least some aspects of these promises?[44] To pave the way for such an understanding, it is not difficult to imagine the promises as already pertaining to the world and the status now belonging to Christ the promiser—he plainly indicates as much with regard to the prerogative to rule the nations, which he *has received* from his Father (2: 27), and the royal session he *now holds* on the Father's throne (3: 21). The rewards promised to the conquerors then might easily belong to the heavenly world where Christ now is. Crowns are promised to the saints in 2: 10; 3: 11, thrones in 3: 21 and white garments in 3: 4–5. We find the twenty-four elders around the heavenly throne in possession of all three (4: 4) and we behold the white garments adorning the martyrs (6: 11) and the innumerable multitude (7: 9, 13–14; 19: 8, 14) in heaven. The affinity of the rewards to the present situation in heaven is also suggested by the mention of the temple in 3: 12. The problem that the new Jerusalem, once it descends from heaven, has no need of temple (21: 22) may not be an insuperable barrier to one who wishes to regard the promise in 3: 12 as fulfilled in a future state of glory.[45] But why should the promise not be related to that temple which, throughout the book until 21: 1 ff., exists in heaven? In fact, the only promise which resists being referred to the intermediate state is the obviously outstanding prospect of smashing the nations as an iron rod smashes pottery (2: 27).[46] But even this promise is

[43] Boring, 267, 'Especially important is the key term *nikao*, "conquer"/"overcome," used repeatedly to sum up both Jesus' christological mission and the essence of the Christian life, which in both cases means "suffer and die".'

[44] 2. 10, 'be faithful unto death and I will give you the crown of life' (Cyprian, *Ep.* xii. 1 [503]) and 3. 21, the promise to him who conquers that he will be granted to sit with Christ on his throne (Cyprian, *Mort.* 22; the Roman confessors, *Ep.* xxxi. 4; Origen, *ScholApoc.* xxiv; Tertullian, *Scorpiace* 12 (the martyrs only, of course) received this application in the third century.

[45] Charles, *Revelation*, i. 91, and others.

[46] Some, of course, understand this as symbolic of the conquering of the nations by the word of the gospel.

joined to a 'power over the nations' which Jesus already commands (2: 27, 'even as I myself have received power from my Father'). The extension of this present authority to the exercise of final judgement in reference to Psalm 2: 9 awaits the end of Christ's conquest (19: 15)[47] but its exercise over the nations in other respects, evidently, does not. We find no compelling reason to prevent us seeing the promises to the conquerors as blessings with Christ in the heavenly world, a foretaste of which may indeed be experienced by the faithful in this life, but which are to be inherited in a new way when the believer has 'conquered' in death.

(d) The Open Door.   If the approach taken here has any validity then we might also see the oracle of 3: 8 in a new light. Here Jesus, who has 'the key of David, who opens and no one shall shut, who shuts and no one opens' (2: 7, cf. Isa. 22: 22; 9: 6), announces that he has set before the Philadelphians who have not denied his name 'an open door, which no one is able to shut'. Beckwith argued that instead of indicating an 'opportunity for an effective preaching of the gospel', this open door denoted 'admission into a place or state, cf. Rev. 3[20], 4[1], Acc. 14[27], Jno. 10[7,9]', in this instance, a 'sure entrance into his kingdom'.[48] It is interesting that we are actually shown an open door in the next chapter (4: 1) and that it is an open door in heaven. We have already been told that Christ has the keys of Death and Hades (1: 18). This could very easily mean that Christ now also holds the key to heaven, the 'key of David'[49] from Isaiah 22: 22 thus becoming in Revelation 3: 7 no longer the key to the administration of the earthly Jerusalem (as in Isa. 22: 22) but rather of the heavenly Jerusalem mentioned a few verses later in 3: 12. The open door laid before the Philadelphians then could well be understood as a promise of reception into the heavenly city for those who do not deny the name of Jesus (cf. 2 Tim. 2: 11–12). Once

---

[47] Ps. 2: 9 is applied to the last judgement as well in *PsSol* 17. 23, 24; *SibOr.* VIII. 248.

[48] Beckwith, 480. Hemer, 162, reminds us that the two views need not completely exclude each other, though he believes the reference to evangelism would have been more immediate to the original recipients.

[49] Are the keys of Death and Hades of 1: 18 equated with the key of David in 3: 7? Not precisely. But there is surely some connection, for in the introduction to each of the other letters the sender is identified by allusion to a description of the risen Christ in chapter one (2: 1 cf. 1: 12, 13, 20; 2: 8 cf. 1: 18; 2: 12 cf. 1: 16; 2: 18 cf. 1: 14–15; 3: 1 cf. 1: 4, 15, 20; 3: 14 cf. 1: 5). His identity in 3: 7 as 'the holy one, the true one, who has the key of David' must bring us back to 1: 18.

he has entered into this heavenly Jerusalem the Philadelphian conqueror is promised that he will be made a pillar in its temple, and 'never shall he go out of' that temple (the open door is now shut behind him and no one can open it). The Christ who has conquered death and who has the keys of Death and Hades has also the key to the heavenly Jerusalem and he will open its gate to those who die victoriously in faith, so that they might take their irremovable places in the heavenly temple (cf. John 14: 2; 2 Cor. 5: 1–5; Heb. 12: 22–4).

It may be concluded then that whereas the vision of the martyrs in 6: 9–11 is calculated to impart strength and consolation in the face of horrible conditions which might call Christians to martyrdom, one's own life's blood is by no means the only 'key which unlocks paradise' (Tertullian). The book of Revelation presents instead a very full conception of post-mortem blessedness in heaven for innumerable multitudes of 'saints, apostles, and prophets' surrounding the throne of the Lamb. This results in at least a highly plausible background for one more vision of saints (whether martyrs only or others as well) reigning as priests in heaven with Christ during the interadvent era, as could be the case in Revelation 20: 4–6.

On the other hand, there must be noted in this background the fundamental contrast with the representations of the intermediate state in the two contemporary works which are often laid alongside Revelation as examples of chiliast eschatology, namely, 4Ez. and 2Bar. In these are heard no human choirs in heaven joining in the celebration of the righteous acts of God and the Lamb, no saints sitting on heavenly thrones, as Christ has sat down on his Father's throne in heaven, no human liturgy before God's throne and the heavenly altar, no prospects of being clad in white garments or of being made a pillar in God's heavenly temple. *Not even to martyrs,* but only to those extremely few privileged to have been taken from this world before death is there the blessing of awaiting the end with the (pre-existent) Messiah in heaven. What we encounter for the rest is a uniform conception of sedentary repose in the chambers of the netherworld. The highest we rise toward the doctrine of the book of Revelation is the idea in 4Ez. 7 that the soul, before settling into its subterranean chamber, is allowed a seven-day glimpse at the glory of God to contemplate the blessings it will have in the resurrection.[50]

---

[50] It was already suggested by Strack–Billerbeck, iv. 1026–8 that this is a compromise position between an older view of the dead in sheol and a newer one which

2. The Chiliastic and Non-Chiliastic Contexts

The evidence examined above weighs heavily against the likelihood that the author of the NT Apocalypse would have cherished a chiliastic hope. His view of the place of deceased saints sets him clearly apart from the chiliastic pattern of eschatology and just as clearly within the tradition of non-chiliastic thought. And, interestingly, there is to be seen in his presentation of the intermediate state a natural context for a non-chiliastic exegesis of chapter 20, some early remnants of which we have observed in our study.

With this in mind it will be instructive to re-examine the context which the assumption of chiliasm provides for the book's eschatology. This assumption has the historical advantage that the two unmistakably chiliastic Jewish documents, 4Ez. and 2Bar., appear to have been written more or less contemporaneously with Revelation.[51] Yet the chiliasm of these books throws up two perennial problems: (1) Revelation 20 exhibits, positively, some important divergences from Jewish chiliasm, the one to which we draw attention here being the place occupied by the resurrection of the just, and (2) this chapter lacks almost all of the most familiar features of chiliasm.

1. For the Jewish chiliasts the temporary, earthly, political kingdom of Israel would be the closing chapter of God's dealings in history, transpiring *before* the resurrection and judgement at the end of time.[52] None of the resurrected would have a part in the penultimate, Messianic reign. For Christian chiliasts who saw in the Apocalypse of John a Christian form of this eschatology, this order of 'kingdom then resurrection' was to cause never-ending problems. For Revelation 20 has its 'first resurrection' *concurrent* with its thousand-year kingdom; its kingdom is above all a kingdom of the resurrected (however this resurrection is conceived of).[53]

This meant that for later Christian chiliasts to accept John's scheme they had to choose one of two options. They could say with

would have allowed them into heaven. This suggestion becomes acutely interesting in the light of Bogaert's theory (BETL, 59, 61, 66–7) that the author of 4Ez. knew Revelation. Could John's Apocalypse then have been the 'new' foil against which the author of 4Ez. was reacting?

[51] See, in particular, the work of Bogaert, BETL.

[52] See Bietenhard, *Reich*, 42, 66; Volz, 256.

[53] Fiorenza, *BL*, 121–3 thus understands John to be placing this thousand-year reign not at the conclusion of this aeon but in the new aeon. An analysis too seldom considered is that this kingdom belongs to the overlap of the two aeons.

Irenaeus and Lactantius that those people about whom all the 'earthly' things are spoken, in prophecies thought to relate to the millennium, are the number of the faithful who survive the parousia of Christ, who maintain connubial bonds and continue to beget children,[54] etc.,[55] on the millennial earth. Or they had to say with Cerinthus, Commodianus, and the chiliasts opposed by Origen and Dionysius that it is the resurrected themselves who in their resurrected bodies retain these their natural bodily functions and participate in physical pleasures (with more or less sobriety).[56] In the first case chiliasts would have trouble with Paul's insistence that the resurrection of the dead in Christ and the transformation of the faithful alive at Christ's return would occur together at the last trumpet, 'in the twinkling of an eye' (Paul allowing no opportunity for resurrected and non-resurrected to coexist on a millennial earth, one group living 'like the angels of God in heaven', the other like humans of former days). Victorinus, seeking a solution within this framework, would accordingly forge a distinction between the 'trumpet' of 1 Thessalonians 4: 16 and the 'last trumpet' of 1 Corinthians 15: 52 and would place the millennium between them.[57] In the second case the chiliasts would run up against the Gospel objection that in the resurrection they neither marry nor are given in marriage, but are like the angels of God in heaven.[58] Both positions, and especially the latter one, were bound to give offence to other Christians.

2. We find in Revelation 20, on the other hand, no mention of some of the commonest features of chiliasm: the luxuriant superabundance of earth's produce,[59] the animal world's mutual reconciliation and peaceful submission to mankind,[60] increased human

---

[54] Daniélou is quite mistaken in claiming that Irenaeus makes no reference 'to the continuance of procreation during the Messianic reign' (*TJC*, 394), see *AH* v. 35. 1.

[55] Even Irenaeus, however, refers promises of eating and drinking (Matt. 26: 27–9) to the real consumption of material food by the resurrected disciples (*AH* v. 33. 1).

[56] A new trail was blazed by Methodius' idiosyncratic revision of chiliasm, which dropped all the 'earthly' items altogether and on the basis of the sabbatical nature of the millennium stated that both procreation and agriculture will then be permanently suspended (*Sympos.* 9. 1).   [57] Victorinus, *CA* 20. 2.

[58] Filaster, *DivHer.* LIX, raises this objection against the *Chiliontaëtitae*.

[59] *1En.* 10. 19, *2Bar.* 29. 5–8; 74. 1; Papias, Irenaeus, *AH* v. 33. 3, Commodianus, *Instr.* I. 44; Lactantius, *DInst.* VII. 24.

[60] *2Bar.* 73. 6, Papias, Irenaeus, *AH* v. 33. 3, 4; Lactantius, *DInst.* VII. 24. Daniélou is wrong in limiting this feature to 'Asiatic' chiliasm as its presence in *2Bar.* and Lactantius shows (*TJC*, 383).

longevity,[61] a rebuilt Jerusalem,[62] the servitude of the nations,[63] the return of the ten tribes.[64] The only reference to any earthly conditions during the millennium concerns the inability of the serpent to deceive the nations to gather them for the final battle. All of this is the more striking if, as P.-M. Bogaert's theory holds, John knew 2*Bar*.[65]

The nub of this second problem makes itself felt when it is noticed that the closest approximations to some of these 'chiliastic' characteristics in the closing sections of Revelation are in fact found not in chapter 20 but in chapters 21 and 22, which describe the postmillennial and eternal new heavens and new earth (cf. 2 Pet. 3: 13).

It is this disorientating fact which in part fired R. H. Charles's indomitable zeal to reconstruct the last chapters of Revelation.[66] Völter, Weyland, J. Weiss, Spitta, Erbes, and Bousset had all tried to meet the difficulty with competing theories of multiple authorship. Charles, however, was convinced that the last three chapters just as much as the first nineteen bore the marks of authorial unity. Still he felt constrained to admit that, 'In 20⁴–22 . . . the traditional order of the text exhibits a hopeless mental confusion and a tissue of irreconcilable contradictions'.[67] He thus found it necessary to hypothesize that after finishing 20: 3 the author had died, causing the task of the final arrangement of the book's closing materials to fall, 'to the misfortune of all students of the Apocalypse, into the hands of a very unintelligent disciple' who was 'profoundly ignorant of his master's thought'.[68] Material which should have followed 20: 3 was thus scattered in nonsensical fashion throughout the remainder of the prophecy.

One can understand, if one does not care to endorse, Charles's

---

[61] *1En*. 10. 17; *2Bar*. 73. 3; Justin, *Dial*. 81.

[62] Justin, *Dial*. 80, Irenaeus, *AH* v. 34. 4; 35. 2; for Cerinthus (Eusebius *HE* III. 28. 5) and Apollinarius (cf. Basil, *Ep*. 263. 4), complete with the restored sacrificial cult.

[63] Commodianus, *Instr*. II. 35. 15–16; *CarmA* 998; Victorinus, *CA* 20. 2; Lactantius, *DInst*. VII. 24.

[64] 4*Ez*. 13. 40–7; (possibly Irenaeus, *AH* v. 35. 1, citing *Baruch* 4. 36–7); Commodianus, *Instr*. I. 42; *CarmA* 941–6, 959–61.

[65] P.-M. Bogaert, BETL, 47–68.

[66] It is true that one may detect in Charles's work the desire to clear the Apocalypse of the charge of teaching anything but the absolute disappearance of wickedness and the wicked in the world to come, but even so, the means for fulfilling this desire lay in the assumption that the author was a chiliast.

[67] Charles, *Revelation*, i. 1. See also Charles, 'Solution'.

[68] Charles, *Revelation*, i. xxii. See also ii. 147.

reaction in the face of a real conundrum. The descriptions of the 'millennial' Jerusalem are in the wrong chapter.[69] 'There must be a fitting seat on earth for the kingdom of Christ during the Millennial reign with the glorified martyrs in their heavenly bodies.'[70] Since we find no such seat in chapter 20 and since the heavenly Jerusalem of 21: 9–22: 2 presents the closest facsimile, we should assume that the latter verses belonged originally to the subject of chapter 20. Likewise, only a millennial kingdom on earth where the reigning Christ is present will suffice, according to Charles, for a base of operations from which to execute the task of world evangelization, the like of which is presumed to be foretold in 14: 7; 15: 3–4, and 21: 24–22: 2.[71] Charles was noticeably irritated by 21: 27 and 22: 15 in their present contexts, both easily interpreted as signifying the continued existence of various forms of evil after the new heavens and new earth have made their glorious appearance. But the difficulty evaporates if these too may be transposed to the middle of chapter 20 and understood to pertain to the earthly millennial kingdom—for, as we learn from 4Ez. 7. 26–8; 13. 32–6, in the rejuvenated but still imperfect world of the Messianic kingdom the holy city will coexist with the godless nations round about.[72] The tree of life appearing in 22: 14, 19 is also manifestly out of place, as its purpose (assumed to be self-evident?) 'was to sustain the blessed that were converted from amongst the nations during the Millennial Kingdom ($22^{2.14}$) and not in the heavenly Jerusalem which came down on the new earth, where no such sustenance was needed'.[73]

During this era of some very prodigious scholarship, when Charles and his predecessors were constructing intricate critical solutions (variety of authors, derangement of texts) certain of their

---

[69] 'whereas the vision [of 21: 9–22: 5] as a whole looks to the descent from heaven from God of a New Jerusalem, several verses within it seem to envisage rather a renewal of the "earthly" Jerusalem', Wilcox, 206.

[70] Charles, *Revelation*, ii. 154.   [71] Ibid. 154, 155, 172, 457, etc.

[72] Ibid. 148, 158. See 149, 'Thus in many books in Judaism the hope is entertained, as in our text, that the Gentiles would turn to the worship of the true God, when either the earthly Jerusalem was rebuilt or a Heavenly Jerusalem set up on earth, or when the Messiah established His Kingdom upon the earth. It is true that Judaism associated this expectation with the First Advent of the Messiah; for it looked for no second. But in Christianity it was different. What had not been realized on the First Advent of Christ is, according to many a Christian prophet and Seer, as also to our author, to be realized in a far higher degree when Christ came the second time in glory.'

[73] Charles, 'Solution', 123. He could make no sense of the threat of 22: 19 even in the context of an earthly millennium and thus regarded it as interpolated.

dispensationalist contemporaries in Britain and America, committed to the integrity of the received textual order, were labouring to explain and defend John's 'retrogressions' in chapters 21 and 22 to the topic of the millennium, which John had treated in chapter 20.[74] Both groups of expositors, operating on the assumption that chapter 20 must teach chiliasm, were accounting in their respective ways for the fact that the best 'millennial' teachings in Revelation are not found in the chapter on the millennium.[75]

But these nineteenth- and twentieth-century interpreters were not the first to point up the problem. The practice of reverting to chapters 21 and 22 for details somehow left out of chapter 20 had had a long history. Pseudo-Barnabas 15. 7 draws upon Revelation 21: 5 for his expectation that 'all things will be made new' in the *seventh* millennium, before the beginning of the eternal eighth. Justin interpreted the proclamation of a 'new heaven and new earth' in Isaiah 65: 17–18a as prophecy of the millennium (*Dial.* 81), notwithstanding John's adoption of this vision for the eternal state.[76] Irenaeus faithfully referred it to its correspondent in Revelation 21–2 but assigned the verses immediately following, Isaiah 65: 18b ff., along with the words of Isaiah 54: 11–14, to the millennial city despite John's obvious application of the later passage to the city of Revelation 21: 18–21 (*AH* v. 34. 4; 35. 2). According to Origen, the literalists taught that the precious stones named in Revelation 21: 18–21 would adorn the earthly city of Jerusalem and that the resurrected saints would then live on the wealth of the

---

[74] See Kelly, *Lectures*, 571–6: Rev. 21: 9–22: 5 describes the city as, 'the holy vessel of divine power for governing the earth during the millennium'; idem, *Revelation*, 248 ff.; Bennett, 278–99; Gaebelein, 158–70: the city of 21: 9–22: 5 is suspended over its duplicate, the earthly Jerusalem, during the millennium.

[75] Even Beasley-Murray, *Revelation*, 328, says 'The primary application of verses 24 ff. [of ch. 21] is in the kingdom of Christ on earth, but is equally true of the kingdom of God and the Lamb in the transcendent order of the new creation' and again of 22: 2, 'The symbolism is more suitable to the order of life in the kingdom of Christ than in the new creation' (332). See also Zahn, *Offenbarung*, 611–25, who regards the vision of 21: 9–22: 7 as an 'Aufklärung' of the one in 20: 1–21: 8. It is true that 21: 9 begins a new vision (cf. 1: 9; 4: 1; 17: 1). But this vision elaborates on the material of 21: 1–8 not the material of 20: 4–6. Ladd aptly says that to assume that we have in 21: 9–22: 5 a description of the millennial Jerusalem of ch. 20 'raises more difficulties than it solves' (280).

[76] See Skarsaune, 402–7. 'He has so to speak combined Rev 20: 4–6 and Rev 21f to one concept. This means that Justin has problems with defining the difference in content between the millennium and the eternal life following afterwards, and a termination of the millennium as described in Rev 20: 7–10 has no parallel in Justin' (Skarsaune, 402).

nations (*Princ.* II. 11. 2). Tertullian speaks of the millennial Jerusalem not as being rebuilt on earth but as being 'let down from heaven', a description reserved by John (Rev. 21: 2, 10) for the new world after the millennium and the last judgement (*Marc.* III. 24). Victorinus (*CA* 21. 1–6) and Commodianus both follow Tertullian's lead here, Commodianus then proceeding to describe the earthly city by an indiscriminate borrowing from John's picture of the new Jerusalem in Revelation 21: 16, 22–7 (*Instr.* I. 44).[77]

The persistence of this tendency would be almost enough to make us reconsider Charles's textual theory, had not Irenaeus' citations in *AH* v. 35. 2 already proved that the order of the last chapters in his copy of Revelation is the present canonical one. Charles's theory of textual displacement (though not his nightmarish account of its process) was indeed revived and slightly modified by Paul Gaechter in 1949 and then again in J. Massyngberde Ford's commentary in 1975.[78] It has suffered rejection by the great majority of interpreters.[79] Most, on the contrary, will find it necessary to conclude that the author of Revelation represents the ultimate, glorified state of the redeemed world in figures familiar to himself and other readers of the OT and borrowed from those OT Scriptures.[80] The founding of the new Jerusalem on precious stones, its inexhaustible source of light being the glory of the Lord and not sun or moon, the vision of the nations bringing their glory and honour into the city of God, even the ugly spectacle of the wicked and incorrigibly rebellious still seeming to exist 'outside', so repugnant to every purely transcendent conception of perfected glory, show that the author cannot shake free of the language and imagery of the prophets.

But if John takes over these aspects of Israel's future hope, so prominent in the Judaism of his day, so seemingly earthbound in their original conception, and applies them along with notions altogether more ideal and sublime to the eternal state of the age to come, how then, it must be asked, does he conceive of the interim

[77] See Bietenhard, *SJT*, 24.   [78] Gaechter; Ford, 38–9.
[79] See e.g. the comments of Beckwith, *Apocalypse*, 770; Giblin, 500–1; Lambrecht, BETL, 103, 'the visionary part of Rev [i.e. 4: 1–22: 5] is by no means a patchwork of unconnected traditions but an impressive coherent whole, the work of a great mind'; Rowland, 413–14, 417; Kealy, 250, 'In general, one can say that there is a reasonable consensus that the Apocalypse as we have it is a theological unity, the careful product of one author.'
[80] See especially Rissi.

reign of the Messiah which he outlines so controversially in Revelation 20: 4–6?

The non-chiliastic tradition in early Christian thought looked to the already inaugurated, celestial reign of the risen and ascended Christ rather than to earth for the setting of 20: 4–6 and seems to have read these verses within the framework of the book's other disclosures of the intermediate state.[81] Is this how John himself understood his vision? When it is recalled that we are extremely hard-pressed to find any remotely contemporary Jewish or Christian writing (apocalyptic or non-apocalyptic) whose eschatology combines a clear notion of an intermediate state in heaven with a clear notion of an interim earthly kingdom, an affirmative answer will at the very least not fall under the charge of mistaking 'the nature of apocalyptic prophecy'.[82]

In this section we have attempted only a prelude to an exegesis of Revelation 20: 1–10 itself. There are many exegetical issues passed over here,[83] and no final solution can be arrived at respecting the question of chiliasm in that passage from the material presented here. We have none the less drawn attention to some quite ponderous historical–theological obstacles facing the argument for a chiliastic context for Revelation 20 and, on the other hand, to the high degree of compatibility which exists between Revelation's individual eschatology and that of other non-chiliastic authors.

[81] Several modern exegetes have favoured a heavenly setting for vv. 4–6, without knowledge of the early patristic evidence studied in the present work, including Hengstenberg, ii. 277–83, 296–8; Warfield, *PTR*; Lesètre, 1093–4; Sickenberger, *Merkle*, 300–15 and *Johannesapokalypse*, 179–83; Gliblin, 501; J. A. Hughes, 281–302; Kline, *WTJ* 37 and *WTJ* 39; Gourgues, 676–81 (cf. Allo, *Apocalypse*, 186–287).

[82] Beckwith, *Apocalypse*, 738. The question must be asked, to which type of apocalypse does Revelation bear the most resemblance eschatologically? Is it closer to *4Ez.* and *2Bar.* or to the *Similitudes of Enoch* and the (Christian) *AscIsa* 6–11 (see § II.3.1 above)?

[83] Of particular importance is the issue of the sequence, chronological or recapitulatory, of 19: 11–21 and 20: 1–10. On which see Bornkamm, Giblin, and, most recently, White.

IV

SUMMARY AND CONCLUSIONS

1. MILLENNIUM AND INTERMEDIATE STATE

Our study began with Irenaeus' contention that the belief in an immediate removal of the soul to the presence of God and Christ at death was a stumbling block to orthodox acceptance of chiliasm, and with his counter proposal that the chiliastic hope was properly accompanied and corroborated by belief in a subterranean detainment for the soul until the time of resurrection.

Following this lead, we observed in §§ I. 1 and I. 2 the extraordinary regularity with which the doctrine of a subterranean intermediate state in fact shows up in the writings of other Christian chiliasts (see the Table of Eschatological Views below),[1] often appearing as well with some form of polemic against the opposing view. The alliance between chiliasm and the subterranean view is developed most conscientiously by Irenaeus, with perhaps the best constructive integration by Tertullian and with the highest exegetical ingenuity by Victorinus of Pettau.

Observing this close association between the doctrines leads to the conclusion that in Christian chiliastic circles they played complementary roles in an essentially homogeneous eschatological outlook. With the discovery of the well-spring of this association in a particular strand of Jewish apocalyptic piety, best exemplified by 2Bar. and 4Ez. (§ I. 3), it will appear that chiliasm from its very inception entailed this notion of the repose of godly souls in underworldly treasuries pending the resurrection. This type of eschatological system also appeared to have had a distinctive understanding of the residents of paradise, according to which, the otherworldly

---

[1] The table is by no means intended to give a definitive number of chiliasts or non-chiliasts in our period. Since its common denominator is the existence of a classifiable notion of the intermediate state, certain known chiliasts, such as Cerinthus, Nepos, and Coracion, and other known non-chiliasts, such as Gaius of Rome and the grandsons of Jude, do not appear on it because they have not left us information concerning their views of the afterlife.

paradise preserved only those humans who had been translated before death (see the Table of Eschatological Views). The association had to be developed with some independence from its sources, however, when Christian chiliasts, following John's Apocalypse, placed the resurrection of the just at the beginning and not at the end of the millennium.

The underworld as the abode of the departed was a common enough conception in Antiquity,[2] and by no means was it customarily joined with the hope of a temporary golden age to precede an eternal 'world to come'. Even in Judaism, the first 36 chapters of 1En., for example, attest a subterranean waiting place but anticipate an eternal state of earthly glory with no deference to an interim, provisional kingdom. But we may say first that in Judaism the chiliastic scheme, when it arose, seems to have been wedded to this conception of the intermediate state, and second that Christian chiliasm retained both eschatological teachings side by side as it found them in its sources (and, perhaps, as some Jews themselves carried them from Judaism to Christianity). Thus, though the connection may not have been an absolute logical necessity, it did exist and it had a rationale. In those Jewish apocalyptic documents where it is found, an intermediate waiting place in the netherworld helped to keep the eschatological emphasis on the world to come, after a longed-for, supreme act of deliverance for the nation by God. The eschatological *summa* of the presence of God was kept aloof from man until the final stages of redemption (however these were perceived) had run their course. In the Christian chiliasm of Irenaeus this doctrine of an intermediate state under the earth kept man from overstepping the purpose of the millennium—it was the task of the millennium to supply the necessary further training for the entrance into God's spatial presence. To allow that the saints could already be enjoying the celestial life would be to eliminate the need for a future, earthly millennium.

We have also found confirmation of Irenaeus' remarks by observing the reverse pattern in early Christian eschatology. In Chapter II we discovered a very remarkable lack of any chiliastic expectation, sometimes discernible alternative views and sometimes overt

---

[2] Though for some the ancient Greek idea of a subterranean Hades had fallen into disfavour and had been allegorized (Hades is this world or the wicked in this life) or transferred to the sublunar regions, see e.g. Cumont, *Afterlife*, 70–90; Culianu, 40–2.

opposition to chiliasm in those documents from early Christianity which preserve the NT hope of an immediate removal to Christ's presence in heaven at death, whether or not a despoiling of Hades was involved (see again the Table of Eschatological Views). More results from Chapter II will be summarized in the next section.

As an epilogue to this section we may briefly note the later history of the connection between chiliasm and an infernal intermediate state. Where chiliasm sprang up after the theological developments of the fourth and fifth centuries—particularly the development of a more rigid Christian doctrine of heaven—it often did so at a place somewhat removed from its original roots. In those places the conjunction of our two doctrines is not always found. Certain developments at the time of the Reformation, however, would forge a new but not unfamiliar doctrinal alliance in the West. No longer were men so confident that there lay deep within the bowels of our own earth yawning caverns into which sentient souls could be gathered for the reception of their allotted griefs or pleasures. But the weight of many centuries' elaboration on the doctrines of purgatory and saints' merit finally became too much for the Christian world to bear. For some in an attempt to resolve a philosophical difficulty in Christian anthropology and for many others as a violent corrective to the Church's freighted teachings on the afterlife, a doctrine of the soul's sleep (or death)[3] between death and the resurrection was engendered, much to the consternation of the larger (Roman and reformed) Church.[4] In many instances this doctrine was promulgated along with new breeds of chiliasm. Norman Burns, in his study of English 'mortalism'[5] in the sixteenth and seventeenth centuries, has noted the congruency which was perceived between the two eschatological ideas.

They, like Tyndale, wanted no part of any doctrine that detracted from the importance of the great eschatological drama, and in this period some chiliasts decided that if the imagination was to give the drama of the Kingdom its due attention the idea that souls are presently in bliss must be eliminated. These chiliasts 'searched the Scriptures,' of course, but they found there what others, more interested in the immediacy of the Christi-

---

[3] Cf. § II. 7. 3 above.

[4] See Williams, *Radical Reformation*, the references under psychopannychism in the index.

[5] Under 'mortalism' are included both the notion of the soul's preservation in a dormant state until the resurrection and the view that the soul passed completely out of existence along with the body until God would recreate both at the eschaton.

an's reward, could not find: the doctrine of the sleep of the soul.... The troubled social situation of the middle years of the seventeenth century brought on, then, not only an increase in chiliasm, but a smaller, parallel increase in Christian mortalism. In the years before Hobbes linked soul sleeping with the Millennium, a number of English Christians anticipated him.[6]

The connection between soul-sleep and chiliasm has been maintained not only by individuals but was institutionalized in several nineteenth- and twentieth-century Christian sects such as Mormonism, Seventh Day Adventism, and the Jehovah's Witnesses. Time and again the validity of the doctrinal connection observed by Irenaeus in the late second century has been reconfirmed. The belief in an immediate experience of heaven at death was not only inimical to the original chiliastic eschatology but it has repeatedly proved troublesome for many chiliasts throughout Christian history.

2. DISTRIBUTION OF ESCHATOLOGICAL VIEWS

We saw in the Introduction that Justin had referred to 'pure and pious' Christians whom he could not say were pleased with chiliasm. Christians of like description were known also to Irenaeus. May we not believe that we can now identify some who would have belonged to these parties?

The express statements of Hermas, the authors of *2Clem.*, the *EpApost.*, and the *ApocPet.*, as well as Hippolytus, Clement of Alexandria, Origen, Dionysius of Alexandria, and Cyprian concerning general eschatology enable us to say with little or no hesitation that all held amillennial expectations of the return of Christ. All of these also held to some form of a heavenly intermediate state, and this fact further verifies that we have to do in early Christianity with competing patterns or 'complexes' of eschatological teaching. This verification has a reflexive impact on our interpretation of several other authors. It makes possible the inference that Clement of Rome, Ignatius, Polycarp, Melito of Sardis, the authors of *AscIsa.* 6–11, *5Ez.*, *OdesSol.*, *EpDiogn.*, *MartPolyc.*, *EpV&L*, and *ActThom.* would not have been at home within the chiliast camp, for, though we have found only half the bones of

[6] Burns, 133; see 33–5; 132–9.

their eschatological 'skeleton', the skeleton to which these bones belong is of the non-chiliastic species. It is of course possible that another species existed, formed with half the bones of one known species, half the bones of the other. All we can say is that we possess no clear examples of such a hybrid. This metaphor is of course imperfect and cannot reflect the fact, which comes into play with Irenaeus, Tertullian, and perhaps Justin, that eschatological opinions shift and evolve within a single author and at a given moment may not be consistent. The fact remains, however, that what the eleven authors mentioned above have left us of their views of the intermediate state conforms with the non-chiliastic but not with the chiliastic trajectory within early Christian eschatological thought.

It is important, in the light of current scholarly trends, to emphasize that the early, non-chiliastic trajectory does not appear to have held any prejudice whatsoever against the belief in a future resurrection of the body. In Gnosticism, of course, and at its fringes,[7] a 'heavenly' afterlife was certainly combined with antagonism to the salvability of the flesh. But this antagonism flowed from other impulses. It will be recalled that neither Justin nor Irenaeus charges orthodox non-chiliasts with denial of the resurrection of the body, Irenaeus merely faults them for being ignorant of the chiliastic, twofold *order* of the resurrection. Likewise, the analysis which holds that a heavenly intermediate state 'is only artificially compatible with' 'belief in resurrection',[8] we can only judge, would have surprised the apostle Paul. The ground motive for the heavenly view within Christianity was not a radically dualistic anthropology (most chiliasts were every bit as 'dualistic' as most non-chiliasts in this respect) but rather the deep and persistent conviction of a fellowship with Christ which even death could not sever.

One sometimes encounters the related assumption that anybody in the early Church who believed the parousia was 'near' (less frequently, anybody who believed in the parousia at all) qualifies for the designation 'chiliast'. Harnack went so far as to assert that

---

[7] Some would see the author of *AscIsa*. 6–11 creeping towards these fringes (§ II. 3. 1 above). See also our comments on Clement of Alexandria in II. 6 above. Origen's doctrine of the bodily resurrection caused notorious adverse reactions, but his teaching was at worst a reinterpretation (it is generally believed now that Methodius' criticism was somewhat rash, see e.g. Crouzel, *Origène*, 303, 321 ff.); he certainly did not seek to get rid of this doctrine which he considered essential to the Christian faith.   [8] Schürer, ii. 542.

the words 'he shall come again to judge the living and the dead' presupposed chiliasm and that outside of chiliasm these words could be nothing more than a 'rhetorical flourish'.[9] Yet Cyprian, for one, more so than Tertullian, Irenaeus, Justin, Pseudo-Barnabas, or Papias, believed he was living at the remotest edge of human history (*Ep.* LVIII. 1; *Demetr.* 3; *Mort.* 25; 27; *Epp.* LIX. 13, 19; LX. 3). This did not make him a chiliast.[10] It should be recognized once and for all that neither the immediacy nor the fervency of an author's eschatological expectation is a reliable criterion for judging whether he was a chiliast. It would be much easier, in fact, to move to the other extreme and say that faith in the last Christological article of the creed logically presupposed non-chiliasm. If the return of Christ is expressly for the purpose of judging both living *and* dead, this judgement is the final assize and does not acknowledge a penultimate millennial reign on earth.

Nor should it be thought permissible to portray all opposition to early chiliasm as 'Greek', 'allegorizing', or 'spiritualizing'. Doubtless chiliastic hopes must have seemed a chimera to any who were favourably disposed to Platonism but the eschatological scheme which looked for a return of Christ to be followed, without an interregnum, by a last judgement and an eternal state was no less 'realistic', no less 'historical' and no more 'allegorical', 'mystical' or 'Greek' than was chiliasm.

All of this should substantially alter common appraisals of the distribution and influence of Christian eschatological views in the first through the third centuries. The link between the teaching of a heavenly intermediate state and non-chiliasm permits the judgement that this eschatological pattern, traces of which have to be recognized in many NT writings,[11] was quickly and widely diffused.

---

[9] Harnack, *Lehrbuch* i. 615, n. 1 (with respect to Cyprian in particular, whom Harnack admitted was not a chiliast (*Lehrbuch* i. 616, n. 1), this amounts to something rather brutal). Cf. also 620, 'Along with chiliasm, living faith in the imminent return of Christ was also lost.' This is manifestly untrue. Richard Landes's recent and very important article demonstrates (whether intentionally or not) that imminent expectation of the end of the world fomented towards the fulfilment of each proposed date of the year 6000 *anno mundi* (usually *c.* AD 500 or 800), even at times when traditional chiliasm could not have been a particularly vital force. To cite from his article one example, 'At the sack of Rome in 410, Augustine tells us that some exclaimed: "Behold, from Adam all the years have passed, and behold, the 6000 years are completed . . . and now comes the Day of Judgment" (*Sermo* 113, 8; PL 38 c. 576)'. In the chiliast scheme 'the Day of Judgment' comes after the 7,000th year.

[10] See also our notes on the *EpApost.*, in II. 3. 4 above.

[11] It is at least to be marvelled at how, according to Harnack's construction (*EB*, 496), chiliasm could have been 'inseparably bound up with the Christian faith down

In Rome and, no doubt, in many other places where Christianity first took root, it had become conventional perhaps long before a coherent, Christian chiliasm was formulated.[12] The infernal intermediate state cannot be called 'the common' Christian view of this period, it is better labelled (within Christian circles) the 'chiliastic' view. Nor is it possible any longer to characterize 'the whole ancient Christian eschatology' as 'chiliasm',[13] or even to say that 'Chiliasm is the rule, not the exception, with the Christian writers of the second century.'[14]

With our broadened understanding of chiliasm and non-chiliasm as competing patterns or complexes of eschatological teaching, and with the discovery of the existence of an early non-chiliastic interpretation of Revelation 20, we also are made to recognize a neglected factor in the ultimate decline of chiliasm in the patristic period (see the Introduction above). A solidly entrenched and conservative, non-chiliastic eschatology was present in the Church to rival chiliasm from beginning to end. The discovery of this factor, moreover, has stemmed from an 'inner' analysis, one made by a participant in the controversy, namely, Irenaeus.

3. IRENAEUS AND CHILIASM

An interesting conclusion emerges from our study in relation to Irenaeus himself. It appears certain that he did not grow up in his Christian life a self-conscious chiliast and there is every reason to believe his chiliasm was not received from Polycarp. Instead he seems to have made his decisive adoption of chiliasm, with its peculiar notion of the intermediate state, sometime in the midst of writing (probably the fourth book of) his *Against Heresies*. If I am

to the middle of the 2nd century', when it is admitted that 'Nowhere in the discourses of Jesus is there a hint of a limited duration of the Messianic kingdom. The apostolic epistles are equally free from any trace of chiliasm ...'!

[12] The time between the two Jewish revolts seems to have been the time when Jewish, chiliastic Messianism came to full flower, when a clearly demarcated, interim kingdom introductory to the age to come, came into prominence. The Revelation of John probably belongs to this period but it must be asked how John answers this rising eschatological expectation. Does he adopt it with Christian modifications or does he counter it with a (by now) standard Christian explanation that the Messiah's 'temporary' kingdom has already begun, centred in the heavenly Jerusalem?

[13] Harnack, *EB*, 495.   [14] Lightfoot, *Supernatural*, 151.

not mistaken, the first three books and most of the fourth book contain nothing which would point unequivocally to belief in an earthly millennium,[15] while they contain on the other hand much that might be thought to be at odds with it.[16] It is in the fifth book where he finally settles on his chiliastic understanding of the subterranean intermediate state.[17]

Our study of the *MartPolyc.* and the *EpV&L* above lends support to this proposal. Both reflect the form of afterlife expectation Irenaeus opposes in the last chapters of *AH* v but to which he seems to give credence in earlier portions of that work (see III. 11. 8; 16. 4; 22. 4; 23. 1; IV. 31. 3; 33. 9 (cf. Fr. 26)). Irenaeus' knowledge of both these martyrological writings was quite intimate indeed. He certainly would have been aware of the doctrine imputed to the pastor of his youth by the *MartPolyc.*, a doctrine consistent with Polycarp's own letter to Philippi. Our manuscripts of the *MartPolyc.* purport to have been derived ultimately from Irenaeus' personal copy. The delivery of the *EpV&L* to Rome and perhaps even the writing of the epistle itself were entrusted to none other than Irenaeus by the Churches of Gaul.[18] If the theory that he authored the letter is not accepted, his role as its courier to the outside world might at least be seen as a tacit approval of its contents in general. And if indeed, as is entirely possible, he was the author, this would

---

[15] It is perhaps not until IV. 20. 10 (but possibly as early as IV. 16. 1) that we have a distinguishable reference to an interim, earthly kingdom of tranquillity.

[16] e.g. in II. 33. 5 he speaks of *one* resurrection of the righteous and the unrighteous (as he does also in I. 10. 1 and III. 23. 7), after which 'Both classes shall then cease from any longer begetting and being begotten, from marrying and being given in marriage'; in II. 22. 2 the 'acceptable year of the Lord' is 'the whole time from His advent onwards to the consummation', after which there follows 'the day of retribution', that is, 'the judgement'; as late as IV. 4. 2 we read, 'And therefore Jerusalem, taking its commencement from David, and fulfilling its own times, must have an end of legislation, when the new covenant was revealed.' In V. 34. 4–35. 2, by contrast, he insists that the earthly city must be rebuilt.

[17] It has been pointed out that Irenaeus accepts a non-chiliastic exegesis of Isa. 11 in the *Proof* 61 and this is sometimes seen as a retraction of his former chiliasm (e.g. by Hanson, *CHB* i. 433). It may be however, as Bardenhewer (i. 409) has suggested, that the *Proof* (which refers in ch. 99 to *AH*) was in fact issued sometime after the publishing of books I–III of the *AH* but before the completion of book v. From his statements in the preface to book III it is clear that the first two books had been issued already, and the preface to the fourth book seems to presuppose that the third had left the copyists some time ago. The *Proof* might then belong to the period before Irenaeus had finally made up his mind on the matter of chiliasm. (*Proof* 39 can easily be read as signifying that Christ's descent to Hades allows those liberated therefrom to follow him to heaven.)

[18] See above, § II. 4.

further establish the fact that his later statements in *AH* v represent an abandonment of an eschatology formerly held.

In Chapter I we determined that when he wrote *AH* v. 31 Irenaeus was countering both heretical and orthodox dissenters from chiliasm. We may, from our analysis above, be confident that he knew very well with whom he was differing. Judging from the *EpV&L*, they included many from his own churches in Gaul. They must have included his venerated master Polycarp, Clement of Rome, whose letter to the Corinthians Irenaeus knew and esteemed (*AH* III. 3. 4), and Hermas (IV. 20. 2),[19] whose proliferation of imagery depicting a heavenly intermediate state he could hardly have missed. And we are in the interesting position of knowing that when Irenaeus wrote the last book of the *AH*, when he at last settled upon his view of the millennium and the intermediate state, he was cognizant of the eschatology of Ignatius, whom he styles, 'one of our own'. He quotes from *Romans* 4. 1 in *AH* v. 28. 4:

As a certain man of ours said, when he was condemned to the wild beasts because of his testimony with respect to God: 'I am the wheat of Christ, and am ground by the teeth of the wild beasts, that I may be found the pure bread of God.'

Irenaeus is unavoidably acquainted then with Ignatius' hope of 'attaining God' by his death. Ignatius is called a man 'condemned to the wild beasts because of his testimony with respect to God.'[20] Only four chapters later (v. 32. 1), in words fairly echoing those just cited, Irenaeus asserts that those who 'were slain because of their love to God' (*interfecti sunt propter Dei dilectionem*) must rise for the millennium before they will be made worthy, gradually, to 'arrive at' or 'take possession of' God (*capere Deum*)! It is just possible that the Latin *capere Deum* translates a lost Greek original τυχεῖν or ἐπιτυχεῖν θεοῦ, the words used so often and so distinctively by Ignatius.[21] But even if not, the idea represented by *capere Deum* must be very close to what Ignatius meant by his 'attaining God'. What is most remarkable is not simply that Irenaeus personally

---

[19] Irenaeus prefaces his only reference to the *Shepherd* of Hermas with the words, Καλῶς οὖν εἶπεν ἡ γραφὴ ἡ λέγουσα . . .

[20] Διὰ τὴν πρὸς τὸν θεὸν μαρτυρίαν κατακριθεὶς πρὸς θηρία (*propter martyrium in Deum adjudicatus ad bestias*). The Greek is from *Fragment 22* (Rousseau, SC, 360–2).

[21] *Capere Patrem* appears in III. 20. 2, *capiendum Deum* in IV. 37. 7, *pertingentes usque in Deum* in IV. 20. 6, and *particeps Dei* in IV. 28. 2 (cf. IV. 29. 7). In none of these instances does the Greek survive.

rejects this hope (even for martyrs) but that he does so, as the similarity of language in these two passages suggests, very probably with Ignatius himself in mind.[22]

This all leads to the somewhat puzzling conclusion that Irenaeus had to have known he was departing from a very widespread, traditional, Christian eschatological hope when he undertook his rigorous defence of chiliasm. Only one momentous cause, towering above all others, is capable of accounting for this departure: the increasing urgency of the confrontation with Gnosticism.[23]

Irenaeus tells us that he has given himself to the study of heterodox theology like none of his predecessors had done (IV. praef. 2). In the years which had passed since the persecution reported in the *EpV&L*, Irenaeus had discovered a natural point of contact between the gnostic troublemakers and the flock entrusted to his care. The non-chiliastic eschatology of his parishioners and his former self, which allotted to the Christian dead a place in heaven with God and the Lamb, could easily provide a way of access to Gnostics who not only held to a heavenly intermediate state but who denied the redeemability of the material world. It must be remembered that Marcionite and Valentinian eschatologies depended on the outlines of existing Church eschatology. Marcion had begun in typically radical fashion, taunting the orthodox with the claim that Christ had removed from Hades only those who were enemies of the OT God (*AH* I. 27. 3). In other words, Marcion evidently agreed that Christians were now in heaven, only they were Marcionite Christians and not catholics. It is interesting that when Irenaeus in *AH* I records this Marcionite teaching, he criticizes Marcion only for 'saying all things in direct opposition to the truth', again indicating that when he wrote book I, Irenaeus did not yet object to the idea of a removal from Hades but only to Marcion's switching of the identities of those removed. The Valentinians on the other hand felt free to admit Catholics into heaven,[24] but their

---

[22] Grant, *Apologists*, 184, believes that Irenaeus does not cite Ignatius by name because 'he disagreed with basic elements of his theology'.

[23] The prominent role of anti-Gnosticism in Irenaeus' millennialism, recognized by many scholars, e.g. J. T. Nielsen, 93, O'Rourke Boyle, 9–13, Daniélou, *TJC*, 386, is patent throughout the defence.

[24] MacRae, 321, 'Influenced by their position within—or on the margin of—Christianity, the Valentinians allow a place of intermediate repose or salvation . . . for the 'psychic' class of people who are other, non-Valentinian Christians.'

taunt was the claim that the seventh heaven these 'psychics' occupied with the Creator (Demiurge) was far inferior to the eighth
heaven of the Valentinian pneumatics (*AH* I. 7. 1). Both apostate
eschatologies presuppose an orthodox teaching of post-mortem
blessedness in heaven—notwithstanding Irenaeus' deduction
(v. 31. 1; 32. 1) that this teaching had entered orthodoxy from heresy. To do away with both types of heretical boasting Irenaeus had
simply to decide to champion the chiliastic eschatology with which
he was familiar from the writings of Papias, Justin, Pseudo-Barnabas, and, possibly, certain Jewish apocalyptic literature, thereby
cutting off the heretics and their platform within orthodoxy in one
fell swoop. This is not at all to suggest that Irenaeus was less than
sincere when he defended chiliasm. Indeed, the last five chapters
in the *AH* do, in a way, form a fitting capstone to his whole 'pro-
materialist' polemic against heresy.[25] The doctrine of chiliasm was
tailor-made for refuting Gnostics, providing at once a tremendous
apologetic for the goodness of the material creation and, with its
attendant conception of the intermediate state, an antidote to the
aggravating Gnostic pretensions to a super-celestial existence after
death.

4. A NON-CHILIASTIC EXEGESIS OF REVELATION 20

We have observed the existence, long before Tyconius, Jerome, and
Augustine, of a non-chiliastic interpretation of Revelation 20: 4–6.
Important aspects of this interpretation indeed were inherited intact
by its fourth- and fifth-century descendants, though some distinctive traits did not apparently survive. An indication of how this
early interpretation fitted within a larger set of texts thought to
speak of the heavenly world of Christ's kingdom, and how these
contributed to martyrological thought, may be gained from the
Appendix and from various places in our study. Here is a review
of the major components of the millennial scene of Revelation
20: 1–10 as they appear in the non-chiliastic exegesis examined
above.[26]

[25] O'Rourke Boyle, 16, believes that his chiliasm was of a piece with his other
prime, anti-Gnostic concerns, 'the unity of God in salvational history, and the
knowledge of God as mediated in and through Christ'. The role of his chiliasm in
these areas is not as apparent to me.
[26] There are obviously many exegetical points passed over here, but few of these
can be readily addressed from the early history of the book's exegesis.

1. The Binding and Release of Satan, 20: 1–3, 7–8

We have noticed at several points the theme, especially popular in Christian preaching, of Satan's binding during the present era (cf. 2Clem. 20. 4; Melito, PP 102; Claudius Apolinarius (Eusebius, ChronPasc. praef.); Irenaeus, *AH* III. 18. 6; III. 23. 1, 7; V. 21. 3; Hippolytus, CD IV. 33. 4–5. GospNicod. 22). Though the exegetical starting point for this was usually Matthew 12: 29 (pars.) it is *prima facie* doubtful whether the tremendous soteriological weight fastened to this binding could have been sustained from this Gospel account alone. The binding is for example associated not with its Gospel setting in the earthly life of Jesus but with the destruction of death and the trampling down of Hades by Christ (Melito PP 102; Irenaeus, *AH* III. 23. 1) and with the liberation not just of the demon-possessed during Jesus' Palestinian ministry but of 'humanity' (Irenaeus, *AH* V. 20. 3; Hippolytus, CD IV. 33. 4–5). That Matthew 12: 29 and Revelation 20: 1–3 were seen as complementary is attested when Irenaeus himself uses them interchangeably (*AH* III. 23. 1, 7). Even Revelation 20, which speaks after all of Satan's release after the thousand years, may not at first glance seem to supply all this added theological weight. But an important clue is that the abyss in that passage was interpreted as Hades.[27] For the binding is sometimes closely associated with the treading down of Hades (Satan's 'house' of Matt. 12: 29, Melito, PP 102; Origen, CRom. v. 10) and the bearing aloft of the redeemed to heaven (Melito, PP 102),[28] and Satan is even presented as bound and imprisoned in Hades (Origen, HomGen. 1; GospNicod. 22). The connection with Hades comes not from the Gospels but from Revelation 20: 3. Thus a rationale from Revelation 20 for the soteriological significance of the binding is seen—Satan's hegemony over death is broken once and for all (Heb. 2: 14–15), the keys of death and Hades are now in the Redeemer's hand—and even a subsequent loosing of Satan from his prison would not then be tantamount to a relapse of salvation history. The form of reference in 20: 2 to the devil, 'the dragon, that ancient serpent', an overt recollection of the Genesis

---

[27] Cf. 'the key of the abyss', 20: 1 with 'the keys of death and of Hades', 1. 8. Jerome (Victorinus' commentary, Haussleiter, 143) and Augustine (CivDei xx. 7), by contrast, understood the abyss to be the hearts of the wicked.

[28] Probably to be read in this light is Irenaeus' comment, in connection with the binding of the strong man, that Christ was a man 'contending for the fathers' (*AH* III. 18. 6).

story, would not have been lost on these early interpreters who saw in Satan's binding an overturning of the sentence of death which had come about through his instigation.[29] As put by Hippolytus, Christ is the one 'who drew out of the nethermost Hades the man first-formed of the earth, lost and held by the bonds of death; he who came down from above and bore upward him who was below unto the things above ... And having been suspended on the tree he made him (man) lord over him who had conquered...' (*Song*, fr. 1).

This evidence for a present reference of the binding should be coupled with the Vienne and Lyons churches' interpretation of the horrible bloodletting they had experienced as the raging of a restrained adversary, the devil, who would one day come without restraint (ἀδεῶc) against the Church. We have proposed that the choice of this word was influenced by the binding of Satan in Revelation 20: 1–3, and if so, reflects an early non-chiliastic approach to that chapter. Thus the attack of Gog and Magog at the close of the millennium (Rev. 20: 7–9) had, it can be said, a natural and highly plausible application to this unrestrained coming, the final persecution of the Church, the 'war' expected to take place just before the parousia (cf. Rev. 16: 14; 17: 14; 19: 19; 2 Thess. 2: 3–11).

2. The Reign, 20: 4–6

As to the identity of the participants in the millennial reign, there is not a great difference between chiliast and non-chiliast, both admitting the righteous of all ages.[30] The one real difference was that the martyrs, whose special mention in Revelation 20: 4 was reflected in the prominent place given them in early non-chiliast exegesis, received no similar distinction in chiliasm. As heaven was the scene of the reign in the non-chiliastic view, such a focus on

---

[29] The throwback to Genesis would have been aided by the mention of 'deception' in 20: 3, cf. Gen. 3: 13 (and 2 Cor. 11: 3; 1 Tim. 2: 14). Though the specific goal of the deception in chapter 20 is the gathering of Gog and Magog for battle.

[30] Prigent, *L'Apocalypse*, 311, states that Cyprian seems to have been the first to interpret the faithful in this passage as not being all martyrs. Cyprian is rather the first to say so explicitly. Justin assumes that the patriarchs as well as the just of all ages are resurrected to participate in the millennial reign (*Dial.* 80) as does Irenaeus. Further, early portrayals of the intermediate state in heaven assume the presence there of non-martyrs and martyrs together.

the martyrs was merely in keeping with so many of the early Christian representations of heaven, as martyrs are customarily found in the first ranks of the redeemed populating the celestial kingdom.

If the identity of the participants was non-controversial the same cannot be said of their 'state' of existence. The ψυχαί of 20: 4 were to the non-chiliasts 'disembodied' souls, pre-eminently those of the martyrs, already in heaven.[31] There they shared in the kingdom of Christ, participating in his ruling and judging and serving the heavenly altar as priests in the heavenly sacerdocy (Clement, *Strom.* VI. xiii. 106. 2; Hippolytus, *CD* II. 37. 4; Origen, *ExhMart.* 30 (cf. 28, 37); Dionysius (Eusebius *HE* VI. 42. 5); Cyprian, *Fortunatum* 12; the Roman confessors, Cyprian's *Ep.* XXXI. 3).

We know that Augustine, in continuity with the non-chiliastic tradition, still reserved a large place in his exegesis for the 'Church triumphant' in heaven. He understands 'the souls of those who had been beheaded' to be Christian martyrs (who also stand for the rest of the Christian dead) now in heaven, who reign, 'though not as yet in conjunction with their bodies' (*CivDei* XX. 9). But a point should be made concerning the 'first resurrection' of 20: 5–6. Tyconius, Jerome, and Augustine understand the first resurrection to be the resurrection of the soul to new life in baptism.[32] We have seen, however, that at least twice in previous Christian literature the first resurrection seems to have been understood as the rising of the soul to heaven at death (Hippolytus, *CD* II. 37. 4; Origen, *HomJer.* II. 3; cf. Ignatius *Eph.* 11. 2; *Rom.* 4. 3). This understanding of the first resurrection of Rev. 20: 5–6 was apparently accepted by Ambrose of Milan.[33] To my knowledge, it does not surface again, after Augustine's epoch-making exposition of the passage, until Berengaudus, a commentator of the eighth or perhaps the twelfth century.[34] Berengaudus knows the Augustinian exegesis but care-

---

[31] By the chiliasts no special notice is taken of the 'souls' mentioned here, for the first resurrection was understood as the bodily 'resurrection of the just' a thousand years (or a part thereof, according to individual merit, in the view of Tertullian) before the bodily resurrection of the wicked.

[32] Tyconius, Bonner, 3, 28, and in Gennadius, *De Viris Illustribus* 18; Jerome, Haussleiter, 141; Augustine, *CivDei* XX. 6–7, 9.

[33] *In Ps.* 1. 47–54, according to Brian Daley, 195–6. Daley's *EEC* article on chiliasm came to my notice too late for me to pursue this lead. Perhaps one will find more on Ambrose and Rev. 20 in Daley's forthcoming book, *The Hope of the Early Church: Eschatology in the Patristic Age* (Cambridge).

[34] *PL* 17, cols. 930–1, noted by Botte, 7. Kretschmar, 137, note 379, 150, favours the twelfth century for Berengaudus (on whom see Moreau; Levesque).

fully and cogently argues that the 'first resurrection' takes place for the elect at death,[35] for not every person who receives the 'resurrection' of baptism (Rom. 6: 4; Col. 3: 1) is in fact 'blessed and holy' and immune from the power of the second death (Rev. 20: 6), for some show themselves to be reprobate.

It is important, finally, to realize that the prevalence of this early non-chiliastic interpretation may have been greater than the relatively few actual citations from Revelation 20 in the literature of our period might lead us to think. Account must be taken of the primitive and very widely attested belief in the heavenly, divine presence or kingdom as the lot of believers and especially of martyrs between death and the resurrection. This belief shows no indebtedness to the chiliastic eschatology but rather, formed the natural framework for the early non-chiliastic interpretation of (shall we say, for the actual composition of?) Revelation 20: 4–6.

5. ESCHATOLOGY IN THE NEW TESTAMENT

Chiliasm is sometimes assumed to have been a driving force in the shaping of the eschatological consciousness of several NT figures, Jesus included. But when express eschatological statements are tabulated, only Paul and the author of Revelation, and sometimes only the latter, customarily pass the tests. If the NT documents are examined in the light of the fuller understanding of chiliast and non-chiliast eschatologies as each involving distinctive notions of the intermediate state, we shall find great difficulty in concluding that even these qualify to be classed as chiliastic. The Gospels of Luke and John, Hebrews, 2 Peter, some at least of the letters of Paul and, perhaps most importantly, the book of Revelation, by virtue of their conceptions of the dead in Christ, would place themselves within the stream of non-chiliastic eschatological thought.[36] Are there indications of chiliasm in Paul and Revelation strong enough to override the presumption created by this historical–theological typology?

We have noted two of the obstacles which face the acceptance of the chiliastic *2Bar.* and *4Ez.* as parallels to the eschatology of

---

[35] Misconstrued by Swete, ccxii.

[36] We also noted on several occasions the general failure on the part of chiliasts to deal with the NT passages which speak of an intermediate state in heaven.

Revelation. The millennium of Revelation 20 is a kingdom of the resurrected, whereas in its Jewish counterpart all inheritors of Messiah's kingdom are flesh-and-blood mortals. And, a close likeness between these kingdoms in other respects can only be achieved by mining details from John's description of the new heavens and new earth and studding the millennium with them. That these are not incidental problems is shown by our review of the interpretative difficulties each has brought forth for ancient and modern chiliast interpreters.

It will have to be admitted that there is at the very least a sharp contrast between the notions of the intermediate state of the just held by the author of Revelation on the one hand and by the authors of *2Bar.* and *4Ez.* and the virtually unanimous body of early Christian chiliasm on the other. Further, documents, whether apocalyptic or not, which are roughly contemporary and which share with Revelation a heavenly notion of the intermediate state are virtually unanimously not interested in a chiliastic expectation. Easy assumptions about chiliasm being 'canonically formulated'[37] in John's Revelation cannot stand unchallenged.

Finally, this issue is recast yet again by the discovery of an early non-chiliastic interpretation of Revelation 20, an interpretation which itself, as we have seen, grew out of the type of 'non-chiliastic' notion of the intermediate state which John himself accepted in contradistinction to that of the Jewish chiliasts.

[37] Maier, 105.

TABLE. Table of Eschatological Views

	Definite chiliast	Subterranean intermediate state	Paradise only for the translated	Definite non-chiliast	Heavenly intermediate state	Indefinite on chiliasm
Pseudo-Philo		X	X			X
2 Baruch	X	X	X			
4 Ezra	X	X	X			
Papias	X	X	X			
Justin	X	?				
Pseudo-Barnabas	?					
Irenaeus	X	X	X			
Clementine Recognitions		X	X			X
Tertullian	X	X	X[a]			
Novatian		X				X
Commodianus	?	X				
Methodius	?				X	
Victorinus	X	X	X			
Lactantius	X	X				
I Clement					X	X
Ignatius					X	X
Polycarp					X	X
Hermas				X	X	
II Clement				X	X	
Ascension of Isaiah 6–11					X	X
Epistula Apostolorum				X	X	
Apocalypse of Peter				X	X	
5 Ezra					X	X
Odes of Solomon					X	X
Acts of Thomas					X	X

Melito	X	X	
Epistle to Diognetus	X	X	
Martyrdom of Polycarp	X	X	
Epistle of Vienne and Lyons	X	X	
Hippolytus		X	
Clement of Alexandria		X	X
Origen		X	X
Dionysius of Alexandria			X
Cyprian			X

[a]Tertullian also allows martyrs into paradise.

APPENDIX

CYPRIAN, THE CARTHAGINIAN CONFESSORS, AND REVELATION 20

I append here, for its worth in illustrating an aspect of the then-current theology of martyrdom and the place of Revelation 20 in it, an excursus into the background of the problems with the confessors in Carthage during the episcopate of Cyprian. Though the details of chronology and personality cannot be certified, I hope to give in what follows sufficient evidence for many of the ideas involved and their claims to exegetical bases.

Lying behind the succession of events in Carthage in the years 250–1 we may see a pre-existing, assumed, if nowhere fully articulated, theology of martyrdom which owed something at least to a non-chiliastic use of Revelation 20. Though shared by Cyprian himself, this theology was capable of being exploited and taken to new lengths by those anxious to find ways of undermining his authority and ensconcing their own. As the Decian persecution erupted there was already current a belief that departed martyrs could partake in some way and in some measure in the process of divine remission of sins (evidence will be stated presently). On this scheme, living confessors would only be able to formulate recommendations that a given penitent be admitted to communion, subject always to clerical approbation.[1] Cyprian cannot deny this practice outright, his only complaint, though it was a large one, concerned the lack of discretion exercised by the examining confessors.

But another course also lay open to those on the path of martyrdom. They could promise that once they had departed this life in martyrdom and had arrived in heaven they would do what would then be in their power to remit the sins in question. We may learn this much from Ep. xxi (531), the letter of Celerinus to Lucian written early in AD 250. Celerinus was a Carthaginian who at the time of writing was in Rome where he had suffered bonds for confessing the name of the Lord (Eusebius, HE vi. 43. 5–6) and been subsequently released. Lucian is a confessor imprisoned in Carthage and acting as aid and secretary to other confessors. Celerinus, in this 'ill-judged appeal' (Benson), beseeches peace for his lapsed sisters,

---

[1] Benson, DCA, 983.

For I have heard that you have received the ministry of the purpled ones. . . . I ask, therefore my lord, and I entreat by our Lord Jesus Christ, that you will refer the case [i.e. of my sisters] to the rest of your colleagues, your brethren, my lords, and ask from them, that whichever of you is first crowned, should remit (*remittant*) such a great sin to those our sisters, Numeria and Candida.

Celerinus himself, though a confessor, does not assume to himself on this basis the power to remit sins but reserves his request for whichever sufferer will be the first to be crowned, that is, to die and be received into heaven. The idea is that once a martyr is in heaven he has attained a position 'like unto the apostles' (Origen, *On Prayer* 28. 9; *ExhMart.* 34),[2] who had been commissioned to pronounce the binding and loosing of sins. This is again clear when in *Ep.* xxxvi. 1 (AD 250) the presbyters and deacons in Rome express astonishment to Cyprian that the lapsed who have been granted peace by the confessors have the audacity to claim that they 'already have it in heaven', reflecting a claim for martyr authority made on the basis of Matthew 18: 18 of sins being loosed 'in heaven'. Such a claim had surfaced at least as early as the persecutions in Gaul some 70 years earlier (cf. *EpV&L.*, 'they released all and bound none', Eusebius *HE* v. 2. 5; cf. v. 1. 45) and was being allowed to martyrs (probably in Rome) in the first decades of the third century according to Tertullian (*Pud.* 22). Where had this idea come from?

Several NT sayings of Jesus played their parts in shaping conceptions of the glories of the martyr, including Matthew 20: 20–3, where it is hinted that sitting at Jesus' right or left in his kingdom has to do with first drinking the cup of martyrdom (*MartPolyc.* 14; Tertullian, *Scorpiace* 12; Origen, *ExhMart.* 28); Matthew 10: 32, where confessing Jesus before men is rewarded by his confessing the faithful one before the Father in heaven (Origen, *ExhMart.* 34–35; Cyprian, *Epp.* xii. 1 [503]; xxxi. 2 [508], the Roman confessors); Revelation 2: 10, 'Be faithful unto death and I will give you the crown of life' (*Ep.* xii. 1 [503]); and Revelation 3: 21, the promise to him who conquers that he will be granted to sit with Christ on his throne (Cyprian, *Mortalitate* 22; the Roman confessors, *Ep.* xxxi. 4; Origen, *ScholApoc.* xxiv; Tertullian, *Scorpiace* 12).

---

[2] 'The following exhortations to martyrdom in Matthew are not addressed to any but the twelve. We too must hear them, and by so doing we shall be brothers of the apostles who heard them and be numbered with the apostles', Origen, *ExhMart.* 34.

Another text which was accepted as information about the exalted status of the martyr in heaven was Revelation 20: 4–6. We have observed that this text is explicitly called upon by Origen when he says that deceased martyrs, the 'beheaded', who assess with Christ at the heavenly altar mediate forgiveness of sins as priests subject to the High Priest (*ExhMart.* 30, cf. 37). Cyprian himself stopped well short of allowing to even the glorified martyr in heaven, let alone to the worthy confessor in prison, the power to absolve sins (e.g. *Laps.* 18 [250].[3] He will concede, however, that martyrs are 'friends of the Lord, and hereafter to exercise judgement with Him' (*Ep.* xv. 3, [515], cf. *Ep.* xxxi. 3 [559]). This concession, may also have something to do with Revelation 20: 4. The precise time referent for this judging with Christ is unspecified; it might look ahead to a time after Christ's second coming (as in *Fort.* 13 [346]). But since in *Ep.* XV he is addressing the 'martyrs and confessors' it is more likely that Cyprian understands this capacity to be something which begins with their withdrawal from the world. This finds confirmation in the words of Moyses, Maximus, Nicostratus, and the other Roman confessors writing to Cyprian from prison concerning martyrdom (*Ep.* xxxi. 3 [559]):

For what more glorious, or what more blessed . . . Than to have mounted to heaven with the world left behind? Than, having forsaken men, to stand

---

[3] As long as the other-worldly activity of the martyrs on behalf of those here below could be conceived as limited to intercession, Cyprian himself would have ratified appeals to the confessors. He asks the virgins to 'remember us at that time, when virginity shall begin to be rewarded in you' (*Hab.* 24 [205. 4]). That the deceased Christian may continue in heaven a life of prayer for those on earth is seen again in *Ep.* LX. 5 (695) (to Cornelius in exile) 'Let us on both sides always pray for one another. Let us relieve burdens and afflictions by mutual love, that if any one of us, by the swiftness of divine condescension, shall go hence the first, our love may continue in the presence of the Lord, and our prayers for our brethren and sisters not cease in the presence of the Father's mercy.' There is here still no hint that those on earth may communicate their thoughts to the saints in the Lord's presence. Hence the reminders on this side of death to remember each other then. See also Eusebius, *PalMart.* 7 and *Acta Fructuosi* 5.

There is not with Cyprian as there was evidently with Origen a benefit to be gained in this life from the sacrifice of the martyrs, though confessors possessed a 'prerogative . . . with God' (*Ep.* XVIII. 1 [523, 524]), the assumed greater efficacy of their prayers (*Ep.* LXXVI. 7 [833]). We have his firm declaration that 'the merits of martyrs and the works of the righteous' avail with the Judge only on the final day of judgement (*Laps.* 17 [249, 250]). In the meantime, the wishes of the martyrs cannot be admitted without confirmation of the clergy (*Epp.* XVIII. 1 [523–524]; XIX. 2 [527]). See Benson, *Cyprian,* 97.

among the angels?[4] Than, all worldly impediments being broken through, already to stand free in the sight of God (*in conspectu Dei*)? Than to enjoy the heavenly kingdom without any delay? Than to have become an associate of Christ's passion in Christ's name? Than to have become by the divine condescension the judge of one's own judge (*quam iudicis sui diuina dignatione iudicem factum fuisse*)?

These last words point to a judging status acquired immediately upon one's departure in martyrdom. And this must remind us of the words of another Roman (?), Hippolytus, writing half a century earlier in *CD* II. 37. 4, who had said that he who departs worthily in martyrdom 'is no longer judged at all but judges, possessing his own portion in the first resurrection'. The idea seems to be the same: the martyr's victory over his persecutor is somehow reflected in his elevation to the station of judge in the other world. Hippolytus ties this in directly to the prerogative belonging to the participant of the 'first resurrection' of Revelation 20: 5–6, where 'judgement' is given to those who sat on thrones. Similarly, in the view of the Roman martyrs, this judging is placed in a complementary way alongside attainment to the *caeleste regnum*. The important statement of Dionysius supports our analysis. In language which strongly evokes the passage Revelation 20: 4–6 Dionysius also speaks of the divine condescension which elevates the martyrs in heaven to the present office of being 'assessors of Christ', who 'share the fellowship of his kingdom, and are partakers of his decisions and judge along with him' (*HE* VI. 42. 5). Once again martyrs are believed to enjoy a particularly close association with Christ in his kingdom above and participate in his judging activity in the present age. We are also reminded of Clement's view that those enrolled in the heavenly presbyterate are 'judging the people' (*Strom.* VI. xiii. 106. 2).

From Cyprian's own treatment of Revelation 20: 4–6 we already know that its thousand-year reign informed his conception of the lot of the martyrs and others in heaven after death. We have just seen some suggestion of how widespread this approach to Revelation 20: 4–6 might have been in his day.

Back to Carthage, with these and similar ideas of martyrdom

---

[4] In para. 2 (558) the confessors tell Cyprian, 'Thus, from your letter, we saw those glorious triumphs of the martyrs; and with our eyes in some sort have followed them as they went to heaven, and have contemplated them seated among angels, and the powers and dominions of heaven.'

afloat it was not long before clever minds devised the system we see in operation with Paulus and Lucian, whether conceived by them or by others. About to die and stirred up by a generous if bungling spirit of good-will, Paulus left with his attendant Lucian the assurance that anyone who henceforth asked peace from Lucian could be granted it in Paulus' name (*Ep.* xxii. 2 [534]). Cyprian was quick to perceive the import of this. Now, at any rate, if not before, the lapsed could claim the right of immediate restoration simply by obtaining the mercy of the deceased Paulus through certificates written by Lucian (*Ep.* xxvii. 1 [541]). Lucian had become a direct channel of divine forgiveness. Until due order could be restored, the bishop and the entire ecclesiastical machinery of discipline could be treated as entirely obsolete.

At some point in the mêlée refractory members of the clergy saw the opportunity of measuring swords with Cyprian by actually admitting to communion without any regard to the bishop and his instructions those who had obtained *libelli* from the confessors.[5] This encouragement and, no doubt, flattery of the confessors may then have led to more inflated claims that a proleptic assumption of 'martyr authority' is conferred before the consummation of martyrdom through the act of confessing itself. It requires some such prolepsis, whether this came relatively late in Carthage or, as other evidence might suggest, was indeed present from the beginning,[6] for the confessor before he dies to presume to restore penitents to communion.

A final outrage to Church order came when some confessors began not only dispensing forgiveness to individual penitents but saying, 'Let such a one be received to communion along with his friends.' Now this, says Cyprian, 'was never in any case done by the martyrs' (*Ep.* xv. 4 [516]).

The importance of this crisis for the study of early Christian eschatology lies not only in the part occupied in this theology of

---

[5] Benson, *DCA*, 983.

[6] In *Pud.* 22 Tertullian shows that absolution was already being given by martyrs. The situation narrated by Dionysius in his letter to Fabius also presupposes that during the Decian persecution in Alexandria martyrs had, before they died, granted ecclesiastical restoration to penitents. Compare Apollonius' question to the Montanist false prophet and false martyr, 'Does the prophet absolve the martyr of robbery or the martyr forgive the prophet for avarice?' (Eusebius, HE v. 18. 7). *ApostConst.* viii. 23 shows that church legislation was deemed necessary in order to strip away clerical dignity snatched unlawfully by unordained confessors.

martyrdom by Revelation 20 but also in the witness thus borne to the *acceptance* of this eschatology. It was common ground between Cyprian and the confessors, though it was taken to unprecedented lengths by those opposed to Cyprian; to deny the martyr's heavenly status was unthinkable in Rome or North Africa at this time (even by Tertullian's time). This is made the more remarkable by the realization that there existed in chiliasm an eschatology which, had he chosen to employ it, would have given Cyprian a powerful means for overthrowing the claims of his opponents. Tertullian already had been unable to assert a complete chiliasm on to North African soil, but Victorinus would have been able to do so with a little ingenuity and a new interpretation of Revelation 6: 9. Cyprian makes no such attempt.

SELECT BIBLIOGRAPHY

EDITIONS AND TRANSLATIONS OF PRIMARY SOURCES[1]

ANDERSEN, F. I., '2 (Slavonic Apocalypse of) Enoch (Late First Century A.D.), Appendix: 2 Enoch in *Merilo Pravednoe: A New Translation and Introduction'*, *OTP* i, 91–221.   = Andersen, OTP

ANDERSON, H., '3 Maccabees (First Century B.C.): A New Translation and Introduction', *OTP* i, 509–29.   = Anderson, '3Macc.'

BARDY, GUSTAVE, *Hippolyte Commentaire sur Daniel*, Introd. by Bardy, text established and trans. by Maurice Lefèvre, SC 14 (Paris, 1947). = Bardy–Lefèvre, SC

BERTRAND, DANIEL A., *La Vie grecque d'Adam et Eve: Introduction, texte, traduction et commentaire*, Recherches intertestamentaires 1 (Paris, 1987).   = Bertrand

Βιβλιοθήκη Ἑλλήνων Πατέρων καὶ Ἐκκλησιαστικῶν Cυγγραφέων, 62 vols. (Athens, 1955–82).

BIHLMEYER, KARL, *Die apostolischen Väter Neubearbeitung der Funkschen Ausgabe*, SQ, 3rd edn. with supplement by Wilhelm Schneemelcher, Part 1 (Tübingen, 1970).   = Bihlmeyer

BOGAERT, PIERRE, *Apocalypse de Baruch: Introduction, traduction du syriaque et commentaire*, 2 vols.: 1, SC 144 (Paris, 1969).   = Bogaert, SC 144

ii, SC 145 (Paris, 1969).   = Bogaert, SC 145

BONWETSCH, G. NATHANAEL, *Methodius*, GCS 27 (Leipzig, 1917).

—— and ACHELIS, HANS, *Hippolytus Werke*, i. *Exegetische und homiletische Schriften*, GCS (Leipzig, 1897).   = Bonwetsch–Achelis

BOX, G. H., *The Ezra-Apocalypse* (London, 1912).   = Box, Ezra-Ap.

BRAUDE, WILLIAM G., trans., *Pesikta Rabbati: Discourses for Feasts, Fasts, and Special Sabbaths*, 2 vols., Yale Judaica Series 18 (New Haven/ London, 1968).

BRIÈRE, MAURICE, MARIÈS, LOUIS, and MERCIER, B.-CH, *Hippolyte de Rome, Sur les Bénédictions d'Isaac, de Jacob et de Moïse*, PO 27, Parts 1,2 (Paris, 1957).   = Brière–Mariès–Mercier

BRIGHT, PAMELA, trans., *Early Christian Spirituality*, ed. Charles Kannen-

---

[1] Including those which contain commentaries. Commentaries on Biblical books appear in the next section.

giesser, Sources of Early Christian Thought (Philadelphia, 1986).
= Bright, *Early Christian Spirituality*

BROCK, SEBASTIAN, 'Some New Syriac Texts Attributed to Hippolytus', *Mus.* 94 (1981), 177–200.   = Brock

CAMELOT, P. TH., *Ignace d'Antioch, Polycarpe de Smyrne, Lettres, Martyre de Polycarpe Texte grec, introduction, traduction et notes*, SC 10, 4th edn. (Paris, 1969).   = Camelot

CASEY, ROBERT PIERCE, *The Excerpta ex Theodoto of Clement of Alexandria*, SD 1 (London, 1934).   = Casey, *Excerpta*

CHADWICK, HENRY, *Origen, Contra Celsum: Translated with an Introduction and Notes* (Cambridge, 1953).   = Chadwick, *CCels*

CHARLES, R. H., *The Ascension of Isaiah: Edited with Introduction, Notes, and Indices* (London, 1900).   = Charles, *Ascension*

COHEN, A., ed., *The Minor Tractates of the Talmud*, 2 vols. (London, 1965). = Cohen

COLLINS, J. J., 'Sibylline Oracles (Second Century B.C.–Seventh Century A.D.): A New Translation and Introduction', *OTP* i, 317–472. = Collins, *OTP*

CONYBEARE, F. C., 'Newly Discovered Letters of Dionysius of Alexandria to the Popes Stephen and Xystus', *EHR* 25 (1910), 111–14. = Conybeare

CROUZEL, HENRI, *Origène, Traité des principes*, tome ii. *Livres I et II. Commentaire et fragments*, SC 253 (Paris, 1978).   = Crouzel, SC 253

—— *Origène, Traité des principes*, tome iii. *Livres III et IV. Texte critique et traduction*, SC 268 (Paris, 1980).   = Crouzel, SC 268

—— *Origène, Traité principes*, tome iv. *Livres III et IV. Commentaire et fragments*, SC 269 (Paris, 1980).   = Crouzel, SC 269

—— *Origène, Traité des principes*, tome v, SC 312 (Paris, 1984). = Crouzel, SC 312

CROUZEL, HENRI, FOURIER, FRANÇOIS, and PÉRICHON, PIERRE, *Origène, Homélies sur S. Luc: Texte latin et fragments grecs: introduction et notes*, SC 87 (Paris, 1962).   = Crouzel–Fourier–Périchon, SC 87

CROUZEL, HENRI, and SIMONETTI, MANLIO, *Origène, Traité des principes*, tome i. *Livres I et II. Introduction, texte critique et traduction*, SC 252 (Paris, 1978).   = Crouzel–Simonetti, SC 252

CRUSE, FREDERICK, trans., *The Ecclesiastical History of Eusebius Pamphilus Bishop of Cesarea, in Palestine, with An Historical View of the Council of Nice* by Isaac Boyle (Grand Rapids, 1962 repr. of 1850 original). = Cruse

DE LUBAC, HENRI, and DOUTRELEAU, LOUIS, *Origène, Homélies sur la Genèse*, SC 7, 2nd edn. (Paris, 1976).   = de Lubac–Doutreleau

DIBELIUS, MARTIN, *Der Hirt des Hermas*, HNT Ergängzungs-Band. Die apostolischen Väter, 4 (Tübingen, 1923).   = Dibelius

EPSTEIN, ISIDORE, *Hebrew–English Edition of the Babylonian Talmud*, 20 vols. to date (London, 1969–84).   = Epstein

EVANS, ERNEST, Q. *Septimii Florentis Tertulliani de resurrectione carnis liber: Tertullian's Treatise on the Resurrection. The text edited with an Introduction, Translation and Commentary* (London, 1960).

—— Q. *Septimii Florentis Tertulliani de carnis Christi liber: Tertullian's Treatise on the Incarnation. The text edited with an Introduction, Translation and Commentary* (London, 1956).

—— *Tertullian adversus Marcionem* (i. Books 1 to 3; ii. Books 4 and 5), OECT (Oxford, 1972).

FAUSSET, W. YORK, *Novatiani Romanae urbis presbyteri de trinitate liber: Novatian's Treatise on the Trinity* (Cambridge, 1909).   = Fausset

FELTOE, CHARLES LETT, Διονυσίου λείψανα: *The Letters and Other Remains of Dionysius of Alexandria* (Cambridge, 1904).   = Feltoe, *Dionysius*

FREEDMAN, H., and SIMON, MAURICE, eds., *Midrash Rabbah* (London, 1961 repr. of 1939 original).   = Freedman–Simon, *MidRab.*

GARITTÈ, GÉRARD, *Traités d'Hippolyte sur David et Goliath, sur le Cantique des Cantiques et sur l'Antéchrist*, CSCO (Louvain, 1965).   = Garittè, CSCO

GEBHARDT, OSCAR DE, and HARNACK, ADOLFUS, *Clementis Romani ad Corinthios quae dicuntur epistulae: textum ad fidem codicum et Alexandrini et Constantinopolitani nuper inventi recensuereunt et illustraverunt*, Patrum Apostolicorum Opera, 2nd edn., (Leipzig, 1876).   = Gebhardt–Harnack

GOODSPEED, EDGAR J., *The Apostolic Fathers: An American Translation* (New York, 1950).   = Goodspeed

GRANT, ROBERT M., *Ignatius of Antioch*, ApF, iv (London, 1966).   = Grant, *Ignatius*

GRANT, ROBERT M., and GRAHAM, HOLT, H., *First and Second Clement*, ApF, ii (Toronto/New York/London, 1965).   = Grant–Graham, *Clement*

GWYNN, JOHN, 'Hippolytus and his "Heads Against Gaius" ', *Herm.* 6 (1888), 397–418.   = Gwynn

HALL, STUART GEORGE, *Melito of Sardis On Pascha and Fragments*, OECT (Oxford, 1979).   = Hall

HANNAN, MARY LOUISE, *Thasci Caecili Cypriani De mortalitate: A Commentary, with an Introduction and Translation*, CUAPS 36 (Washington, 1933).   = Hannan

HARNACK, ADOLF VON, *Das Schreiben der römischen Kirche an die korinthische aus der Zeit Domitians (I. Clemensbrief): Übersetzt und den Studierenden erklärt*, EK (Leipzig, 1929).   = Harnack, *I. Clemensbrief*

HARRINGTON, D. J., 'Pseudo-Philo (First Century A.D.): A New Translation and Introduction', *OTP* ii, 297–377.   = Harrington

206 *Select Bibliography*

HARTEL, GUILELMUS, S. *Thasci Caecili Cypriani opera omnia*, CSEL 3 (Vienna, 1871). = Hartel

HARVEY, W. WIGAN, *Sancti Irenæi episcopi Lugdunensis libros quinque adversus haereses*, 2 vols. (Cambridge, 1862). = Harvey

HAUSSLEITER, JOHANNES, *Victorini episcopi Petavionensis opera* CSEL 49 (Vienna/Leipzig, 1916). = Haussleiter

HOLL, KARL, *Fragmente vornicänischer Kirchenväter aus den Sacra Parallela*, TU neue Folge 5 (Leipzig, 1901) [*De universo*, no. 353, pp. 137–143]. = Holl

HORT, FENTON JOHN ANTHONY, and MAYOR, JOSEPH B., *Clement of Alexandria Miscellanies Book VII* (London, 1902). = Hort–Mayor, *Miscellanies*

HUSSON, PIERRE, and NAUTIN, PIERRE, *Origène, Homélies sur Jérémie*, trans. Husson and Nautin, ed., introd., and annotated by Nautin, i, *Introduction et Homélies I–XI*, SC 232 (Paris, 1976). = Husson–Nautin, SC 232

—— *Origène. Homélies sur Jérémie*, trans. Husson and Nautin, ed., introd., and annotated by Nautin, ii, *Homélies XII–XX et Homélies latines, Index*, SC 238 (Paris, 1977). = Husson–Nautin, SC 238

ISAAC, E., '1 (Ethiopic Apocalypse of) Enoch: A New Translation and Introduction', *OTP*, i, 5–89. = Isaac

JAMES, M. R., *The Biblical Antiquities of Philo*, Translations of Early Documents, ser. 1, Palestinian Jewish Texts (Pre-Rabbinic) (London/New York, 1917). = James, *Antiquities*

—— *The Apocryphal New Testament* (Oxford, 1926, first issued 1924). = James, *ANT*

—— introd. to Bensly, *The Fourth Book of Ezra: The Latin Version Edited from the MSS*, TS 2. 2 (1985). = James, *TS*

JAUBERT, ANNIE, *Clément de Rome, Épître aux Corinthiens: Introduction, texte, traduction, notes et index*, SC 167 (Paris, 1971). = Jaubert

JOLY, ROBERT, *Hermas, Le Pasteur: Introduction, texte critique, traduction et notes*, SC 53, 2nd edn. (Paris, 1968). = Joly

KIDD, B. J., *Documents Illustrative of the History of the Church*, 2 vols. (London/New York, 1920). = Kidd

KISCH, GUIDO, *Pseudo-Philo's Liber antiquitatum biblicarum*, Publications in Mediaeval Studies, The University of Notre Dame 10 (Notre Dame, Ind., 1949).

KLOSTERMANN, ERICH, *Origenes Werke XII. Origenes Matthäuserklärung III Fragmente und Indices*, GCS 41 (Leipzig, 1941). = Klostermann

KLIJN, A. F. J., '2 (Syriac Apocalypse of) Baruch (Early Second Century A.D.): A New Translation and Introduction', *OTP* i, 615–52. = Klijn, *OTP*

KNIBB, M. A., Martyrdom and Ascension of Isaiah (Second Century B.C.— Fourth Century A.D.): A New Translation and Introduction', *OTP* ii, 143–76. = Knibb, *OTP*

KOETSCHAU, P., *Origenes Werke I. Die Schrift vom Martyrium, Buch I–IV gegen Celsus*, GCS 2 (Leipzig, 1899). = Koetschau

LAKE, KIRSOPP, *The Apostolic Fathers: With an English Translation*, LCL, 2 vols. (Cambridge, Mass./London, 1912, 1913). = Lake, *ApF*

——— OULTON, J. E. L., and LAWLOR, H. J., *Eusebius, The Ecclesiastical History*, LCL, 2 vols.: i, ET by Kirsopp Lake (Cambridge, Mass./London, 1925); ii, ET by J. E. L. Oulton, taken from the edition published in conjunction with H. J. Lawlor (Cambridge, Mass./London, 1930). = Lake *Eusebius*

LAWLOR, HUGH JACKSON, and OULTON, JOHN ERNEST LEONARD, *Eusebius Bishop of Caesarea, The Ecclesiastical History and the Martyrs of Palestine: Translated with Introduction and Notes*, 2 vols. (London, 1954 repr. of 1927 edn.). = Lawlor–Oulton, *Eusebius*

LAWSON, R. P., *Origen, The Song of Songs Commentary and Homilies*, ACW 26 (Westminster, Md./London, 1957).

LIGHTFOOT, J. B., *The Apostolic Fathers: Clement, Ignatius, and Polycarp. Revised Texts with Introductions, Notes, Dissertations, and Translations*, 2nd edn., 2 Parts in 5 vols. (Grand Rapids, 1981 reprint of 1889–90 edn.). = Lightfoot, *AF*

MARTIN, JOSEPH, *Commodiani Carmini*, CC 78, 1960. = Martin, CC

MARX, FRIDERICUS, *Sancti Filastrii episcopi Brixiensis diversarum hereseon liber*, CSEL 38 (Vienna/Prague/Leipzig, 1898).

MATTER, E. ANN, 'The Pseudo-Alcuinian "de septem sigillis": An Early Latin Apocalypse Exegesis', *Traditio* 36 (1980), 111–37. = Matter

MEECHAM, HENRY G., *The Epistle to Diognetus: The Greek Text with Introduction, Translation and Notes*, Publications of the University of Manchester, 305 Theological Series 7 (Manchester, 1949). = Meecham

MÉHAT, ANDRÉ, *Origène: Homélies sur les Nombres*, SC 29 (Paris, 1951). = Méhat, SC 29

METZGER, B. M., 'The Fourth Book of Ezra (Late First Century A.D.) with the Four Additional Chapters: A New Translation and Introduction', *OTP* i, 516–59. = Metzger, *OTP*

Midrash Rabbah, 2 vols. (Wilna, Romm, 1887).

MILIK, J. T., *The Books of Enoch: Aramaic Fragments of Qumran Cave 4* (Oxford, 1976). = Milik

MUSURILLO, H., *St. Methodius, The Symposium: A Treatise on Chastity*, ACW 27 (Westminster, Md./London, 1958). = Musurillo, *Methodius*

——— *The Acts of the Christian Martyrs: Introduction, Texts and Translations* (Oxford, 1972). = Musurillo, *Acts*

MYERS, JACOB, *I and II Esdras: Introduction, Translation and Commentary*, AB (Garden City, NY, 1974). = Myers

OEHLER, FRANCISCUS, *Quinti Septimii Florentis Tertulliani quae supersunt omnia*, 3 vols. (Lipsiae, i and iii, 1853, ii, 1854).

OULTON, JOHN ERNEST LEONARD, and CHADWICK, HENRY, *Alexandrian Christianity*, LCC, ii (London, 1954). = Oulton–Chadwick, LCC

PARMENTIER, LÉON, *Theodoret Kirchengeschichte*, GCS 19 (Leipzig, 1911).

PEEL, MALCOLM LEE, *The Epistle to Rheginos* (London, 1969).

PERLER, OTHMAR, *Méliton de Sardes Sur la Pâque et fragments: Introduction, texte critique, traduction et notes*, SC 123 (Paris, 1966). = Perler, SC

Peshitta Institute, Leiden, *The Old Testament in Syriac According to the Peshitta Version*, Part 4, fascicle 3, *Apocalypse of Baruch, 4 Esdras* (Leiden, 1973).

PRIGENT, PIERRE, *Épître de Barnabé*, SC 172, introd., trans., and notes by Prigent, Greek text established and introd. by Robert A. Kraft (Paris, 1971). = Prigent, SC

RAMSBOTHAM, A., 'The Commentary of Origen on the Epistle to the Romans', *JTS* 13 (1912), 215–24; 357–68.

REHM, BERNHARD, and PASCHKE, FRANZ, eds., *Die Pseudoklementinen. II Rekognitionen in Rufins Übersetzung*, GCS 51 (Berlin, 1965).

ROBINSON, J. M., ed., *The Nag Hammadi Library in English* (Leiden, 1977). = Robinson, NHLE

ROUSSEAU, ADELIN, and DOUTRELEAU, LOUIS, *Irénée de Lyon: Contre les Hérésies Livre i*, 2 vols., SC 263–4 (Paris, 1979); *Livre ii.* 2 vols., SC 293 (Paris, 1982); *Livre iii.* 2 vols., SC 210–11 (Paris, 1974).

ROUSSEAU, ADELIN, HEMMERDINGER, B., MERCIER, C., and DOUTRELEAU, L., *Irénée de Lyon: Contre les Hérésies Livre iv*, 2 vols., SC 100 (Paris, 1965).

ROUSSEAU, ADELIN, DOUTRELEAU, LOUIS, and MERCIER, CHARLES, *Irénée de Lyon: Contre les Hérésies Livre v.*, 2 vols., *152–3 (Paris, 1969)*. = Rousseau

SAGNARD, FRANÇOIS, *Clément d'Alexandrie, Extraits de Théodote*, SC 23 (Paris, 1948, repr. 1970). = Sagnard

SALVATORE, ANTONIO, *Commodiani Carmen apologeticum*, CP 5 (Torino, 1977). = Salvatore

SCHOEDEL, WILLIAM R., *Polycarp, Martyrdom of Polycarp, Fragments of Papias*, ApF v (London/Camden, NJ/Toronto, 1967). = Schoedel, ApF

—— *Ignatius of Antioch: A Commentary on the Letters of Ignatius of Antioch*, Hermeneia (Philadelphia, 1985). = Schoedel, Ignatius

SEDLACEK, I., *Dionysius bar Salibi in Apocalypsim, Actus et Epistulas catholicas*, CSCO, Scriptores syri, 2, ci (1909 [text], 1910 [Latin version]). = Sedlacek

Sifre Bamidbar Dibarim (Wilna, 1966).

SMITH, JOSEPH P., trans. and annotator, *St. Irenaeus, Proof of the Apostolic Preaching*, ACW 16 (New York/Ramsey, NJ, 1952). = Smith, Proof

SNYDER, GRAYDON F., *The Shepherd of Hermas*, ApF vi (London/Camden, NJ/Toronto, 1968). = Snyder, ApF

Stählin, Otto, *Clemens Alexandrinus*, i. *Protrepticus und Paedagogus*, GCS 12, dritte, durchgesehene Aufl. von Ursula Treu (Berlin, 1972, 1st edn., Leipzig, 1905).

—— Früchtel, Ludwig, *Clemens Alexandrinus*, ii. *Stromata Buch I–VI*, GCS 52 (15) (Berlin, 1960).

—— Früchtel, Ludwig, and Treu, Ursula, *Clemens Alexandrinus*, iii. *Stromata Buch VII und VIII, Excerpta ex Theodoto, Eclogae propheticae, Quis diues salvetur, Fragmente*, GCS 17 (Berlin, 1970).

Staniforth, Maxwell, trans., *Early Christian Writings: The Apostolic Fathers* (Middlesex, 1968).   = Staniforth

Thackeray, H. St J. *et al.*, *Josephus*, 9 vols. (10th vol. added, 1981), LCL (Cambridge, Mass./London, 1926–81).

Tisserant, Eugène, *Ascension d'Isaie: Traduction de la version éthiopienne avec les principales variantes des versions greque, latines et slave. Introduction et notes*, Documents pour l'étude de la Bible (Paris, 1909). = Tisserant

Trollope, W. S., *Justini philosophi et martyris cum Tryphone Judæo dialogus, pars altera, colloquium secundi diei continens* (Cambridge, 1842).   = Trollope.

Turner, C. H., 'An Exegetical Fragment of the Third Century', *JTS* 5 (1904), 218–41.   = Turner, 'Fragment'

—— 'The *Liber eclesiasticorum dogmatum* Attributed to Gennadius', *JTS* 7 (1906), 78–99.   = Turner, 'Gennadius'

Violet, B., *Die Ezra-Apocalypse (IV Ezra), I. Teil: Die Überlieferung*, GCS 18 (Leipzig, 1910).

Waszink, J. H., *Quinti Septimi Florentis Tertulliani de anima* (Amsterdam, 1947).   = Waszink, *Anima*

Williamson, G. A., trans., *Eusebius, The History of the Church from Christ to Constantine* (Minneapolis, 1975, repr. of 1965 original). = Williamson

Wintermute, O. S., 'Jubilees (Second Century B.C.): A New Translation and Introduction', *OTP*, ii, 35–142.

SECONDARY SOURCES

Allo, E.-B., *Saint Jean, L'Apocalypse*, ÉBib. (Paris, 1921).   = Allo, *Apocalypse*

—— *Saint Paul, Seconde Épître aux Corinthiens*, ÉBib. (Paris, 1956). = Allo, *Corinthiens*

Altaner, Berthold, 'Neues zum Verständnis von I. Klemens 5,1–6, 2/Der Apostel Petrus, römischer Märtyrer', *HJb* 62–9 (1949), 25–30. = Altaner, *HJb*

—— and Stuiber, Alfred, *Patrologie: Leben, Schriften und Lehre der*

Kirchenväter, 7th, fully rev. edn. (Freiburg/Basel/Vienna, 1960). = Altaner–Stuiber

AMANN, É., 'Mélèce de Lycopolis', *DTC* (Paris, 1928), x. 1, cols. 531–6. = Amann

ATTRIDGE, HAROLD W., *The Epistle to the Hebrews: A Commentary on the Epistle to the Hebrews*, Hermeneia (Philadelphia, 1989). = Attridge

AUDET, J.-P., 'Affinités littéraires et doctrinales du Manuel de discipline', *RB* 60 (1953), 41–82. = Audet

AUNE, DAVID EDWARD, *The Cultic Setting of Realized Eschatology in Early Christianity*, Suppl. *NovT*, 28 (Leiden, 1972). = Aune

BACON, BENJAMIN W., 'Date and Habitat of the Elders of Papias', *ZNW* 12 (1911), 176–87. = Bacon

BAILEY, J. W., 'The Temporary Messianic Reign in the Literature of Early Judaism', *JBL* 53 (1934), 170–87. = Bailey

BAMBERGER, BERNARD J., 'Paradise and Hell in Later Jewish Thought', *EJ* 13, 82–5. = Bamberger

BAMMEL, ERNST, 'Papias', *RGG*, 3rd edn. (1961), v, cols. 47–8. = Bammel

BARDENHEWER, OTTO, *Geschichte der altkirchlichen Literatur* (Darmstadt, 1962 repr. of 1913 original). = Bardenhewer

BARDY, G., 'Millénarisme', *DTC* (Paris, 1929), x. 2, cols. 1760–3. = Bardy

BARNARD, L. W., 'Hermas and Judaism', *StudPatr.*, iv, part 2, ed. F. L. Cross (Berlin, 1961), 4–10. = Barnard, *StudPatr.*

—— *Studies in the Apostolic Fathers and Their Background* (Oxford, 1966). = Barnard, *Studies*

—— *Justin Martyr: His Life and Thought* (Cambridge, 1967). = Barnard, *Justin*

—— 'In Defence of Pseudo-Pionius' Account of Saint Polycarp's Martyrdom', in *Kyriakon: Festschrift Johannes Quasten*, ed. Patrick Granfield and Josef A. Jungmann, 2 vols., (Münster, 1970), i, 192–204. = Barnard, *Kyr.*

BARNES, TIMOTHY D., 'Pre-Decian *Acta Martyrum*', *JTS* NS 19 (1968), 509–31. = Barnes, *JTS*

BAUCKHAM, RICHARD, 'The Great Tribulation in the Shepherd of Hermas', *JTS* NS 25 (1974), 27–40. = Bauckham, *JTS*

—— 'The Martyrdom of Enoch and Elijah: Jewish or Christian?', *JBL* 95 (1976), 447–58. = Bauckham, *JBL*

—— 'The Two Fig Tree Parables in the Apocalypse of Peter', *JBL* 104 (1985), 269–87. = Bauckham, *JBL* (1985)

——*Jude, 2Peter*, WBC 50 (Waco, 1983). = Bauckham, *Jude, 2Peter*

BAUER, W., 'Chiliasmus', *RAC* (1954), ii, cols. 1073–8. = Bauer, *RAC*

BAUERNFEIND, OTTO, "τυγχάνω κτλ.", *TDNT*, viii, 238–45. = Bauernfeind

BAUMEISTER, THEOFRIED, *Die Anfänge der Theologie des Martyriums*, MBT 45 (Münster, 1980). = Baumeister

BEASLEY-MURRAY, GEORGE R., The Book of Revelation, NCB (London, 1974).
= Beasley-Murray, Revelation
—— Jesus and the Kingdom of God (Grand Rapids/Exeter, 1986).
= Beasley-Murray, Jesus
BECKWITH, ISBON T., The Apocalypse of John (Grand Rapids, 1967 repr. of
1919 original). = Beckwith, Apocalypse
BENNETT, EDWARD, The Visions of John in Patmos (London, 1892).
= Bennett
BENSON, EDWARD WHITE, 'Libelli', DCA (London, 1880), ii, 981–3.
= Benson, DCA
—— Cyprian: His Life, his times, his work (London, 1897). = Benson,
Cyprian
BETTENCOURT, ESTÉVAO, 'Millenarianism', SM (London, 1969), iv, 43–4.
= Bettencourt
BIENERT, WOLFGANG A., Dionysius von Alexandrien: Zur Frage des Origen-
ismus im dritten Jahrhundert, PTS 21 (Berlin/New York, 1978).
= Bienert
BIETENHARD, HANS, Die himmlische Welt im Urchristentum und Spätjuden-
tum, WUNT 2 (Tübingen, 1951). = Bietenhard, Welt
—— Das tausendjährige Reich (Zurich, 1955). = Bietenhard, Reich
—— 'The Millennial Hope in the Early Church', SJT 6 (1953), 12–30.
= Bientenhard, SJT
BLACK, M., 'The Eschatology of the Similitudes of Enoch', JTS NS, 3 (1952),
1–10. = Black, JTS
—— 'The Account of the Essenes in Hippolytus and Josephus', in The
Background of the New Testament and Its Eschatology, ed. W. D. Davies
and D. Daube (Cambridge, 1956), 172–5. = Black, 'Essenes'
BLUM, GEORG GÜNTER, 'Chiliasmus II. Alte Kirche', TR vii (Berlin/New
York, 1981), 729–32. = Blum
BOGAERT, P.-M., 'Les Apocalypses contemporaines de Baruch, d'Esdras et
de Jean', in L'Apocalypse johannique et l'Apocalyptique dans le Nouveau
Testament, ed. J. Lambrecht, BETL 53 (Leuven, 1980), 47–68.
= Bogaert, BETL
BONNER, GERALD, Saint Bede in the Tradition of Western Apocalyptic
Commentary, Jarrow Lecture 1966. = Bonner
BORING, M. EUGENE, 'The Theology of Revelation "The Lord Our God the
Almighty Reigns"', Interpretation 40 (1986), 257–69. = Boring
BORNKAMM, G., 'Die Komposition der apokalyptischen Visionen in der
Offenbarung Johannis', ZNW 36 (1937), 132–49. = Bornkamm
BOTTE, B., 'Prima resurrectio: Un vestige de millénarisme dans les liturgies
occidentales', RTAM 15 (1948), 5–17. = Botte
BOUSSET, WILHELM, Die Offenbarung Johannis, MeyerK 16, 6th edn. (Göt-
tingen, 1906). = Bousset

BOWER, RICHARD A., 'The Meaning of *EPITUGCHANO* in the Epistles of St. Ignatius of Antioch', *VC* 28 (1974), 1–14.   = Bower

BREWER, HEINRICH, 'Kommodian von Gaza: Ein arelatensischer Laiendichter aus der Mitte des fünften Jahrhunderts, *FLDG* 6, 1–2 (Paderborn, 1906).   = Brewer

BRIGHT, PAMELA, 'Origenian Understanding of Martyrdom and its Biblical Framework', in *Origen of Alexandria: His World and His Legacy*, ed. Charles Kannengiesser and William L. Peterson, Christianity and Judaism in Antiquity 1 (Notre Dame, Ind., 1988), 180–99.   = Bright

BUCHANAN, GEORGE WESLEY, *To the Hebrews*, AB (Garden City, NY, 1972).   = Buchanan

BUONAIUTI, ERNESTO, 'The Ethics and Eschatology of Methodius of Olympus', *HTR* 14 (1921), 255–66.   = Buonaiuti

BULTMANN, RUDOLF, *The Gospel of John: A Commentary* (ET, Oxford, 1971).   = Bultmann, *John*

BURCHARD, CHRISTOPH, 'Zur Nebenüberlieferung von Josephus' Bericht über die Essener Bell 2,119–161 bei Hippolyt, Porphyrius, Josippus, Niketas Choniates uhd anderen', in *Josephus-Studien: Untersuchungen zu Josephus, dem antiken Judentum und dem Neuen Testament, Otto Michel zum 70. Geburtstag gewidmet*, ed. Otto Betz, Klaus Haacker, and Martin Hengel (Göttingen, 1974), 77–96.   = Burchard

BURNETT, FRED W., "Philo on Immortality: A Thematic Study of Philo's Concept of παλιγγενεσία", *CBQ* 46 (1984), 447–70.   = Burnett

BURNS, NORMAN T., *Christian Mortalism from Tyndale to Milton* (Cambridge, Mass.) 1972.   = Burns

BUTTERWORTH, ROBERT, review of Josef Frickel, *Das Dunkel um Hippolyt von Rom. Ein Lösungsversuch: Die Schriften Elenchos und contra Noëtum*, Grazer Theologische Studien (Graz, 1988), in *JTS* NS 41 (1990), 236–9.   = Butterworth

CAVALLIN, HANS CLEMENS CAESARIUS, *Life After Death: Paul's Argument for the Resurrection of the Dead in I Cor 15. Part 1 An Enquiry into the Jewish Background*, ConB. New Testament Series 7. 1 (Lund, 1974).   = Cavallin

CHADWICK, HENRY, *Early Christian Thought and the Classical Tradition: Studies in Justin, Clement, and Origen* (Oxford, 1966).   = Chadwick, *Classical Tradition*

—— 'Philo and the Beginnings of Christian Thought', in *The Cambridge History of Later Greek and Early Medieval Philosophy*, ed. A. H. Armstrong (Cambridge, 1967), 137–57.   = Chadwick, 'Philo'

CHARLES, R. H., 'A Solution of the Chief Difficulties in Revelation xx–xxii', *ExpT* 26 (1914, 1915), 54–57, 119–123.   = Charles, 'Solution'

—— *A Critical and Exegetical Commentary on The Revelation of St. John: With Introduction, Notes, and Indices, also the Greek Text and English Translation*, ICC, 2 vols. (Edinburgh, 1920).   = Charles, *Revelation*

CHARLESWORTH, JAMES HAMILTON, *The Old Testament Pseudepigrapha and the New Testament: Prolegomena for the Study of Christian Origins*, Society for New Testament Studies Monograph Series 54 (Cambridge et al.) 1985.   = Charlesworth, SNTS

CHERNUS, IRA, *Mysticism in Rabbinic Judaism*, Studia Judaica. Forschungen zur Wissenschaft des Judentums 11 (Berlin/New York, 1982).   = Chernus

CLEMEN, CARL, *Niedergefahren zu den Toten: Ein Beitrag zur Würdigung des Apostolikums* (Giessen, 1990).   = Clemen

COGGINS, R. J., and KNIBB, M. A., *The First and Second Books of Esdras: Commentary on 1 Esdras by R. J. Coggins and Commentary on 2 Esdras by M. A. Knibb*, The Cambridge Bible Commentary on the New English Bible (Cambridge et al., 1979).   = Coggins–Knibb, *Esdras*

COHN, NORMAN, *The Pursuit of the Millennium: Revolutionary Millenarians and Mystical Anarchists of the Middle Ages*, rev. and expanded edn. (London, 1970, 1st edn. 1957).   = Cohn

COLLINS, J. J., 'Apocalyptic Eschatology as the Transcendence of Death', *CBQ* 36 (1974), 21–43.   = Collins, *CBQ*

CORWIN, VIRGINIA, *St. Ignatius and Christianity in Antioch*, (New Haven, Conn., 1960).   = Corwin

CROUZEL, HENRI, 'L'Exégèse origénienne de 1 Cor. 3, 11–15 et la purification eschatologique', in *EPEKTASIS* (1972), 273–83.   = Crouzel, *EPEKTASIS*

—— 'La "première" et la "seconde" résurrection des hommes d'après Origène', *Didaskalia* 3 (1973), 3–19.   = Crouzel, *Didaskalia*

—— Les Prophéties de la résurrection selon Origéne', in *FF* (Turin, 1975), 980–92.   = Crouzel, *FF*

—— 'Mort et immortalité selon Origéne', *BLE* 79 (1978), 19–23, 86–96, 181–96.   = Crouzel, *BLE*

—— *Origène* (Paris, 1985).   = Crouzel, *Origène*

CULIANU, IOAN PETRU, *Psychanodia I. A Survey of the Evidence Concerning the Ascension of the Soul and its Relevance*, ÉPROER 99 (Leiden, 1983).   = Culianu

CUMONT, FRANZ, *After Life in Roman Paganism: Lectures Delivered at Yale University on the Silliman Foundation* (New York, 1959 repr. of 1922 original).   = Cumont, *After Life*

CURTI, CARMELO, 'Il regno millenario in Vittorino di Petovio', *Aug.* 18 (1978), 419–33.   = Curti

DALEY, BRIAN E., 'Chiliasm', in *EEC* (New York/London, 1990), 193–7.   = Daley

D'ALÈS, ADHÉMAR, *La Théologie de Tertullien*, 2nd edn. (Paris, 1905).   = d'Alès, *Tertullien*

—— *La Théologie de saint Cyprien* (Paris, 1922).   = d'Ales, *Cyprien*

214   *Select Bibliography*

DANIÉLOU, JEAN, A History of Early Christian Doctrine Before the Council of Nicaea, 3 vols.: i, The Theology of Jewish Christianity, (ET, London, 1964).   = Daniélou, TJC
ii, Gospel Message and Hellenistic Culture (ET, London, 1973).   = Daniélou, GM
iii, The Origins of Latin Christianity (ET, London, 1977).   = Daniélou, OLC
—— 'La Typologie millénariste de la semaine', VC 2 (1948), 1–16.   = Daniélou, VC
—— Primitive Christian Symbols (ET, London, 1964).   = Daniélou, Symbols
—— 'Millenarianism', in Bauer Encyclopedia of Biblical Theology, ed. Johannes B. Bauer (London, 1978), 582–4.   = Daniélou, BEBT
DAVENPORT, GENE L., The Eschatology of the Book of Jubilees, Studia Post-Biblica 20 (Leiden, 1971).   = Davenport
DAVIES, PHILIP R., 'Eschatology at Qumran', JBL 104 (1985), 39–55.   = Davies, JBL
DE BRUYNE, L., review of Stuiber, A., Refrigerium interim, die Vorstellungen vom Zwischenzustand und die frühchristliche Grabeskunst Theoph. 11 (Bonn, 1957) in RivAC 34 (1958, 87–118).   = de Bruyne
DE JONGE, H. J., "bótrui boǵiei: The Age of Kronos and the Millennium in Papias of Hierapolis", in Studies in Hellenistic Religions, ed. M. J. Vermaseren, ÉPROER 78, (Leiden), 37–49.   = de Jonge
DEVREESSE, ROBERT, Les Anciens Commentateurs grecs de l'octateuque et des rois (fragments tirés des chaînes), ST 201 (Città del Vaticano, 1959).   = Devreesse
DODD, C. H., The Interpretation of the Fourth Gospel (Cambridge, 1953).   = Dodd Interpretation
DOIGNON, JEAN, 'Le "Placitum" eschatologique attribué aux stoïciens par Lactance ("Institutions divines" 7, 20) résumé de la communication', Lactance et son Temps: Recherches actuelles: Actes du IVe Colloque d'Études Historiques et Patristiques Chantilly 21–23 septembre 1976, ed. J. Fontaine and M. Perrin, ThH 48 (Paris, 1978), 165–70.   = Doignon, Lactance
—— 'Le Placitum eschatologique attribué aux Stoïcens par Lactance ("Institutions divines" 7, 20)', RPh (1977) 43–55.   = Doignon, RPh
DOLAN, J. P., 'Millenarianism (in Church History)', NCE ix, 852–4.   = Dolan
DONFRIED, KARL PAUL, The Setting of Second Clement in Early Christianity, Suppl. NovT 38 (1974).   = Donfried
DUNBAR, DAVID G., 'The Eschatology of Hippolytus of Rome' (unpublished dissertation, Drew University, 1979).   = Dunbar, 'Eschatology'
—— 'Hippolytus of Rome and the Eschatological Exegesis of the Early Church', WTJ 45 (1983), 322–39.   = Dunbar, WTJ

DUREL, JOACHIM, *Commodien: Recherches sur la doctrine, la langue et le vocabulaire du poète* (Paris, 1912). = Durel

ELLINGWORTH, PAUL, 'Hebrews and I Clement: Literary Dependence or Common Tradition', *BibZ* 23 (1979), 262–9. = Ellingworth

ERMONI, V., 'Les Phases successives de l'erreur millénariste', *RQH* 70 (NS 26) (1901), 353–88. = Ermoni

FÀBREGA, VALENTIN, 'Die chiliastische Lehre des Laktanz: Methodische und theologische Voraussetzungen und religionsgeschichtlicher Hintergrund', *JbAC* 17 (1974), 126–46. = Fàbrega

FAHEY, MICHAEL ANDREW, *Cyprian and the Bible: A Study in Third-Century Exegesis*, Beiträge zur Geschichte der biblischen Hermeneutik 9 (Tübingen, 1971). = Fahey

FARGES, JACQUES, *Les Idées morales et religieuses de Méthode d'Olympe: Contribution à l'étude des rapports du Christianisme et de l'Hellénisme à la fin du troisième siècle*, BAP (Paris, 1929). = Farges

FINÉ, HEINZ, *Die Terminologie der Jenseitsvorstellungen bei Tertullian: Ein semasiologischer Beitrag zur Dogmengeschichte des Zwischenzustandes* Theoph. 12 (Bonn, 1958). = Finé

FIORENZA, ELIZABETH SCHÜSSLER, 'Eschatology and Composition of the Apocalypse', *CBQ* 30 (1968), 537–69. = Fiorenza, *CBQ*

—— Die tausendjährige Herrschaft der Auferstandenen (Apk 20, 4–6)', *BL* 13 (1972), 107–24. = Fiorenza, *BL*

FISCHER, JOSEPH A., *Studien zum Todesgedanken in der alten Kirche: Die Beurteilung des natürlichen Todes in der kirchlichen Literatur der ersten drei Jahrhunderte, i* (Munich, 1954). = Fischer, *Todesgedanken*

FISCHER, ULRICH, *Eschatologie und Jenseitserwartung im hellenistischen Diasporajudentum* (Berlin/New York, 1978). = Fischer, *Eschatologie*

FITZMYER, JOSEPH A., *The Gospel According to Luke (X–XXIV)*, AB (Garden City, NY, 1985). = Fitzmyer, *Luke (X–XXIV)*

FORD, J. MASSYNGBERDE, *Revelation*, AB (Garden City, NY, 1975). = Ford

FREND, W. H. C., *Martyrdom and Persecution in the Early Church: A Study of a Conflict from the Maccabees to Donatus* (Oxford, 1965). = Frend, *Martyrdom*

—— *The Rise of Christianity* (Philadelphia, 1984). = Frend, *Rise*

FULLER, JOHN MEE, 'Meletius (2)', *DCB* III, 890–1. = J. M. Fuller

FURNISH, VICTOR PAUL, *II Corinthians*, AB 32A (Garden City, NY, 1984). = Furnish

GAEBELEIN, ARNO C., *The Revelation* (New York, 1915). = Gaebelein

GAECHTER, PAUL, 'The Original Sequence of Apocalypse 20–22', *ThSt.* 10 (1949), 485–521. = Gaechter

GAGÉ, JEAN 'Commodien et le moment millénariste du IIIᵉ siècle (258–62 ap. J.-C.)', *RHPR* 41 (1961), 355–78. = Gagé

GAUTHIER, NANCY, 'Les Images de l'au-delà durant l'antiquité chrétienne', *Revue des études augustiniennes* 33 (1987) 3–22. = Gauthier

GELIN, 'Millénarisme', in *Suppl DB*, (Paris, 1957), v, cols. 1289–94. = Gelin

GIBLIN, C. H., 'Structural and Thematic Correlations in the Theology of Revelation 16–22', *Biblica* 55 (1974), 487–504. = Giblin

GIBSON, ELSA, The *'Christians for Christians' Inscriptions of Phrygia: Greek Texts, Translation and Commentary*, HTS 32 (Missoula, Mont., 1978). = Gibson

GLASSON, T. F., *Greek Influence in Jewish Eschatology* (London, 1961). = Glasson

GOODENOUGH, EDWIN R., *The Theology of Justin Martyr* (Amsterdam, 1968 repr. of 1923 original). = Goodenough, *Theology*

—— 'Philo on Immortality', *HTR* 39 (1946), 89–108. = Goodenough, *HTR*

GOURGUES, MICHAEL, 'The Thousand-Year Reign (Rev. 20: 1–6): Terrestrial or Celestial?' *CBQ* 47 (1985), 676–81. = Gourgues

GRANT, FREDERICK C., 'The Eschatology of the Second Century', *AJT* 21 (1919), 193–211. = F. C. Grant

GRANT, ROBERT M., *Eusebius as Church Historian* (Oxford, 1980). = Grant *Eusebius*

—— *Greek Apologists of the Second Century* (Philadelphia, 1988). = Grant, *Apologists*

GRY, LÉON, *Le Millénarisme dans ses origines et son développement* (Paris, 1904). = Gry, *Millénarisme*

—— 'Le Papias des belles promesses messianiques', *VP* 3 ser. (1943–4), 112–24. = Gry, *VP*

GSCHWIND, KARL, *Die Niederfahrt Christi in die Unterwelt: Ein Beitrag zur Exegese des Neuen Testamentes und zur Geschichte des Taufsymbols*, NtAbh ii numbers 3–5 (Münster, 1911). = Gschwind

GUARDUCCI, MARGHERITA, 'La statua di "Sant'Ippolito"' in *Ricerche su Ippolito*, Studia Ephemeridis 'Augustinianum', 13 (Rome, 1977), 17–30. = Guarducci

GUNDRY, ROBERT H., '"In my Father's House are Many Μοναί"' (John 14: 2)', *ZNW* 58 (1967), 68–72. = Gundry

GUNTHER, JOHN J., 'Syrian Christian Dualism', *VC* 25 (1971) 81–93. = Gunther

HAENCHEN, ERNST, *John 2: A Commentary on the Gospel of John Chapters 7–12*, Hermeneia (ET, Philadelphia, 1984). = Haenchen, *John 2*

HAEUSER, PHILIPP, *Der Barnabasbrief, neu untersucht und neu erklärt*, FLDG 11² (Paderborn, 1912). = Haeuser

HAGNER, DONALD ALFRED, *The Use of the Old and New Testaments in Clement of Rome*, Suppl. *NovT* 34 (Leiden, 1973). = Hagner

HALL, ROBERT G., 'The *Ascension of Isaiah*: Community Situation, Date, and Place in Early Christianity', *JBL* 109 (1990), 289–306. = Hall, 'Ascension'

HAMILTON, WILLIAM, 'Many Mansions for God', *ExpT* 25 (1913–14), 75.
= Hamilton

HAMMOND BAMMEL, C. P., 'Ignatian Problems' *JTS* NS 33 (1982), 62–97.
= Hammond Bammel

HANHART, KAREL, *The Intermediate State in the New Testament* (Groningen, 1966).   = Hanhart, *Intermediate*

—— 'Paul's Hope in the Face of Death', *JBL* 88 (1969), 445–57.
= Hanhart, *JBL*

HANSON, R. P. C., *Allegory and Event: A Study of the Sources and Significance of Origen's Interpretation of Scripture* (London, 1959).   = Hanson, *Allegory and Event*

—— 'Biblical Exegesis in the Early Church', in P. R. Ackroyd and C. F. Evans, eds., *The Cambridge History of the Bible*, 3 vols. (Cambridge, 1970), i, *From the Beginnings to Jerome*, 412–53.   = Hanson, *CHB*

HARNACK, ADOLF, *Geschichte der altchristlichen Litteratur bis Eusebius*, Part 1, *Die Überlieferung und der Bestand* (Leipzig, 1893).   = Harnack, *Geschichte*

—— *Lehrbuch der Dogmengeschichte*, 4th edn., 3 vols. (Tübingen, 1909).
= Harnack, *Lehrbuch*

—— 'Millennium', *EB*, 14th edn. (Chicago/London/Toronto, 1945), xv. 495–7.   = Harnack, *EB*

HARRIS, MURRAY J., *Raised Immortal: Resurrection and Immortality in the New Testament* (London, 1983).   = Harris

HEMER, COLIN, *The Letters to the Seven Churches of Asia in Their Local Setting*, JSNT Suppl. 11 (Sheffield, 1986).   = Hemer

HENGSTENBERG, E. W., *The Revelation of St John, Expounded for those who Search the Scriptures*, Clark's Foreign Theological Library 22 and 26, 2 vols. (ET, Edinburgh, 1851–2).   = Hengstenberg

HENESSEY, LAWRENCE R., 'The Place of Saints and Sinners after Death', in *Origen of Alexandria: His World and his Legacy*, ed. Charles Kannengiesser and William L. Peterson, Christianity and Judaism in Antiquity I (Notre Dame, Ind., 1988), 295–312.   = Hennessey

HÉRING, JEAN, 'Étude sur la doctrine de la chute et de la préexistence des ames chez Clément d'Alexandrie', *BÉHÉSR* 38 (Paris, 1923), 1–45.
= Héring, *BÉHÉSR*

—— *L'Épitre aux Hébreux*, CNT 12 (Neuchatel/Paris, 1954).   = Héring, *Hébreux*

—— 'Eschatologie biblique et Idéalisme platonicien', in *Background of the New Testament and its Eschatology: Studies in Honour of C. H. Dodd*, ed. W. D. Davis and D. Daube (Cambridge, 1956), 444–63.

HERMANS, ALBERT, 'Le Pseudo-Barnabé est-il Millénariste?', ALBO ser. 3. fasc. 15 (Bruges/Paris, 1960), 849–76.   = Hermans

HILL, CHARLES E., 'Paul's Understanding of Christ's Kingdom in I Corinthians 15: 20–18', *NovT* 30 (1988), 297–320.   = Hill, *NovT*

——— 'Hades of Hippolytus or Tartarus of Tertullian? The Authorship of the Fragment *De Universo*', VC 43 (1989), 105–26.   = Hill, VC

HILL, MICHAEL, *A Sociology of Religion*, Heinemann Studies in Sociology (London, 1973).   = Michael Hill

HILLS, JULIAN, *Tradition and Composition in the* Epistula Apostolorum, Harvard Dissertations in Religion (Philadelphia, 1990).   = Hills

HINSON, E. G., 'Evidence of Essene Influence in Roman Christianity: An Inquiry', StudPatr., xvii, part 2, ed. Elizabeth Livingstone (Oxford, 1982), 697–701.   = Hinson

HODGE, CHARLES, *An Exposition of the Second Epistle to the Corinthians* (Grand Rapids, 1953, repr.).   = Hodge

HORNSCHUH, MANFRED, *Studien zur Epistula Apostolorum*, PTS 5 (Berlin, 1965).   = Hornschuh

HORBURY, WILLIAM, 'Messianism among Jews and Christians in the Second Century', Aug. 28 (1988), 71–88.   = Horbury, Aug.

HUGHES, J. A., 'Revelation 20: 4–6 and the Question of the Millennium', WTJ 35 (1973), 281–302.   = J. A. Hughes

HUGHES, PHILIP EDGCUMBE, *A Commentary on the Epistle to the Hebrews* (Grand Rapids, 1977).   = Hughes, Hebrews

ISENBERG, SHELDON R., 'Millenarism in Greco-Roman Palestine', Religion 4 (1974), 26–46.   = Isenberg

JAMES, J. COURTNEY, 'Mansiones Multae', ExpT 27 (1915–16), 427–8.   = J. C. James

JAY, PIERRE, 'Saint Cyprien et la doctrine du purgatoire', RTAM 27 (1960), 133–6.   = Jay

JEREMIAS, JOACHIM, "ᾅδης", TDNT, i, 146–9.   = Jeremias, "ᾅδης"
——— "ἄβυccoc", TDNT, i, 9–10.   = Jeremias, "ἄβυccoc"
——— "παράδειcoc", TDNT, v, 765–73.   = Jeremias, "παράδειcoc"

JEWETT, ROBERT, *The Thessalonian Correspondence: Pauline Rhetoric and Millenarian Piety*, Foundations and Facets (Philadelphia, 1986).   = Jewett

KELLY, WILLIAM, *Lectures Introductory to the Study of the Acts, the Catholic Epistles, and the Revelation* (London, 1870).   = Kelly, Lectures
——— *The Revelation* (London, 1904).   = Kelly, Revelation

KIRCHNER, MORISS, 'Die Eschatologie des Irenäus', TSK 36 (1863), 315–58.   = Kirchner

KLIJN, A. F. J., *The Acts of Thomas: Introduction—Text—Commentary*, Suppl. NovT 5 (1962).   = Klijn, Acts
——— and REININK, G. J., *Patristic Evidence for Jewish-Christian Sects*, Suppl. NovT 36 (Leiden, 1973).   = Klijn–Reinink

KLINE, MEREDITH G., 'The First Resurrection', WTJ 37 (1975), 366–75.   = Kline, WTJ 37
——— 'The First Resurrection: A Reaffirmation', WTJ 39 (1976), 110–19.   = Kline, WTJ 39

KNOCH, OTTO, *Eigenart und Bedeutung der Eschatologie im theologischen Aufriß des ersten Clemensbriefes: Eine auslegungsgeschichtliche Untersuchung*, Theoph 17 (Bonn, 1964). = Knoch

KÖRTNER, ULRICH, H. J., *Papias von Hierapolis: Ein Beitrag zur Geschichte des frühen Christentums*, FRLANT 133 (Göttingen, 1983). = Körtner

KRAFT, H., 'Chiliasmus', *RGG*, 3rd edn. (Tübingen, 1957), i, cols. 1651–3. = H. Kraft

KRAFT, ROBERT A., 'Towards Assessing the Latin Text of "5 Ezra": The "Christian" Connection', *HTR* 79 (1986), 158–69. = Kraft, *HTR*

KRETSCHMAR, GEORG, *Die Offenbarung des Johannes: Die Geschichte ihrer Auslegung im 1. Jahrtausend*, CTM B.9 (Stuttgart, 1985). = Kretschmar

KUHN, HEINZ-WOLFGANG, *Enderwartung und gegenwärtiges Heil: Untersuchungen zu den Gemeindeliedern von Qumran mit einem Anhang über Eschatologie und Gegenwart in der Verkündigung Jesu*, SUNT 4 (Göttingen, 1966). = Kuhn, *Enderwartung*

KUHN, KARL GEORG, *Der tannaitische Midrasch: Sifre zu Numeri*, Rabbinische Texte, second series, *Tannaitische Midraschim: Übersetzung und Erklärung*, iii (Stuttgart, 1959). = Kuhn, *Sifre*

LADD, GEORGE ELDON, *A Commentary on the Revelation of John* (Grand Rapids, 1972). = Ladd

LAGUIER, LOUIS, 'Le Millénarisme de saint Justin', *Revue de clergé français* 39 (1904), 182–93. = Laguier

LAMBRECHT, J., 'A Structuration of Revelation 4,1–22,5' in *L'Apocalypse johannique et l'Apocalyptique dans le Nouveau Testament*, ed. J. Lambrecht, BETL 53 (Leuven, 1980), 77–104. = Lambrecht, BETL

—— 'Structure and Line of Thought in 1 Cor. 15: 23–8', *NovT* 32 (1990), 143–51. = Lambrecht, *NovT*

LANDES, RICHARD, 'Lest the Millennium be Fulfilled: Apocalyptic Expectations and the Pattern of Western Chronography 100–800 CE', in *The Use and Abuse of Eschatology in the Middle Ages*, ed. Werner Verbeke, Daniel Verhelst, and Andries Welkenhuysen, Mediaevalia Lovaniensia Series 1, Studia 15 (Leuven, 1988), 137–211. = Landes

LANG, FRIEDRICH GUSTAV, *2. Korinther 5, 1–10 in der neueren Forschung*, Beiträge zur Geschichte der biblischen Exegese 16 (Tübingen, 1973). = Lang

LAURIN, ROBERT B., 'The Question of Immortality in the Qumran Hodayot', *JSS* 3 (1958), 344–55. = Laurin

LECLERCQ, H., 'Millénarisme', *DACL* (Paris, 1933), xi. 1, cols. 1181–95. = Leclercq

LESÈTRE, H., 'Millénarisme', in *DB* (Paris, 1908) iv, cols. 1090–7. = Lesètre

LEVESQUE, E., 'Berengaud', in *DB* (Paris, 1895), i, cols. 1610–11. = Levesque

LIEBERMAN, SAUL, 'Some Aspects of After Life in Early Rabbinic Literature',

Harry Austyn Wolfson Jubilee Volume (at 75), 3 vols. (Jerusalem, 1965), ii, 495–532. = Lieberman

LIENHARD, JOSEPH T., 'The Christology of the Epistle to Diognetus', *VC* 24 (1970), 280–9. = Lienhard

LIGHTFOOT, J. B., *Essays on the Work Entitled Supernatural Religion Reprinted From The Contemporary Review*, 2nd edn. (London/New York, 1893). = Lightfoot, *Supernatural*

LILLA, SALVATORE R. C., *Clement of Alexandria: A Study in Christian Platonism and Gnosticism*, OTM (Oxford, 1971). = Lilla

LOI, VINCENZO, 'L'identità letteraria di Ippolito di Roma', in *Ricerche su Ippolito*, 67–88. = Loi, 'L'identità

—— *et al.*, *Ricerche su Ippolito*, Studia Ephemeridis 'Augustinianum', 13 (Rome, 1977). = Loi, *Ricerche*

McCAFFREY, JAMES, *The House with Many Rooms: The Temple Theme of John 14,2–3*, Analecta Biblica 114 (Rome, 1988). = McCaffrey

MacCULLOCH, J. A., *The Harrowing of Hell* (Edinburgh, 1930). = MacCulloch

McGINN, BERNARD, *Visions of the End: Apocalyptic Traditions in the Middle Ages* (New York, 1979). = McGinn

MacRAE, GEORGE, 'Apocalyptic Eschatology in Gnosticism', in *Apocalypticism in the Mediterranean World and the Near East: Proceedings of the International Colloquium on Apocalypticism, Uppsala, August 12–17, 1979*, ed. David Hellholm (Tübingen, 1983), 317–25. = MacRae

MAIER, GERHARD, *Die Johannesoffenbarung und die Kirche*, WUNT 25 (Tübingen, 1981). = Maier

MARSH, H. G., The Use of μυστήριον in The Writings of Clement of Alexandria with Special Reference to His Sacramental Doctrine', *JTS* 37 (1936), 64–80. = Marsh

MARTIN, JOSEF, *Studien und Beiträge zur Erklärung und Zeitbestimmung Commodians*, TU 39 (Leipzig, 1913), i–142. = Martin, *Studien*

MASON, A. J., 'Tertullian and Purgatory', *JTS* 3 (1902), 598–601. = Mason, *JTS*

MÉHAT, ANDRÉ, 'Le "lieu supracéleste" de Saint Justin à Origène', *FF*, 282–94. = Méhat, *FF*

MELONI, PIETRO, 'Ippolito e il Cantico dei cantici', in *Ricerche su Ippolito*, Studia Ephemeridis 'Augustinianum', 13 (Rome, 1977), 97–120. = Meloni

MILIKOWSKY, CHAIM, 'Which Gehenna? Retribution and Eschatology in the Synoptic Gospels and in Early Jewish Texts', *NTS* 34 (1988), 238–49. = Milikowsky

MOFFATT, JAMES, 'Cyprian on the Lord's Prayer', *The Expositor*, 8th ser. 18 (1919) 176–89. = Moffatt, *Expos*

—— *A Critical and Exegetical Commentary on the Epistle to the Hebrews*, ICC (Edinburgh, 1924). = Moffatt, *Hebrews*

MONTEFIORE, HUGH, *A Commentary on the Epistle to the Hebrews*, BNTC (London, 1964). = Montefiore

MONTGOMERY, J. W., 'Millennium', *ISBE* (Grand Rapids, 1986) iii, 356–61. = Montgomery

MOORE, GEORGE FOOT, *Judaism in the First Centuries of the Christian Era: The Age of the Tannaim*, 2 vols. (Cambridge, Mass., 1927). = Moore, *Judaism*

MOREAU, 'BERENGAUD', *DHG* (Paris), viii, cols. 358–9. = Moreau

MOULE, C. F. D., 'The Influence of Circumstances on the Use of Eschatological Terms', *JTS* 15 (1964), 1–15. = Moule, *JTS*

NAUTIN, PIERRE, *Hippolyte et Josipe* (Paris, 1947). = Nautin, *Josipe*

—— *Le Dossier d'Hippolyte et de Méliton dans les florilèges dogmatiques et chez les historiens modernes* (Paris, 1953). = Nautin, *Dossier*

—— *Lettres et écrivains chrétiens des IIe et IIIe siècles*, Patristica 2 (Paris, 1961). = Nautin, *Lettres*

NICHOLSON, O. P., 'The Source of the Dates in Lactantius' *Divine Institutes*', *JTS* NS 36 (1985), 291–310. = Nicholson

NICKELSBURG, GEORGE W. E., *Jewish Literature between the Bible and the Mishnah* (London, 1981). = Nickelsburg, *Literature*

—— *Resurrection, Immortality, and Eternal Life in Intertestamental Judaism*, HTS 26 (Cambridge, Mass./Oxford, 1972). = Nickelsburg, *Resurrection*

NIELSEN, CHARLES M., 'The Epistle to Diognetus: Its Date and Relationship to Marcion', *ATR* 52 (1970), 77–91. = Nielsen, *ATR*

—— 'Papias: Polemicist Against Whom?', *ThSt.* 35 (1974), 529–35. = Nielsen, *ThSt.*

NIELSEN, J. T., *Adam and Christ in the Theology of Irenaeus of Lyons* (Assen, 1968). = J. T. Nielsen

NILSON, J., 'To Whom is Justin's *Dialogue with Trypho* Addressed?', *ThSt.* 38, (1977), 538–46. = Nilson

NORRIS, FREDERICK W., 'Alogoi', *EEC* (New York/London, 1990), 27. = Norris

ORBE, ANTONIO, 'Adversarios anónimos de la *Salus carnis* (Iren. adv. haer. V,2,2s)', *Greg.* 60 (1979), 9–53. = Orbe

O'HAGAN, A. P., 'The Great Tribulation to Come in the Pastor of Hermas', *StudPatr.*, iv, part 2, ed. F. L. Cross (Berlin, 1961), 305–11. = O'Hagan

O'ROURKE BOYLE, MARJORIE, 'Irenaeus' Millennial Hope: A Polemical Weapon', *RTAM* 36 (1969), 5–16. = O'Rourke Boyle

OSBORN, ERIC FRANCIS, *Justin Martyr*, BHT 47 (Tübingen, 1973). = Osborn, *Justin*

—— 'Clement of Alexandria: A Review of Research, 1958–1982', *SCent.* 3 (1983). = Osborn, *SCent.*

PERLER, OTHMAR, 'Das vierte Makkabäerbuch, Ignatius von Antioch und

die ältesten Martyrerberichte', *RivAC* 25 (1949), 47–72.   = Perler,
RivAC

PERNVEDEN, LAGE, *The Concept of the Church in the Shepherd of Hermas*,
STL 27 (Lund, 1966).   = Pernveden

PERRIN, MICHEL, *L'Homme antique et chrétien: L'Anthropologie de Lactance
250–325*, ThH 59 (Paris, 1981).   = Perrin

PRIGENT, PIERRE, *Les Testimonia dans le christianisme primitif: L'Épître de
Barnabé I–XVI et ses sources*, ÉBib (Paris, 1961).   = Prigent, *Testimonia*

—— *Justin et l'ancien testament*, ÉBib (Paris, 1964).   = Prigent, *Justin*

—— 'Le Millennium dans l'Apocalypse johannique', *L'Apocalyptique*,
Universitè des sciences humains de Strasbourg, Centre de recherches
d'histoire des religions, *Études d'histoire des religions*, 3 (Paris, 1977).
= Prigent, 'Le Millennium'

—— 'Hippolyte, Commentateur de l'Apocalypse', *VC* 28 (1972), 391–412.
= Prigent, 'Hipolyte'

—— *L'Apocalypse de Saint Jean*, CNT 14 (Lausanne/Paris, 1981).
= Prigent, *L'Apocalypse*

QUASTEN, JOHANNES, *Patrology*, 3 vols. (Westminster, Maryland, 1984, repr.
of 1950 original).   = Quasten

RAHNER, KARL, 'Die Bußlehre des hl. Cyprian von Karthago', *ZKTh* 74
(1952) 257–76; 381–438.   = Rahner, *ZKTh*

REBELL, WALTER, 'Das Leidensverständnis bei Paulus und Ignatius von
Antiochien', *NTS* 32 (1986), 457–65.   = Rebell

RICHARD, MARCEL, 'Hippolyte de Rome (saint)', *DS* (Paris, 1969), vii, cols.
531–71.   = Richard, 'Hippolyte'

—— 'Les Difficultés d'une édition des œuvres de S. Hippolyte', *StudPatr.*,
xii, part I, TU cxv, ed. Elizabeth A. Livingstone, (Berlin, 1975), 51–70.
= Richard, *StudPatr.*

RICHARDSON, PETER, and SHUKSTER, MARTIN B., 'Barnabas, Nerva, and the
Yavnean Rabbis', *JTS* NS 34 (1983), 31–55.   = Richardson–Shukster

RISSI, MATHIAS, *The Future of the World*, SBT 2nd ser. 23 (E.T. London,
1972).   = Rissi

ROBERTS, C. H., review of Karl Paul Donfried, *The Setting of Second
Clement in Early Christianity*, *JTS* NS 26 (1975), 460–2.   = Roberts

ROBINSON, JOHN A. T., *Jesus and His Coming*, 2nd edn. (London, 1979).
= Robinson, *Coming*

RORDORF, WILLY, 'La "diaconie" des martyres selon Origène' in *EPEKTASIS*
(1972), 395–402.   = Rordorf, *EPEKTASIS*

ROWLAND, CHRISTOPHER, *The Open Heaven: A Study of Apocalyptic in
Judaism and Early Christianity* (London, 1982).   = Rowland

RUSSELL, D. S., *The Method and Message of Jewish Apocalyptic 200 BC–
AD 100*, The Old Testament Library (Philadelphia, 1964).   = Russell,
Method

—— *The Jews from Alexander to Herod*, The New Clarendon Bible: Old Testament, v (Oxford 1982 repr. of 1967 original). = Russell, *Jews*

SALDARINI, ANTHONY J., 'Apocalyptic and Rabbinic Literature', *CBQ* 37 (1975), 348–58. = Saldarini

SANDEEN, ERNEST R., art. 'Millennialism' in *The New Encyclopaedia Britannica*, 30 vols., 15th edn., *Macropaedia* (Chicago, London, Toronto, et al., 1975), xii, 200–3. = Sandeen

SANDERS, LOUIS, *L'Hellénisme de saint Clément de Rome et le paulinisme*, StudHell (Louvain, 1943). = L. Sanders

SCHMIDT, CARL, *Gespräche Jesu mit seinen Jüngern nach der Auferstehung* (Hildesheim, 1967, repr. of 1919 original). = Schmidt

SCHMÖLE, KLAUS, *Läuterung nach dem Tode und pneumatische Auferstehung bei Klemens von Alexandrien*, MBT 38 (Münster, 1973). = Schmöle

SCHNACKENBURG, RUDOLF, *The Gospel According to St. John*, Herder's Theological Commentary on the New Testament, 3 vols. (ET, London and Tunbridge Wells, 1982). = Schnackenburg, *John*

SCHULTZ, D. R., 'The Origin of Sin in Irenaeus and Jewish Pseudepigraphical Literature', *VC* 32 (1978), 161–90. = Schultz

SCHÜRER, EMIL, *The History of the Jewish People in the Age of Jesus Christ (175 B.C.–A.D. 135)*, new Eng. version rev. and ed. by Geza Vermes, Fergus Millar, Martin Goodman, Pamela Vermes, and Matthew Black, 3 vols. in 4 (Edinburgh, 1973–87). = Schürer

SCHWARTZ, HILLEL, 'Millenarism: An Overview', *ER* (New York/London, 1987), ix, 521–32. = Schwartz

SEMISCH and BRATKE, 'Chiliasmus', *RE*, 3rd edn. (Leipzig, 1897), iii, 805–17. = Semisch–Bratke

SICKENBERGER, JOSEPH, 'Das Tausendjährige Reich in der Apokalypse', *Festschrift für Sebastian Merkle* (Düsseldorf, 1922), 300–15. = Sickenberger, *Merkle*

—— *Erklärung der Johannesapokalypse*, 2nd edn. (Bonn, 1942). = Sickenberger, *Johannesapokalypse*

SIMONETTI, MANLIO, 'A modo di conclusione: una ipotesi di lavoro', in *Ricerche su Ippolito*, Studia Ephemeridis 'Augustinianum', 13 (Rome, 1977), 151–6.

SKARSAUNE, OSKAR, 'The Conversion of Justin Martyr', *StTh* 30 (1976), 53–73. = Skarsaune, 'Conversion'

—— *The Proof from Prophecy: A Study in Justin Martyr's Proof Text Tradition: Text-type, Provenance, Theological Profile*, Suppl. *NovT* 56 (Leiden, 1987). = Skarsaune

SMITH, MORTON, 'The Description of the Essenes in Josephus and the Philosophumena', *HUCA* 29 (1958), 273–313. = Smith, *HUCA*

SOUTER, A., 'Reasons for Regarding Hilarius (Ambrosiaster) as the Author of the Mercati-Turner Anecdoton', *JTS* 5 (1904), 608–21. = Souter

SPICQ, C., *L'Épitre aux Hébreux*, 2 vols., ÉBib (Paris, 1953).   = Spicq

STANTON, G. N., '5 Ezra and Matthean Christianity in the Second Century', *JTS* NS, 28 (1977), 67–83   = Stanton

STRACK, H. L., and BILLERBECK, P., *Kommentar zum Neuen Testament aus Talmud und Midrash*, 4 vols. (Munich, 1922–8).   = Strack–Billerbeck

STONEHOUSE, NED BERNARD, *The Apocalypse in the Ancient Church: A Study in the History of the New Testament Canon* (Goes, 1929). = Stonehouse

STUIBER, A., *Refrigerium interim, die Vorstellungen vom Zwischenzustand und die frühchristliche Grabeskunst*, Theoph. 11 (Bonn, 1957). = Stuiber

SWETE, HENRY BARCLAY, *The Apocalypse of St. John*, 3rd edn. (London, 1911).   = Swete

TALMON, YONINA, 'Millenarism', *IESS* (1968), x, 349–62.   = Talmon

THRAEDE, KLAUS, 'Beiträge zur Datierung Commodians', *JbAC* 2 (1959), 90–114.   = Thraede

TIXERONT, *History of Dogmas*, 3 vols., trans. from the 5th French edn. by H. L. B., 2nd edn. i, *The Antenicene Theology* (St Louis/London, 1921). = Tixeront

TURNER, JOHN D., 'The Gnostic Threefold Path to Enlightenment', *NovT* 22 (1980), 324–51.   = J. D. Turner, *NovT*

TUVESON, ERNEST, 'Millenarianism', *DHI* (New York, 1973), iii, 223–75. = Tuveson

URBACH, EPHRAIM E., *The Sages: Their Concepts and Beliefs*, trans. by Israel Abrahams, 2 vols., 2nd edn. (Jerusalem, 1979).   = Urbach

VAN HARTINGSVELD, L., *Die Eschatologie des Johannesevangeliums*, Van Gorcum's theologische Bibliotheek 36 (Assen, 1962).   = Van Hartingsveld

VAN UNNIK, W. C., 'The Authority of the Presbyters in Irenaeus' Works', in *God's Christ and His People: Studies in Honour of Nils Alstrup Dahl*, ed. Jacob Jervell and Wayne Meeks (Oslo, 1977), 248–60.   = van Unnik

VOLZ, PAUL, *Die Eschatologie der Jüdischen Gemeinde im neutestamentlichen Zeitalter: Nach den Quellen der rabbinischen, apokalyptischen und apokryphen Literatur* (Hildesheim, 1966 repr. of 1934 original).   = Volz

WARFIELD, BENJAMIN BRECKENRIDGE, 'The Millennium and the Apocalypse', *PTR* 2 (1904), 599–617.   = Warfield, *PTR*

WELBORN, L. L., 'On the Date of First Clement', *BR* 29 (1984), 35–54. = Welborn

WENGST, KLAUS, *Tradition und Theologie des Barnabasbriefes*, AK 42 (Berlin/New York, 1971).   = Wengst

WESTCOTT, BROOKE FOSS, *The Epistle to the Hebrews*, 3rd edn. (London, 1920).   = Westcott

WHITE, R. FOWLER, 'Reexamining the Evidence for Recapitulation in Rev 20: 1–10', *WTJ* 51 (1989), 319–44.   = White

WIDENGREN, GEO, 'En la maison de mon Père sont demeures nombreuses', *SEÅ* 37–8 (1972–3), 9–15.   = Widengren

WILCKE, HANS-ALWIN, *Das Problem eines messianischen Zwischenreichs bei Paulus*, ATANT 51 (Zurich/Stuttgart, 1967).   = Wilcke

WILCOX, MAX, 'Tradition and Redaction of Rev 21, 9–22,5', in *L'Apocalypse johannique et l'Apocalyptique dans le Nouveau Testament*, ed. J. Lambrecht, BETL 53 (Leuven, 1980), 205–15.   = Wilcox

WILKEN, ROBERT, 'Early Christian Chiliasm, Jewish Messianism, and the Idea of the Holy Land', *HTR* 79 (1986), 298–307.   = Wilken

WILLIAMS, GEORG HUNSTON, *The Radical Reformation* (London, 1962). = Williams, *Radical Reformation*

WILLIS, WAYNE, 'Martyr Eschatology: Ignatius' Use of *Epitugchanō*', *RestQ*, 10 (1967), 81–8.   = Willis

WISE, MICHAEL O., 'The Eschatological Vision of the Temple Scroll', *JNES* 49 (1990), 155–72.   = Wise

WOLFSON, HARRY AUSTYN, *Philo: Foundations of Religious Philosophy in Judaism, Christianity, and Islam*, 2 vols. (Cambridge, Mass., 1947). = Wolfson

WOOD, A. SKEVINGTON, 'The Eschatology of Irenaeus', *EvQ* 41 (1969), 30–41. = Wood

WÜNSCHE, AUG. 'Die Vorstellungen vom Zustande nach dem Tode nach Apokryphen, Talmud und Kirchenvätern', *JPT* 6 (1880), 355–83; 495–523. = Wünsche

WYTZES, 'Paideia and Pronoia in the Works of Clemens Alexandrinus', *VC* 9 (1955), 146–58.   = Wytzes

YOUNG, EDWARD MALLET, 'Commodianus', *DCB*, I, 610–11.   = Young

ZAHN, THEODORE, *Die Offenbarung des Johannes*, 2 vols. (Leipzig, 1924–26). = Zahn, *Offenbarung*

GENERAL INDEX

Modern authors are listed only when cited in the main body of the text.

Abbahu 54
Abel 30–1, 42
Abraham, bosom of 25, 36 n., 131, 139, 156
Achamoth 11, 12, 17 n.
Acts of Thomas 103–4
Adam 51, 110
ἀδεῶς 109–10, 190
Akiba 49 n.
Alogi 2
Ambrose of Milan 56, 191
amillennialism, *see* non-chiliasm
Andersen, F. I. 51
Antichrist 35, 36 n., 108 n., 122, 145 n., 150
Apocalypse of Peter 97–8
Arabot 54, 55
Ascension of Isaiah 94–7
Augustine:
  his exegesis of Revelation 20   2, 65, 191
  his influence on eschatological thought 2 n., 3

Bacon, B. W. 19
Bar Cochba 1 n., 23, 62, 97, 98
Barnard, L. W. 20–1
2 (Syriac) Baruch 41–3
Basilides, Basilidians 11
Bauckham, R. J. 97
Beckwith, I. T. 169
Benson, E. W. 196
Berengaudus 191–2
Bertrand, D. A. 51
Bettencourt, E. 5
Bietenhard, H. 3, 33, 116
Blum, G. G. 38
Book of the Watchers (*1 Enoch* 1–36) 42
Bogaert, P.-M. 58, 173
Bornkamm, G. 104
Bratke 3
Bright, P. 109
Burns, N. 180

Celerinus 196–7
Cerinthus 33 n., 101
Charles, R. H. 96, 173–4, 176
Chernus, I. 56
chiliasm:
  in *2 (Syriac) Baruch* 43–4, 58–9
  of Commodianus 29, 58
  definition 5–6
  of *4 Ezra* 43–4
  influence in Christian history 1, 2–4
  of Irenaeus 6, 9, 12, 59, 184–8
  of Justin 20
  of Lactantius 38
  of Methodius 33–4
  of Papias 18, 58–9
  of Pseudo–Philo 45
  reasons given for its decline 3, 184
  sociological definitions of 1–2
  of Tertullian
  of Victorinus 35
Claudius Apolinarius of Hierapolis 93 n., 119, 189
Clementine *Homilies* 61 n.
Clementine *Recognitions* 60–1
Clement of Alexandria 120–7
2 Clement 87–9
Clement of Rome 6, 66–72
Commodianus 29–31
confessors, and absolution 196–201
cosmic-week theory 35, 38 n., 113–14, 116, 132 n., 144, 164 n.
Creeds:
  Apostles' 183
  Old Roman 3
Crouzel, H. 133
Cruse, R. 109
Curti, C. 112
Cyprian of Carthage 143–53

Daniélou, J. 80, 99, 100, 102, 113
Davenport, G. L. 48
Davies, P. R. 48
Demiurge 9, 11, 12, 31 n., 188
Dibelius, M. 84

Dionysius of Alexandria 101 n., 141–3
Dionysius Bar Salibi 113, 115
dispensationalists 175
distribution of eschatological views in
    early Christianity 2–6, 181–4
Domitian 4
Donaldson, J. 109

Eliezer ben Jose the Galilean 55, 56
Elijah 19, 27 n., 35, 37, 45, 60
Elisha 15, 37
Elmenhorst 91
Enoch 27 n., 37 n., 51, 60
Epistle to Diognetus 6, 89–90
Epistle to Rheginos 11
Epistle of Vienne and Lyons 107–11
Epistula Apostolorum 101–4
('Eπι)τυγχάνω 73–4, 88, 90, 106 n.,
    186–7
4 Ezra 43–4
5 Ezra 98-100

Filaster 172 n.
Finé, H. 62
Fischer, J. A. 66–7
Ford, J. M. 166, 176
Frickel, J. 112
Furnish, V. P. 159

Gaechter, P. 176
Gaius of Rome 101 n., 115
    his opposition to chiliasm 2, 4, 115,
    120
Georgi, D. 104
Goodspeed, E. J. 109
Grant, R. M. 111
Gry, L. 34, 90, 92
Gospel of Nicodemus 29
Gwynn, J. 119

Hades:
    baptism in 86 n., 102, 104
    harrowing of 15 (Irenaeus), 25
    (Tertullian's opponents), 29
    (Gospel of Nicodemus), 78
    (Ignatius), 86 (Hermas), 92–4
    (Melito), 102 (Epistle of the
    Apostles), 103 (Odes of Solomon,
    Acts of Thomas, Acts of
    Thaddeus, Ignatius, Tr.), 116
    (Hippolytus), 123 (Clement of
    Alexandria), 138, 139 (Origen),
    147 n. (Cyprian), 159 n. (Paul?),

    185 n. (Irenaeus), 187 (Marcion)
    keys of 169–70
    in Luke 16: 19–31   156
    preaching in 12, 86
    see also intermediate state
Harnack, A. 2, 3, 89, 90, 91, 182
heaven, as kingdom 14, 15 n. (Irenaeus),
    20, 22–3 (Justin), 26, 28
    (Tertullian's opponents), 90
    (Epistle to Diognetus), 96–7
    (Ascension of Isaiah), 99–100 (5
    Ezra), 104 (Acts of Thomas), 106–7
    (Martyrdom of Polycarp, Origen,
    Tertullian, Clement of Alexandria),
    117 (Hippolytus), 124–7 (Clement
    of Alexandria), 129–30, 137
    (Origen), 142–3 (Dionysius of
    Alexandria), 145–7, 150–3
    (Cyprian), 156 (Luke), 160 (Paul),
    162–3 (2 Peter), 168–9
    (Revelation), 191 (non-chiliasts
    generally), 198–9 (the Roman
    confessors)
    see also intermediate state, paradise
Hegesippus 4, 87 n.
Hermas, The Shepherd 80–7
Hippolytus 111–20
Hiyya, sons of 56
Hobbes, T. 181
Horbury, W. 62

Ignatius 6, 72–8
intermediate state 6–7
    in Acts of Thomas 103–4
    in Apocalypse of Peter 98
    in Ascension of Isaiah 6–11   95–7
    in 2 (Syriac) Baruch 43
    in 3 Baruch 50 n.
    in 2 Clement 88
    Clement of Alexandria's view 123–7
    Clement of Rome's view 66–72
    Commodianus' view 29–31
    connection with general eschatology
    7, 14, 17–18, 28, 39, 40, 41, 63, 64,
    87, 127–8, 131, 154–5, 178–81,
    194–5
    Cyprian's view 147–52, 196–201
    Dionysius of Alexandria's view 142–3
    in the Epistle to Diognetus 90
    in the Epistle of Vienne and Lyons
    107
    in the Epistula Apostolorum 102
    Essene views 47

in 4 Ezra 43
in 5 Ezra 99–100
Gnostic views 14, 17, 187–8
in Hebrews 161–2
Hermas' view 82–7
Hippolytus' view 116–18
Ignatius' view 73–8
Irenaeus' view 12, 14–16
in John's Gospel 157–8
Josephus' view 71
Justin's view 21–3
Lactantius' view 38–9
in Luke's Gospel 155–7
in 2 Maccabees 46 n.
in 3 Maccabees 46 n.
in 4 Maccabees 53
in Martyrdom of Polycarp 106
Melito's view 92–4
Methodius' view 32
Novatian's view 32
Origen's view 129–37
Papias' view 19–20
in 2 Peter 162–3
Pharisaical view 46
Polycarp's view 79–80
Pseudo-Philo's view 45
in Paul 158–61
in Rabbinic sources 53–7
in Revelation 163–70
the Roman confessors' view 198–9
at Qumran 48–9
Sadducean view 47
in Similitudes of Enoch 50
Tertullian's view 16, 24–8
Victorinus' view 35–7
in Wisdom of Solomon 52–3
Irenaeus 9–18, 184–8

Jay, P. 148
Jehovah's Witnesses 181
Jeremiah 37
Jeremiah apocryphon 29
Jerome 34, 65, 191
Johanan 54
Johanan ben Zakkai 56
Josephus 46, 47, 71
Jude, grandsons of 4, 6, 20
Justin Martyr 20–4

Kidd, B. J. 109
kingdom, see heaven, chiliasm, non-
    chiliasm

κλῆρος, κληρονομία:
  in Ignatius 76, 80
  in Paul and Polycarp 79–80
Knibb, M. A. 99
Knoch, O. 67, 68, 70

Lactantius 37–9
Lake, K. 109
Lang, F. G. 159
Leclercq, H. 92
Lesètre, H. 33
Life of Adam and Eve 50–1
Lightfoot, J. B. 19, 77, 109, 113
Loi, V. 112, 119
Lucian (of Carthage) 196–7, 200

McGiffert, A. C. 109
Marcion, Marcionites, 10 n., 12, 22 n.,
    26, 28, 187
martyr, martyrdom 14, 15, 16, 22–3, 27,
    36, 39, 40 n., 42, 60, 68, 73–4, 80,
    83–5, 86, 87, 93, 100, 102, 105, 107,
    117, 118, 124, 136–7, 139, 148–9,
    150–2, 164–70, 197–9
Martyrdom of Polycarp 105–7
Meletians 'Melitans', 91–2
Meletius of Lycopolis 91–2
Melito of Sardis 90–4
Meloni, P. 112
Millennium, millennialism, see chiliasm
Montanism 3, 28, 200 n.
Mormonism 181
mortalism 180–1
  see also thnetopsychiasm
Moses 37
Moule, C. F. D. 21
Myers, J. 99

Nautin, P. 111, 112
Nero 36 n.
Nickelsburg, G. W. E. 49
non-chiliasm 2
  definition 6
  of Ascension of Isaiah 6–11   94–7
  of Apocalypse of Peter 97–8
  of 2 Clement 87–8
  of Clement of Alexandria 122
  of Clement of Rome 66, 72
  of Cyprian 144–7
  of Dionysius of Alexandria 141
  of Epistle of Vienne and Lyons
      110–11
  of Epistula Apostolorum 101–2

non–chiliasm (*cont.*):
  of Hermas 80–2
  of Hippolytus 113–16, 117–20
  of Jude's grandsons 4
  of *Martyrdom of Polycarp* 107
  of Origen 127–41
  of *Sibyilline Oracles* I–II 98 n.
  mentioned by Irenaeus 4, 9–13,
    17–18
  mentioned by Justin 3–4
Novatian 31–2

Orbe, A. 10–12
one hundred and forty-four thousand
  35, 108, 166
Origen 127–41
  his opposition to chiliasm 2, 4, 115,
    127–31
Oulton, J. E. L. 109

Papias 18–20, 58
Paradise 60–1, 178–9
  in *Apocalypse of Abraham* 52
  in *Apocalypse of Peter* 98
  in *2 (Syriac) Baruch* 43, 156–7
  amongst chiliasts 59–60, 178–9
  Cyprian's view 150, 151–2
  in *2 Enoch* 51
  in *4 Ezra* 44, 156–7
  Irenaeus' view 16 n., 19–20
  in *Life of Adam and Eve* 50–1
  in Luke 23: 42–3   156–7
  other Jewish views 44 n., 56, 60 n.
  Origen's view 130, 132, 134–5, 136,
    137
  Papias' view 19–20
  Pseudo-Philo's view 45–6
  Rabbinic views 56
  in Revelation 168
  in *Similitudes of Enoch* 50
  Tertullian's view 27
  Victorinus' view 37
  see also intermediate state; two
    witnesses
Paulus (of Carthage) 200
Pernveden, L. 80, 81
Perpetua 27, 163 n.
Philo 52
Phinehas 45
Plato, Platonism 10, 33, 52, 126, 183
Polycarp 6, 78–80, 105–7
Pratten, B. P. 109
Pseudo-Barnabas 40 n., 58

Pseudo-Philo, *Biblical Antiquities* 45
purgatory 6 n., 28 n., 121 n., 148–9

Quasten, J. 23, 119

Resh Lakish 54 n., 55
resurrection, incorporeal 11 n., 77, 78,
    120, 136, 191
Revelation, book of:
  divergences from chiliasm 171–7
  its doctrine of the intermediate state
    163–70
  non-chiliastic exegesis of
    ch. 20   188–93
Richard, M. 29, 31, 119
Roberts, A. 109

Sabbath 9, 33, 113, 114, 164 n., 172 n.
  see also cosmic-week theory
Salvatore, A. 29
Satan, binding of 89, 91, 93, 110,
    118–19, 137–9, 189–90
Saturnilians 12
Schmöle, K. 123
Schoedel, W. R. 77, 109
Schmidt, C. 101
Semisch 3
Seventh Day Adventism 181
sheol, *see* Hades, intermediate state
Shepherd, M. H. Jr. 109
Similitudes of Enoch (1 Enoch 37–71)
    50
Simonetti, M. 112
Sibylline Oracles II: 44–5
Snyder, G. F. 82
soul, pre-existence of 39, 47, 52
soul-sleep 181
  see also mortalism, thnetopsychiasm
Staniforth, M. 109
Stanton, G. 98
Stoicism 38–9

ten lost tribes, return of 44, 58, 173
Tertullian 16, 24–8, 201
Theodoret of Cyrus 92
Theophilus of Antioch 114
thnetopsychiasm 139–40
  see also mortalism
Turner, C. H. 91
twenty-four elders of Revelation 96,
    125–6, 168
two witnesses, of Rev. 11: 3–12   37
Tyconius 2 n., 65, 191

Tyndale, W. 180

Valentinians 10, 11, 12, 13, 17 n., 28, 31 n., 187–8
Victorinus of Pettau 34–7, 201
Vettius Epagathus 108

Waszink, J. H. 26
Williamson, G. A. 109
world-week theory, *see* cosmic-week theory

Zahn, T. 82

INDEX OF SCRIPTURAL PASSAGES TREATED

2 KINGS
6: 6 — 15

PSALMS
2: 9 — 169
86: 23 — 14

ECCLESIASTES
4: 14 — 137

ISAIAH
11: — 185 n.
22: 22 — 169
26: 20 — 67
54: 11–14 — 175
65: 17–18 — 175

JEREMIAH
1: 5 — 37

EZEKIEL
37: 12 — 67–8

MATTHEW
2: 16 — 26
5: 10 — 98
5: 23–4 — 36
5: 26 — 28, 148, 149 n.
10: 32 — 197
11: 12 — 124
11: 40 — 14
12: 29 — 93, 110, 119, 189
18: 18 — 197
19: 28 — 104, 130, 138
19: 29 — 35
20: 22–3 — 105, 137, 197
26: 27–9 — 35, 172 n.

MARK
10: 38–9 — 105

LUKE
14: 12–14 — 134
16: 9 — 125
16: 16 — 124
16: 19–31 — 131–2, 139, 156–7
16: 26 — 36 n.
19: 17–19 — 130
23: 42–3 — 93, 98, 132, 156–7

JOHN
12: 24–6 — 158
14: 2–4 — 157–8
14: 2 — 68, 130
17: 24 — 131
17: 25 — 158

ROMANS
8: 18–25 — 60

1 CORINTHIANS
15: 20–8 — 161
15: 51–3 — 35, 59, 172

2 CORINTHIANS
5: 1 — 32
5: 1–10 — 158–9, 160
5: 6–8 — 27 n.

EPHESIANS
4: 9 — 14

PHILIPPIANS
1: 23 — 26, 130, 159–60
3: 12–21 — 159
3: 14 — 159

COLOSSIANS
1: 12 — 76, 160

1 THESSALONIANS
4: 16 — 172

HEBREWS
12: 22–4 — 71, 161–2, 166

1 PETER
3: 19–22 — 162 n.

2 PETER
1: 11 — 162–3

REVELATION
chs. 2–3 — 167–9
2: 10–11 — 106
3: 8 — 169
3: 21 — 85, 197
5: 3–4 — 35, 36 n.
5: 6–11 — 166
6: 9–11 — 27, 36, 163–6, 201
6: 11 — 164 n., 167
7: 9–17 — 100, 166
11: 3–12 — 37
11: 3 — 97, 100 n.
12: 10 — 167
12: 12 — 166, 167
14: 1–7 — 100, 166
14: 4 — 108
14: 13 — 164 n.
16: 7 — 165
19: 2 — 165–6
20: 1–3 — 89, 91, 118, 137–9, 189–90
20: 2 — 110
20: 4–6 — 35, 118, 120, 133–6, 137, 142, 150, 153, 170, 177, 190–1
20: 4 — 96, 125, 136, 164, 199
20: 5–6 — 199
20: 6 — 97
20: 7–10 — 110
20: 7–8 — 189
21: 9–22: 2 — 174–5

INDEX OF OTHER ANCIENT SOURCES TREATED

Christian Sources

Acta Pauli	102 n.
Acts of Thaddeus (Eus. HE I. 13. 20)	103 n.
Acts of Thomas	103–4
Apocalypse of Peter	97–8
Apocalypse of Weeks (1 Enoch 91. 12–17; 93. 1–10)	5 n.
Apostolic Constitutions	
VIII. 23	200 n.
Ascension of Isaiah	94–7
Augustine, de Civitate Dei	
XX. 7	114
XX. 9	191
Carmen adversus Marcionem	
III. 245–6	37 n.
IV. 172–91	36 n.
Claudius Apolinarius, Concerning the Passover (Eus. ChronPasc. praef.)	93 n., 119, 189
Clementine Homilies	61 n.
Clementine Recognitions	60–1
I. 52. 4–5	40 n., 61
2 Clement	87–9
5. 1, 5–6	88
17. 4–7	88
19. 4	88
20. 4	89, 189
Clement of Alexandria	
Paedagogus	
I. vi. 28. 3	123
II. iv. 41. 4	123
Quis diues saluetur	
32. 1–6	124
42. 15	123
Stromata	
IV. iv. 13. 2	124
IV. iv. 14. 2	124
IV. iv. 14. 3	124
IV. iv. 15. 3	124
IV. xv. 104. 1	124
VI. ix. 75. 1–2	124
VI. xiii. 106. 2	125, 126, 199
VII. x. 56. 7–57. 1	124
VII. x. 56. 5–6	125

Clement of Rome, 1 Clement	
5. 4–7	69–71
5. 7	76–7
20. 5	67
34. 3	66
36. 3–6	66
42. 3	6
44. 1	85 n.
49. 5	68
50. 3	66, 68
50. 3–4	67–8
Commodianus	
Instructions	
I. 24. 18–21	30
I. 26. 33–4	30
I. 34. 18–19	31
I. 35. 6	31
I. 36. 8–10	31 n.
I. 44	⸴176
II. 13. 19, 20	31 n.
Carmen Apologeticum	
314	29
669–72	31
Cyprian	
Ad Demetrianum	
5	147
16	148
23	147
25	148
Epistula	
XV. 3	198
XV. 4	200
XXI	196–7
XXXI. 3	198–9
LV	147–9
LX. 5	198 n.
LXI. 4	145
LXIII. 18	145
Ad Fortunatum (De exhortatione martyrii)	
12–13	150–1
De habitu uirginum	
21	148 n.
24	198 n.
De lapsis	
17	198 n.
de mortalitate	
2	145–6

3	146
5	146
18	145, 146
26	151–2
De dominica oratione	
13	147
De catholicae ecclesiae unitate	
27	145
Dionysius of Alexandria	
To Fabius (Eus. *HE*	
VI. 42. 5)	142–3, 199, 200 n.
On Promises	142–3
To Stephen on Baptism	143
5 Ezra	98–100
2. 18	37 n.
Epistle to Diognetus	89–90
Epistle of Vienne and Lyons	107–11
(Eus. *HE* V. 2. 5)	197
Epistula Apostolorum	101–4
Filaster	
Diversarum heresion liber	
LIX	172 n.
Gennadius of Marseilles	
Liber ecclesiasticorum dogmatum	91
Gospel of Nicodemus	29
22	189
Hermas, *The Shepherd*	
Visions	
2. 2. 6	86
3. 2. 1	30 n., 71, 84
3. 5. 2	86
3.9. 5–6	81
Mandates	
12. 4. 6	83
Similitudes	
1.	82–3
5. 6. 7	81
5. 7. 1	81–2
8	85, 100
9. 15–16	85–6
9. 16. 2–3	104
9. 25. 2	86–7
9. 28. 2–4	85
Hippolytus	111–20
On Christ and Antichrist	
59	117

The Blessings of Moses	
pp. 197–9	115
Commentary on Daniel	
II. 37. 4	117, 199
IV. 11. 4	115
IV. 23	114
IV. 33. 4–5	119, 189
Chapters Against Gaius	116, 118–20
On the Great Song fr. 1	190
Ignatius	
To the Ephesians	
11. 2	77
To the Magnesians	
5. 1	76 n.
9. 2	78
To the Romans	
2. 2	76–7
4. 1	186
4. 1–3	77
6. 1	76 n.
6. 2	75, 76, 160
To the Smyrnaeans	
4. 2	75
To the Trallians	
9	103
13. 3	75
Irenaeus	
Adversus Haereses	
I. 7. 1	188
I. 7. 5	17 n.
I. 27. 3	187
II. 22. 2	185 n.
II. 33. 5	185 n.
III. 11. 8	15 n.
III. 16. 4	14, 26
III. 18. 6	189
III. 23. 1	110–11, 189
III. 23. 7	110, 189
IV 4. 2	185 n.
IV. 16. 1	185 n.
IV. 20. 10	185
IV. 31. 3	15–16
IV. 33. 9	14–15
V. 2. 2–3	10
V. 4. 1	12
V. 5. 1	14 n., 16 n., 19
V. 5. 2	19
V. 17. 4	15
V. 21. 3	189
V. 28. 4	186
V. 30. 4	9
V. 31–2. 1	4, 16

Adversus Hacreses (cont.):
  v. 31. 1   10–12, 29
  v. 32. 1   13, 16, 17, 59, 186
  v. 33. 3   18, 35
  v. 34. 4–35. 2   185 n.
  v. 34. 4   175
  v. 35. 1   59
  v. 35. 1–2   17
  v. 35. 2   175, 176
Demonstration of the Apostolic
    Preaching
  39   185 n.
  61   185 n.
Fragment 26   15–16, 94 n.

Justin
  1 Apology
    10. 2–3   22, 23
    11. 1–2   20, 23
    52   20
    57   3, 23
  2 Apology
    2. 18, 19   21
  Dialogue with Trypho the Jew
    5. 3   30
    35   12, 13 n.
    45. 4   20
    80   3, 12, 20
    81   175
    99. 3   22, 47
    113. 3–5   20
    139. 5   20

Lactantius
  The Divine Institutes
    VII. 7. 7   39
    VII. 20   39
    VII. 21. 7   39
    VII. 24   38

Martyrdom of Saint Justin
    and his Companions
  5   21
Martyrdom of Polycarp   105–7
Melito of Sardis
  New Fragment II. 12. 107–19 93–4 n.
  New Fragment II. 15–17   93 n.
  New Fragment III. 5. 24–36   93
  On the Devil and the Revelation
      of John   91, 111 n.
  Peri Pascha 102. 760–4   93, 119, 189

Methodius of Olympus
  Treatise on the Resurrection of
    the Body
    II. 15. 7   32
  The Symposium
    9. 1   34 n.
    9. 5   33
  On Things Created
    12   132 n.

Novatian
  On the Trinity
    I. 1   32

Odes of Solomon   103–4
  42. 15   12 n.
Origen
  Contra Celsum
    VII. 28   131
    VII. 29   129
  Commentary on Romans
    v. 10   138
  Dialogue with Heraclides
    24   137
  Exhortation to Martyrdom
    30   136, 197
    34   197
    36   137
  Fragment on Luke
    83   134
  Homilies on Genesis
    I   138
  Homilies on Jeremiah
    II. 3   134–5
  Homilies on Luke
    XXIV. 2   134–5
  Homilies on Numbers
    XXVI. 4   131–2
  On Prayer
    28   137
    37   137
  De principiis
    II. 11   126, 127, 129–30, 131,
                                175–6

Papias   18–20, 58
Polycarp, To the Philippians
  5. 2   78
  7. 1   22 n., 80
  9. 2   69–70, 79
  12. 2   79, 160
Pseudo-Barnabas
  11. 9   58

15. 3–8   40 n.
15. 7   175
19. 1   40 n.
Pseudo-Cyprian, *De laude martyrii*
    13   149 n.

De septem sigillis   36 n.

Tertullian
    De anima
        53. 6   31 n.
        55   24–5, 26, 27, 120
        56   27, 30
        57. 11   27
        58. 1   27
    Apology
        47. 13   26
    De exhortatione castitatis
        11   26 n.
    Adversus Marcionem
        III. 24   176
    De monogamia
        10   27 n.
    De pudicitia
        22   157, 200 n.
    De resurrectione carnis
        2. 2   25
        43   27 n., 160
    Scorpiace
        6   26
        10   26
    De universo   24 n., 30, 37, 112, 116n,
                                            119
Theodoret of Cyrus, *Ecclesiastical
    History*   92

Victorinus of Pettau
    Commentary on the Apocalypse
        5. 1   35–6
        6. 4   36
        11. 3   37
        11. 4   37
        12. 1   37
        12. 4   35
        20. 2   35
        21. 1–6   176
        21. 5–6   35
    De fabrica mundi
        6   35

Non-Christian Sources

'Aboth d'Rabbi Nathan, version A   54

Apocalypse of Abraham   52
2 *Baruch*   41, 42–3
    25. 1–4   43
    29. 5–8   58
    40. 3   59
    74. 2   59
3 *Baruch*   50 n.
The Dead Sea Scrolls   47–50

1 *Enoch*
    1–36 (The Book of the
        Watchers)   5 n., 42, 179
        10. 17–19   42, 58
        22   42, 49
    37–71 (The Similitudes of
        Enoch)   50
    102–4   50 n.
    108   50 n.
2 *Enoch*   51
4 *Ezra*   43–4
    6. 26   44
    7. 29   44
    7. 80   43
    10. 7   83 n.
    14. 9   44

Genesis Rabbah XII. 10   54

Josephus
    Antiquitates Judaicae
        XVIII. 14   46
        XVIII. 16   47
        XVIII. 18   47
    Bellum Judaicum
        II. 155–6   47
        II. 163   46
        II. 165   47
        III. 374   71
Life of Adam and Eve   50–1
2 *Maccabees*   46 n.
3 *Maccabees*   46 n.
4 *Maccabees*   53

Philo   52
Pseudo-Philo, *Biblical Antiquities*   45–6

Sibylline Oracles
    II. 170–6   44–5
    III   5 n.
    VII. 145–9   33 n.
Sifre on Numbers 139   55

TB Berakot 18b   56   Testament of Judah
TB Shabbat 152a   55   25. 1–5   5 n.
TB Shabbat 152b–53a   54   Testament of Levi
TB Hagigah 12b   54, 55   3. 8   49
Testament of Asher
  6. 5   49   Wisdom of Solomon   52–3